Analysis of Machine Elements
Using SolidWorks Simulation 2009

John R. Steffen, Ph.D., P.E.
Valparaiso University

ISBN: 978-1-58503-493-2

SDC
PUBLICATIONS

Schroff Development Corporation

www.schroff.com

Trademarks and Disclaimer

SolidWorks, SolidWorks Simulation, and its family of products are registered trademarks of Dassault Systemes, SolidWorks Corporation. Microsoft Windows®, Excel®, and its family of products are registered trademarks of the Microsoft Corporation.

Every effort has been made to provide an accurate, error free text. The author and manufacturers shall not be held liable for any parts developed or designed based on this book or for errors appearing in this text.

About the Cover

Two-Stage Compressor, pencil on hard-board by Michael R. Steffen

An artistic interpretation of a mechanical device is chosen for the cover because, although finite element analysis is a highly sophisticated, mathematically based software program, its application requires a certain amount of art to be used properly.

Examination Copies

Books received as examination copies are for review purposes only and may not be made available for student use. Resale of examination copies is prohibited.

Electronic Files

Any electronic files associated with this book are licensed to the original user only. These files may not be transferred to any other party.

Dedication

For family and friends who have provided guidance, inspiration, encouragement, and much delight. Especially my wife Marolyn, and children Amy and Michael.

About the Author

Dr. John Steffen obtained his B.S.M.E. from Valparaiso University, M.S.M.E. from The University of Notre Dame, and Ph.D. from Rutgers, The State University of New Jersey. His areas of interest include Machine Design, Mechanisms and Mechanism Synthesis, Finite Element Analysis, and Experimental Stress Analysis. Dr. Steffen is Professor Emeritus of Mechanical Engineering and the Alfred W. Sieving Chair, Emeritus, in Engineering at Valparaiso University, Valparaiso IN. He is an active member of the American Society of Mechanical Engineers (ASME) and the American Society for Engineering Education (ASEE).

Acknowledgements

The author would like to acknowledge the following individuals and corporations for their support, encouragement, and invaluable assistance in preparation of this book.

- The SolidWorks Corporation, especially Mr. Joe Galliera and Ms Magdalen Fryatt and the SolidWorks Solution Partner team for their support and assistance.
- Mr. Stephen Schroff and Ms. Mary Schmidt of Schroff Development Corporation, for their guidance and assistance preparing the manuscript for publication.
- Mr. Michael A. Steffen and Mr. Carl Jurss for their assistance with preparation of many SolidWorks models and drawings. Mr. Ed Spanopulos photographic credit.
- Ms. Cami Gudino, Administrative Assistant in the College of Engineering, for text entry and knowing the answers to numerous logistical questions.
- Mr. Ross Mack, for assistance within both SolidWorks and SolidWorks Simulation, and Prof. Scott Duncan, Ph.D. for suggesting revisions.
- Valparaiso University and the College of Engineering who provided an environment that encouraged and supported this effort.

This publication marks the 4th edition of a learner centered, step-by-step guide to using SolidWorks Simulation. Every attempt has been made to make this book error free so that it best serves first-time SolidWorks Simulation users. In many instances, the software provides alternative approaches to perform the same tasks. Some alternatives are presented; however, it is not possible to include every option while keeping the text of manageable length. In an effort to improve future editions of this text, the author welcomes error corrections and suggestions to improve the presentation at john.steffen@valpo.edu.

NOTES:

Table of Contents

Chapter 2
Curved Beam Analysis

Chapter 3
Stress Concentration Analysis

Chapter 6
Contact Analysis in a Trunion Mount

Chapter 7
Bolted Joint Analysis

APPENDIX A

INDEX

NOTES:

PREFACE

Intended Audience for This Text

This text is written primarily for first-time SolidWorks Simulation® users who wish to understand finite element analysis capabilities applicable to stress analysis of mechanical elements. The focus of examples is on problems commonly found in an introductory, undergraduate, Design of Machine Elements or similarly named courses. Also, depending upon the primary textbook used for a Mechanics of Materials course, many examples contained herein can also be introduced in those courses. However, those courses are usually so packed with new concepts that adding finite element analysis to the mix of topics only serves to dilute the understanding of both subjects. Other novice users of SolidWorks Simulation, possessing the background described above, will also benefit by using the self-study format employed throughout this text.

Many chapter example problems are accompanied by problem solutions based on the use of classical equations for stress determination. This approach amplifies two fundamental tenets of this text. The first is that a better understanding of course topics related to stress determination is realized when classical methods *and* finite element solutions are considered together. The second tenet is that finite element solutions should always be verified by checking, whether by classical stress equations or experimentation.

Although it is assumed that readers have working knowledge of SolidWorks, practicality dictates that many users will be new to the SolidWorks/SolidWorks Simulation work environment or transitioning to it from other finite element software programs. For these reasons, this text is organized so that individuals with no prior SolidWorks or SolidWorks Simulation experience will be successful. To assist overcoming any lack of SolidWorks familiarity, models of parts or assemblies for all examples and end of chapter problems can be downloaded from: http://www.schroff.com/resources/.

Using this SolidWorks Simulation User Guide

Each chapter of this text begins with a list of *Learning Objectives* related to specific capabilities of the SolidWorks Simulation program introduced in that chapter. Most software capabilities are repeated in subsequent examples so that users become familiar with their purpose and are capable of applying them to future problems. However, successive use of repeated steps is typically accompanied by briefer explanations. This approach is used to minimize document length, to permit users to work more at their own pace, and to devote more emphasis to new concepts being introduced.

Unlike many step-by-step user guides that only list a succession of steps, which if followed correctly lead to successful solution of a problem, this text attempts to provide insight into *why* each step is performed in a "just-in-time" manner. A consequence of this approach is somewhat lengthier explanations of new topics. However, these explanations ensure a deeper understanding and ultimately enhance knowledge about the software and the finite element method.

Numerous traditional design of machine elements textbooks[1,2,3,4,5,6] were reviewed prior to embarking on the writing of this SolidWorks Simulation user guide. The goal was to identify common organizational schemes such that this text would be compatible with the bulk of commonly used undergraduate machine design texts. However, considerable organizational differences between textbooks, compounded by the fact that course outlines often vary by instructor, made it unlikely that a common format would accommodate all organizational needs. Perhaps the only common theme found is that chapters in the first-half of the referenced texts focus on topics related to special states of stress found in mechanical elements.

For these reasons, this text begins with problems that can be solved with a basic understanding of mechanics of materials. Problem types quickly migrate to include states of stress found in more specialized situations common to a design of mechanical elements course. Paralleling this progression of problem types, each chapter introduces new software concepts and capabilities. Therefore, it is recommended that chapters be followed in the sequence presented. However, despite this recommendation, each chapter is self-contained, thus examples can be worked in any order.

Each example is divided into several major sections that are designated by a descriptive title or a sub-title. This division of topics is done to focus attention upon a specific overall task within each section. For example, individual sections are devoted to: material selection, application of fixtures and applied loads, meshing the model, etc. Each section is subdivided into a series of numbered steps intended to lead the user through a logical sequence of actions necessary to accomplish the overall goal of a specific section. However, numbed steps do not necessarily imply a rigid order to an analysis. Rather, the numbers are to serve as "location finders" when working back-and-forth between this user guide and a computer screen. Each menu selection is printed in **bold font** to facilitate locating the exact word or phrase on the computer monitor.

Because SolidWorks Simulation is a Windows® based program, the left mouse button serves the usual purposes of clicking to select an item or clicking-and-dragging to draw a line and/or to create or select a geometric shape. References to left mouse button selections are simply denoted by the words "click" or "select." Clicking the right mouse button provides access to numerous pull-down menus within SolidWorks Simulation. A "right-click" is always specifically indicated where applicable. Selections from within pull-down menus are always made with the left mouse button.

---

[1] Collins, J.A., Mechanical Design of Machine Elements and Machines, John Wiley & Sons, Inc, 2003.
[2] Hamrock, B., Schmid, S.R., Jacobson, B., Fundamental of Machine Elements, 2nd ed., McGraw-Hill, 2005.
[3] Mott, R.L., Machine Elements in Mechanical Design, 4th ed., Pearson-Prentice Hall, 2004.
[4] Budynas, R.G., Nisbett, J.K., Shigley's Mechanical Engineering Design, 8th ed., McGraw-Hill, 2008.
[5] Spotts, M., Shoup, T.E., Hornberger, L. Design of Machine Elements, 8th ed., Pearson-Prentice Hall, 2004.
[6] Ugural, A.C., Mechanical Design an Integrated Approach, McGraw-Hill, 2004.

It is frequently necessary to reorient SolidWorks models or assemblies by zooming, rotating, or otherwise manipulating the model to facilitate application of loads or restraints to specific geometric entities. To facilitate these operations without the need for menu or icon selections, the following "short-cut" key and mouse combinations are summarized in Table 1.

Table1 - Short-cut key and mouse button selections

Key and Mouse Button Combinations	Resulting Model Motion
Roll the Middle Mouse Button (MMB) 'up' or 'down.'	Zoom 'out' or 'in' on the model, respectively, in *incremental* steps.
[Shift] + MMB and push mouse 'away' from or 'toward' the user.	Zoom 'in' or 'out' on the model respectively, by *smooth* motion.
Press MMB and move the mouse.	Rotates the model rotates in 3-dimensions.
[Ctrl] + MMB and move the mouse.	Model moves left or right and/or up or down on the graphics screen.

Instructors Preface

This text is intended for use by students with background in an introductory Mechanics of Materials course. However, the focus of most examples and end of chapter problems is on topics commonly found in a Design of Machine Elements or similarly named course.

While it is fairly common knowledge that virtually anyone with a technical background can become proficient at using a finite element program, what is frequently lacking is the ability to discern meaningful results from the copious output produced by such programs. To address this perceived weakness, this text and its end-of-chapter problems consistently attempt to compare finite element results to results found using classical stress equations.

To accommodate organizational differences between design of machine elements textbooks and between individual course outlines, chapters of this text can be worked in any order. However, it is strongly recommended that Chapters 1 and 2 serve as a common starting point. While subsequent chapters may refer to techniques mastered in earlier (skipped) chapters, all necessary analysis steps are included so that users are able to complete each example. Also, due to default software output that uses von Mises stress plots, this topic is briefly introduced in Chapter 2. Instructors should be aware of this fact and attempt to fill in any gaps in understanding until von Mises stress is addressed in your course.

Finally, "check sheets" are provided to facilitate grading all end-of-chapter problems. These check sheets are created in MS Word® and, thus, can be edited to emphasize (add or delete) particular aspects of a problem and/or to change point values to emphasize the importance of specific portions of an analysis. Check sheets can be downloaded at the publisher's web site: http://www.schroff.com/resources. This is the same web site where model files for all textbook problems are found. It can be instructional to provide these sheets to students when problems are assigned so that expectations are clearly understood.

NOTES:

INTRODUCTION

Finite Element Analysis

Finite element theory was introduced over sixty years ago. However, implementation of this theory only became practical with the advent of high-speed computers. This section introduces one method of understanding the numerous sets of simultaneous equations that must be solved as part of the finite element method, and therefore, why this technique requires computer solution. Other more refined mathematical formulations exist; however, they are not the subject of this text. Suffice it to say that finite element theory applied to the solution of any realistic problem results in a computationally intensive exercise. Additional insight into the number of equations that must be solved in a finite element analysis is related to the number of nodes and elements in a model as described in the next section.

The following discussion provides a simplified overview of the mathematical basis of a finite element solution based on the *stiffness* approach. Begin by considering a simple member of original length **L** subject to an external axial load **F** as shown in Fig. 1. Due to force **F**, the member undergoes an axial deformation shown as **ΔL**. For this simple case, the well-known equation relating force and deformation is given by equation [1].

$$\Delta L = \frac{FL}{AE} \qquad [1]$$

Notice that the material property (**E** = modulus of elasticity) along with the applied force **F**, length **L**, and cross-sectional area **A**, must be known to solve for **ΔL**.

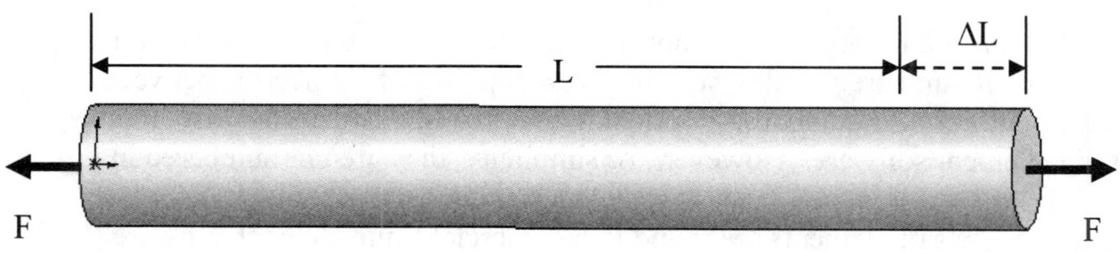

Figure 1 – A simple member subject axial force **F** to illustrate the relationship that exists between the applied force and the resulting deformation **ΔL**.

The next step in a stiffness formulation is to compute strain based on the deformation determined using equation [1] above. To do so the simple definition of strain is used; it can be expressed verbally as:

strain = (change of length) / (original length)

or

mathematically as:

$$\varepsilon = \frac{\Delta L}{L} \quad [2]$$

Finally, since the goal of analysis is determination of stress in a member, stress can be can be determined from the classic stress-strain relationship listed below.

$$\sigma = E\varepsilon \quad [3]$$

Of course, equation [3] is valid only in the elastic region where stress is proportional to strain. This fact is fundamental to *linear* finite element analysis described in this text.

Thus, finite element analysis begins with a basic mathematical description of deformation and proceeds to the solution of member stresses. Other formulations of finite element equations exist, but, they are not described here.

Nodes, Elements, Degrees of Freedom, and Equations

To permit mathematical analysis by the finite element method requires simplification of modeled parts. If the cylindrical member, shown in Fig. 1, were divided into an arbitrary number of *nodes* and *elements*, its model might appear as shown in Fig. 2.

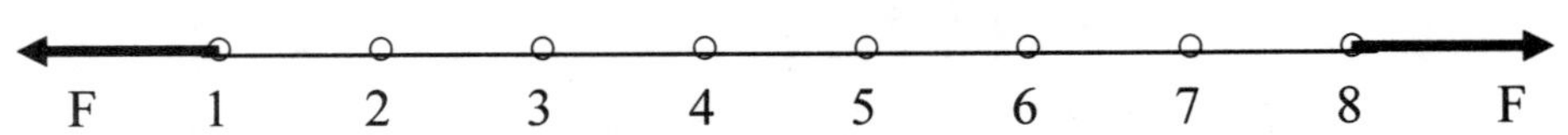

Figure 2 – Simplified model of the cylindrical member sub-divided into a series of nodes and elements.

In Fig. 2, *elements* are represented by short line segments between successive numbered points. The small numbered circles, which represent points of connection between adjacent elements, are called *nodes*. For tracking purposes, elements are also numbered within finite element software. However, for simplicity, they are not numbered in Fig. 2.

Many different types of elements are found in commercial finite element software. SolidWorks Simulation beam elements can be used to model the part shown in Figs. 1, 2 and 3. Beam elements are included here to introduce the concepts of *degrees of freedom* and the *number of equations* that result during a finite element solution. To assist with this understanding, we isolate an arbitrary element and its two nodes (n and n+1) from Fig. 2 to obtain an enlarged view of a single element and its two nodes shown in Fig. 3.

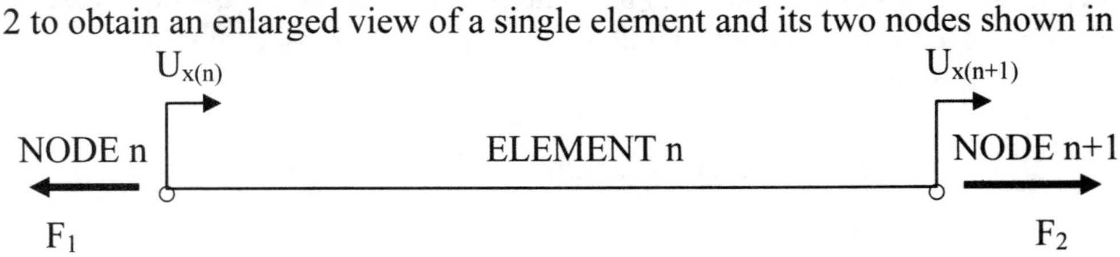

Figure 3 – A simple one-dimensional model represented using nodes and an element.

First, we assume that displacements at nodes n and n+1 are restricted to lie in the X-direction. This restriction ensures that the problem is one-dimensional (i.e., displacements are limited to a single direction, the X-direction). $U_{x(n)}$ and $U_{x(n+1)}$ represent displacements in the X-direction at *each* node. These displacements correspond to one *degree of freedom* at each node. Thus, since displacement at *each* node results in one set of equations, like equations [1, 2, 3] above, it is logical to conclude that two sets of equations result for the element shown in Fig. 3. (one set of equations for each node). If one were to extrapolate the above observation to all seven elements, each with two nodes, for the model shown in Fig. 2, it is evident that:

(7 elements)*(2 nodes/element)*(1 degree of freedom/node) = 14 degrees of freedom [4]

A mathematical solution for the fourteen displacements requires simultaneous solution of fourteen equations to solve this very simple problem. The following section examines other element types currently available in SolidWorks Simulation.

SolidWorks Simulation Elements

Having established a fundamental understanding of nodes, elements, and degrees of freedom, we next introduce the various types of elements available within SolidWorks Simulation. Basic element types include a *Solid* element, a *Shell* element, and *Beam* or *Truss* elements. *Solid* and *shell* elements are available as either a first-order or a second-order element types while *Beam* elements have unique characteristics as described in a later section. Descriptions of each element type follow.

Solid Elements

The majority of components analyzed by finite element methods are 3-dimensional models based on solid geometry used to define boundaries of a part or assembly. In this context *solid* refers to parts or assemblies that have significant volume or thickness relative to other component dimensions. The SolidWorks Simulation *solid* elements used to model this type of geometry are named tetrahedral elements. A first-order tetrahedral element, shown in Fig. 4, is comprised of six straight sides, four flat faces, and four nodes that the join edges at each of its four corners. All sides of first-order elements remain straight and flat after deformation. First-order elements are also called "draft quality" elements.

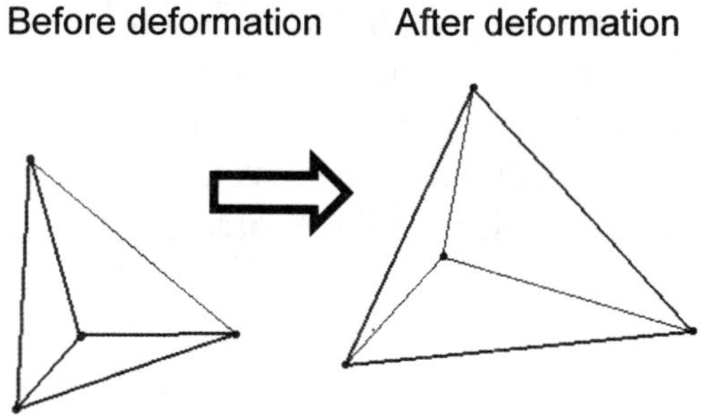

Figure 4 – First-order tetrahedral element before and after deformation.

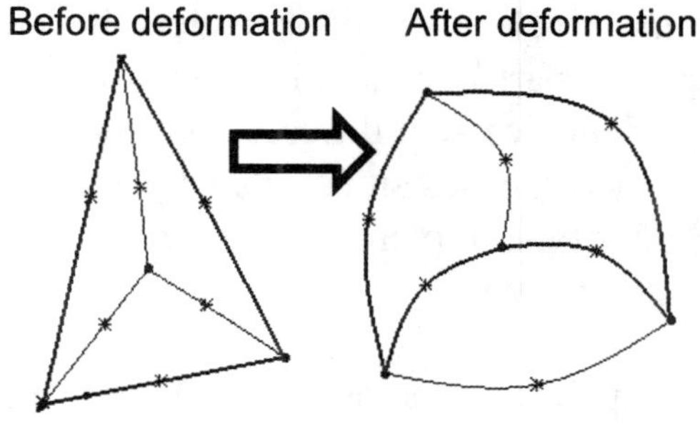

Figure 5 – Second-order tetrahedral element before and after deformation.

A second-order tetrahedral element, illustrated in Fig. 5, is characterized by the addition of another node on each edge of the element for a total of ten nodes per element. These additional nodes, often called "mid-side nodes," permit edges and surfaces to conform and deform in a second-order (curved) manner. The obvious advantage of second-order elements is their ability to provide better mapping of curved surfaces. And, a better fit of elements ensures improved modeling of deformations, strains, and hence stresses computed within modeled parts. Whether a first-order (draft quality mesh) or second-order (high quality mesh) is used, the overall mesh density (i.e., total number of elements) is essentially the same for identical model geometry. However, second-order elements yield better results at the expense of greater computational resources.

Solid Element Degrees of Freedom

Both first-order and second-order tetrahedral elements within SolidWorks Simulation allow three degrees of freedom at each node. These degrees of freedom permit *displacements* in the X, Y, and Z directions. The number of degrees of freedom for each element type is summarized below.

First-order element –
(3 degrees of freedom/node) * (4 nodes/element) = 12 degrees of freedom/element [5]

Second-order element –
(3 degrees of freedom/node) * (10 nodes/element) = 30 degrees of freedom/element [6]

Recalling the relationship between degrees of freedom and the corresponding number of simultaneous equations requiring solution for each degree of freedom, it is easily seen that computational intensity increases dramatically as model size and order of the element type increase. Although more computationally intensive, second-order elements yield more accurate results and are typically recommended.

Shell Elements

The second type of element available within SolidWorks Simulation is the *shell* element. As implied by its name, *shell* elements are primarily used to analyze thin-walled components such as sheet metal parts or other thin parts (surfaces) regardless of material. Examples of components that might be modeled using shell elements include a motorcycle gas tank or fenders, beverage containers, thin-wall pressure vessels, many plastic parts, or the oil pan on your car. Although the above examples may appear to present clear-cut differences between uses for *solid* and *shell* elements, in reality there exist numerous situations where a "thin" member can be modeled equally well using either type of element. Usually the nature of desired results dictates the choice of element type.

As with solid elements, *shell* elements are also available as first-order "draft quality" or second-order "high quality" mesh types. Figure 6 illustrates a first-order shell element. This element appears two dimensional with straight sides, a flat surface, and one node at each of its three corners. Figure 7 illustrates a second-order shell element with its additional mid-side nodes yielding a total of six nodes per element.

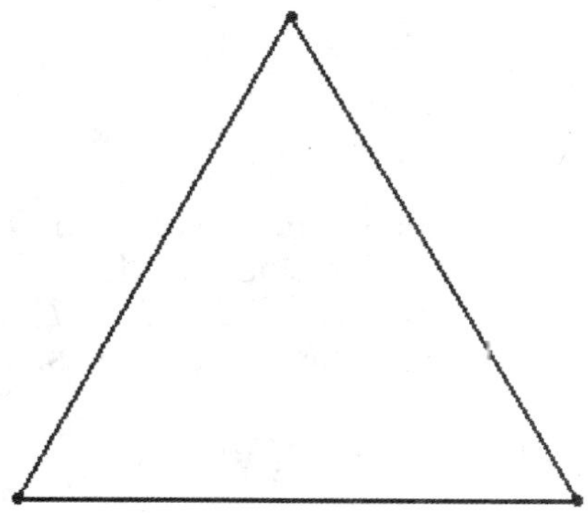

Figure 6 – First-order shell element.

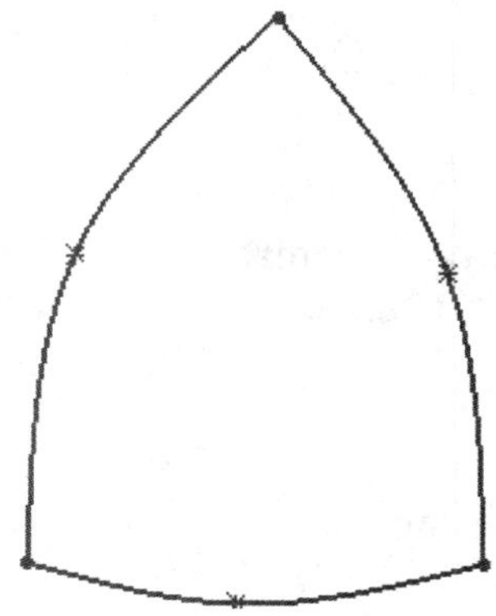

Figure 7 – Second-order shell element showing additional mid-side nodes.

Once again, mid-side nodes permit shell elements to conform to curved geometry of the original component and to better model curvature associated with displacements in deformed parts. Although shell elements are considered two dimensional, a thickness must be associated with them to properly model a part. There are two ways to define a shell mesh. One method creates a shell mesh based on the *mid-surface* of a part while the other approach allows the user to select the surface to be meshed. Since assignment of mesh thickness varies according to how a shell mesh is defined, this topic is investigated further in an illustrative example in Chapter 4.

Shell Element Degrees of Freedom

Because shell elements are two dimensional, it might be presumed that they have fewer degrees of freedom (i.e., displacements) allowed at each node point. However, just the opposite is true because, in addition to translational displacements at each node, thin members (shells or membranes) may be subject to bending displacements. Therefore, each node of a shell element has six degrees of freedom. They include three displacements (X, Y, Z) and three rotations, one about each of the global X, Y, Z axes.

Beam and Truss Elements

Beam or truss elements are the logical choice when modeling structural members due to the significantly reduced number of nodes and elements required to create a model. Beam elements are used where length of the member is large when compared to its cross sectional dimensions. For example, beam elements are typically used where the length to height ratio is 20:1 or greater. To gain an appreciation for simplicity of beam elements, consider Figs. 8 (a, b, c). If the structural channel shown schematically in Fig. 8 (a) were created using solid or shell elements, thousands of nodes and elements would be required to model each beam as shown in Fig. 8 (b). However, use of beam elements reduces model size to a series of cylinders (the elements) connected end-to-end (by nodes) shown in Fig. 8 (c). Smaller model size results in a reduction of computational resources used during an analysis while still yielding needed results.

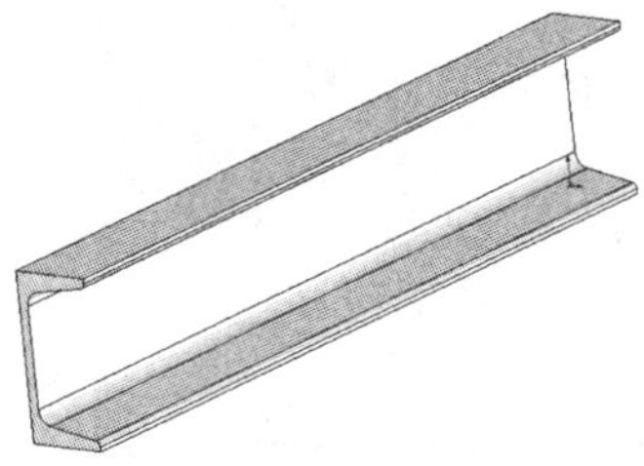

Figure 8 (a) - Schematic of a structural channel.

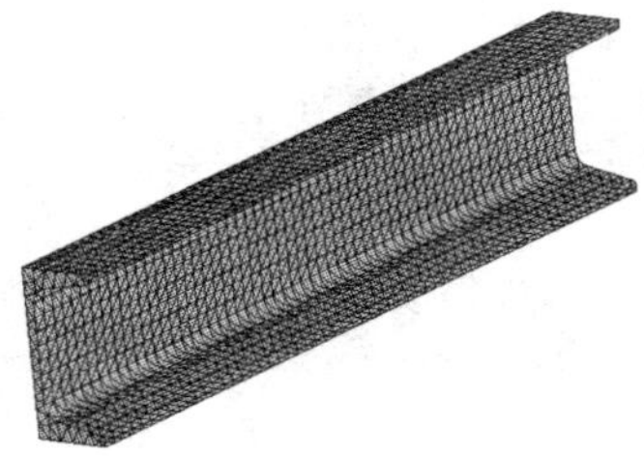

Figure 8 (b) - Channel modeled using solid tetrahedral elements consists of over 19,000 nodes.

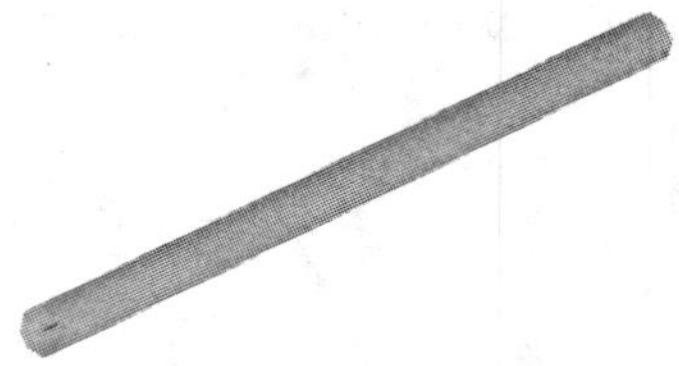

Figure 8 (c) – Simplified beam element model consists of 59 nodes 57 elements and two joints.

Extensive tables of common beam cross-sections are available within SolidWorks.

Beams are defined by a straight line of beam *elements* connected by *nodes* and with one *joint* at each end. Also, definition of beam cross-section dimensions is needed to so that the program can compute moment of inertia and neutral axis location. No matter what the shape of the original structural member is, when represented as a beam or truss element, it appears like the cylinder illustrated in Fig. 8 (c).

Based upon their application, these structural members can be defined as either *truss* or *beam* elements. The difference between these definitions lies in the connections defined between the members. For example, a *truss* consists of a structural member connected by pin joints at both ends. As such, truss members are classified as two force members that carry only axial loads (tension or compression). A *beam*, on the other hand, assumes rigid connections between members. These rigid connections are capable of transmitting not only axial loads, but also bending moments, and even torsion between connected members.

Because beam elements are not investigated in this text, this brief introduction should suffice to alert the interested reader to their existence and general use.

Meshing a Model

The process of subdividing machine elements into an organized set of nodes and elements is called *meshing,* or creating a *mesh,* on a model of the component to be analyzed. As implied above, mathematical solution of a finite element analysis depends upon sets of simultaneous equations that describe small displacements at the element level. Therefore, subdividing a model into a continuous set of nodes and elements, i.e., meshing a model, is a necessary prerequisite in the solution process. Fortunately, within SolidWorks Simulation meshing occurs automatically. However, users have the ability to apply mesh controls as is investigated in an example in Chapter 3.
To understand this process it is helpful to outline the progression from an actual part to a meshed finite element model. This process is illustrated in Figs. 9, 10, and 11. Typically

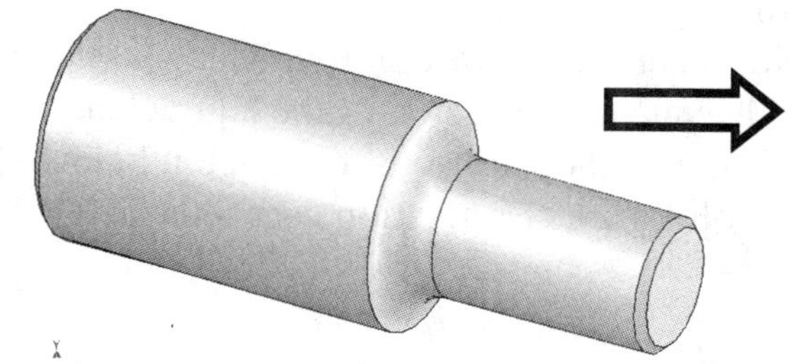

Figure 9 – Solid model of an actual machine shaft to be meshed prior to FEA.

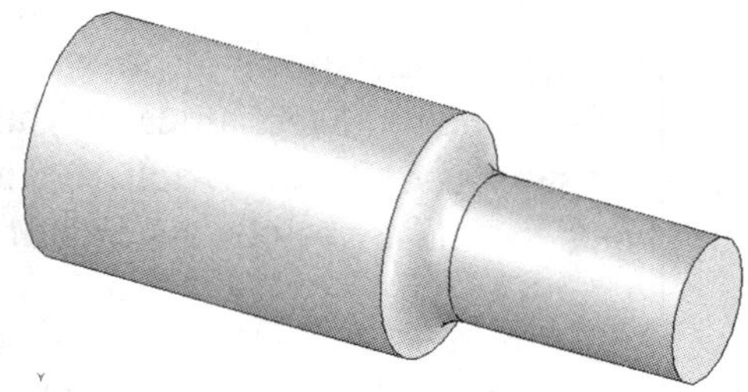

Figure 10 – Solid model of shaft modified to simplify its geometry prior to meshing. (two end chamfers are deleted)

actual part geometry is simplified to reduce or eliminate geometric features that have little or no impact on the ensuing analysis. This step is known as "defeaturing" the model. In this example, 45° chamfers are removed from both ends of the shaft shown in Fig. 9, which leads to the simplified model illustrated in Fig. 10. This may seem like a small change, but an accumulation of similar small changes made to a complex part or assembly can significantly reduce model complexity and hence solution time. Of course, the user must use good engineering judgment when weighing whether or not simplifying changes alter important aspects of stress within a model.

Figure 11 shows the simplified shaft model after meshing it using first-order, solid tetrahedral elements. The model below consists of approximately 1543 elements and 7192 nodes. Automatic meshing of this part was accomplished in less than three seconds using SolidWorks Simulation 2009 and a Pentium IV® PC.

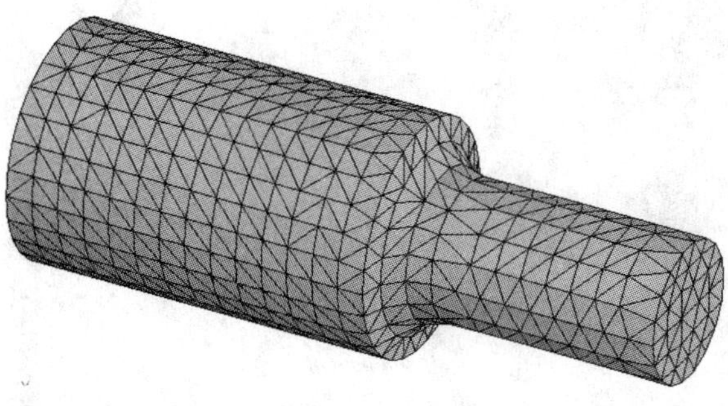

Figure 11 – Meshed model of the shaft using first-order (draft quality) tetrahedral elements.

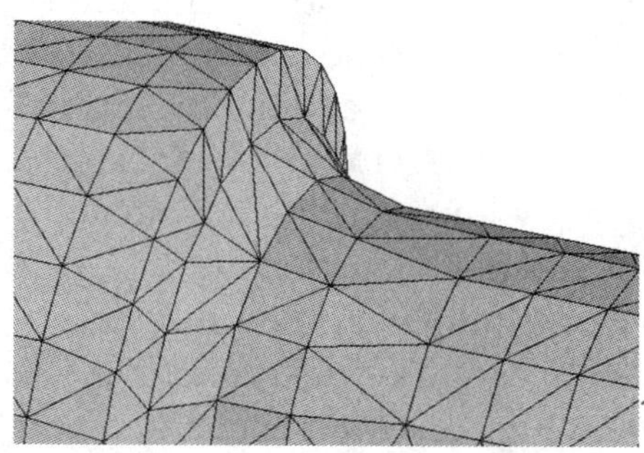

Figure 12 – Close-up of the fillet reveals the approximate nature of first-order tetrahedral elements.

Figure 12 shows a close-up view of the fillet at the transition between small and large shaft diameters. This image reveals the approximate nature of first-order tetrahedral element edges (straight edges) when used to model a curved surface. The modeling errors that are visible when first-order elements are used contribute to larger approximations in computed results of a finite element analysis. For this reason, second-order (high quality) elements are recommended to achieve more accurate results. Remaining steps of a finite element analysis are analogous to steps involved when solving stress related problems by long-hand methods. In particular, loads and restraints are applied to the model (like creating a free-body diagram), and material properties are selected so that stress levels can be compared to material strength at the conclusion of a solution. Because these aspects of problem solution are familiar to individuals who have completed a fundamental Mechanics of Materials course, discussion of the equivalent finite element steps is deferred to actual examples. For these reasons, discussion below shifts emphasis to define various aspects of the SolidWorks Simulation user interface.

Introduction to the SolidWorks Simulation User Interface

Perhaps the most awkward part of getting started using SolidWorks, SolidWorks Simulation, or any other complex software program, is finding your way around in a new software work environment. Because some users might be new to both SolidWorks Simulation *and* SolidWorks, this introduction begins by providing orientation to the SolidWorks work environment, also known as a Graphical User Interface or GUI.

Proficient SolidWorks users can skip the SolidWorks orientation section below. However, the toolbars shown in Figs. 13 and 15 should be examined. These toolbars are important because many SolidWorks icons are also useful when working in SolidWorks Simulation.

Orientation and Set-up of the SolidWorks Work Environment

First time users of the combined SolidWorks / SolidWorks Simulation software must become acquainted with both the vocabulary and the location of items in the work environment. Thus, we begin by investigating how to add or delete menus to the default SolidWorks graphical user interface. The default SolidWorks screen is shown in Fig. 13. Most menu items are inactive (grayed out) at this time.

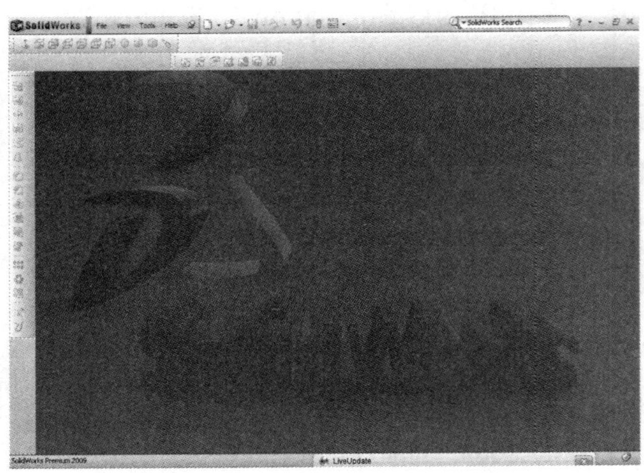

Figure 13 – SolidWorks start-up screen showing default menus and toolbars.

Depending upon your work environment, particularly at public access computers, the default SolidWorks work environment may have been altered by previous users. Therefore, this section outlines how to return all settings to the factory default settings followed by steps to customize the work environment.
Begin by opening the main menu and permanently displaying it on the screen as outlined below.

1. If the **Main Menu**, labeled on Fig. 14, appears at the top left of the s… to step 3. Otherwise, move the cursor over the  button at top … the screen. This action opens the main menu illustrated in Fig. 14.

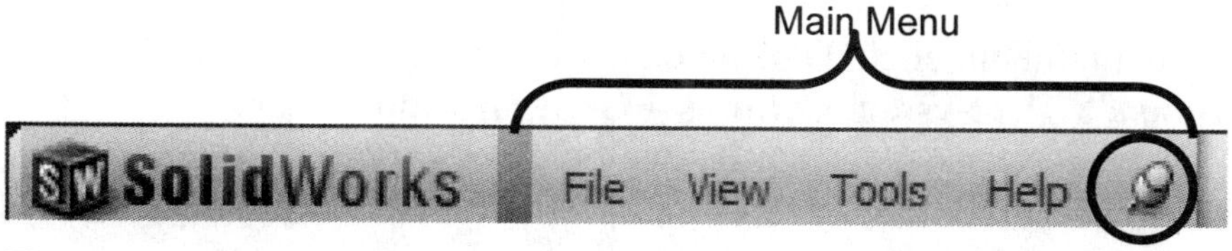

Figure 14 – The SolidWorks button provides access to the **File**, **View**, **Tools**, and **Help** items in the main menu.

2. Because these menu items are used frequently, click to select the "push-pin" icon, circled in Fig. 14. This action permanently displays the main menu.

The next step is to reset to the system default settings. Begin by opening a *new part* file in SolidWorks as follows.

3. In the SolidWorks main menu, click **File**, and from the pull-down menu select **New…**. The **New SolidWorks Document** window opens. Within this window, click the **Part**  icon.

4. Click **[OK]** to open this *new* part. The **New SolidWorks Document** window closes and the default SolidWorks screen appears similar to that in Fig. 15.

Various areas of the *default* SolidWorks start-up screen are labeled in Fig. 15. Also, explore the *tabs* beneath the **Sketch** toolbar. SolidWorks users will notice a tab for the familiar **Featrures** toolbar. After exploring several tabs, return to the **Sketch** tab.

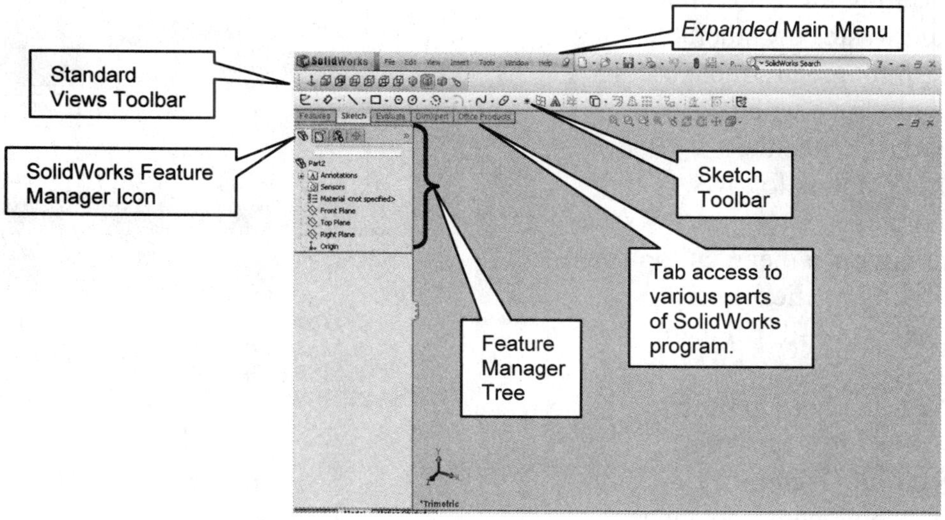

Figure 15 – Definitions identifying basic portions of the SolidWorks screen. Several default toolbars are shown.

If your screen looks like Fig. 15, skip to the section titled **Customizing the SolidWorks Screen** immediately below. If not, proceed to the next step where the default screen settings are reset.

5. In the main menu, click **Tools** and near the bottom of the pull-down menu, select **Options…** The **System Options – General** widow opens.

6. At the lower left corner of this window, click the **[Reset All]** button. Immediately the **SolidWorks** confirmation window opens as shown in Fig. 16.

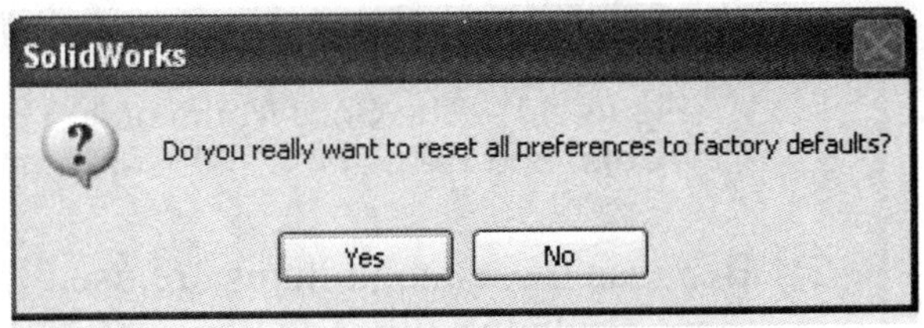

Figure 16 – SolidWorks confirmation window.

7. Select the **[Yes]** button to return SolidWorks to the factory default settings.

8. Click **[OK]** to close the **System Options – General** widow.

Customizing the SolidWorks Screen

If the large graphics area of the screen appears grey, blue, or some other shaded color, continue to the next paragraph. However, if the background color is *white*, skip to the sentence following step 7.

Because a shaded background can mask details of a screen image and because printing images on this background wastes considerable ink/toner (think green), most users prefer to work on a white background. Change the background color as follows.

1. In the main menu, at top left of screen, click **Tools** to open a pull-down menu.

2. Near the bottom of this menu, click **Options…** The **System Options - General** window opens and appears similar to Fig. 17.

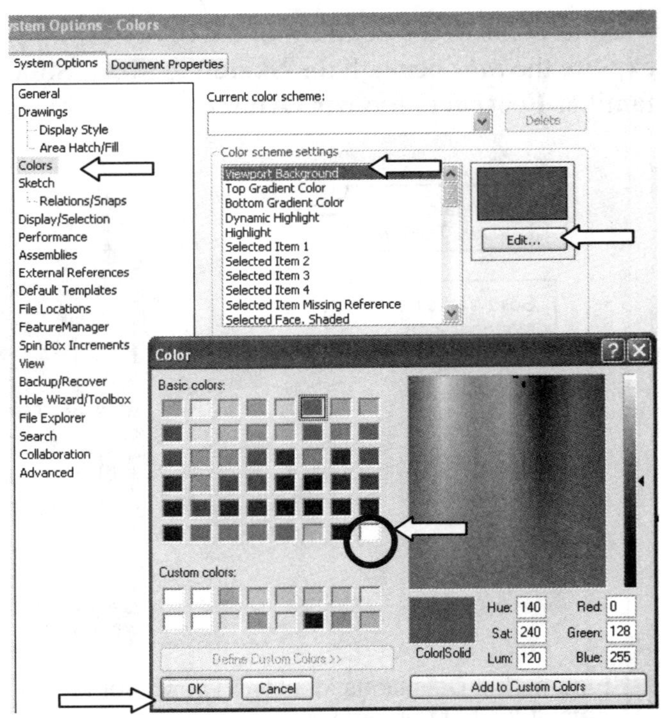

Figure 17 – Selections used to change the **Viewport Background** color.

3. Beneath the **Systems Options** tab, select **Colors** and immediately the right half of the window appears similar to that shown in the background of Fig. 17.

4. Within the **Color scheme settings** box, the top entry should read, **Viewport Background**. Click to select **Viewport Background** (if not already selected).

5. To the right of the previous selection, click the **[Edit...]** button. The **Color** window opens as also shown in Fig. 17.

6. Within the **Basic colors:** section, select the *white* color box; then click **[OK]** to close the **Color** window.

7. Finally, click **[OK]** to close the **System Options - Color** window.

The next task leads you through the addition of various toolbars to the screen and the modification of some existing toolbars.

8. From the main menu, click **View**. Then from the pull-down menu select **Toolbars ▶**. This action opens the Command Manager pull-down menu shown in the partial screen image of Fig. 18. *CAUTION: Two **Toolbars** options exist! Choose the one indicated by an arrow.*

The **Standard Views** icon, circled in Fig 18, corresponds to the **Standard Views** toolbar that already appears at the top of the graphics window in Fig. 15. Note that the **Standard Views** icon appears depressed (darker shading) thereby indicating it is active. *NOTE: It may be necessary to scroll down the list to locate the **Standard Views** icon.*

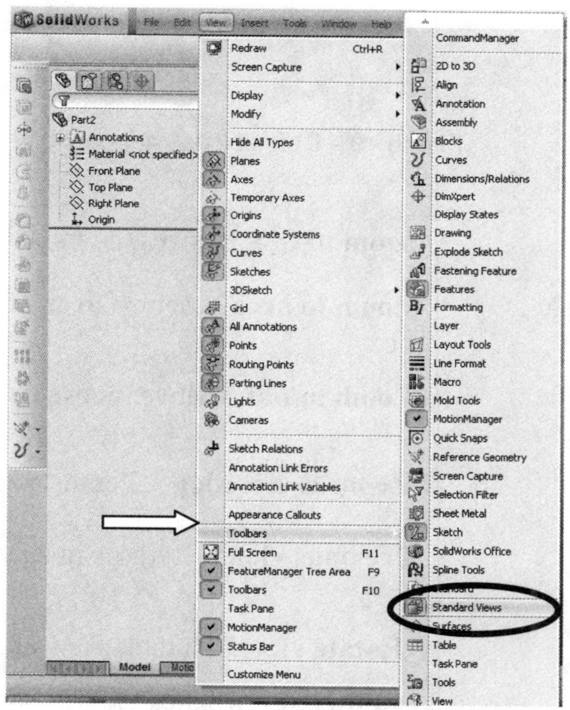

Figure 18 – The Command Manager menu from which toolbars are selected for display.

Although the following steps detail how to add toolbars to the menu, be aware that most necessary toolbars already appear on the screen due to default settings within SolidWorks. Thus, to gain practice with this procedure, follow steps below to *turn off* the toolbars and subsequently to *turn them back on.*

9. Click **Standard Views** (see circled menu item in Fig. 18). The menu closes and the **Standard Views** toolbar is deleted from the top of the screen.

10. Once again open the Command Manager pull-down menu again, but this time use the following shortcut. Right-click anywhere in the light grey area on the top menu bar. This shortcut opens directly to the Command Manager menu.

11. Locate and select the **Standard Views** icon. The Command Manager closes and the **Standard Views** toolbar is again added to the top of the screen.

12. To gain familiarity with this process, repeat steps 10and 11 but, this time select the **Sketch** icon. The **Sketch** toolbar is typically placed along the right edge of the graphics window. If it does not appear there initially, its location can be adjusted by clicking-and-dragging a toolbar drag handle located at the top or right side of the toolbar.

Finally, observe the icons appearing at the top-middle of the graphics screen shown in Fig. 19. These icons allow the user to perform various graphic manipulations on part models. A brief description of each is provided below.

Figure 19 – Default icons appearing at top-middle of the start-up screen

 **Zoom to fit** – Resizes the model and places it at the center of the screen.

 **Zoom to area** – Zooms to an area of the model enclosed in a user defined box.

 **Zoom in/out** – Move mouse up or down to zoon 'out' or 'in' on the model.

 **Zoom to selection** – Zooms to selected part or sub-assembly.

 **Previous view** – Returns image to previous view.

 **Rotate view** – Rotates view about 3-dimensional axes.

 **Roll view** – Rotates view about a specific X, Y, or Z axis.

 **Pan** – Moves model left/right, up/down, or diagonally.

 **Standard views** – The ▼arrow provides access to multiple standard views. These views are also accessible using **Standard Views** icons on the upper menu.

13. By right-clicking on any of these icons a pull-down menu containing the above icons, and several additional, icons is opened.

14. Within this menu, icons can be removed from the screen by clicking to remove the check mark "✓" adjacent to an icon name. Conversely, icons can be added by the reverse process. Make no changes to the icons shown.

15. Close the pull-down menu by clicking anywhere outside the menu.

Although short-cut methods for manipulating the model were introduced in the Preface, (see **Table 1**, page ix), new users may find the visual display of icon capability helpful.

Seasoned SolidWorks users might choose to place additional toolbars on the screen, or to customize those now appearing by adding or removing specific icons. The procedure to do this is much the same as adding or removing icons in any Windows® program. For this reason it is not uncommon for slight differences of screen images to occur. Some blank areas on the upper toolbar menu will be filled in with SolidWorks Simulation icons as demonstrated in the next section.

Orientation to the SolidWorks Simulation Work Environment

Following procedures like those outlined above, essential SolidWorks Simulation toolbars are next added to the screen. However, it is first necessary to deal with the possibility that the *Simulation* (i.e., finite element) component of SolidWorks has not yet been added to the work environment. Thus, proceed as follows to activate SolidWorks *Simulation*.

1. In the main menu, click **Tools** and from the pull-down menu select **Add-Ins...** The **Add-Ins** window opens as shown in Fig. 20.

2. Within the **Add-Ins** window, click to place a check mark to the *left* of ☑ **SolidWorks Simulation** and also in the **Start Up** column located to the *right* of **SolidWorks Simulation** ☑.

3. Click **[OK]** to close the **Add-Ins** window.

This action adds the name "**Simulation**" to the main menu at the top of the screen. At this time it may be necessary for first time users to **[Accept]** the SolidWorks Simulation license agreement. Also, depending upon the version of SolidWorks being used, a **Welcome to SolidWorks Simulation** window may open. Review the videos as time permits.

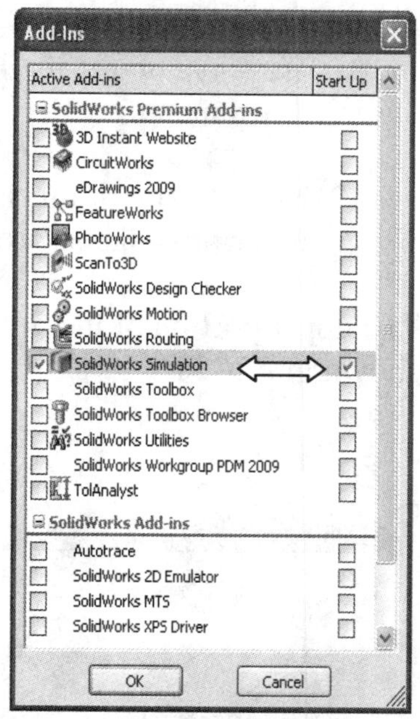

Figure 20 – Activating the SolidWorks Simulation software.

4. Click **Simulation** in the main menu to open a pull-down menu of capabilities available within the finite element portion of the program.

Because there are simpler ways to access Simulation capabilities, the approach used in the previous step will be used rarely.

5. Click anywhere outside the menu to close it.

6. Right-click on any of the *tabs* near the top left of the screen. A pull-down menu opens. This menu contains other tabs that can be added to or deleted from those currently displayed.

Proceed as follows to remove unneeded tabs and to add more important tabs.

7. Right-click *any tab* near the top left of screen. This action opens a pull-down menu.

8. In the pull-down menu clear the check mark "✓" adjacent to ☐ **DimXpert**. The menu closes automatically and **DimXpert** is removed from the list of tabs.

9. Once again, right-click any tab. In the pull-down menu place a check mark adjacent to ☑ **Simulation**. This action causes the **Simulation** tab to appear at the top of the screen.

10. Click the **Simulation** tab to display icons used during a finite element analysis.

11. Because these icons are unfamiliar to new users, right-click anywhere in the light grey area on the top menu bar to once again open the Command Manager pull-down menu.

12. Near the top of this menu, select **Use Large Buttons with Text** and immediately, descriptive labels are added beneath each icon.

The upper portion of the SolidWorks Simulation window should now appear like that shown in Fig. 21.

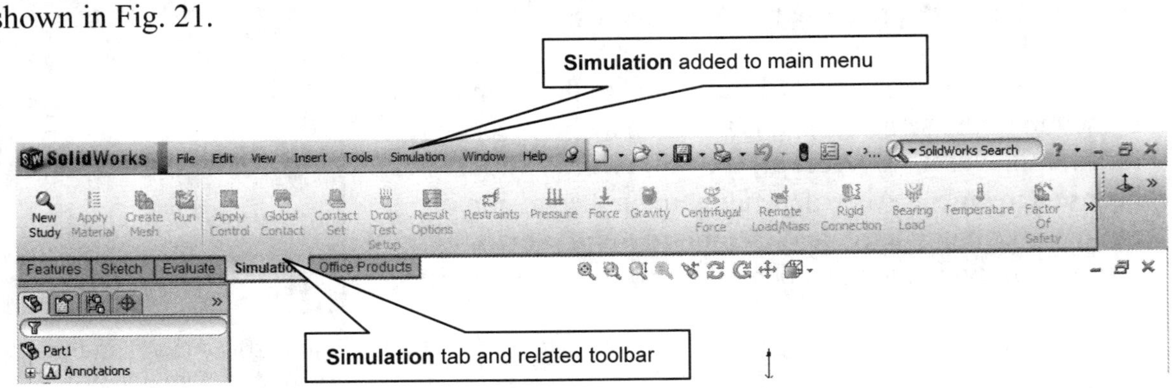

Figure 21 – Work environment modified by the addition of the SolidWorks Simulation toolbars.

Property Managers and Dialogue Boxes

Property managers and dialogue boxes are, perhaps, the most frequently used items when developing a finite element analysis within SolidWorks Simulation. The importance of these two interfaces cannot be overstated because the specific meaning of each aspect of the finite element modeling process is defined within them. However, these interfaces are only encountered when defining an actual analysis. For this reason, this section only attempts to define their location on the screen and provide basic insight to their general role in an analysis. Because an actual analysis is not currently being performed, this section is descriptive in nature only and does not require user interaction.

When opened, a *property manager* is typically located at the left side of the graphics screen, shown boxed in Fig. 22. Numerous property managers exist and each is somewhat unique. However, the general observations included below apply to each. The property manager, shown boxed in Fig. 22, is enlarged in Fig. 23.

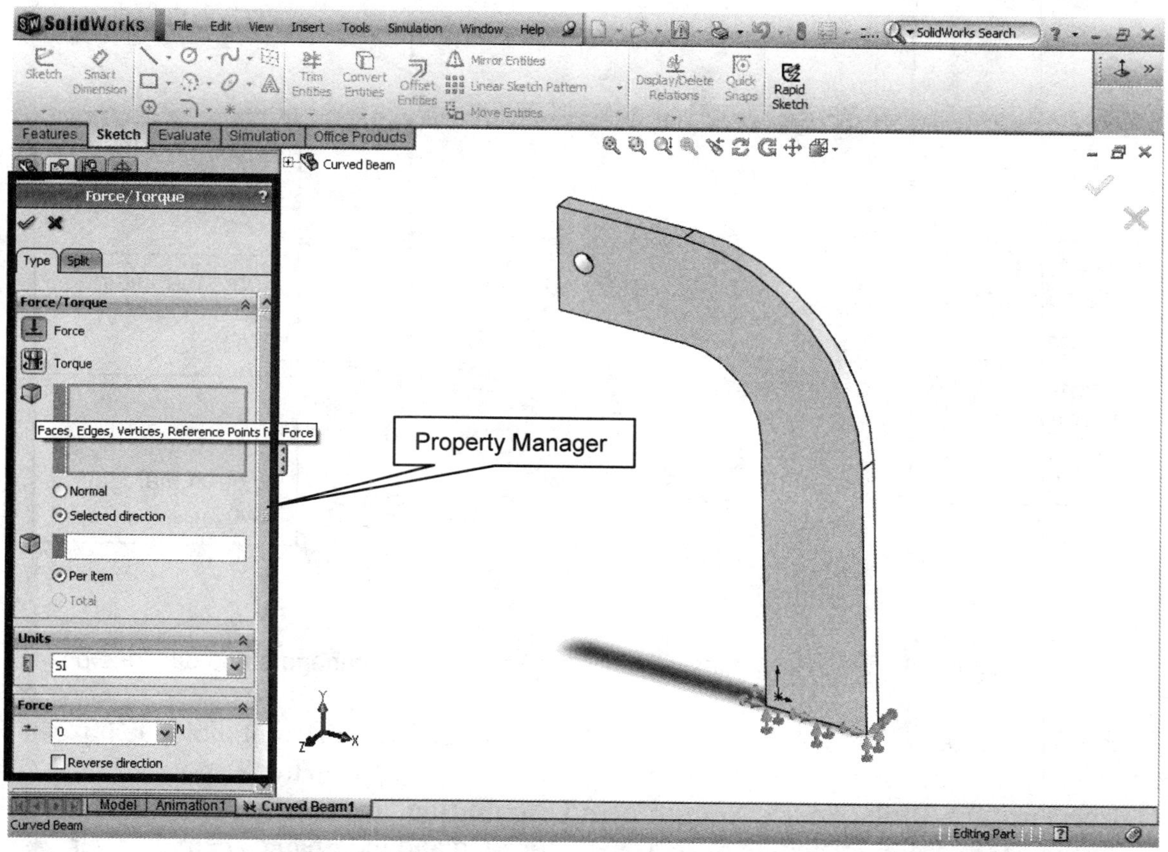

Figure 22 – Image showing the location of a property manager in the SolidWorks Simulation graphical user interface.

Figure 23 shows an example of the **Force/Torque** property manager with its name prominently displayed at the top. This property manager is used when defining different types of loads applied to a finite element model.

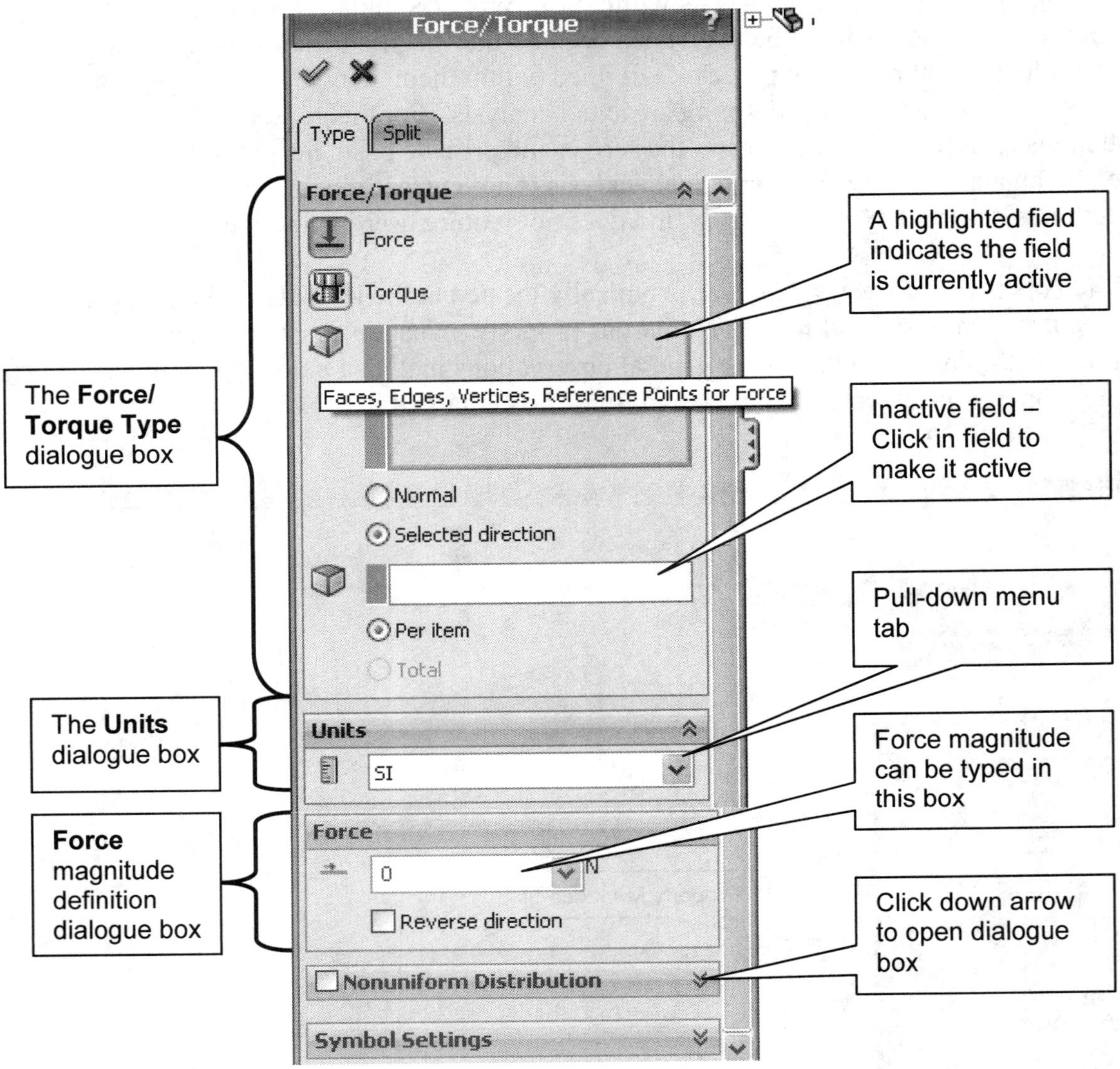

Figure 23 – Overview of features common to property managers and dialogue boxes.

Each *property manager* contains several *dialogue boxes*. Five different dialogue boxes appear in the **Force/Torque** property manager shown above, they are: **Type (Force/Torque)**, **Units**, **Force**, **Nonuniform Distribution**, and **Symbol settings**. Dialogue boxes group related items in a single location and their names help the user quickly locate items to be defined.

For example, the **Type** dialogue box lists various types of forces or torques that can be selected by clicking within the ⊙ symbol to the left of a specific load type. Also within the **Type** dialogue box are two *fields*. Moving the cursor over a field, or the icon adjacent to a field, causes specific field information to appear much like occurs for other Windows® icons. In Fig. 23, the name of the upper field is displayed as "**Faces, Edges,**

Vertices, Reference Points for Force". This field is also highlighted (here shown in grey), which indicates it is currently "active" and awaiting user input.

Many dialogue boxes contain pull-down menus, which can be accessed by clicking the symbol adjacent to the field. For example, the **Units** dialogue box in Fig. 23 permits the user to switch between **English (IPS)**, **SI**, or **Metric (G)** units. Some boxes, such as the **Force** dialogue box, permit the user to type a force value into a data box. And finally, as is often the case, insufficient space is available to display the contents of all dialogue boxes simultaneously. Therefore, only the titles of some dialogue boxes appear. In these instances the user must click the symbol to display the contents of the dialogue box. Such is the case for the **Nonuniform Distribution** and the **Symbol Settings** dialogue boxes at the bottom of Fig, 23.

This completes the introduction to underlying fundamentals of finite element analysis and the SolidWorks and SolidWorks Simulation graphical user interfaces. Familiarize yourself with this work environment so that you are able to work comfortably within it.

Examples focusing on the application of SolidWorks Simulation to solve finite element modeling problems begin in the next chapter.

NOTES:

CHAPTER #1

STRESS ANALYSIS USING SOLIDWORKS SIMULATION

This chapter is intended to familiarize first-time users of SolidWorks Simulation with basic software capabilities. Particular aspects of the software to be mastered are listed below. This example problem also serves as a model for subsequent Finite Element Analysis (FEA) problems because, once mastered, the sequence of solution steps is fairly consistent. These steps closely parallel the first six learning objectives outlined below.

Learning Objectives

Upon completion of this unit, users should be able to:

- Create and execute a linear, static Finite Element Analysis (FEA) using SolidWorks Simulation. This process is named a *"Study."*
- Assign *Material Properties* using the SolidWorks material editor.
- Apply *Fixtures* and *External Loads* to a model.
- Use the default *Mesh* definition to subdivide a part into nodes and elements.
- Execute a standard *Solution* to a FEA problem.
- Selectively view appropriate stress *Results* of a Finite Element Analysis.
- Use the *Probe* feature to create graphs of stress variation within a part.
- Develop insight into practical decisions that influence how a *Study* is defined to obtain desired results.

Problem Statement

The goal of this example is to determine stresses in the reciprocating cam follower illustrated in Fig. 1. In particular, stresses to be determined are those in the circled region near the upper end of the cam follower where it passes through its support in the frame.

Positions of the cam and follower shown in Fig. 1 and Fig. 2 are assumed to correspond to the locations of maximum cam pressure angle and maximum dynamic load on the cam follower. Although not shown here, a dynamic analysis should be performed using SolidWorks Motion and the resulting dynamic loads used here.

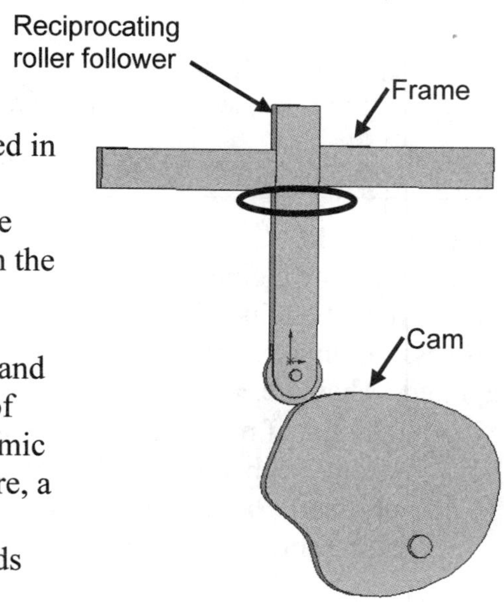

Figure 1 – Concept sketch showing the region of interest on the cam follower.

Figure 2 shows specific dimensions and loads applied to the cam follower. Force components F_x = -368 lb and F_y = 1010 lb exerted by the cam on the follower in the X and Y directions are applied on the roller-pin at the bottom of the follower. Because a static stress analysis is to be performed, the upper-end of the cam follower is considered "fixed", analogous to the fixed end of a cantilever beam, and corresponding reaction forces R_x, R_y, and a resisting moment M_z are shown at the upper support. We will soon discover one of these end conditions is not possible if solid tetrahedral elements are used to model the cam follower.

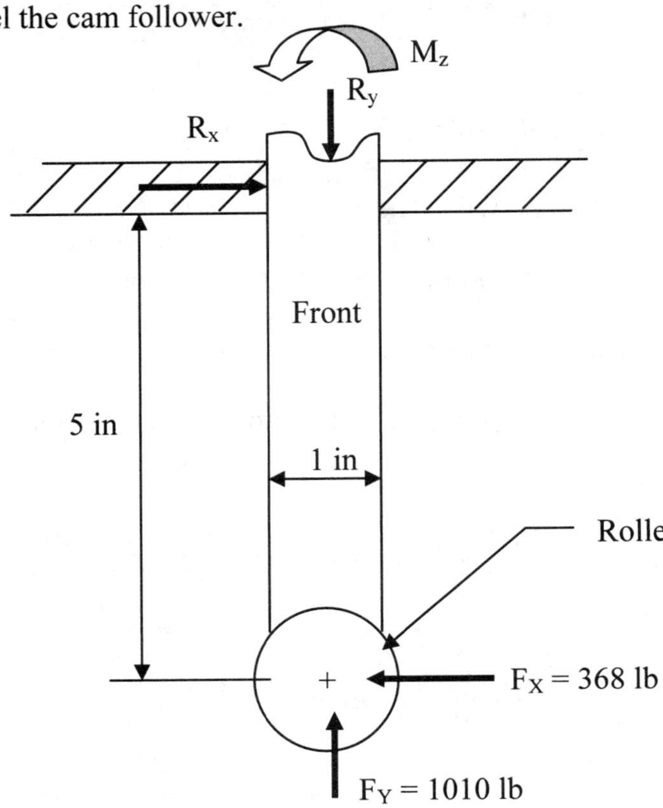

Figure 2 – Two-dimensional model of the reciprocating cam follower. The *Front* surface is labeled for later reference. The follower stem is ½ in deep into the page.

Design Insight

Although finite element programs are powerful computational tools, you should be aware that engineering assumptions are often necessary to advance the design process. In this example, at least three significant engineering assumptions are applied. They are:

- The list of possible materials must be narrowed to a group that provides a strong yet heat-treatable class of steels. Heat treatment is important to produce a hard, long wearing surface for contact between the cam follower and frame.

- Because the focus of this analysis is on stresses at the *upper* end of the cam follower, modeling of the roller and its pin connection to the follower can be neglected at a considerable saving of effort.

- Assuming the upper-end of the cam follower is "fixed" results in significant simplification for this initial example (i.e. a static rather than a dynamic analysis results).

Creating a Static Stress Analysis (Study)

Before proceeding, download and unzip chapter examples and end-of-chapter problems from the publisher's web site at: **http://www.schroff.com/resources**

1. Open SolidWorks by making the following selections. These steps are similar to opening any Windows program. (*Note:* The "/" is used to separate successive menu selections.)

Start/All Programs/SolidWorks 2009 (or) Click the **SolidWorks** icon on your screen.

2. When SolidWorks opens, select **File / Open...** Then use procedures common to your computer environment to open the file named **Cam Follower (Part)**.

If a pop-up SolidWorks window appears and states: **The following documents will be converted when saved: Cam Follower (Part).SLDPRT**, click **[OK]** to close the window. The cam follower part should now appear as shown in Fig. 3.

NOTE: If SolidWorks **Simulation** is not listed in the main menu of the SolidWorks screen, then in the main menu click **Tools / Add-Ins...** Next, in the **Add-Ins** window place check marks "✓" in the left *and* right columns adjacent to ☑ **SolidWorks Simulation** ☑ then click **[OK]** to close the **Add Ins** window. The **SolidWorks Simulation** License Agreement appears *(for first-time users only).* Click **[Accept]**.

At this point **Simulation** is added to the main menu displayed at the top of the screen. If the main menu is not displayed, go to the top of page I-9 of the Introduction and perform step 1. In fact, if the graphical user interface is not set up as outlined on pages I-8 through I-14 of the Introduction, it is *strongly recommended* to do so at this time because instructions below are based on the work environment defined there.

3. In the main menu, select **Simulation**. Then from the pull-down menu select **Study...** Alternatively, in the **Simulation** tab, near top of the screen, click to select the **New Study** icon. The **Study** property manager opens as shown in Fig. 4.

4. In the **Name** dialogue box, replace "**Study 1**" by typing a descriptive name. For this example type, "**Cam Follower #1**."

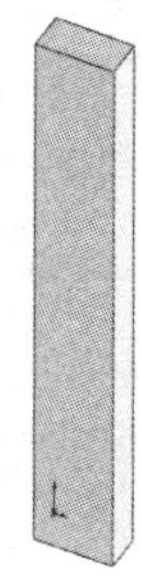

Figure 3 – Solid model of the cam follower.

5. Next, in the **Type** dialogue box, verify that the system default **Static** analysis icon appears shaded to indicate it is selected.

6. Click **[OK]** ✓ (the green check mark) to close the **Study** Property manager.

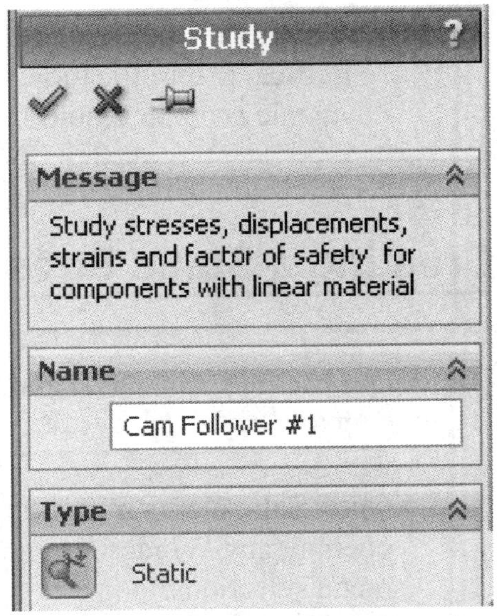

Figure 4 – Initial selections shown in the **Study** property manager.

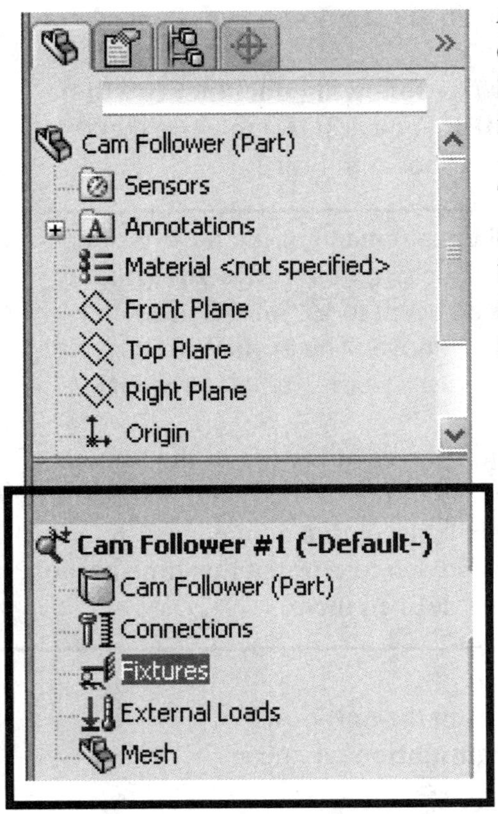

Figure 5 – The **SolidWorks Simulation** manager showing various components used to define a Study.

After completing the above steps, an outline of the current Study is created at the bottom of the SolidWorks Simulation manager tree, shown boxed in Fig. 5.

The Study name, **Cam Follower #1 (-Default-)**, appears in bold font at the top of the box. Beneath this name is the **Cam Follower (Part)** folder. This folder contains the SolidWorks model of the cam follower. Also shown are:

a. The **Connections** icon, where interactions between parts are defined. Connections are not applicable to this example because only one part exists,

b. Next is the **Fixtures** icon where restraints are applied to the model,

c. The **External Loads** icon is next. This is where forces, torques, pressures, etc. are applied to a model,

d. Finally, the **Mesh** icon.

The finite element analysis steps outlined in Fig. 5 proceed in a logical order. Thus, this sequence of steps is followed in all subsequent examples. It is, however, worth noting that steps shown in the outline can be executed in any order.

Assigning Material to the Model

Begin by defining the material of which the cam follower is made. To do this, proceed as follows. *NOTE: For simplicity in the remainder of this text, the SolidWorks Simulation manager will be referred to as the Simulation manager.*

1. In the Simulation manager right-click the **Cam Follower (Part)** folder; see Fig. 6, and from the pull-down menu, select **Apply/Edit Material...** The **Material** window opens as shown in Fig. 7.

2. Near the top-left of the **Material** window, beneath **Select material source**, do the following:

   a. Click to select ⦿ **From library files:**.

   b. From the pull-down menu adjacent to **From library files:**, select the **solidworks materials** option (if not already selected).

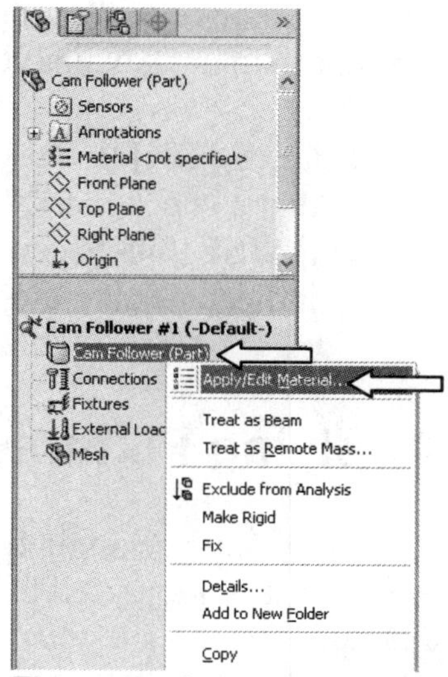

Figure 6 – Selecting the part to which material properties are assigned.

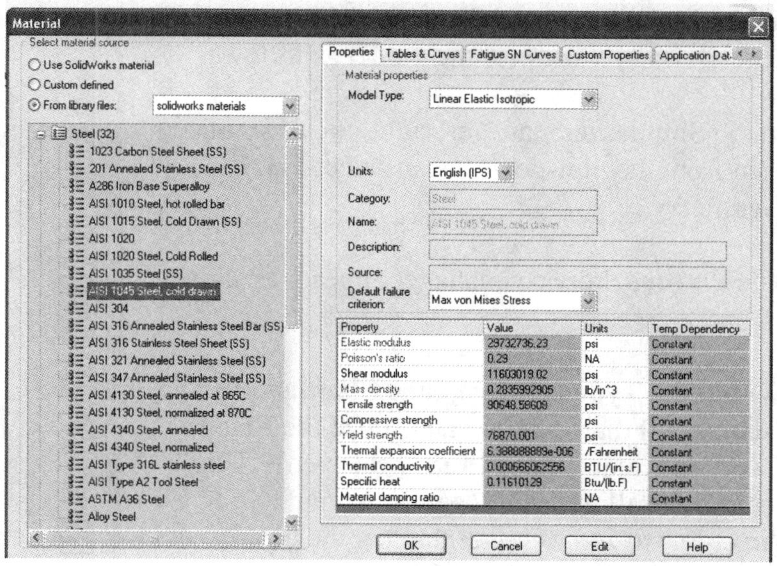

Figure 7 – Material properties of a part are specified in the **Material** window.

   c. Click the plus sign next to "+" **Steel (32)** and scroll down the list to select **AISI 1045 Steel, cold drawn**. Immediately, properties of 1045 steel appear in the right half of the table.

d. If material properties are listed in SI units, click the **Units:** pull-down menu. From the list, select the **English (IPS)** system of units, where IPS indicates units of inches, pounds, and seconds.

Familiarize yourself with information in the table by reading **Property** names listed in the left-hand column and their corresponding magnitudes in the **Value** column. For example, **Yield strength** = **76870.001 psi** for AISI 1045 cold drawn steel. Obviously, greater precision is indicated than is truly known for this material. This is because S.I. units are default within SolidWorks Simulation and extra digits frequently occur when values are converted to English units. Examine other values listed in the table to become familiar with data available in the material library.

3. Click **[OK]** to close the **Material** window. In the Simulation manager tree, notice that a check mark "✓" now appears on the **Cam Follower (Part)** folder and **(-AISI 1045 Steel, cold drawn-)** is associated with this part. The check mark indicates that material properties have been defined.

Applying Fixtures

Restraints must be applied to stabilize and support the model as it is supported in its actual application. In this example, the top surface of the model, i.e., the location where the cam follower enters the frame, is assumed to be "fixed." This restraint is consistent with a cam follower whose upper end is located in a near-zero clearance slot in the frame and for which a static analysis is assumed. Define fixtures for the model as follows.

1. In the Simulation manager, right-click **Fixtures**, then from the pull-down menu select **Fixed Geometry…**

   The **Fixture** property manager appears as shown in Fig. 8

2. Within the **Type** tab, locate the **Standard (Fixed Geometry)** dialogue box and select the **Fixed Geometry** icon (if not already selected). This option sets all translations in X, Y, and Z directions to zero. Recall that tetrahedral elements used to model solid parts allow only three degrees of freedom (three translations) at each node.

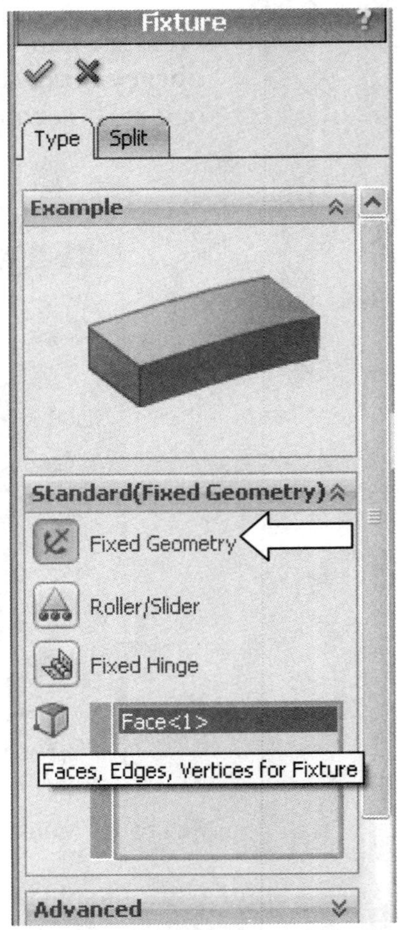

Figure 8 – Selections made in the **Fixture** property manager.

As with other Windows operations, placing the cursor over an icon causes a brief description of the icon to be displayed. Placing the cursor on the icon located to the left of the light-blue colored field in the **Standard (Fixed Geometry)** dialogue box reveals that **Faces, Edges, Vertices for Fixture** can be selected as entities to which restraints can be applied. In this example the top surface of the cam follower is selected as described next.

The light-blue color indicates that the **Faces, Edges, Vertices for Fixture** field is *active* and waiting for the user to specify what part of the model is to be designated as **Fixed**. If, in the following step, selecting the top surface of the model is difficult due its orientation or size, use the graphics controls to rotate, and/or zoom-in on the top surface. If rotate or zoom icons are used, press **[Esc]** to return to the standard cursor (pointer).

3. Move the cursor over the model and when the top *surface* is indicated by a shaded square next to the cursor *and* when **Fixture** symbols appear around the edges of the top surface, click to select the surface.

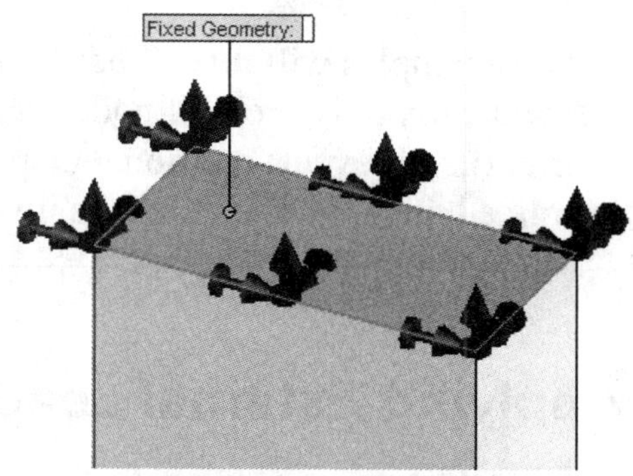

Figure 9 – **Fixed** restraint applied to top surface of the cam follower model.

Fixture symbols appear as arrows in the X, Y, and Z directions shown in Fig. 9 and an information "flag" labels the surface as **Fixed Geometry**. Also, the notation **Face<1>** now appears in the **Fixture** property manager shown in Fig. 8.

If the *bottom* surface (surface with a line on it) or an edge, vertex, or other surface of the model is selected incorrectly, right-click the incorrect item in the dialogue box (light blue field) and select **Delete**. Then repeat step #3.

4. To change color or size of the restraint symbols, click the down-arrow to open the **Symbol Settings** dialogue box located at the bottom of the **Fixtures** property manager. Click the **[Edit Color...]** button to open a color palette. Select the desired color and click **[OK]**. In this example you are encouraged to leave the fixture color as pre-defined because additional symbols applied to the model later in this analysis use different default colors to differentiate fixtures from applied loads. To change symbol size, click the up or down arrows adjacent to the **Symbol Size** spin box. Fixture symbols in Fig. 9 were increased in size to 150 and their color changed for emphasis.

5. Click **[OK]** ✓ (green check-mark) at top of the **Fixture** property manager to accept these restraints and close the window. The above steps render the top face of the cam follower **Immovable** and create an icon named **Fixture-1** beneath the **Fixtures** folder in the Simulation manager.

Aside:
It is important to note that, although the **Fixture** property manager allows the user to specify **Fixed** restraints at desired locations on a model, the effect of this restraint type produces different restraints when applied to different element types. However, the software recognizes the type of element to which restraints are being applied (solid model, shell elements, truss elements, or beam elements), and applies the proper fixture to each type.

In the case of a solid model, such as the cam follower, application of **Fixed** restraints prevents translations of the top surface in the X, Y, and Z directions. This type of restraint is often referred to as being "immovable" because it prevents only three degrees of freedom at each node selected on the model. Note that the moment acting on top of the cam follower in Fig. 2, is *not* restrained by immovable restraints.

Future examples will reveal that **Fixed** restraints, when applied to shell or beam elements, not only prohibit node translations in the X, Y, and Z directions, but also restrict (i.e., prevent) rotational displacement about the X, Y, and Z axes at each restrained node. A shell mesh is investigated in Chapter 4.

Applying External Loads

Following the sequence of steps suggested in the Simulation manager, we next apply external forces to the model. Proceed by defining the X and Y force components one at a time that act at the bottom center of the cam follower. Begin by applying the vertical component of force F_y = 1010 lb that acts upward on the bottom of the cam follower. Proceed as follows.

1. In the Simulation manager, right-click the **External Loads** folder and from the pull-down menu, select **Force...** The **Force/Torque** property manager appears in Fig. 10.

2. Under the **Type** tab, click the **Force** icon. (if not already selected).

3. Beneath the light blue colored field, click to choose ⊙ **Selected direction**. This choice is made to define the direction of the Y-force component in step 5 below.

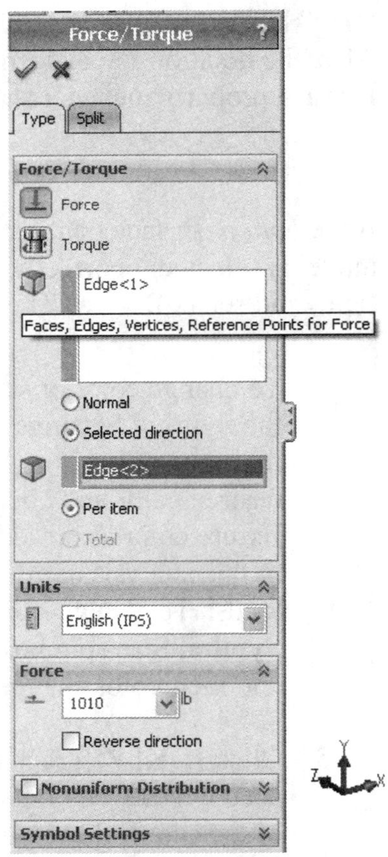

Figure 10 – Definition of force F_y normal to a *Split Line*.

4. Next, place the cursor over the light-blue colored field. The message, **Faces, Edges, Vertices, Reference Points for Force** prompts the user to select the entity to which the Y-component of force is to be applied. In the graphics area, rotate the model and zoom-in on the bottom face. Notice the line that appears at the center of the bottom surface. As you move the cursor onto this line, the message *(Split Line1)* appears. Click to select this line since it is desired to place both X and Y force components at the center of the bottom face. After selecting *(Split Line1)*, **Edge<1>** appears in the top field of the **Force/Torque** dialogue box in Fig. 10 and an information "flag" appears adjacent to the model.

5. Next, click inside the bottom field in the **Force/Torque** dialogue box. This action changes the field color from white to light blue. Placing the cursor on this field prompts the user to select a **Face, Edge, Plane, Axis for Direction**. In other words, to indicate the direction of the Y-force component it is necessary to select a face, edge, or axis in the desired direction. Click to select any *vertical* **Edge** of the model as shown in Fig. 11. **Edge<2>** should appear in the active field and force vectors should appear at both ends of *Split Line 1*. Ignore incorrect Y-directions at this time. If force vectors do not appear, proceed to the next step; otherwise skip to step 7.

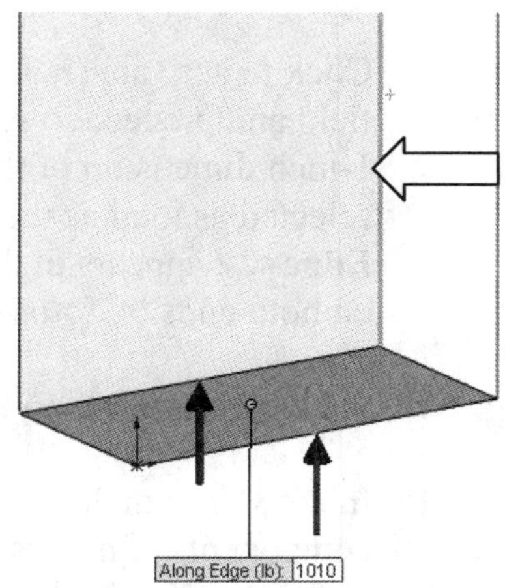

Figure 11 – Vertical force components and the edge used to specify direction of the force acting on Split Line1.

6. Click to open the **Symbol Settings** dialogue box located at the very bottom of the **Force/Torque** property manager. Toggle the ☑ **Show preview** check mark "off" and "on" again to display the force vectors.

7. Next, within the **Units** dialogue box use the pull-down menu set **Units** to **English (IPS)** (if not already selected).

8. In the **Force** dialogue box, type **1010**, which is the magnitude of the Y-force component. Examine the direction of vectors appearing in the graphic image and if they are not directed toward the top of the model, check ☑ **Reverse direction.**

9. Click **[OK]** ✓ (green check-mark) to accept this force definition and close the **Force/Torque** property manager. SolidWorks Simulation applies the 1010 lb force to the model and creates an icon named **Force/Torque-1** beneath the **External Loads** folder in the Simulation manager tree.

Next, apply the X-force component (F_x = -368 lb) to *Split Line 1* on the bottom of the cam follower. Try this on your own. However, a listing of commands is provided in steps 10 through 17 below for those desiring guidance

10. In the Simulation manager tree, right-click the **External Loads** folder and select **Force...** The **Force/Torque** property manager opens.

11. In the **Force/Torque** dialogue box, choose ⊙ **Selected direction.**

12. The active (light blue) field **Faces, Edges, Vertices, Reference Points for Force** prompts the user to indicate where the force is to be applied. Again select *(Split Line1)*. The line is highlighted and **Edge <1>** appears in the active field.

13. Click to activate (light blue color) the **Face**, **Edge**, **Plane**, **Axis for Direction** field and proceed to select an edge parallel to the X-direction (i.e.- parallel to the 1-inch dimension of the cam follower). Any edge, even a top edge, can be selected as long as the edge is in the X-direction. After selecting an edge, **Edge<2>** appears in the direction field and force vectors in the X-direction appear on both ends of *Split Line1*. Ignore incorrect direction at this time.

14. Set the **Units** field to **English (IPS)**.

15. In the **Force** dialogue box , type **368** to define magnitude of the X-force component. If necessary, check ☑ **Reverse direction** to orient force components in the negative X-direction.

16. If the X force component should appear as shown Fig. 12, click **[OK]** ✓ to accept this force and close the **Force/Torque** property manager.

17. An icon named **Force/Torque-2** appears beneath the **External Loads** folder.

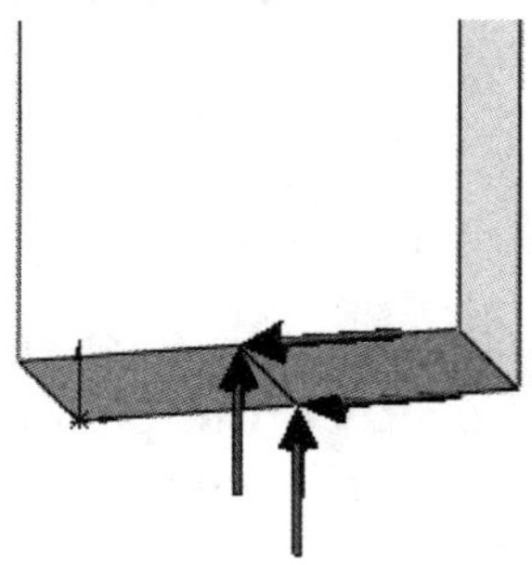

Figure 12 – Front view of cam follower showing force components F_x and F_y applied to the split line.

The model is now complete as far as material property, restraint, and force definitions are concerned. The next step is to Mesh the model as described in the following section.

Aside #1:
Split lines are frequently encountered in the study of SolidWorks, therefore, this example does not review how they are applied to a model. However, they are also extremely useful in Finite Element Analysis, and for that reason, their application is reviewed in future examples.

Aside #2:
As noted in the **Design Insight** section at the beginning of this example, stresses at the *upper end* of the cam follower are to be investigated. For this reason, the very simplified assumption of force loading at the center of the lower end of the model, where the roller is attached to the follower, might be deemed acceptable. After all, why devote considerable time and effort to model contact stress between the roller-pin and cam follower *if* the focus of analysis is to determine stresses elsewhere in the model? On the other hand, if the focus of this analysis were on stresses in the vicinity of the pin that joins to roller to the cam follower, then details of that geometry must be included in the model. Contact stress between a pin and a hole is investigated in Chapter 6.

Meshing the Model

The final task in preparing the model for analysis is to generate a finite element mesh in the solid model. This section explores the meshing process.

1. In the Simulation manager, right-click the **Mesh** icon and from the pull-down menu, select **Create Mesh...** The **Mesh** property manager opens. A partial view of this property manager is shown in Fig. 13.

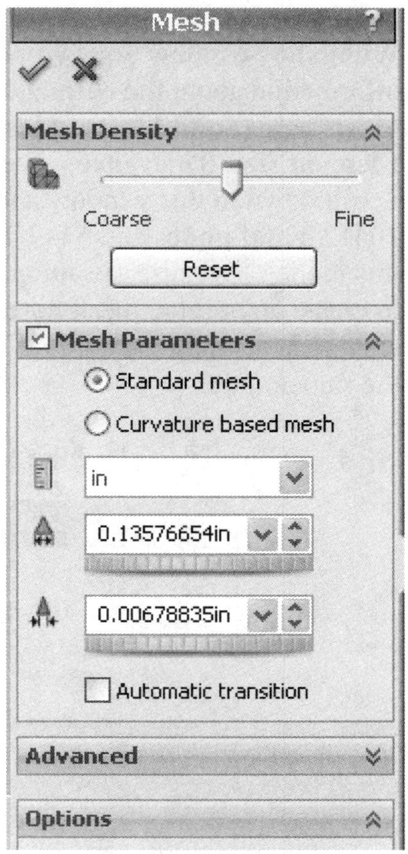

Figure 13 – Mesh parameters, can be altered in the **Mesh** property manager.

The **Mesh Density** dialogue box shows a pointer on a sliding scale between **Coarse** and **Fine** mesh sizes. The default setting is to perform an initial analysis with mesh size set midway between these two extremes.

To learn more about the current mesh (i.e., units, mesh size, and tolerance), click the down arrow to open the **Mesh Parameters** dialogue box also shown in Fig. 13. At the top of this dialogue box observe that ⊙ **Standard mesh** is selected followed by the **Unit** field, where units of inches (**in**) should appear. If not, change units by accessing the **Unit** pull-down menu.

Also within the **Mesh Parameters** dialogue box observe the **Global Size** of the mesh indicated in the middle field as **0.13576654 in**. This value represents the approximate length of each side of a tetrahedral element throughout the model.

The third field from the top indicates the mesh **Tolerance** which expresses the allowable deviation from the specified mesh size. **Tolerance** allows lengths of element sides to deviate from the exact **Global Size** so that the mesh is able to conform to curvature and other discontinuities present in a geometrically complex model. These values are automatically calculated by the software based upon model geometry. As such, these values usually provide sufficient definition of element size to yield acceptable results for an initial finite element analysis.

Although the **Mesh** property manager is unchanged in this example, its use in modifying mesh size is investigated in Chapter 3.

2. Click **[OK]** ✓ to accept the default values and close the **Mesh** property manager.

Meshing starts automatically and the **Mesh Progress** window appears briefly. After meshing is completed, SolidWorks Simulation displays the meshed model as shown in Fig. 14. Also, a check mark "✓" appears on the **Mesh** icon in the Simulation manager tree to indicate meshing is complete.

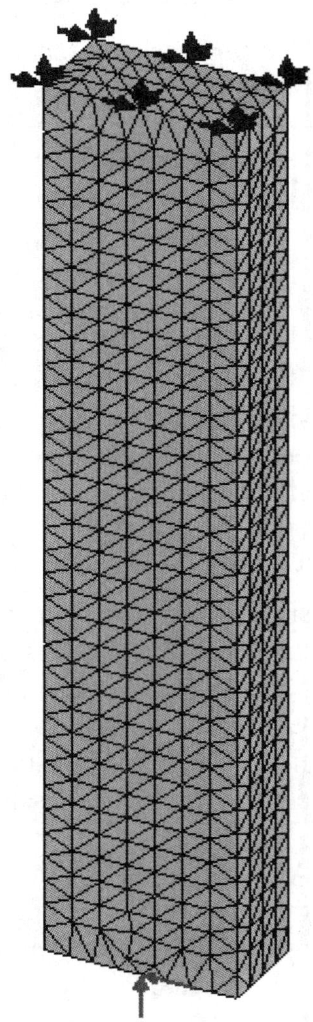

3. To display mesh information, right-click **Mesh** and select **Details...** The **Mesh Details** window opens and is also shown in Fig. 14.

Within this window SolidWorks Simulation displays information about the current model such as its **Study name**, **Mesh type (Solid Mesh)**, **Mesher Used (Standard mesh)**, ..., **Element size**, **Tolerance** values and other data is repeated. Scroll down in this window and notice that approximately 10412 **Total nodes** and 6449 **Total elements** are created for this model. Because the automatic meshing software attempts to create an optimal mesh for each model, the number of nodes and elements may vary slightly between alternate meshing of the same model.

4. Click ☒ to close the **Mesh Details** window.

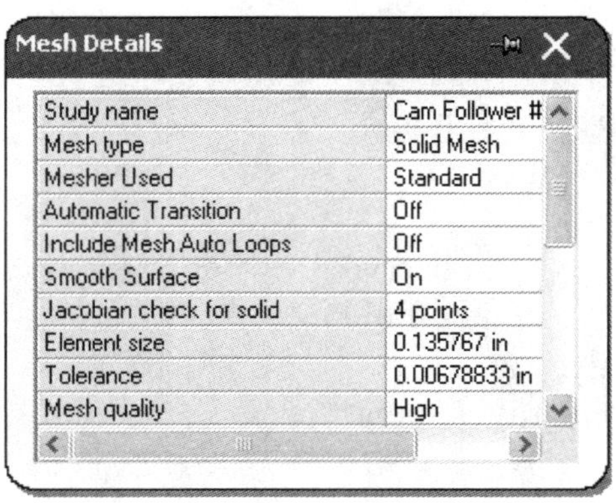

Mesh Details

Study name	Cam Follower #
Mesh type	Solid Mesh
Mesher Used	Standard
Automatic Transition	Off
Include Mesh Auto Loops	Off
Smooth Surface	On
Jacobian check for solid	4 points
Element size	0.135767 in
Tolerance	0.00678833 in
Mesh quality	High

Figure 14 – Cam follower with mesh and boundary conditions illustrated. Also shown is the **Mesh Details** window where mesh information can be reviewed.

5. To hide the mesh, right-click **Mesh** and from the pull-down menu select **Hide Mesh**. Conversely, selecting **Show Mesh** in the pull-down menu returns the mesh display to the model. Try this option, but Hide the mesh before continuing.

> **Aside:**
> As noted earlier, it is permissible to define material properties, fixtures, external loads, and create the mesh in *any order*. However, all these *necessary* steps must be completed prior to running the Solution portion of a study.

Running the Solution

After the model has been completely defined, we are ready to proceed to the *Solution* process. This is the second major portion of a finite element program. It is where the numerous equations that define a Study are solved. For all of its complexity, this portion of a Finite Element Analysis is, perhaps, most deceiving in terms of its seeming simplicity from the user's perspective. Time required for an analysis can vary from several seconds to several hours depending upon overall model complexity and computer hardware used. Most examples in this text should solve in a matter of seconds or a few minutes at most. To solve the current example, proceed as follows.

1. To run the analysis, right-click **Cam Follower #1 (-Default-)** denoted by boldface font near the middle of the Simulation manager tree. Refer to highlighted text in Fig. 15.

2. From the pull-down menu, select **Run** and the solution process begins automatically. A window that tracks progress of the Solution appears, but due to the small size and simplicity of this example, it is displayed only briefly.

After successful solution of the static analysis, SolidWorks Simulation creates a new folder, named "**Results**," at the bottom of the Simulation manager tree. This folder should contain the three sub-folders shown in Fig. 15. These three sub-folders contain default plots resulting from a finite element analysis of the current model. If these folders do *not* appear, follow steps (a) through (f) outlined below. Otherwise skip to the section titled "**Examination of Results**."

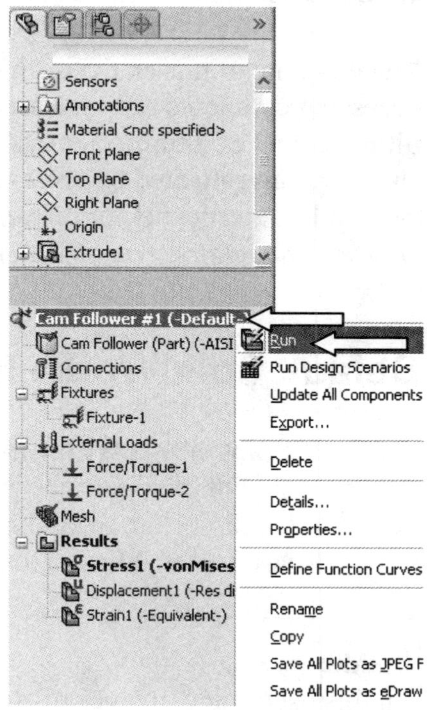

Figure 15 – Folders created as part of the Solution process. Each folder contains solution information indicated by its name

Right-click the **Results** folder and from the pull-down menu, select **Define Stress Plot…** The **Stress Plot** property manager opens.

b) In the **Display** dialogue box, select **VON: von Mises Stress** from the pull-down menu (if not already selected).

c) Also in the **Display** dialogue box, select **psi** from the **Units** pull-down menu.

d) Click **[OK]** ✓ to close the property manager and immediately a plot of the von Mises stress is displayed in the graphics area.

e) Repeat steps (a) through (d), but in step (a) substitute **Define Displacement Plot…**; in step (b) accept the default display item named **URES: Resultant Displacement**; in step (c) change the **Units** pull-down menu to inches (**in**); and in step (d) click **[OK]**✓.

f) Repeat steps (a) through (d) a third time, but in step (a) substitute **Define Strain Plot…**; in step (b) accept the default display item named **ESTRN: Equivalent Strain**; in step (c) take no action because strain is unitless; and in step (d) click **[OK]**✓.

Examination of Results

The outcome of this analysis, in the form of graphs, plots, and data, can be viewed by accessing computed output stored in the various **Results** folders. These results are the ultimate goal of a finite element analysis. It is where validity of finite element results should be investigated by cross-checking them against manual calculations or other verifiable experimental or reference results. *Checking computed results is a necessary step in good engineering practice!*

Default SolidWorks Simulation Graphical Results

1. If a plot of **Stress1 (-vonMises-)** is already displayed then continue to the next step. Otherwise, in the Simulation manager, right-click the **Stress1 (-vonMises-)** folder and from the pull-down menu select **Show**. Alternatively, double-click **Stress1 (-vonMises-)** to display the plot.

Aside:
In this user guide, images of stress within the loaded model are referred to as "stress contour plots" or simply "plots." On the other hand, when an image shows the relationship between two variables in the form of an X-Y line graph, the image is referred to as a "graph."

Either of the actions in step 1 causes a deformed view of the cam follower to appear along with a plot of the von Mises stress distribution, displayed in multiple colors, on the model as shown in Fig. 16.

2. Default information provided near the upper-left corner of the graphics screen, circled in Fig. 16, includes:

- **Model name:** ← Contains the name of the SolidWorks model opened from the parts file at the beginning of this example; it is named **"Cam Follower (Part)."**

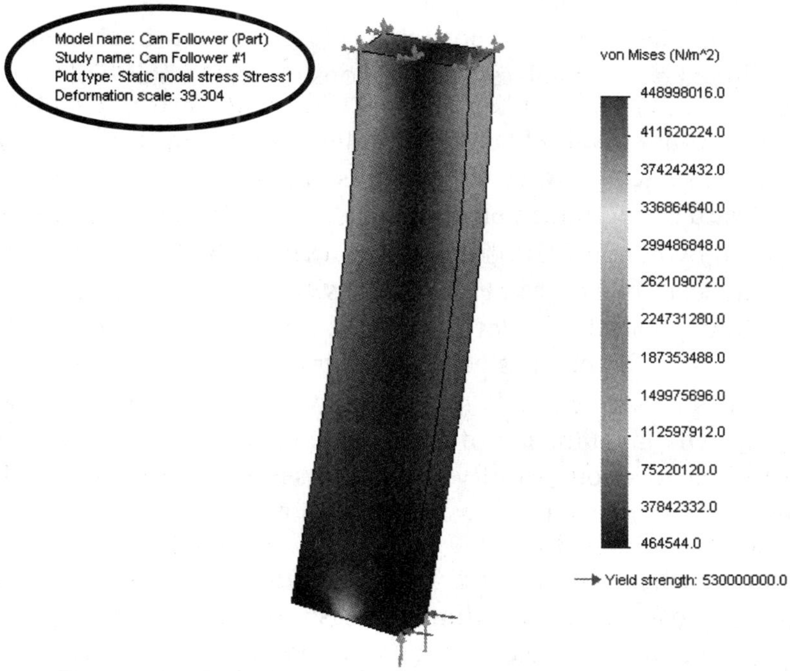

Figure 16 – Default plot of von Mises stress distribution throughout the cam follower model. Stress is shown in SI units.

- **Study name:** ← Lists the name selected and typed into the **Study** property manager at the start of this example. If previous instructions were followed precisely, this name should appear as **"Cam Follower #1**".

- **Plot type:** ← Should indicate **"Static nodal stress Stress1**"

- **Deformation Scale:** ← To illustrate a deformed shape, SolidWorks Simulation scales the maximum deformation of the model to 10% of the diagonal of a bounding box around the model (this box is not visible). A number representing the magnitude of this deformation scale is 39.304 (or similar value) appears on this line. This value indicates that the model is deformed 39.304 *times* its actual deformation. The deformed model is provided to aid visualization of a deformed model and does *not* represent the actual magnitude of part deformation.

- Also included is a color-coded stress scale. Stress magnitudes at various locations throughout the model can be determined by matching colors to those of the color-coded stress scale. Red traditionally corresponds to high stress while dark blue corresponds to algebraically lower stress magnitudes.

Results Predicted by Classical Stress Equations

It is assumed that some users may not yet be familiar with von Mises stress.[1] Therefore, discussion below digresses to examine *other*, more fundamental, stresses that occur within the cam follower model. To accomplish this, a brief, but thorough solution to the current problem is included based on classical equations of stress analysis.

Begin by recalling the original free-body diagram of the cam follower, Fig. 2. That figure revealed the part is subject to force components in both the X and Y directions on its lower end. The upward acting force component F_y = 1010 lb causes an axial compressive stress given by $\sigma_y = F_y/A$ in the Y-direction. Although this stress is shown near the lower end of the cam follower in Fig. 17, classic stress equations assume it is *uniformly distributed* throughout the model from top to bottom. Similarly, the X-component of force, F_x = -368 lb that acts perpendicular to the length of the cam follower, causes bending stress given by $\sigma_y = Mc/I$ shown at the top of the model in Fig. 17. Bending stress is maximum at the top of the model due to maximum length of the moment arm (5.0 in) at this location. Briefly review stress calculations included on Fig. 17 before proceeding. Recall the cam follower is 1.00-in wide by 0.50-in thick.

Because all stresses depicted on Fig. 17 act in the Y-direction, they can be combined by simply adding magnitudes of axial and bending stresses provided proper $\pm$ signs are included. Combining these stresses yields the following results:

Stress at point **A** is in compression due to both axial and bending stresses, thus-

Stress at point **A**: $(\sigma_y)_A = \sigma_{Axial} + \sigma_{Bending}$ = (-2020) + (-22080) = -24,100 psi

Stress at point **B** is in compression due to axial stress, but bending stress is zero on the neutral axis, thus-

Stress at point **B**: $(\sigma_y)_B = \sigma_{Axial} + \sigma_{Bending}$ = (-2020) + (0) = -2,020 psi

Stress at point **C** is compressive due to axial stress, but in tension due to bending stress. Because the "+" bending stress is greater than the "-" axial stress, the resultant stress at point **C** is-

Stress at point **C**: $(\sigma_y)_C = \sigma_{Axial} + \sigma_{Bending}$ = (-2020) + (+22080) = +20,060 psi

[1] It is presumed that use of this SolidWorks Simulation user guide will be introduced near the beginning of a Design of Machine Elements or Mechanics of Materials course. However, most traditional textbooks on these subjects delay introduction of vonMises stress until later chapters. For this reason, early examples in this user guide involve stresses that are more familiar to individuals who have completed a fundamental mechanics of materials course.

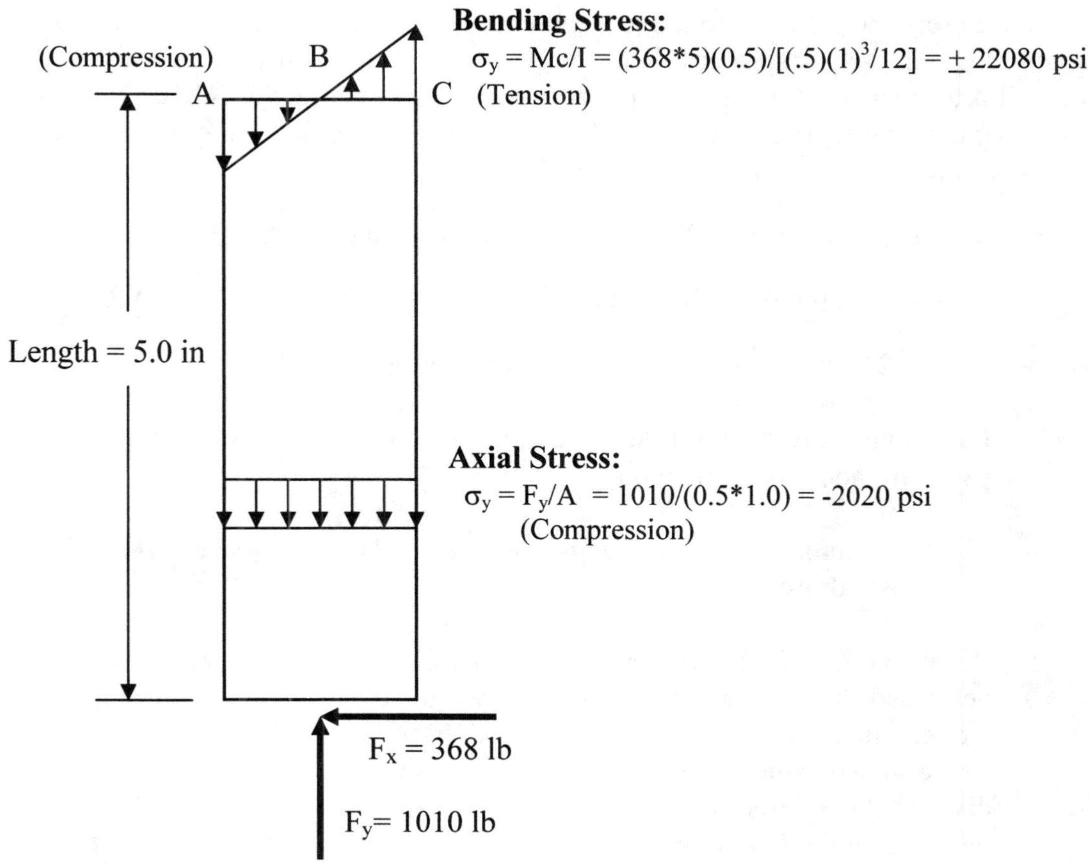

Figure 17 – Schematic of loading and distribution of bending stress (compression on left-side and tension on right-side) and axial stress (compression) in the Y-direction on the cam follower determined using classic stress equations.

SolidWorks Simulation Results for Stress in Y-Direction

The above results are next compared with those determined using the finite element analysis performed in this chapter. To do so, it is meaningful to produce a plot of normal stress in the Y-direction (i.e., σ_y). Proceed as follows.

1. In the Simulation manager tree right-click the **Results** folder and from the pull-down menu select **Define Stress Plot…** The **Stress Plot** property manager opens as shown in Fig. 18.

2. In the **Display** dialogue box**,** click to open the pull-down menu adjacent to the **Component** field. Initially this field shows that the **VON: von Mises Stress** is selected for display. From the list of stresses available in the pull-down menu, locate and highlight **SY: Y Normal Stress**. This selection identifies normal stress in the Y-direction, commonly represented by σ_y, as the stress to be displayed in a new plot. This is the *same* stress determined using classical equations above.

For future reference it is informative to observe all the other stresses available for analysis within the **Component** field. Briefly return to the pull-down menu and note the list of thirteen stresses included there. Although names, rather than Greek symbols are listed, observe what stresses it is possible to select from the following *partial* list of stresses available.

σ_x, σ_y, σ_z = Normal stresses in X, Y and Z directions listed as **SX, SY, SZ.**

τ_{xy} τ_{xz} τ_{zy} = Shear stresses on X, Y, and Z planes, listed as **TXY, TXZ, TYZ.**

σ_1, σ_2, σ_3 = 1st, 2nd, and 3rd Principal stresses listed as **P1, P2, P3.**

3. Beneath the stress **Component** field, verify that **Units** are set to **psi.** If not, select **psi** from the pull-down menu.

4. In the **Advanced Options** dialogue box verify that ⊙ **Node Values** is selected.

5. Because it is often convenient to turn off the deformed shape when viewing stresses within a model, click to *clear* the check mark "✓" from the ☐ **Deformed Shape** dialogue box. Suppressing display of the deformed shape also proves helpful when using the **Probe** feature later in this example.

6. Open the **Property** dialogue box, and click to place a check mark next to ☑ **Include title text** and type a descriptive title such as **Sigma-Y, *Your name***. A descriptive title serves both to identify *what* quantity is plotted and *who* created the study.

7. Click **[OK]** ✓ to accept these changes and close the **Stress Plot** property manager. A default plot of normal stress in the Y-direction (σ_y) now appears on the graphics screen and a new plot, named **Stress2 (-Y normal-)**, appears beneath the **Results** folder. The icon labeled **Stress1 (-vonMises-)** contains a plot of von Mises stresses while **Stress2** contains a plot of normal stress in the Y-direction (σ_y).

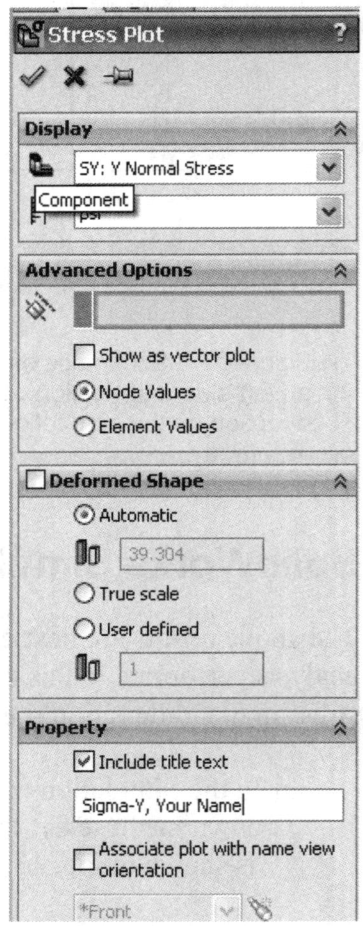

Figure 18 – Selections to specify plotting of a different stress component on the model.

Note that the title entered in step 6 appears at the top-left of the graphics window. Next, visual characteristics of the graphics display are modified to better view the results; to do this proceed as follows.

8. Right-click **Stress2 (-Y normal-)** and from the pull-down menu, select **Settings….** The **Settings** property manager opens as seen in Fig. 19.

9. Within the **Fringe Options** dialogue box, select **Discrete** from the pull-down menu. This action displays stress contours as discrete color bands rather than the rainbow effect created by the **Continuous** display. While on this menu, experiment with other **Fringe Options**, then reset to **Discrete** to correspond with images illustrated in this text.

10. In the **Boundary Options** dialogue box, select **Model**. This option outlines the model with a black line thereby making its edges easier to view.

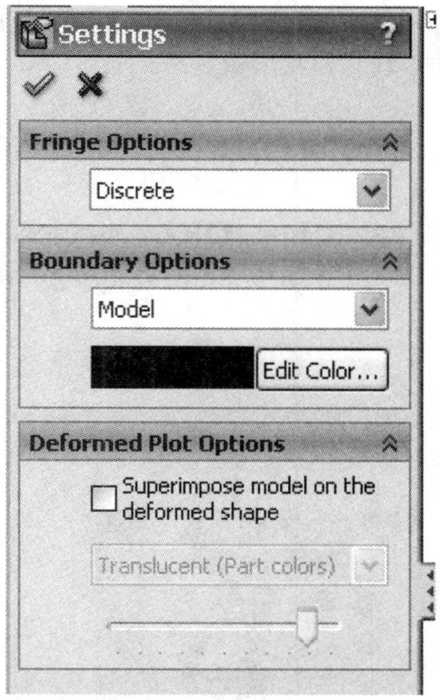

Figure 19 – Altering stress contour display options in the **Settings** property manager.

11. Click **[OK]** ✓ to close the **Settings** property manager. A *partial* image of the **Discrete** fringe plot of normal stress in the Y-direction appears in Fig. 20 (a).

Using the Probe Tool

Although stress contour plots provide a general sense of stress magnitudes throughout the model, it is often desirable to determine stress magnitudes at specific locations. To do this the **Probe** tool is used. To aid in selecting specific points on the model, two changes are introduced to create a second image similar to that of Fig. 20 (b). First, the **Mesh** is superimposed on the model, and second, stress contours are represented by **Lines** rather than **Discrete** full-color fringes.

To alter model appearance, return to the **Settings** property manager as follows.

1. Right-click **Stress2 (-Y normal-)** and from the pull-down menu select **Settings…** This action returns us to the **Settings** property manager.

Aside:
For the next part of this example the **Fringe Options** field is specified as **Line** rather than **Discrete** because color shading makes the **Mesh** difficult to view when printed in black and white. Those who wish to retain the **Fringe Option** as **Discrete** are *encouraged* to do so and *skip* to step 3 below.

2. Within the **Settings** property manager, change the **Fringe Options** field to **Line**. *(Optional)*.

3. Next, change the **Boundary Options** to **Mesh**.

4. Click **[OK]** ✓ to close the **Settings** property manager. The upper portion of the model should appear with the mesh shown as illustrated in Fig. 20 (b).

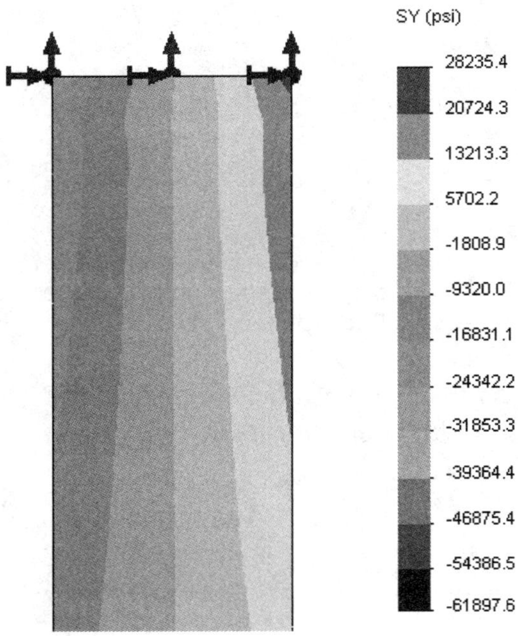

Figure 20 (a) – Upper portion of model showing stress σ_y as **Discrete** fringes.

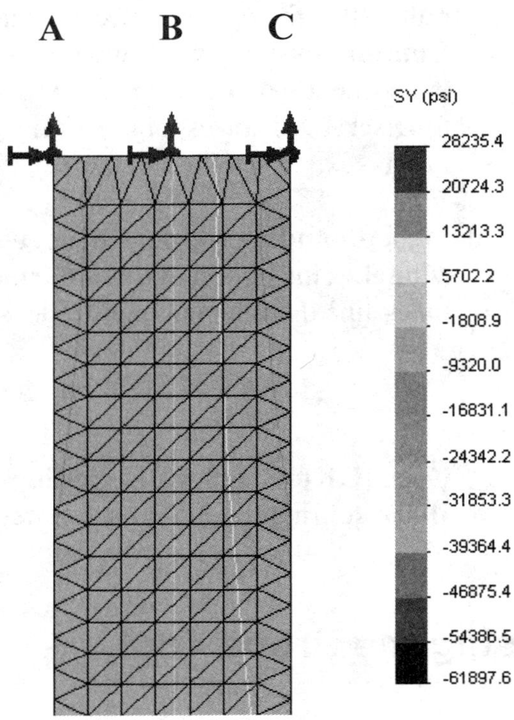

Figure 20 (b) – Upper portion of the model showing normal stress σ_y using the **Line** option. A **Mesh** is superimposed on the model to facilitate using the **Probe** feature.

We are now ready to compare manually calculated stresses with stress values determined using finite element analysis. To facilitate comparisons, stress magnitudes at points **A, B,** and **C** on top of the cam follower, Fig. 20 (b), are repeated below.

Stress at point A: $(\sigma_y)_A = \sigma_{Axial} + \sigma_{Bending} = (-2020) + (-22080) = -24{,}100$ psi

Stress at point B: $(\sigma_y)_B = \sigma_{Axial} + \sigma_{Bending} = (-2020) + (0) = -2{,}020$ psi

Stress at point C: $(\sigma_y)_C = \sigma_{Axial} + \sigma_{Bending} = (-2020) + (+22080) = +20{,}060$ psi

The **Probe** tool is used to determine stresses at points **A**, **B**, and **C** on the model and at all points in-between. It *may* be necessary to approximate the stress at the location of point **B**. The reason for this is that the automatically generated mesh size is somewhat arbitrary. Therefore, nodes, which typically are used as measurement points, may not lie *exactly* at the location of point **B** on the centroidal axis. This will be determined as the analysis proceeds.

Begin by zooming-in on the top of the model. An image similar to that shown in Fig. 20 (a) or (b) should appear on your screen. Two different methods for using the Probe tool are demonstrated below. Proceed as follows to use the **Probe** tool by the first method.

5. In the SolidWorks Simulation manager tree right-click **Stress2 (-Y normal-)** and from the pull-down menu, select **Probe**. The **Probe Result** property manager opens, but does not initially look like Fig. 21. The table in the center of the **Results** dialogue box is initially empty.

6. In the **Options** dialogue box, click to choose ⊙ **On selected entities**. The **Results** dialogue box expands to include the highlighted (light blue) field. This field is active and is awaiting the selection of **Faces, Edges, or Vertices** on the model.

7. In the graphics screen, slowly move the cursor over the model. The symbol adjacent to the cursor changes to a square, a line, or a small circle to represent selection of a **Face**, an **Edge**, or a **Vertex** respectively. Choose the line representing the top, front **Edge** of the cam follower. **Edge<1>** appears in the highlighted field and the **[Update]** button becomes active.

8. Clicking the **[Update]** button automatically fills in the **Results** table with the data seen in Fig. 21 and described below.

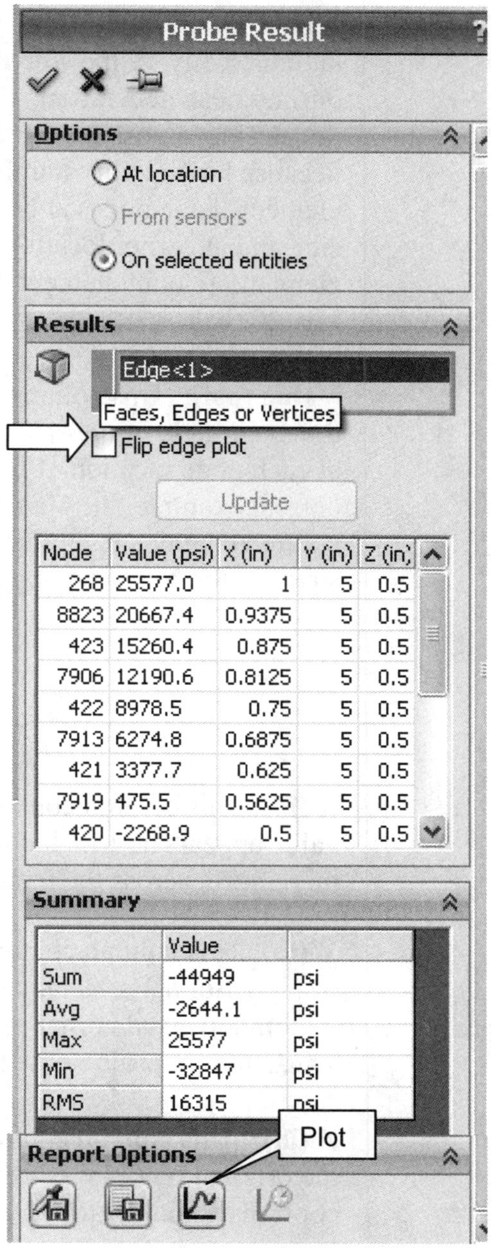

Figure 21 – **Probe Result** table contains stress values at node locations across the top **Edge** of the model.

NOTE: To view complete results, it may be necessary to enlarge the table and individual columns within the table by clicking-and-dragging the right boundary of the ***Probe Result*** *property manager and the individual column boundaries respectively.*
Information contained in each column of the **Results** table, repeated in Fig. 22, includes (from left to right):

- **Node**: This column contains the number of each *sequential* node located across the top front edge of the model. Node numbers are assigned automatically by the software during mesh generation. Seventeen nodes exist across the top edge because high quality tetrahedral elements have nodes at both mid-side and at corner locations on each element. [Count element sides in Fig. 20 (b)].

- **Value (psi)**: This column contains the magnitude of the *selected* stress at each node location. For the current example, the **Value (psi)** column contains magnitude of stress in the Y-direction, (σ_y).

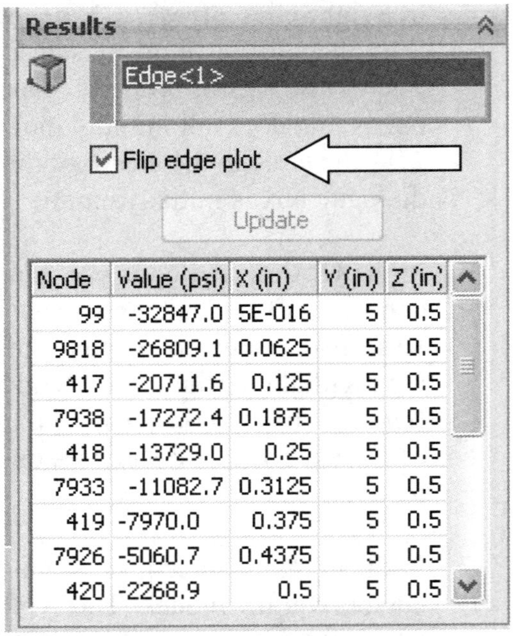

Figure 22 – Values in the **Results** table repeated.

- **X (in)**: This column contains X-coordinates of each node location. The initial value appears as 1 inch and subsequent values decrease in 1/16 inch increments across the model. (Refer to values shown in Fig. 21).

- **Y (in)**: This column contains Y-coordinates of each node location. The original SolidWorks model of the cam follower was created by locating its bottom left-hand corner at the origin of a global X, Y, Z coordinate system. Thus, all points along the top edge lie 5.0 inches above the origin.

- **Z (in)**: This column contains Z-coordinates of each node location. Because the original model was extruded ½ inch in the positive Z direction, all Z-coordinates on the top front edge are located at Z = + 0.5 inches.

9. In the **Report Options** dialogue box, located at the bottom of the **Probe Result** property manager, click the **Plot** icon; see flag in Fig. 21. Immediately a graph of stress σ_y across the top edge of the model is displayed.

Notice, however, that this graph displays tensile (positive) stress on its left-hand side and compressive (negative) stress on its right-side. This is just the reverse of the actual stress distribution across the top of the cam follower. The reason for this is that the top edge is a line with two different ends, but no means is provided to select one end or the other. This logical misrepresentation of data is easily remedied by the following action.

10. First, close the current graph by clicking the ☒ at its upper-right corner.

11. Next, in the **Results** dialogue box, place a check ✓ adjacent to ☑ **Flip edge plot**. See arrow in Fig. 21 or Fig.22.

12. Again, click the **Plot** icon and a corrected graph, showing variation of σ_y across the top edge of the model, from left to right, appears in Fig. 23.

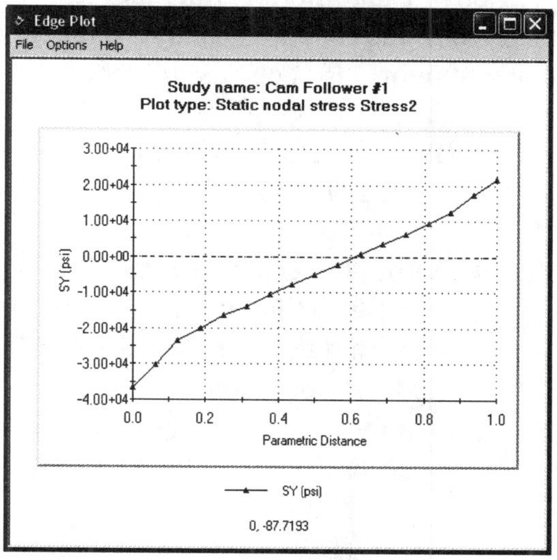

Figure 23 – Graph of stress distribution σ_y from the left side (0.0 in.) to right side (at 1 in.) along top front edge of the cam follower.

The graph in Fig. 23 indicates compressive stress along the left side of the model as expected. This stress gradually decreases to zero near the center of the model and then becomes positive, indicating tensile stress, on the right side of the cam follower. These results are consistent with our understanding of stress distribution on the top edge of the model. However, we next observe that these results do not agree well with classical theory.

OBSERVATIONS:

Table 1 compares results of manually calculated stresses with finite element results obtained using the **Probe** tool at locations **A**, **B**, and **C** at the top-end of the cam follower. Verify results in the Probe Tool Results column of Table 1 by scrolling through values in the **Results** table.

Table 1 – Comparison of stress σ_y computed by classical and finite element methods.

Location	Manual Calculation (psi)	Probe Tool Results (psi)	Percent Difference (%)
Point A	-24100	-32847	26.6 %
Point B	-2020	-2269	10.9 %
Point C	+20060	+25577	21.6 %

Results in Table 1 appear to indicate significant differences between results calculated using classical stress equations and those determined by finite element analysis methods. How can this be?

The above question can be answered by recalling St. Venant's principle, which states that stress predicted by classic equations exists only in regions *reasonably well removed* from points of load application, support locations, or locations of geometric discontinuity. Any of these conditions typically introduces significant *localized* effects. Thus, in these regions, shortcomings of classical stress equations are at odds with the enhanced predictive capability of finite element results. For this reason, the **Probe** tool is used again, but this time it is used to select nodes at locations somewhat removed from the upper support. Proceed as follows.

13. Begin by closing the **Edge Plot** graph. Click ⊠ to close the graph.

14. Within the **Options** dialogue box, click to select ⊙ **At location**. This action clears all data from the **Results** table and changes the mode of operation to one that enables display of results at user selected node locations.

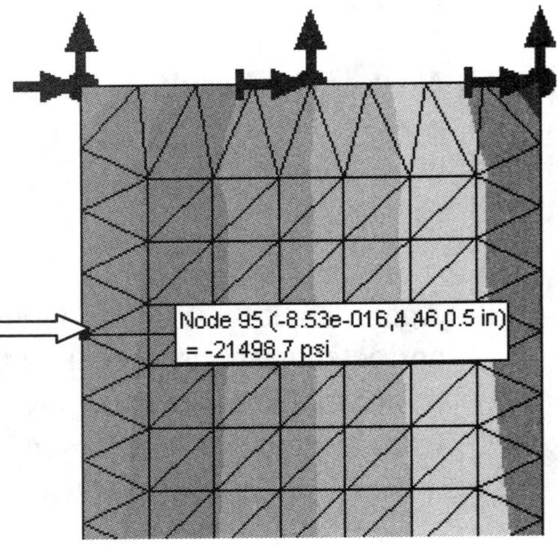

Figure 24 – Close-up view of top end of the model showing the first node selected along an *approximate* straight-line across the model.

15. Move the Probe tool into the graphics area and count down to the 4th node below the top-left corner. See node selected in Fig. 24. This node is somewhat arbitrarily assumed to be "sufficiently removed" from the *immovable* **Fixture** condition previously applied at the top of the cam follower. This location is chosen to avoid the effects predicted by St. Venant's principle.

As you perform the next step, a small text box will appear adjacent to each selected node. (See the information "flag" in Fig. 24). Information in this box lists the *Node Number* followed, in parenthesis, by its *(X, Y, Z)* coordinates. The second line of text lists the stress magnitude at the selected node; units are included with all values. These values are also listed in the **Results** table of the **Probe Result** property manager. Unfortunately, the text-boxes tend overwrite one another for closely spaced nodes. However, when used to identify stress at specific locations on a model, they can be quite useful. Rotate the model as shown in Fig. 25 to facilitate selecting nodes that otherwise would be hidden behind these text boxes.

16. Proceed across the model *from left-to-right* and click to select *only* nodes at element corners as illustrated by darkened dots in Fig. 25. If an error is made when selecting nodes, simply click the ⊙ **At Location** button again. This action clears the **Results** table and the selection process can be repeated.

Aside:
Due to the arbitrary mesh generation scheme it may not be possible to select a row of nodes in a *straight line* across the model. Despite this inconvenience, it is still possible to compute stresses at each node location and compare values obtained using classical stress equations with finite element results listed in the **Results** table.

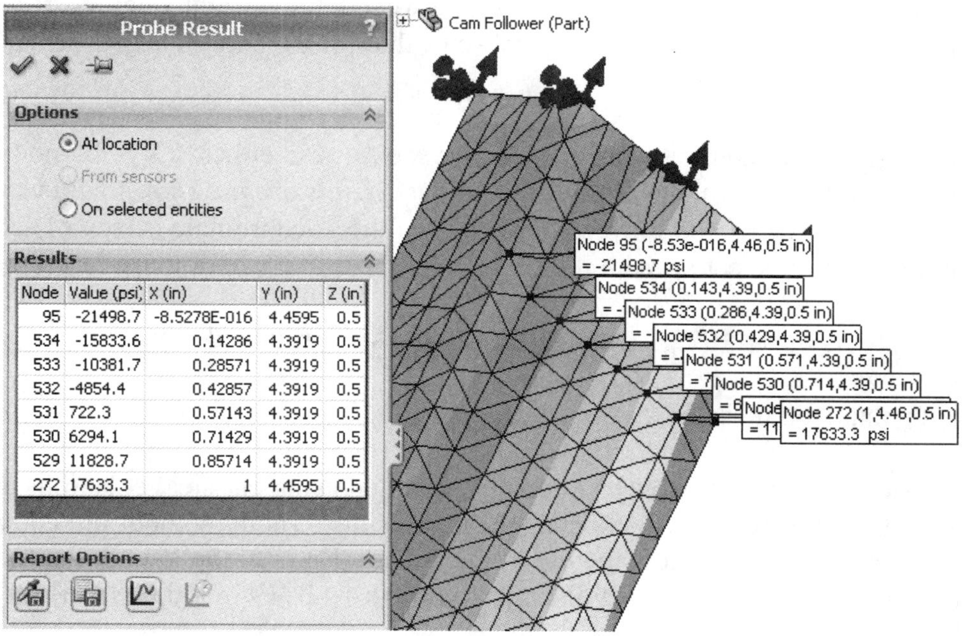

Figure 25 – **Results** table containing σ_y values and node locations for node selection across the model at a distance "sufficiently removed" from support conditions.

17. Within the **Report Options** dialogue box, once again select the Plot icon. The resulting **Probe Result** graph is shown in Fig. 26.

The graph in Fig. 26 reveals the expected variation of stress caused by adding the uniform axial compressive stress to the near linear variation of bending stress. Bending stress varies from compression on left side of the model to tension on the right side.

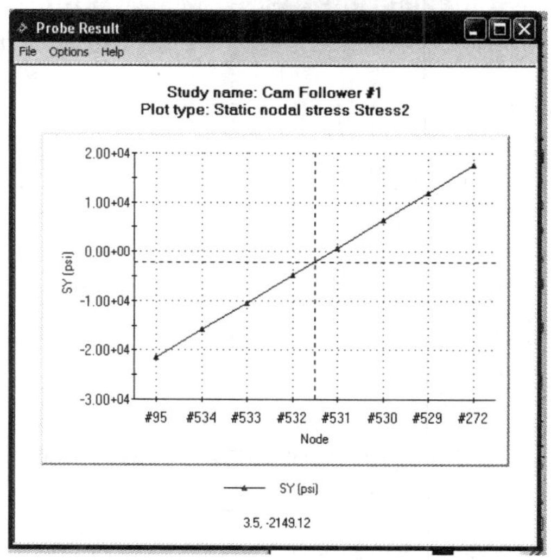

Figure 26 – Plot of combined axial and bending stress variation (σ_y) across the model.

18. Move the cursor onto the graph and note the cross-hairs (two intersecting dashed lines) appear and move with the cursor. On the default graph, stress **SY (psi)** is plotted on the ordinate and node numbers are plotted on the abscissa. As the cross-hairs move, values of the X and Y coordinates at their intersection update automatically beneath the graph.

19. Move the cursor to the intersection of the curve and the centroidal axis of the model. The center of the cam follower, between left and right sides, corresponds to an abscissa value of X = 3.5 nodes; see values at the bottom center beneath the graph.

With the cross-hairs on the curve, the coordinates should read either: (X = 3.5 nodes, Y = -1929.82 psi) or (X = 3.5 nodes, Y = -2149.12 psi). *Units are not shown with values beneath the graph.* The reason for the uncertainty of the Y-coordinate is lack of accuracy in locating its exact intersection with the curve. Thus, the average of these two values –

$$(\sigma_y)_{AVG} = [-1929 + (-2149)]/2 = 2039 \text{ psi} \quad \text{(rounded values)}$$

is used for comparison in Table 2.

Table 2 shows a comparison between stresses calculated using classical equations and those computed using the finite element analysis. Results of both methods are compared at *approximately* 0.6 inches below the top of the model. Refer to the Y-coordinate in the **Results** table of Fig. 25 for the exact distance (5.000 in - 4.3919 in = 0.6081 in) for most nodes.

Table 2 – Comparison of stress σ_y computed by classical and finite element methods at an arbitrary distance below the top of the cam follower.

Location	Manual Calculation (psi)	Probe Tool Results (psi)	Percent Difference (%)
Point A	-21710	-21499	0.98 %
Point B	-2020	-2039	0.93 %
Point C	17670	17633	0.21 %

A significant improvement in the comparison of computed and finite element results is observed in Table 2. Differences are less than 1 % at all points **A**, **B**, and **C**. Based on these comparisons, several observations are included in the Summary section at the end of this chapter.

20. Do *not* close the **Probe Result** graph. Instead, proceed directly to the next section.

Customizing Graphs

Because default information displayed on SolidWorks Simulation graphs is rather terse, as evidenced by graphs of the previous section, this section briefly examines those graphs and explores means to enhance them. Begin by examining differences between graphs shown in Figs. 23 and 26 (repeated below).

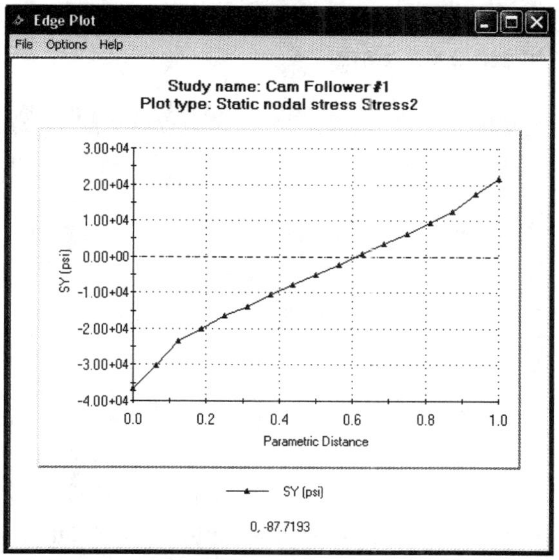

Figure 23 – Repeated

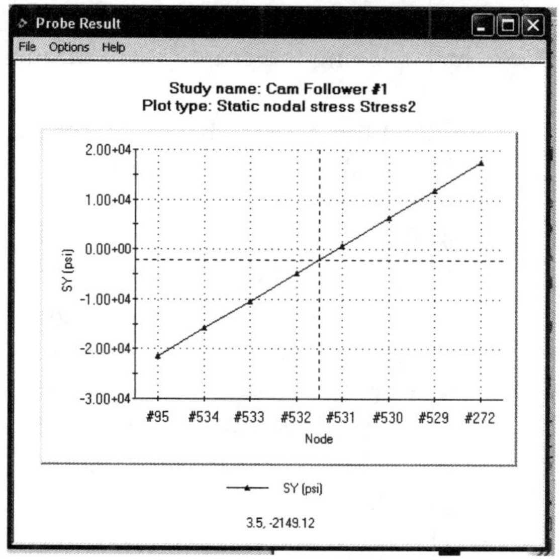

Figure 26 – Repeated

Observations:

- Both graphs bear the same title. Therefore, there is no obvious clue that these graphs represent stress data at different locations on the cam follower.
- The Y-axis label indicates that normal stress in the Y-direction is plotted (**SY** = σ_y), but there is no indication that **SY** is a combination of axial and bending stress.
- The X-axis in Fig. 23 plots the **Parametric Distance**, which in this case begins at 0.0 inches at the left side of the model and increases to 1.0 inch at its right side. Recall, an edge of the model was selected to create Fig. 23.
- The X-axis in Fig. 26 lists the numbers of each **Node** selected as the **Probe** tool moved across the model from left to right.
- A legend, at bottom middle of the graph, indicates the symbols and line color used to plot **SY**. If other lines were plotted on the same graph, additional symbols and colors would appear. Also, because the entire edge was selected for the graph of Fig. 23, both mid-side and corner nodes were selected. Whereas, only corner nodes were selected for the plot in Fig. 26, hence fewer data points are displayed.

Graphing capability within SolidWorks Simulation is rather limited, therefore, steps below outline *only* the most useful tools for customizing graphs. Because the graph shown in Fig. 26 should still be open, proceed as follows.

1. In the menu at the top of the **Probe Result** graph, select **Options**. Then from the pull-down menu select **Properties**. The **2D Chart Control Properties** window opens as shown in Fig. 27.

Begin by replacing the graph title with more descriptive wording.

2. Select the **Titles** tab and within the **Titles** tab, select the **Label** tab.

3. Within the **Text:** box type a descriptive title. Choose wording that fully describes the information displayed on this graph. Press the **[Enter]** key between lines. Compare your title to that shown in Fig. 27. Was all the pertinent information included?

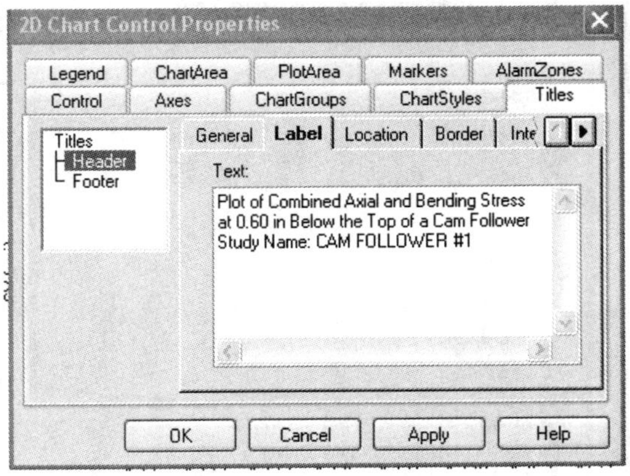

Figure 27 – Creating descriptive graph titles and axis labels within the **2D Chart Control Properties** window.

4. Explore other options within the **Titles** tab as time and interest permit.

Next proceed to alter the axis labels. Once again the goal is to provide more descriptive labels. The following step assumes the **2D Chart Control Properties** window remains open. If not, open it again by repeating step 1.

5. Select the **Axes** tab followed by selection of the **Title** tab. Notice that the **X** axis is highlighted (blue) at the top left corner of the current window.

6. In the **Text:** box, replace the current axis label, "**Node**," using wording such as, "**Node Numbers Across the Cam Follower (Node Nos.)**."

Note that node numbers are the default display when the **Probe** tool is used. The task of altering these values to again represent distance across the width of the cam follower is arduous, but it can be done. It is not demonstrated here because there are seven divisions (seven corner nodes) across the model, and seven does not divide into nice fractional values to display location. Thus, proceed as follows to enhance the Y-axis label.

7. While still on the **Axes** tab, click to highlight **Y** in the **Axes** box located at top left of the **2D Chart Control Properties** window. The **Text:** box changes to show the current Y-axis label, **SY (psi)**.

8. Type a new, more descriptive label for the Y axis into the **Text:** box and click **[OK]** to close the **2D Chart Control Properties** window.

9. Examine the graph titles, then click ☒ to close the **Probe Result** graph.

10. Click **[OK]** ✓ to close the **Probe Result** property manager.

Summary

- The effect of *localized* conditions, also known as "end-conditions" or "boundary conditions" (i.e., at support locations and locations of applied loads), upon finite element results can be significant. These effects are not predicted by classical equations used in manual stress calculations. For this reason care must be exercised when checking finite element results in these regions.

- Excellent agreement typically does exist between finite element analysis and manually computed results at locations *sufficiently removed* from localized conditions (examples of St. Venant's principle).

- The importance of selecting the *appropriate stress* within a finite element analysis when comparing results cannot be overstated. For example, the SolidWorks Simulation default plot of von Mises stress does not, and should not, agree if compared with manually calculated values of stress in the Y-direction (σ_y). Simply stated, *like* stresses must be compared when checking validity of a finite element analysis.

The current example concludes at this point. Most of the software capabilities introduced in this example are fundamental to a successful finite element analysis and will be encountered repeatedly in subsequent examples and end-of-chapter problems.

This file either can be saved or deleted. A brief description of the two options for closing files follows. Because a variety of file structures are found in different computer work environments, the guidelines below are quite general. It is suggested that local system guidelines be followed regarding *where* files are saved (i.e., to a personal USB or "jump" drive, to the hard-drive, or to personal file space allocated on a system network).

<u>CLOSE the file and SAVE it to your account</u>:
To exit SolidWorks Simulation and save a file *to your file space*, select **File** from the main menu. Next select **Save As…** this opens the **Save As** window. When queried, **Save results**, click **Yes** to save the results calculated during the solution process. Since work is to be saved to your personal account space, follow the file handling protocol for your computer system or network. Then, close **SolidWorks** as you would any other Windows® program.

<u>CLOSE the file WITHOUT SAVING</u>: ← *Recommended*
To exit SolidWorks Simulation *without saving your results*, select **File** from the main menu. From the pull-down menu, select **Close**. The **SolidWorks** window opens and displays the message "**Save changes to Cam Follower (Part)?**" choose **[No]**. Close **SolidWorks** as you would any other Windows® program.

EXERCISES

End of chapter exercises are intended to provide additional practice using principles introduced in the current chapter. Future chapters also build upon capabilities mastered in preceding chapters. SolidWorks part files for all example and end-of-chapter problems can be downloaded from: **http://www.schroff.com/resources**. To save time, download all files at one time. Use a USB drive or create a file on your PC or network.

Most exercises include multiple parts. In an academic setting, it is likely that parts of problems will be assigned or modified to suit specific course goals.
╬ ***Designates problems that introduce new concepts. Solution guidance is provided for these problems.***

Default Expectations (unless specified otherwise)

- Include a *descriptive* Study name and *your name* when naming each Study. This approach uniquely labels each printed page with your name.
- Use *discrete* stress contours (colored fringes) and display all plots on an *un-deformed* view of the model.

RECALL: "Plot" – refers to a stress contour plot (i.e., colored fringes depicting stress magnitudes within a model).

"Graph" – refers to a X,Y line-graph that depicts a relationship between two variables.

EXERCISE 1 – Shear Due to Bending in Cantilever Beam

The cantilever beam pictured in Fig. E1-1 is rigidly supported (**Fixed**) at its left-end and is subject to forces F_x and F_y applied to its right-end. Either create a beam model using SolidWorks on your own or open problem file **Cantilever 1-1**, which is available at the publisher's web site (see above). Then, perform a finite element analysis of this beam subject to the following guidelines.

- Material: **AISI 1045 Steel cold drawn**
- Mesh: **High Quality** tetrahedral elements (system default)
- External Load: Assign an axial **Force** F_x = 830 lb that acts **Normal** to the right-end of the beam in the direction shown. Also apply a downward **Force** F_y = 760 lb that acts on the top-right **Edge** of the beam. *Split Lines* are not used.

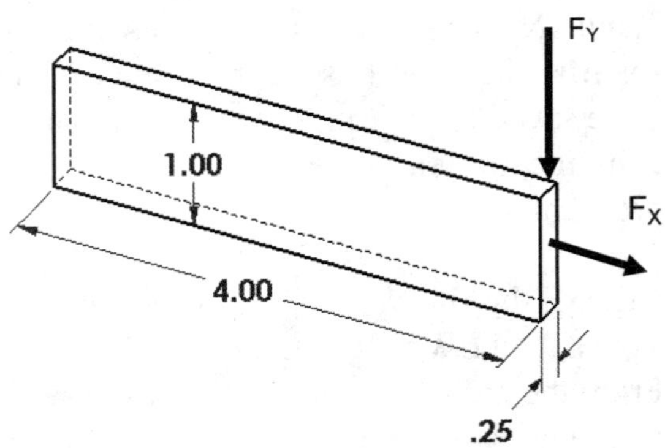

Figure E1-1 – Basic dimensions of a cantilever beam subject to loads F_x and F_y.

- Assign a **Fixed** restraint (not shown in Fig. E1-1) to the left-end of the beam

Determine the following:

a. Create a stress contour plot of shear stress τ_{xy} showing the stress distribution on the front face, which corresponds to the 1.00 x 4.00 in side of the beam. Include a descriptive caption and your name on this plot.

b. Use the **Probe** feature to create a graph of τ_{xy} across the left-front edge of the beam. Create this graph by zooming in on the left end of the model and selecting its left edge; use **Flip edge plot** if necessary.

c. Use the **Probe** feature to create a graph of τ_{xy} across the front face of the beam by selecting successive nodes (from top to bottom) at a location approximately 1-in. to the right of the fixed-end of the model. (Refer to the **Results** table to ensure an X-value corresponding to approximately 1 in. from the left-end of the model is used. *Record the actual value.*). If nodes are not aligned in a straight line across the model, then choose nodes along the best approximation of a straight line. On this plot, manually label the value and location of τ_{xy} used to determine maximum shear due to bending. Customize the graph title and labels for both the X and Y axes on this graph.

d. Calculate the maximum shear stress due to bending using classical stress equations at the fixed end and at the same distance to the right of the fixed end determined in the **Results** table of step (c). Then, use equation [1] below to compute the percent difference between classical and finite element solutions for τ determined at the center of the beam (between top and bottom surfaces) in parts (b) and (c) above.

$$\% \text{ difference} = \frac{(\text{FEA result - classical result})}{\text{FEA result}} * 100 = \qquad [1]$$

e. Briefly state reason(s) why shear stress determined in parts (b) and (c) differ.

f. Use the **Probe** feature to create a graph of σ_x across the front face of the beam (from top to bottom) at approximately 1-in. to the right of the fixed-end. Select *both* corner and mid-side nodes to yield a more uniform graph. In the **Results** table, observe and record the exact X-coordinate of nodes located on the top and bottom edges of the beam. Assign a descriptive title and axis labels to this graph.

g. Use classical stress equations to calculate the *appropriate* normal stress on *both* the top and bottom surfaces of the beam at approximately 1-in. to the right of the fixed-end. Use the "correct distance" to calculate stress at this location. Hint: the X-coordinate of node location(s), determined in step (f) above, should help to determine the "correct distance."

h. Use equation [1] above to compare finite element results for σ_x with manual calculations of σ_x on both top and bottom surfaces of the beam. Clearly label calculations corresponding to "top" and "bottom" surfaces.

i. If results for the comparison of σ_x at 1 in from the left end differ by more than 2% locate and correct the error(s) in either the finite element model and/or in manual stress calculations.

<u>EXERCISE 2</u> – Combined Stress in an "L" Shaped Cantilever Beam

The "L"- shaped cantilever bracket, pictured in Fig. E1-2, is rigidly supported (**Fixed**) at its left end. It is made from **2014-T4** Aluminum and is subject to a concentrated tensile load of F = 6.5 kN applied to a *Split Line* located adjacent to the hole on the right end of the beam. Open the file **Cantilever Bracket**. Use the model provided at the publisher's web site http://www.schroff.com/resources. Create a finite element model of this beam based on the following information.

- Material: **2014-T4** Aluminum (Use S.I. units)
- Mesh: **High Quality** tetrahedral elements (system default)
- External Load: Assign a **Force** F = 6.5 kN, directed to the right and applied on the *Split Line* labeled in Fig. E1-2.
- Fixture: Apply a **Fixed** restraint at the left-end of the model.

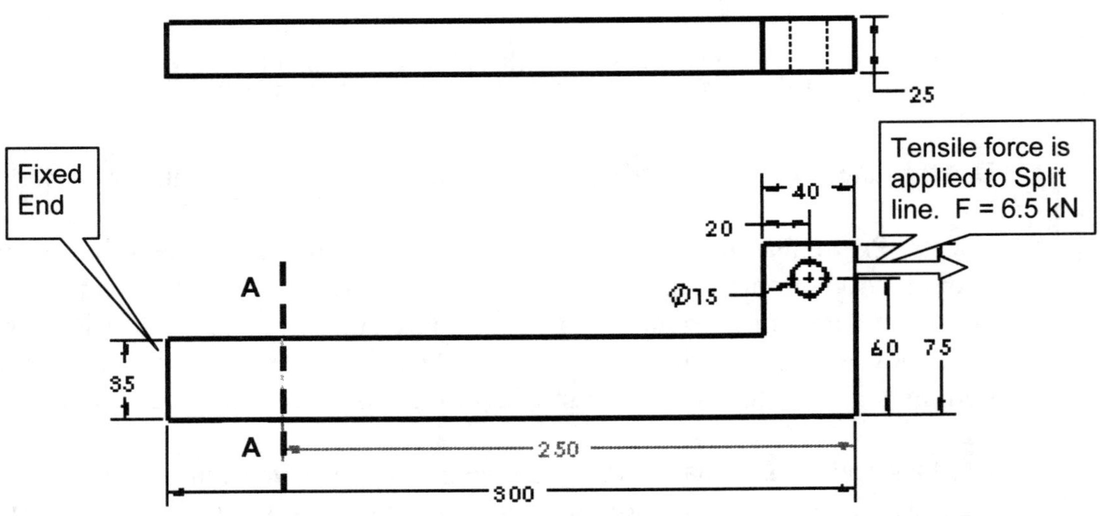

Figure E1-2 – An "L"-shaped cantilever beam "fixed" at its left-end and subject to an axial, tensile force F = 6.5 kN applied at its right end. All lengths in mm.

Determine the following:

a. Create a stress contour plot of the *most appropriate* normal stress distribution on the front face of the beam. Consider the lower image in Fig. 1-2 to be the "front" view. Include your name and a descriptive title on this plot.

b. On the plot of part (a), state whether or not the material yield strength is exceeded. If it is exceeded, circle the region or regions where this occurs and state the reason for your conclusion.

c. Use the **Probe** feature to create a graph of the *most appropriate* normal stress across the front face of the beam by selecting successive nodes (from top to bottom) at location A-A. (Refer to the **Results** table to ensure an X-value corresponding to approximately 50 mm from the left-end of the model is used. *Record the distance value.* If nodes are not aligned in a straight line across the model at location A-A, then choose nodes along the best approximation of a straight line. On this graph, manually label the value and location of stress on the top, centroidal, and bottom surfaces of the beam. Customize the graph title and labels for both the X and Y axes on this graph. The *most appropriate* normal stresses should correspond to those computed in part (d) below.

d. Use classical equations to calculate the axial and bending stresses on the top, centroidal (middle), and bottom surfaces of the beam at location A-A. Clearly label calculations corresponding to each of these surfaces.

e. Use equation [1], below, to compute the percent difference between classical and finite element solutions for stresses determined on the top, centroidal, and bottom beam surfaces determined in parts (c) and (d) above.

$$\% \text{ difference} = \frac{(\text{FEA result - classical result})}{\text{FEA result}} * 100 = \qquad [1]$$

f. If results of part (e) differ by more than 3%, determine the source of the error and, in a brief paragraph, describe the source of the error and how it was rectified.

╬ EXERCISE 3 – Stress Distribution in the Yoshida Buckling Model (Special Topic: Soft Spring Restraint)

The part shown in Fig. E1-3 is often referred to as the "Yoshida Buckling" model by individuals familiar with experimental stress analysis techniques. It is often used as an experimental model in an academic setting due to the interesting stress distribution that exists within the part. In an experimental course, strain gages and/or photoelastic techniques are used to determine strains, and from them, stresses in the part. This exercise investigates the model using finite element analysis.

Open the file: **Yoshida Buckling Model**

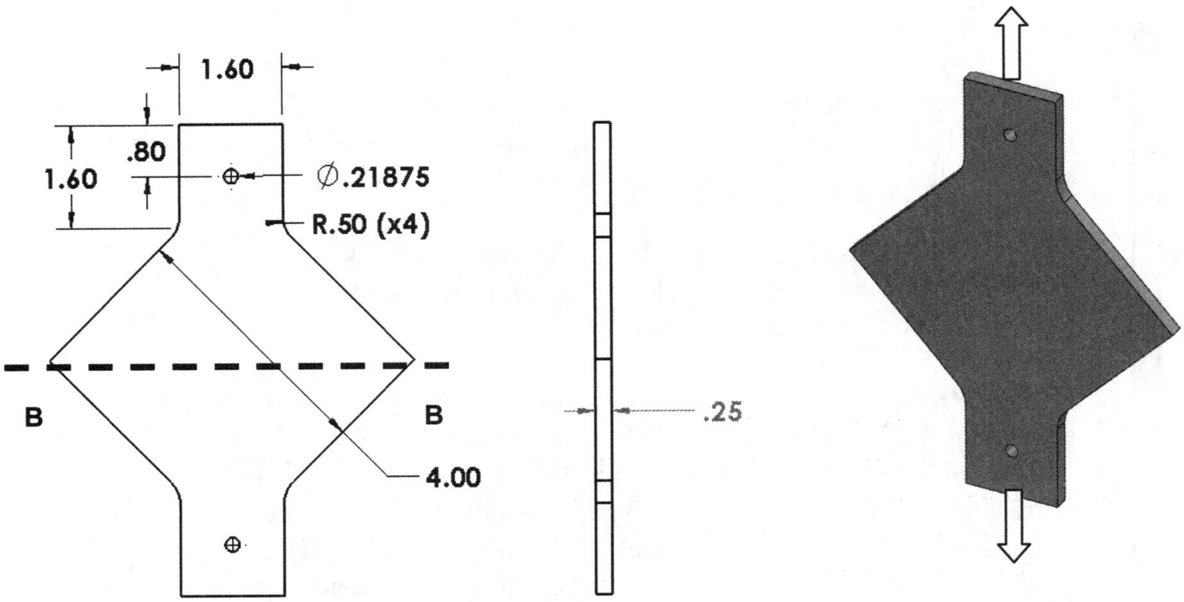

Figure E1-3 – A typical Yoshida Buckling Model. Model dimensions may vary provided proper proportions are retained. Model thickness may vary. Units: inches

Create a model of the above part subject to the following conditions.

- Material: **1060-H18** Aluminum (Use English customary units)
- Mesh: **High Quality** tetrahedral elements (system default)
- External Load: Assign the applied tensile **Force** of **F = 780** lb directed normal to *Split Lines* provided on top and bottom surfaces of the model.

  HINT #1: When applying **External Loads** within the **Force/Torque** property manager, click ⊙ **Selected direction**. Otherwise it is not possible to apply forces to the *Split Lines*.

  HINT #2: **External Loads** must be applied individually. Why? Try applying both forces within the same property manager and see what happens.

In actuality loads are applied by pins passing through holes located at either end of the model. This approach requires somewhat more sophistication than most users have at this time. Alternate methods of load application are investigated in future chapters.

- Support the model using **Soft Springs**. The reason for applying soft springs to the model is that finite element models must be restrained against the possibility of "rigid body motion." It is logical to ask . . . "Why might there be any rigid body motion for the current model? The answer to this question is discussed in the Analysis Insight section.

Analysis Insight

The Yoshida Buckling model is the *only* part file in Chapter #1 that does *not* have a **Fixed** restraint applied somewhere on the part. Recall that **Fixed** restraints, when applied to tetrahedral elements, restrict translations in the X, Y, and Z directions at each node to which they are applied. Thus, equilibrium for externally applied forces in any of those directions is guaranteed due to the **Fixed** restraints. But, that is not the case for the current model where only external forces are applied, but no **Fixtures** are used.

It also might logically be argued that the model is in static equilibrium under the action of equal but opposite forces acting on opposing ends of the model. However, the traditional understanding of equilibrium of forces, such as are applied to a free-body diagram, is subject to subtle differences in a finite element analysis. Those differences include possible asymmetry of the mesh, small inaccuracies in the model, and/or mathematical round-off in calculations. Thus, in a finite element analysis, even the smallest difference from a "zero" force balance results in an unbalanced force acting on the body. And, according to Newton's second law of motion, any unbalanced force acting on a body results in its acceleration in the direction of that unbalanced force. Such motion is not tolerated in a static finite element analysis. Therefore, one way to deal with unbalanced forces is to apply *soft springs* to the model to stabilize it. Instructions in the use of soft springs are provided in the Solution Guidance Section.

Solution Guidance

<u>Soft Spring Restraints</u>

Discussion below provides guidance in the assignment of soft springs to the current model. Soft springs can be assigned any time before the Solution is **Run**.

- Right-click the Study name at top of the Simulation manager tree (not to be confused with the name at top of the SolidWorks Feature manager tree). A pull-down menu appears as shown in Fig. E1-4. From the pull-down menu, select **Properties...** The **Static** window opens as shown in Fig. E1-5.

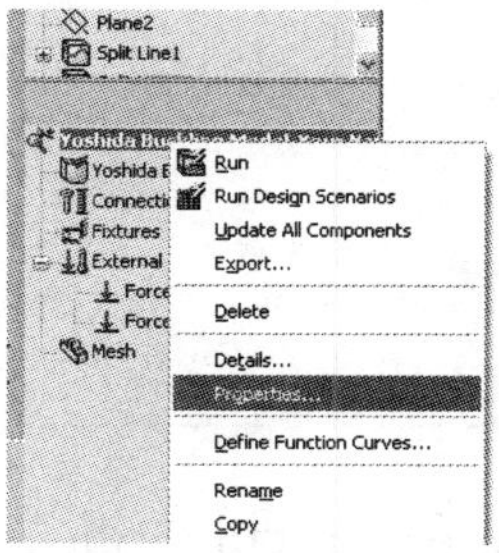

Figure E1-4 – Accessing the Study pull-down menu.

Solution Guidance (continued)

- Within the **Options** tab, select ☑ **Use soft spring to stabilize model**.

- Also select ⊙ **Direct Sparse** as the equation solver method. This solver must be used in conjunction with the soft spring option. Discussion of solver types available within SolidWorks Simulation is beyond the scope of this chapter.

- Click **[OK]** to close the **Static** window.

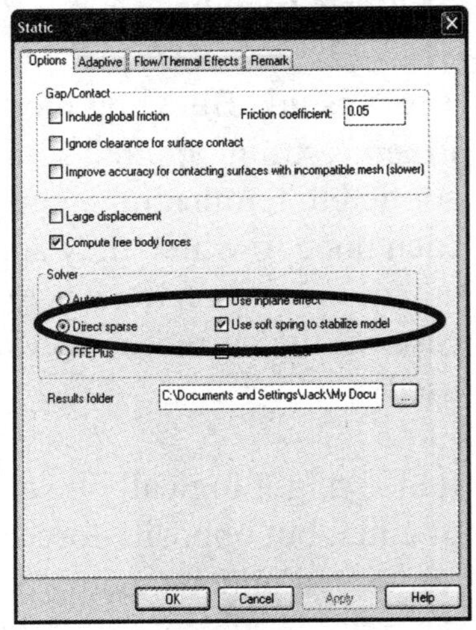

Figure E1-5 – Selecting **Soft Springs** to stabilize the model.

Notice that no springs appear on the screen image of the model. However, they are mathematically present and effectively restrain the model as illustrated in Fig. E1-6.

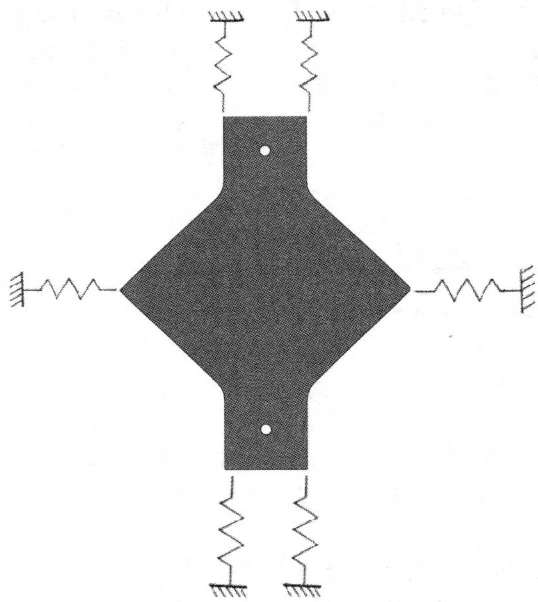

Figure E1-6 – Schematic representation of **Soft Springs** applied to stabilize a model with insufficient **Fixtures**.

Determine the following:

a. Create a plot of von Mises stress throughout the model. On the screen image, zoom in on high stress regions to get an accurate assessment of stress magnitude in the affected region(s). Estimate the maximum stress at top and bottom ends of the model and manually record its magnitude on the plot adjacent to where it occurs. Also, on an image of the entire model, circle the region(s), if any, where the material yield strength is exceeded.

b. Create a plot of stress in the **Y**-direction on the model. Include the mesh on this model.

c. Use the **Probe** tool to create a graph of stress in the **Y**-direction across the middle of the model. Proceed *from right to left* across the model along imaginary line **B-B** shown in Fig. 1-3. Select only corner nodes in as straight a line as possible across the face of the model. Provide a descriptive graph title (include your name) and descriptive labels for both the X and Y axes.

d. Like part (b), except plot stress in the X- direction. Include the mesh on this image.

e. Like part (c), except select nodes along a vertical center-line extending between edges of the two holes that are closest to one another.

f. For the plot of part (a), were the maximum stresses at both ends of the model equal? If not, at what end of the model (top or bottom) is stress the greatest? Knowing that, (Stress) * (Area) = Force, and based on your observation regarding differences, if any, between stresses at opposite ends of the model, discuss whether or not the finite element model is in static equilibrium. Does your finding support or refute the idea that soft springs might be needed to stabilize the model?

g. In one paragraph, discuss general observations regarding the graphs of σ_y and σ_x created for parts (c) and (e) above. Consider common sense questions such as whether or not the distribution of stress magnitude makes sense and "why" or "why not?"

Textbook Problems

It is highly recommended that the above exercises be supplemented by problems from a design of machine elements textbook. A great way to discover errors made in formulating a finite element analysis is to work problems for which the solution is known by independent calculation or experiment. Typical textbook problems, if well defined in advance, make an excellent source of solutions for comparison.

NOTES:

CHAPTER #2

CURVED BEAM ANALYSIS

This example, unlike the first, will lead you quickly through those aspects of creating a finite element Study with which you already have experience. However, where new information or procedures are introduced, additional details are included. For consistency throughout this text, a common approach is used for the solution of all problems.

Learning Objectives

In addition to software capabilities studied in the previous chapter, upon completion of this example, users should be able to:

- Use SolidWorks Simulation *icons* in addition to menu selections.
- Apply a *split line* to divide a selected face into one or more separate faces.
- Simulate *pin loading* inside a hole.
- Use **Design Checks** to determine the *safety factor* or lack thereof.
- Determine *reaction* forces acting on a finite element model.

Problem Statement

A dimensioned model of a curved beam is shown in Fig. 1. Assume the beam material is 2014 Aluminum alloy, and it is subject to a downward vertical force, F_y = 3800 lb, applied through a cylindrical pin (not shown) in a hole near its free end. The bottom of the curved beam is considered "fixed." In this context, the *actual* fixed end-condition is analogous to that at the end of a cantilever beam where translations in the X, Y, Z directions and rotations about the X, Y, Z axes are considered to be zero. However, recall from Chapter 1 that **Fixture** types within SolidWorks Simulation also depend on the type of element to which they are applied. Therefore, because solid tetrahedral elements are used to model this curved beam, **Immovable** restraints are used.

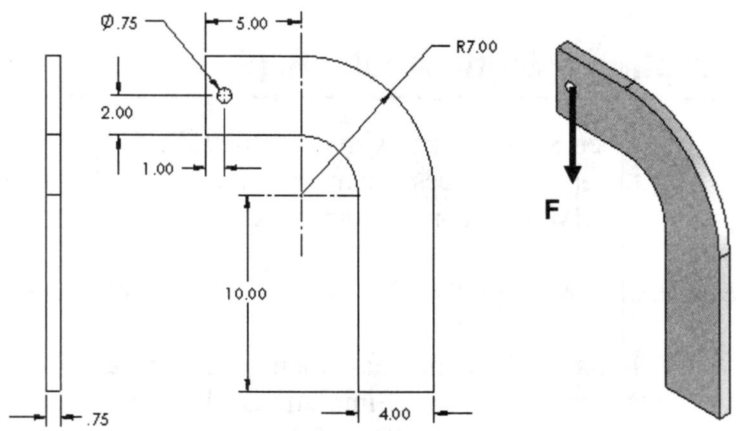

Figure 1 – Three dimensional model of curved beam.

Design Insight
Numerous mechanical elements occur in the shape of initially curved beams. Examples include: C-clamps, punch-press frames, crane hooks, and bicycle caliper brakes, to name a few. This example examines the stress at section A-A shown in Fig. 2. Section A-A is chosen because it is the furthest distance from the applied force **F** thereby creating reaction force **R** = **F** and the maximum bending moment **M** = **F*L** at that location. Accordingly, classical equations for stress in a curved beam predict maximum stress at section A-A. In this example, the validity of this common assumption is investigated while exploring the additional capabilities of SolidWorks Simulation software listed above.

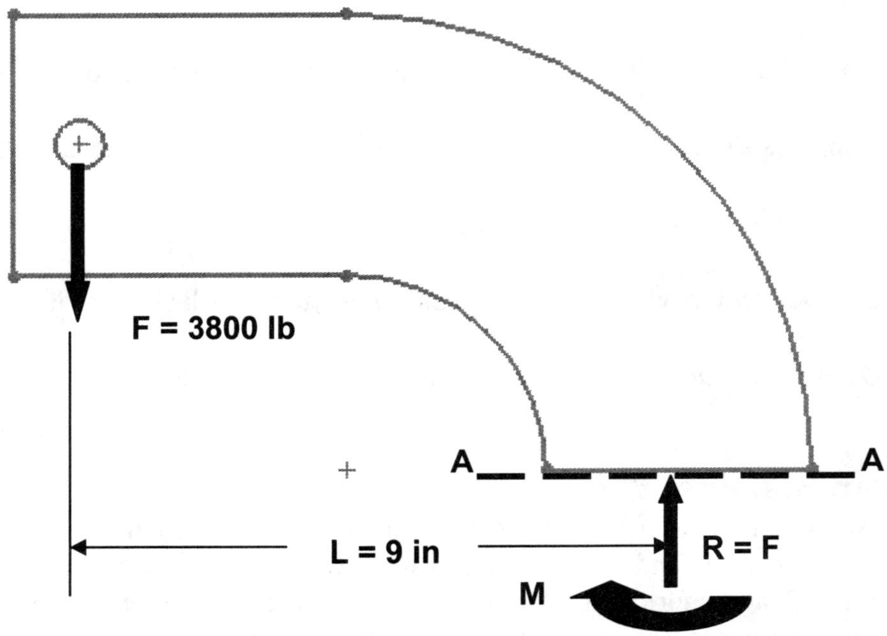

Figure 2 – Traditional free-body diagram of the upper portion of a curved beam model showing applied force **F** acting at a hole, and reactions **R** = **F**, and moment **M** acting on section **A-A**.

Creating a Static Analysis (Study)

1. Open SolidWorks by making the following selections. (*Note:* A "/" is used below to separate successive menu selection). Alternatively, double-click the SolidWorks icon on your desktop.

Start/All Programs/SolidWorks 2009 (or) Click the **SolidWorks** icon on your screen.

2. In the SolidWorks main menu, select **File / Open…** Then browse to the location where SolidWorks Simulations files are stored and select the file named "**Curved Beam**" then click **[Open]**.

If a pop-up window appears and states: **The following documents will be converted when saved "Curved Beam.SLDPRT"**, click **[OK]** to close the window.

> **Reminder:**
> If you do not see **Simulation** listed in the main menu of the SolidWorks screen, click **Tools/Add-Ins…**, then in the **Add-Ins** window check ☑ **SolidWorks Simulation** in both the **Active Add-Ins** and the **Start Up** columns, then click **[OK]**. This action adds **Simulation** to the main menu.

Because one goal of this chapter is to introduce use of SolidWorks Simulation icons, three methods of displaying these icons are outlined below. If Simulation icons already appear on your screen, perform the following steps to investigate all display options available. Proceed as follows.

Display method #1

3. Right-click anywhere on the toolbar at top of the screen. This action opens the SolidWorks Simulation Command Manager menu shown in Fig. 3.

4. Within the Command Manager menu, select **Simulation**, shown at the arrow in Fig. 3. The Simulation toolbar opens; a partial view of it appears in Fig. 4. This toolbar is typically located beneath the main menu. Until a Study is initiated, all icons but one are grayed out (inactive).

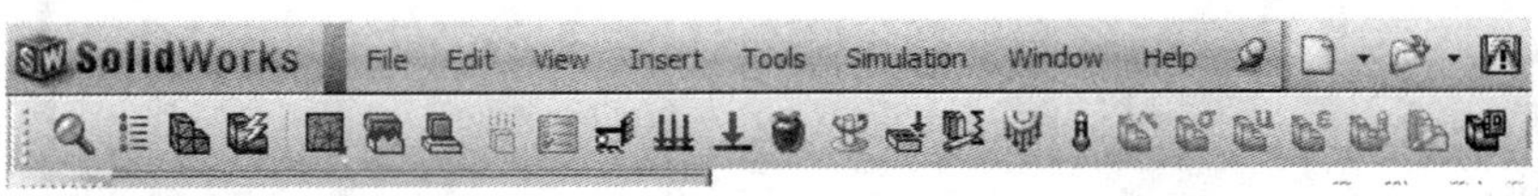

Figure 4 – SolidWorks Simulation icons displayed by selecting **Simulation**.

Additional toolbars may be displayed on your screen. However, the main menu and Simulation toolbars are the focus of Fig. 4, therefore, other toolbars have been removed.

Toolbars can be moved to different locations on the screen. Reposition toolbars by clicking-and-dragging the "handles" located at the left or upper end of each toolbar.

Figure 3 – **Command Manager** pop-up menu.

Display method #2

5. Right-click anywhere on the toolbar at top of the screen. The SolidWorks Simulation Command Manager menu again opens as shown in Fig. 3.

6. At the top of the command manager, click to select **Command Manager**. This action adds a series of *tabs* beneath the main menu. A partial view of the toolbar appears in Fig. 5.

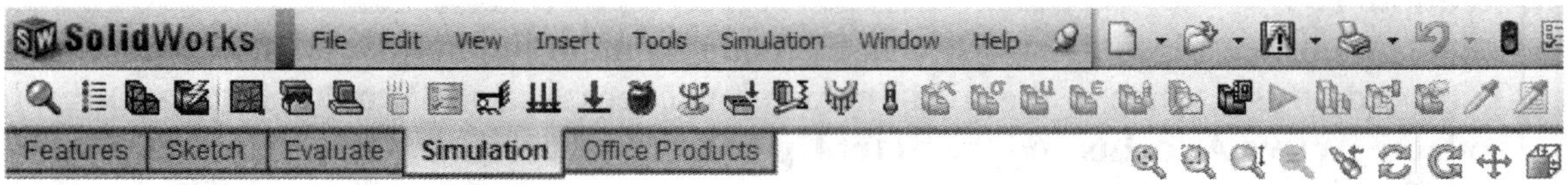

Figure 5 – Partial view of the **Simulation** toolbar, which is available by accessing the **Simulation** tab.

Initially the **Simulation** tab is selected and the same set of SolidWorks Simulation icons is displayed except that now they are accessible only after first selecting the **Simulation** tab.

7. Users familiar with the SolidWorks work environment are encouraged to select the **Features**, and **Sketch** tabs to view familiar icons accessible within these tabs. Return to the **Simulation** tab before continuing.

Display method #3

8. Right-click anywhere on the toolbar at top of the screen to again open the Command Manager.

9. Just below **Command Manager** at top of the pull-down menu, click to select **Use Large Buttons with Text**. This action adds a brief description beneath each icon as illustrated in a partial view of the toolbar displayed in Fig. 6.

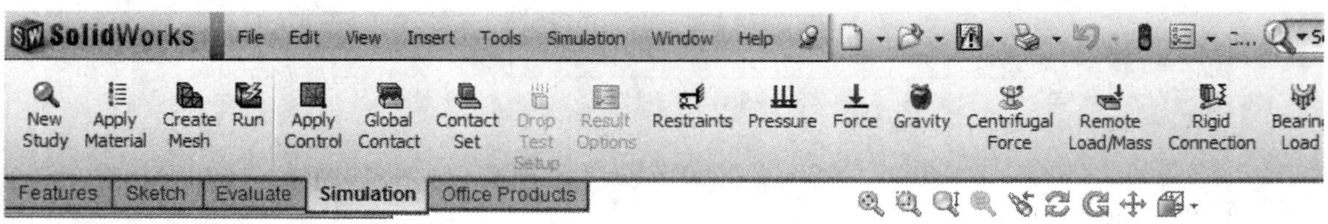

Figure 6 – Partial view of the **Simulation** toolbar with descriptive text applied beneath each icon.

Presuming the **Simulation** icons to be unfamiliar to new users, the display mode illustrated in Fig. 6 is used in throughout this chapter. Now that the work environment is established, a Study of stresses in the curved beam begins below.

10. Within the **Simulation** tab, click to select the **New Study** icon . The **Study** property manager opens (not shown).

11. In the **Name** dialogue box, replace **Study 1** by typing a descriptive name. For this example, type: **Curved Beam Analysis-YOUR NAME**. Including your name along with the Study name ensures that it is displayed on each plot. This helps to identify plots sent to public access printers.

12. In the **Type** dialogue box, verify that **Static** is selected as the analysis type.

13. Click **[OK]** ✓ (green check mark) to close the **Study** property manager. Notice that many of the icons on the **Simulation** tab are displayed in color to indicate they are now active.

The bottom half of the SolidWorks Simulation manager, seen in Fig. 7, is updated to show an outline for the current Study.

As in the previous example, the sequence of steps outlined in Fig. 7 is followed from top to bottom as the current finite element analysis is developed.

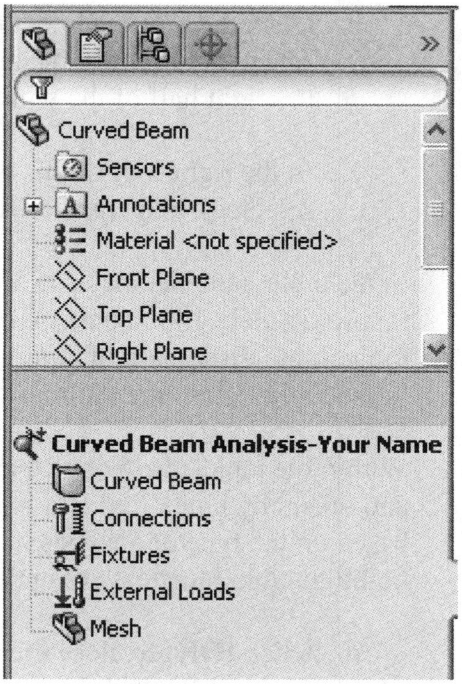

Figure 7 – Basic steps of a Study.

Assign Material Properties to the Model

Part *material* is defined as outlined below.

1. On the **Simulation** tab, click to select the **Apply Material** icon. The **Material** window opens. Alternatively, in the Simulation manager tree, right-click the **Curved Beam** folder and from the pull-down menu select **Apply/Edit Material…** The **Material** window is shown in Fig.8.

   a. Under **Select material source**, click to select ⦿ **From library files:** Then, from the adjacent pull-down menu select **solidworks materials**.

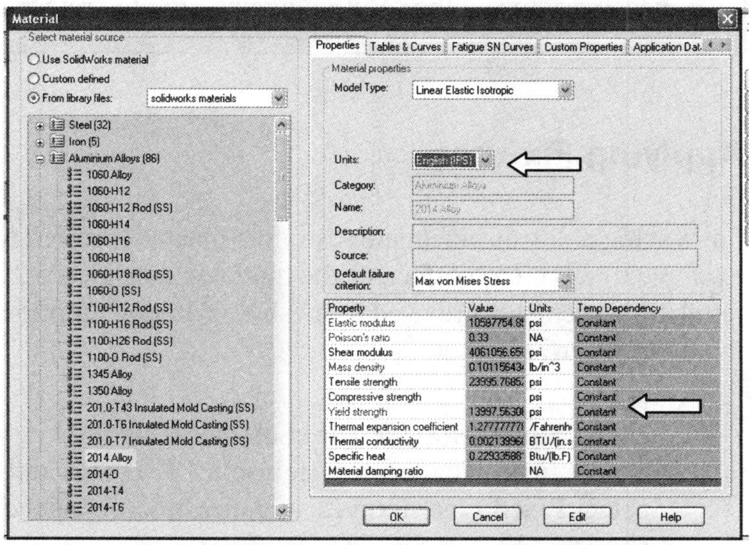

Figure 8 – Material properties are selected and/or defined in the **Material** window.

b. Click the plus sign next to the **Aluminum Alloys (86)** and scroll down to select **2014 Alloy**. The properties of 2014 Aluminum alloy are displayed in the right half of the window.

c. In the right-half of this window, select the **Properties** tab (if not already selected), and change **Units:** to **English (IPS)**.

In the table, note the material **Yield Strength** is a relatively low 13997.56306 psi (approximately 14000 psi). Material with a low yield strength is intentionally chosen to facilitate discussion of *Safety Factor* later in this example. Examine other values in the table to become familiar with data available in the material properties library.

Within the table, also notice that some material properties are indicated by red text and others by blue. Red text indicates a material property that must be specified based on the type of analysis being performed. Conversely, material properties highlighted in blue text are optional, and those in black text are not needed.

d. Click **[OK]** to close the **Material** window. A check mark "✓" appears on the **Curved Beam** folder to indicate a material has been selected. The material type **(-2014 Alloy-)** is also listed adjacent to the model name.

Aside:
If at any point you wish to *change the material specification* of a part, such as during a redesign, right-click the name of the particular part whose material properties are to be changed and from the pull-down menu select **Apply/Edit Material**. The **Material** window is opened and an alternative material can be selected.

However, be aware that when a different material is specified *after* running a solution, it is necessary to run the solution again using the revised material properties.

Applying Fixtures

For a static analysis, adequate restraints must be applied to stabilize the model. In this example, the bottom surface of the model is considered "fixed." However, because tetrahedral elements are used to mesh this model, "immovable" restraints are applied to the bottom surface.

1. In the **Simulation** toolbar click the **Restraints** icon . Alternatively, in the Simulation manager tree, right-click **Fixtures** and from the pull-down menu select **Fixed Geometry…** Either action opens the **Fixture** property manager shown in Fig. 9. *NOTE: The **Restraints** icon may be renamed **Fixtures** in newer software releases.*

2. Within the **Standard (Fixed Geometry)** dialogue box, select the **Fixed Geometry** icon (if not already selected).

3. The **Faces, Edges, Vertices for Fixture** field is highlighted (light blue) to indicate it is active and waiting for the user to select part of the model to be restrained. Rotate, and/or zoom to view the bottom of the model. Next, move the cursor over the model and when the bottom surface is indicated, click to select it. The surface is highlighted and restraint symbols appear as shown in Fig. 10. Also, **Face<1>** appears in the **Faces, Edges, Vertices for Fixture** field.

If an incorrect entity (such as a vertex, edge, or the wrong surface) is selected, right-click the incorrect item in the highlighted field and from the pop-up menu select **Delete**, then repeat step 3.

4. If restraint symbols do not appear, or if it is desired to alter their size or color, click the down arrow to open the **Symbol Settings** dialogue box, at bottom of the **Fixture** property manager and check the ☑ **Show preview** box.

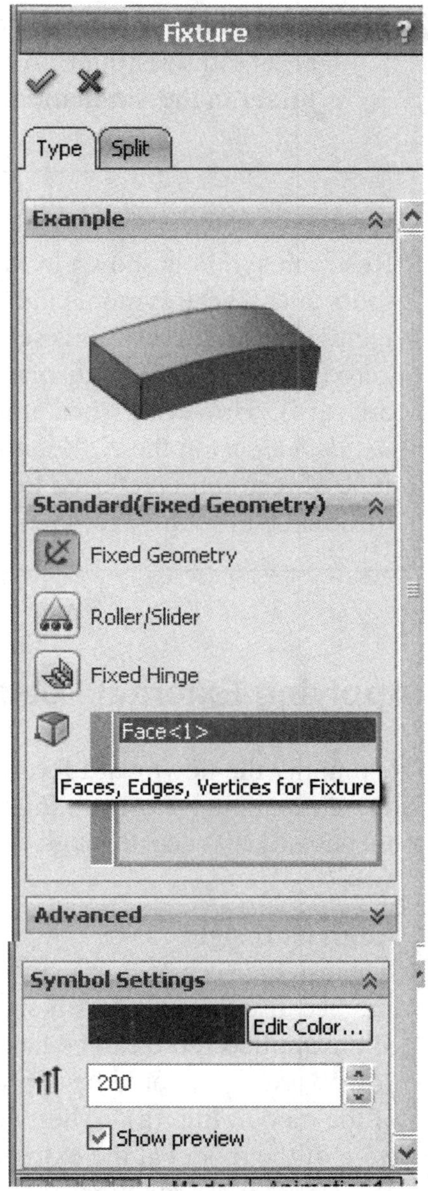

Figure 9 – **Fixture** property manager.

5. Both color and size of the restraint symbols (vectors in the X, Y, Z directions) can be changed by altering values in the **Symbol Settings** field of Fig. 9. Experiment by clicking the up ▲ or down ▼ arrows to change size of restraint symbols. A box of this type, where values can be changed either by typing a new value or by clicking the ▲▼ arrows, is called a "spin box." Restraint symbols shown in Fig. 10 were arbitratily increased to 200%. Experiment with this option.

Figure 10 – Restraints applied to bottom of the curved beam model.

6. Click **[OK]** ✓ (green check mark) at top of the **Fixture** property manager to accept this restraint. An icon named **Fixture-1** appears beneath the **Fixtures** folder in the Simulation manager tree.

Aside:
Restraint symbols shown in Fig. 10 appear as simple arrows with a small disk added to its tail. These symbols indicate **Fixed** restraints when applied to shell or beam elements. **Fixed** restraints set both *translational* and *rotational* degrees of freedom to zero (i.e., both X, Y, Z displacements and rotations (moments) about the X, Y, Z axes are zero). However, when applied to either solid models or truss elements, only *displacements* in the X, Y, and Z directions are restrained (i.e., prevented). This latter type of restraint is referred to as **Immovable**. Watch for this subtle, but important difference in future examples.

Applying External Load(s)

Next apply the downward force, F_y = 3800 lb, at the hole located near the top left-hand side of the model shown in Figs. 1 and 2. This force is assumed to be applied by a pin (not shown) that acts through the hole.

Analysis Insight
Because the goal of this analysis is to focus on curved beam stresses at Section A-A, and because Section A-A is well removed from the point of load application, modeling of the applied force can be handled in a number of different ways. For example, the downward force could be applied to the vertical *surface* located on the upper-left side of the model, Fig. (a). Alternatively, the force could be applied to the upper or lower *edge* of the model at the extreme left side, Fig. (b). These loading situations would require a slight reduction of the magnitude of force **F** to account for its additional distance from the left-side of the model to section A-A (i.e., the moment about section A-A must remain the same).

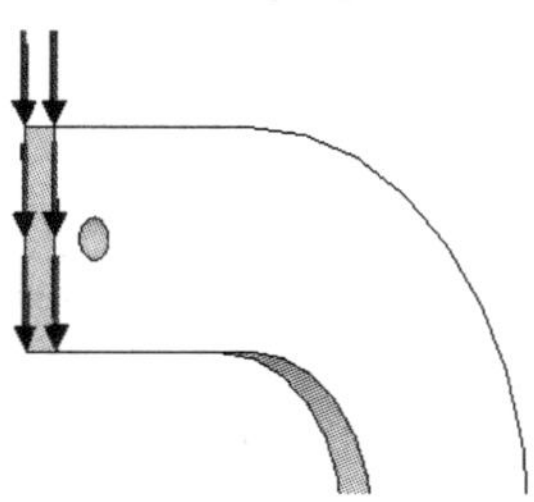

Figure (a) – Force applied to left surface.

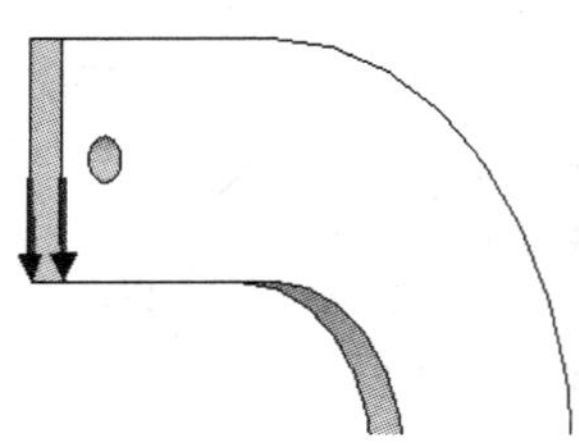

Figure (b) – Force applied to lower edge.

The above loads are simple to apply. However, the assumption of pin loading allows us to investigate use of a *Split Line* to isolate a *portion* of the bottom surface of the hole where contact with a pin is assumed to occur. This surface is where a pin force would be transferred to the curved beam model. The actual contact area depends on a number of factors, which include: (a) geometries of the contacting parts (i.e., relative diameters of the pin and hole), (b) material properties (i.e., hard versus soft contact surfaces of either the pin or the beam), and (c) magnitude of the force that presses the two surfaces together. This example arbitrarily assumes a reasonable contact area so that use of a *Split Line* can be demonstrated. If, on the other hand, contact stresses in the vicinity of the hole were of paramount importance, then determination of the true contact area requires use of *Contact/Gap* analysis. This form of analysis is investigated in Chapter #6.

Inserting Split Lines

The first task is to isolate a portion of the area at the bottom of the hole. This can be accomplished by using a *Split Line*. The method described below outlines the use of a reference plane to insert a *Split Line*.

1. In the drawing toolbar, reorient the model by clicking the **Trimetric** 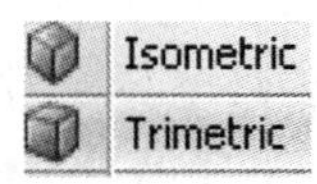

or **Isometric** view icon.

2. From the main menu, select **Insert**. Then, from succeeding pull-down menus make the following selections: **Reference Geometry ▶** followed by **Plane...** The **Plane** property manager opens *and* the SolidWorks "flyout" menu also appears at the upper-left corner of the graphics screen as shown in Fig. 11.

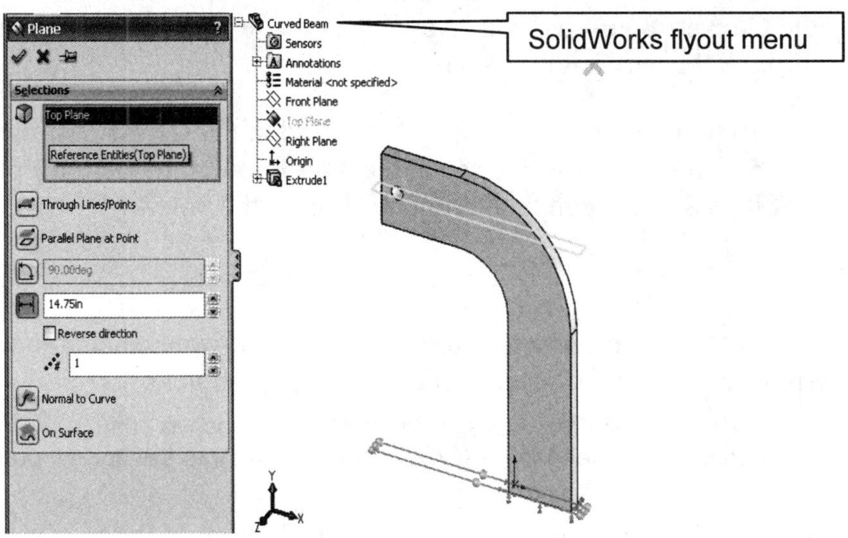

Figure 11 – The **Plane** property manager and menu selections made to create a reference plane that passes through the bottom of the hole.

3. To display the complete "flyout" menu shown in Fig. 11, it may be necessary to click the "+" sign adjacent to the SolidWorks **Curved Beam** icon. Continue to refer to Fig. 11 in steps 4 through 6.

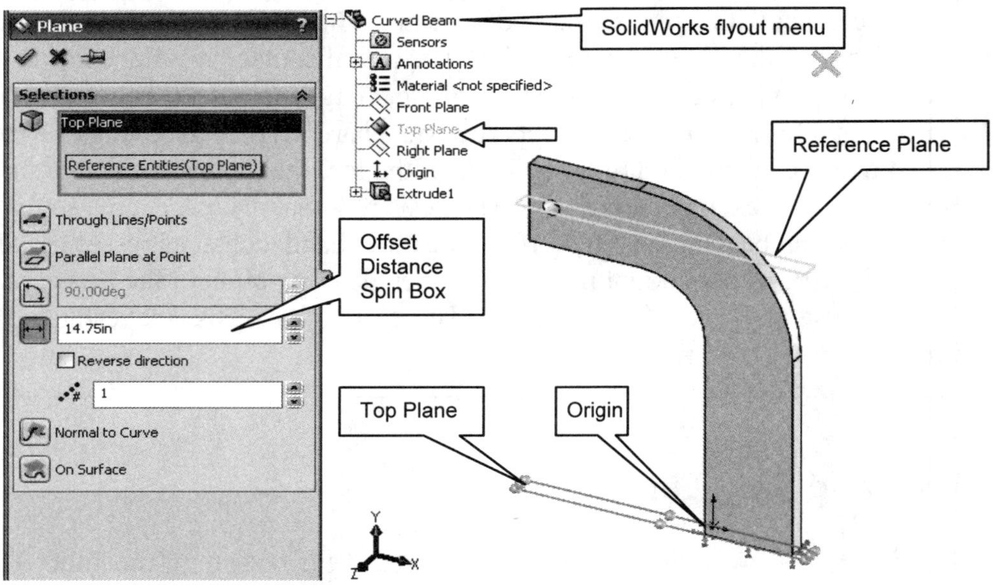

Figure 11(REPEATED) – The **Plane** property manager and various selections made to create a reference plane that passes through the bottom of the hole.

4. Within the **Plane** property manager, under **Selections**, the **Reference Entities** field is highlighted (light blue). Note text appearing in the *Status Line* at bottom left of the screen, which prompts the user to "**Select valid entities to define a plane (plane, face, edge, line or point)**." In the following steps, a horizontal reference plane that passes through the bottom portion of the hole is defined.

5. From the SolidWorks "flyout menu," select **Top Plane**. For users who opened the **Curved Beam** part file available at the textbook web site, the top plane passes through the part origin, which is located on the bottom of the model[1] in Fig. 11.

6. Return to the **Selections** dialogue box and in the **Offset Distance** spin-box, type **14.75**. This is the distance *from* the **Top Plane** to a reference plane located so that it passes through the bottom portion of the hole.

Aside:

The 14.75 in. dimension is determined from the following calculation. Refer to Fig. 1 to determine the source of values used in the equation below.

10 in (height of straight vertical sides) + 3 in (radius of concave surface) + 1.75 in (distance from the horizontal edge beneath the hole and extending into the bottom portion of the hole) = 14.75in.

It is emphasized that the area intersected on the bottom of the hole is chosen *arbitrarily* in this example!

[1] Users who created a curved beam model from scratch can also follow these instructions. The *only* difference being specification of the proper *distance* from the **Top Plane** (used as a reference in *your* model) to the bottom of the hole.

7. Click **[OK]** ✓ to close the **Plane** property manager.

The reference plane created in the preceding steps appears highlighted in the current screen image. In the following steps this plane is used to create *Split Lines* near the bottom of the hole. These *Split Lines* enable us to define a small area on the bottom of the hole where the downward load will be applied.

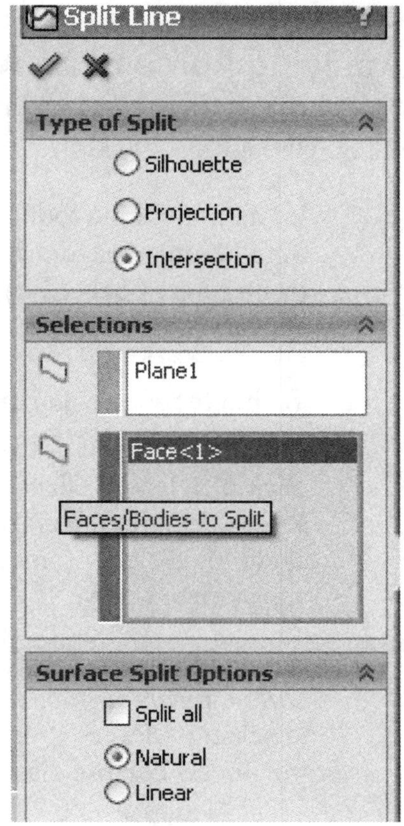

Figure 12 – **Split Line** property manager showing selections.

8. From the main menu, select **Insert**. Then, from the pull-down menus choose: **Curve ►** followed by **Split Line…** The **Split Line** property manager opens as shown in Fig. 12

9. Beneath **Type of Split**, select ⦿ **Intersection**. This choice designates the means by which *Split Lines* are defined for this example (i.e., they will be located where **Plane1** *intersects* the hole).

10. In the **Selections** dialogue box, **Plane1** may already appear in the **Splitting Bodies/Faces/ Planes** field. If **Plane1** does not appear in this field, click to activate the field (light blue), then move the cursor onto the graphics screen and select the upper plane when it is highlighted. **Plane1** now appears in the top field.

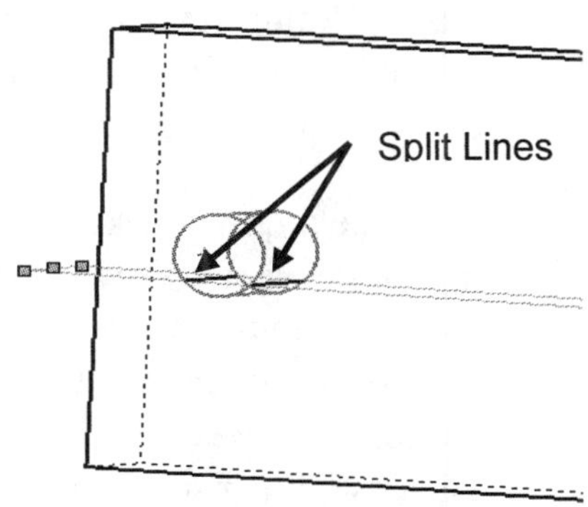

Figure 13 – Close-up view of hole showing *Split Lines* where **Plane1** intersects near the bottom of hole.

11. Next, click inside the **Faces/Bodies to Split** field. This field may already be active (light blue). Then move the cursor over the model and select anywhere on the *inside surface* of the hole. It may be necessary to zoom in on the model to select this surface. Once selected, **Face<1>** appears in the active field. Figure 13 shows a partial image of the model with *Split Lines* appearing where **Plane1** intersects the bottom of the hole.

Remain zoomed-in on the model to facilitate applying a force to the inside of the hole.

12. In the **Surface Split Options** dialogue box, select ⦿ **Natural**. A **Natural** split follows the contour of the selected surface.

13. Click **[OK]** ✓ to close the **Split Line** property manager.

14. If an information "flag" appears adjacent to the *Split Lines*, click ☒ to close it.

Applying Force to an Area Bounded by Split Lines

Now that a restricted area on the bottom of the hole has been identified, the next step is to apply a downward force, F_y = 3800 lb, on this area. Proceed as follows.

1. In the Simulation toolbar, select the **Force** icon. Alternatively, in the Simulation manager, right-click the **External Loads** icon and from the pop-up menu select **Force...** A partial view of the **Force/Torque** property manager appears in Fig. 14.

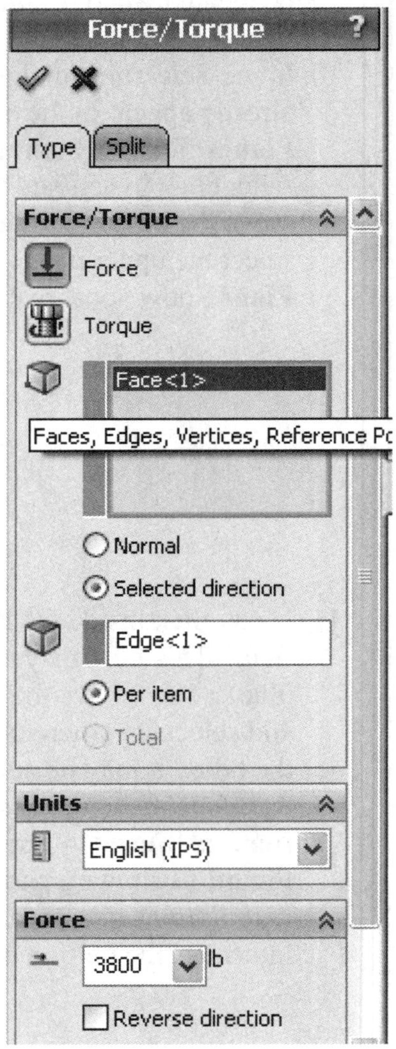

Figure 14 – Specifying a force and its direction on the hole bottom.

2. Within the **Force/Torque** dialogue box, click the **Force** icon (if not already selected). Also, click ⦿**Selected Direction**. Again the **Faces, Edges, Vertices, Reference Points for Force** (light blue) field prompts the user to select an appropriate entity.

3. Move the cursor over the model and when the *bottom inside surface* of the hole is outlined, click to select it. **Face<1>** appears in the active field of the **Force/Torque** dialogue box.

4. Next, click to activate the second field from the top of the **Force/Torque** dialogue box. Passing the cursor over this field identifies it as the **Face, Edge, Plane, Axis for Direction** field. This field is used to specify the direction of the force applied to the bottom of the hole.

   Because a downward, vertical force is to be applied, select a *vertical* edge . . . *any vertical edge* . . . on the model aligned with the Y-direction. After selecting a vertical edge, **Edge<1>** appears in the active field and force vectors appear on the model as seen in Fig. 15.

5. Set **Units** to **English (IPS)**, if not already selected.

6. In the **Force** dialogue box, type **3800**. As noted in an earlier example, it may be necessary to check ☑ **Reverse Direction** if the force is not directed downward.

7. Click **[OK]** ✓ to accept this force definition and close the **Force/Torque** property manager. An icon named **Force/Torque-1** appears beneath the **External Loads** folder in the Simulation manager.

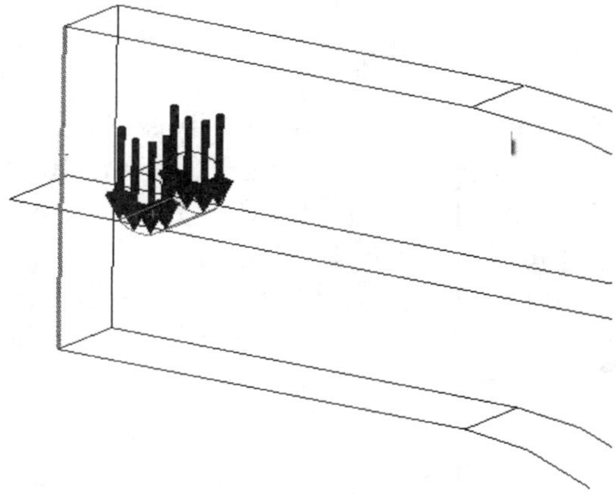

Figure 15 – Downward force applied between *Split Lines* on bottom of hole. A wireframe view of model is shown.

The model is now complete as far as material, restraints, and force definitions are concerned. The next step is to Mesh the model as described below.

Meshing the Model

1. In the Simulation toolbar, select the **Create Mesh** icon. Alternatively, in the Simulation manager tree, right-click **Mesh** and from the pull-down menu select **Create Mesh…** The **Mesh** property manager opens as shown in Figs 16 (a) and (b)

2. Click the down arrow to open the **Mesh Parameters** dialogue box and verify that a ⊙ **Standard mesh** is selected. Also set the **Unit** field to **in** (if not already selected). Accept the remaining default settings (i.e. mesh **Global Size** and **Tolerance**) at the bottom of this dialogue box.

3. Click the down arrow to open the **Advanced** dialogue box, Fig. 15 (b). Verify that **Jacobian points** is set at **4 points**. These settings should produce a good quality mesh. However, verify that the settings are as listed and only change them if they differ.

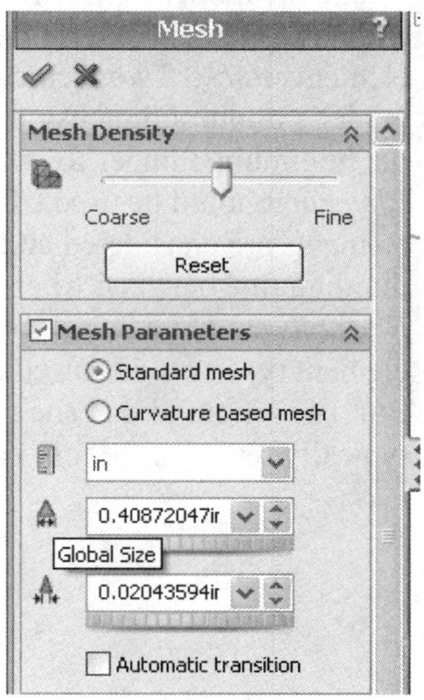

Figure 16 (a) – **Mesh** property manager showing system default **Mesh** settings applied to the current model.

4. Finally, click **[OK]** ✓ to accept these settings and close the **Mesh** property manager.

Meshing starts automatically and the **Mesh Progress** window appears briefly. After meshing is complete, SolidWorks Simulation displays the meshed model shown in Fig. 17. Also, a check mark "✓" appears on the **Mesh** icon to indicate meshing is complete.

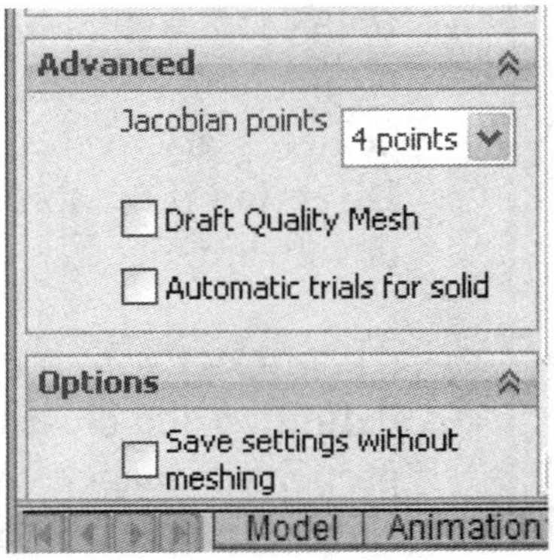

Figure 16 (b) – View of the **Advanced** portion of the **Mesh** property manager.

OPTIONAL:

5. Display mesh information by right-clicking the **Mesh** folder and select **Details....**

The **Mesh Details** window displays a variety of mesh information. Scroll down the list of information an note the number of nodes and elements for this model is 12536 nodes and 7197 elements (numbers may vary slightly due to the automated mesh generation procedure).

Rotate the model as illustrated in Fig. 17 and notice that the mesh is just two elements *thick*. Two elements across the model's thinnest dimension are considered the minimum number for which *Solid Elements* should be used. Thus, two elements are considered an unofficial dividing line between when *Shell* or *Solid Elements* should be used. Therefore, either element type could be used for this model. But, keep in mind that shell elements are typically reserved for thin parts.

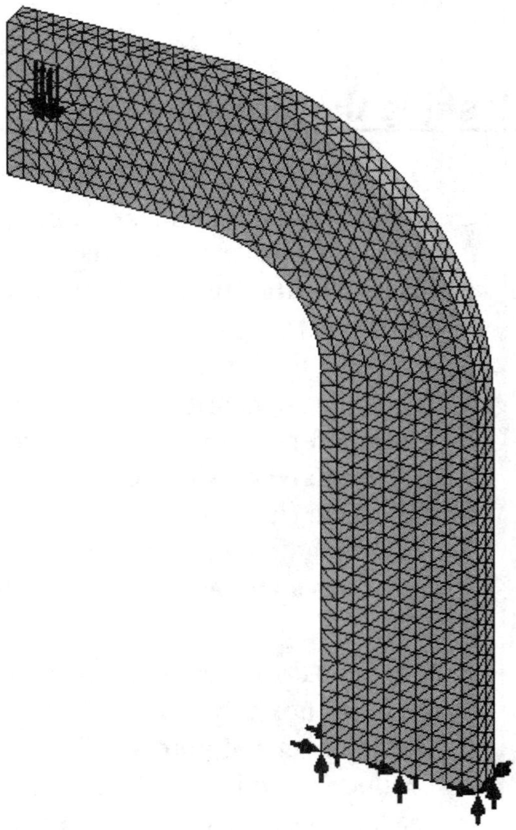

Figure 17 – Curved beam with mesh and boundary conditions illustrated.

> **Reminder**
> Recall that it is permissible to define material properties, fixtures, external loads, and create the mesh in any order. However, all these necessary steps must be completed before running a solution.

Solution

After the model has been completely defined, the solution process is initiated. During a solution the numerous equations defining a Study are solved and results of the analysis are saved for review.

1. On the Simulation tab, click the **Run** icon. Or, right-click the **Curved Beam Analysis - YOUR NAME (-Default-)** folder highlighted in Fig. 18. From the pull-down menu, select **Run**. Either action initiates the solution process.

After a successful solution, a **Results** folder appears at the bottom of the Simulation manager. This folder should include three sub-folders that contain default plots of results saved at the conclusion of each Study. These folders are named as illustrated in Fig. 18. If these folders do *not* appear, follow steps (a) through (f) outlined on page 1-14 of Chapter #1.

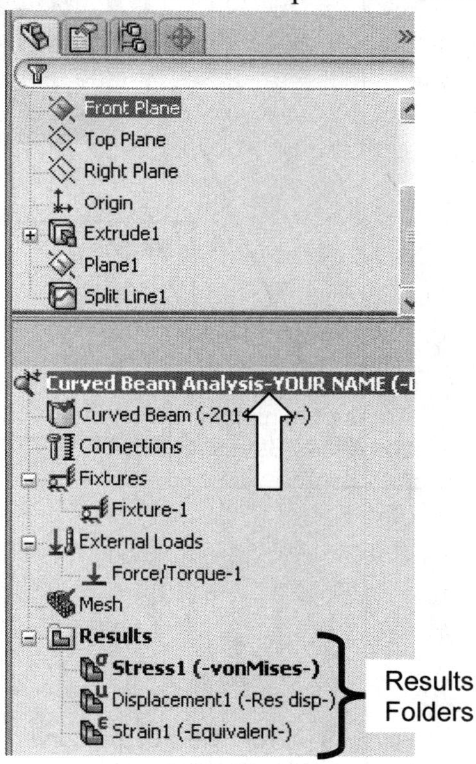

Figure 18 – **Results** folders created during the Solution process.

When the **Results** folders are displayed, alter **Units** for the **Stress** and **Displacement** plots, if necessary, as outlined below.

2. If the von Mises stress plot does not appear, then right-click **Stress1 (-von Mises-)** and from the pull-down menu, select **Show**; a stress plot appears.

3. Again, right-click **Stress1 (-vonMises-)** and from the pull-down menu select **Edit Definition…** In the **Display** dialogue box, verify **Units** are set to **psi**. If not, use the pull-down menu to change **Units** from **N/m^2** to **psi**.

4. Click **[OK]** ✓ to close the **Stress Plot** property manager.

5. Repeat steps (2) through (4), however, in step (2), right-click on **Displacement1 (-Res disp-)** instead of **Stress1 (-vonMises-)** and in step (3) alter the **Units** field from **m** to **in**.

Examination of Results

Analysis of von Mises Stresses Within the Model

Outcomes of the current analysis, in the form of plots, can be viewed by accessing results stored in the various folders listed in the previous section. This is where validity of results is verified by cross-checking Finite Element Analysis (FEA) results against results obtained using classical stress equations. *Checking results is a necessary step in good engineering practice!*

1. In the Simulation manager tree, double-click the **Stress1 (-vonMises-)** folder (or) right-click it and from the pull-down menu, select **Show**. A plot of the vonMises stress distribution throughout the curved beam model is displayed.

Figure 19 reveals an image *similar* to what currently appears on the screen. The following steps convert your current screen image to that shown in Fig. 19.

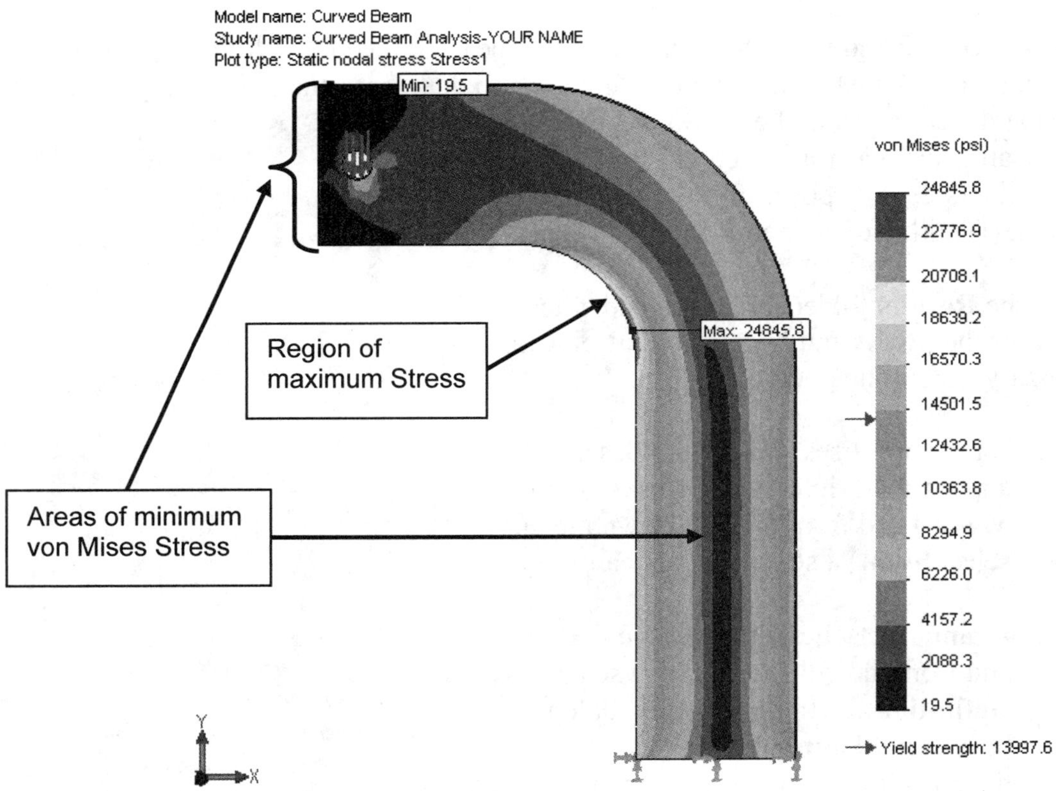

Figure 19 – Front view of the curved beam model showing von Mises stress *after* making changes outlined below. Note arrows indicating Yield Strength on the stress scale at right.

NOTE: *Stress contour plots are printed in black, white, and grey tones. Therefore, light and dark color areas on your screen may differ from images shown throughout this text.*

2. Right-click **Stress1 (-vonMises-)** and from the pull-down menu select **Chart Options….** A portion of the **Chart Options** property manager is shown in Fig. 20.

3. Within the **Display Options** dialogue box, click to place check marks to activate ☑ **Show min annotation** and ☑ **Show max annotation**. This action causes the minimum and maximum von Mises stress locations to be labeled on the model.

4. Click **[OK]** ✓ to close the **Chart Options** property manager.

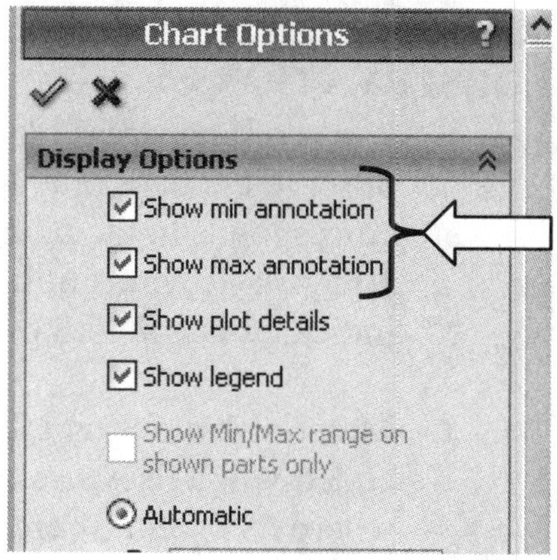

Figure 20 – Upper portion of **Chart Options** property manager showing current selections.

5. Right-click **Stress1 (-vonMises-)** and from the pull-down menu select **Settings….** The **Settings** property manager opens as illustrated in Fig. 21.

6. From the **Fringe options** menu, select **Discrete** as the fringe type to be displayed.

7. Next, in the **Boundary options** pull-down menu, select **Model** to superimpose an outline of the model on the image.

8. Click **[OK]** ✓ to close the **Settings** property manager.

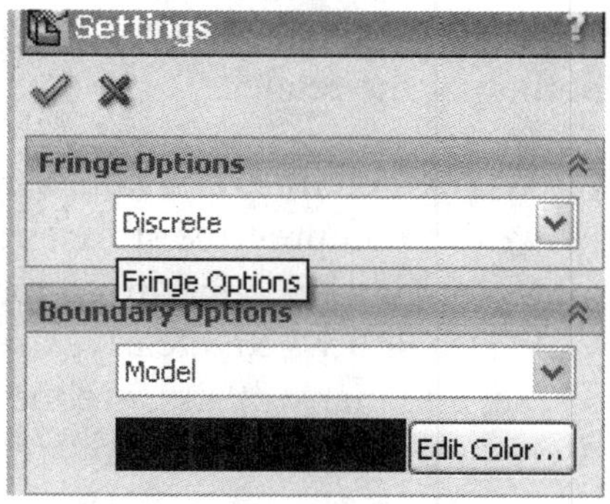

Figure 21 – Selections in the **Settings** property manager.

9. In the Simulation tab, select the **Stress…** icon. Alternatively, right-click **Stress1 (-vonMises-)** and from the pull-down menus select **Edit Definition…** Either action opens the **Stress Plot** property manager, shown in Fig. 22.

10. In the **Deformed Shape** dialogue box, click to "clear" the check-box adjacent to ☐ **Deformed Shape**.

11. Click **[OK]** ✓ to close the **Stress Plot** property manager.

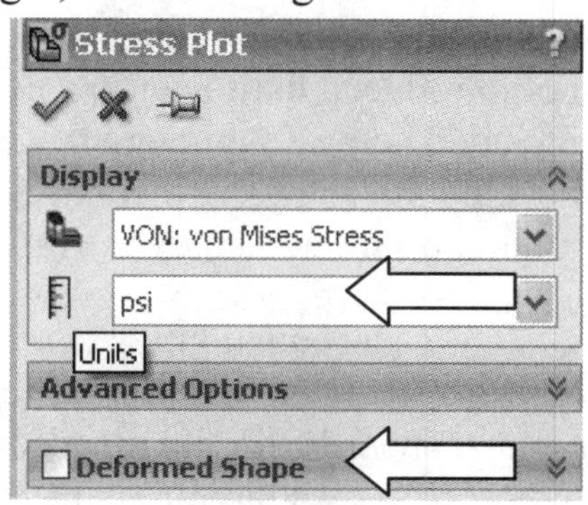

Figure 22 – **Stress Plot** property manager.

The following observations can be made about Fig. 19.

OBSERVATIONS:

- Areas of low stress (dark blue) occur at the top-left side of the model. Also observe the dark blue line through the vertical center of the model. This corresponds to the neutral axis. The lowest von Mises stress is approximately 19.5 psi. Regions of high stress are indicated in red. The maximum stress indicated is 24845.8 psi, which occurs along the concave surface.

- Material *Yield* Strength =13997.6 ≈ 14000 psi is also listed beneath the color-coded **von Mises** stress color bar. An arrow adjacent to the color bar indicates where the Yield Strength lies relative to all stresses within the model. In this instance, it is clear that some stresses in the model *exceed* the material yield strength. *Yield Strength* and *Safety Factor* are investigated below.

Modern finite element software makes conducting a Finite Element Analysis (FEA) and obtaining results deceptively easy. As noted earlier, however, it is the validity of results and understanding how to interpret and evaluate them that is of primary importance. For these reasons, pause to consider two questions that should be intriguing or, perhaps, even bothering the reader.

First, why are all stress values positive in Fig. 19? ("+" values typically indicate tension) However, compressive stresses are known to exist along the concave surface for the given loading. Second, why does the solution show stresses that exceed the material yield strength when, clearly, stresses above the yield strength indicate yielding or failure? These, and many others, are the types of questions that should be raised continually by users of finite element software. Attempts to address these questions are included below.

To answer these questions, we briefly digress to investigate the definition of von Mises stress and a means to determine a *Safety Factor* predicted by the software.

Von Mises Stress -
The example of Chapter 1 skirted the issue about what the von Mises stress is or what it represents. That example further assumed that some readers might not be familiar with von Mises stress. For the sake of completeness and because von Mises stress typically is not introduced until later in a design of machine elements course, its basic definition is included below. Although this SolidWorks Simulation user guide is not intended to develop the complete theory related to von Mises stress, the usefulness of this stress might be summed up by the following statement-

> The equation for von Mises stress "allows the most complicated stress situation to be represented by a single quantity."[2] In other words, for the most complex state of stress that one can imagine (e.g., a three-dimensional stress element subject to a combination of

[2] Budynas, R.G., Nisbett, J. K., Shigley's Mechanical Engineering Design, 8th Ed., McGraw-Hill, 2008, p.216.

> shear and normal stresses acting on every face) these stresses can be reduced to a single number. That number is named the von Mises stress. The number represents a stress magnitude, "which can be compared against the yield strength of the material"[3] to determine whether or not failure by yielding is predicted. As such, the von Mises stress is associated with one of the theories of failure for *ductile* materials; theories of failure are briefly discussed below. The von Mises stress is always a *positive, scalar* number.

The above statement answers the question about the positive nature of von Mises stress shown in Fig. 19. It also should provide some understanding about why the von Mises stress can be used to determine whether or not a part is likely to fail by yielding. *Safety Factor* and failure by yielding are explored further below.

Although the above definition indicates that von Mises stress is always a positive number, that superficial answer might continue to bother readers who intuitively recognize that compressive stresses result along the concave surface of the curved beam.

More fundamentally the issue in question gets to the heart of any analysis, whether it be a finite element analysis or stress calculations based on use of classical equations. The answer, of course, is that one must examine the *appropriate stresses* that correspond to the goals of an analysis. For example, in Chapter 1 it was decided that normal stress in the Y-direction (σ_y) was the only stress component that would yield favorable comparisons with stresses calculated using classic equations. The **Verification of Results** section below reveals the *appropriate stress* for the current example. Before continuing, answer the question, "What is the appropriate stress?" Check your answer below.

Verification of Results

In keeping with the philosophy that it is *always* necessary to verify the validity of Finite Element Analysis (FEA) results, a quick comparison of FEA results with those calculated using classical stress equations for a curved beam is included below.

Results Predicted by Classical Stress Equations

Although not all users may be familiar with the equations for stress in a curved beam, the analysis below should provide sufficient detail to enable reasonable understanding of this state of stress. The first observation is a somewhat unique characteristic of curved beams, namely, for symmetrical cross sections, its neutral axis lies closer to the center of curvature than does its centroidal axis. This can be observed in Fig. 23. By definition the centroidal axis, identified as r_c, is located half-way between the inside and outside radii of

---

[3] Ibid

curvature. However, the neutral axis, identified by r_n, lies closer to the inside (concave) surface. Based upon the above observation, a free body diagram of the upper portion of the curved beam is shown in Fig. 23. Included on this figure are important curved beam dimensions used in the following calculations. Dimensions shown are defined below.

w = width of beam cross-section = 4.00 in (see Fig. 1)
d = depth of beam cross-section = 0.75 in (see Fig. 1)
A = cross-sectional area of beam = w*d = (0.75 in)(4.00 in) = 3.00 in^2
r_i = radius to inside (concave surface) = 3.00 in
r_o = radius to outside (convex surface) = 7.00 in
r_c = radius to centroid of beam = r_i + w/2 = 3.00 + 2.00 = 5.00 in
r_n = radius to the neutral axis = w/ln(r_o/r_i) = 4.00/ln(7.00/3.00) = 4.72 in. [determined by equation for a curved beam having a rectangular cross-section]
c_i = distance from the neutral axis to the inside surface = $r_n - r_i$ = 4.72 – 3.00 = 1.72 in
c_o = distance from the neutral axis to the outside surface = $r_o - r_n$ = 7.00 – 4.72 = 2.28 in
e = distance between the centroidal axis and neutral axis = $r_c - r_n$ = 5.00- 4.72 = 0.28 in

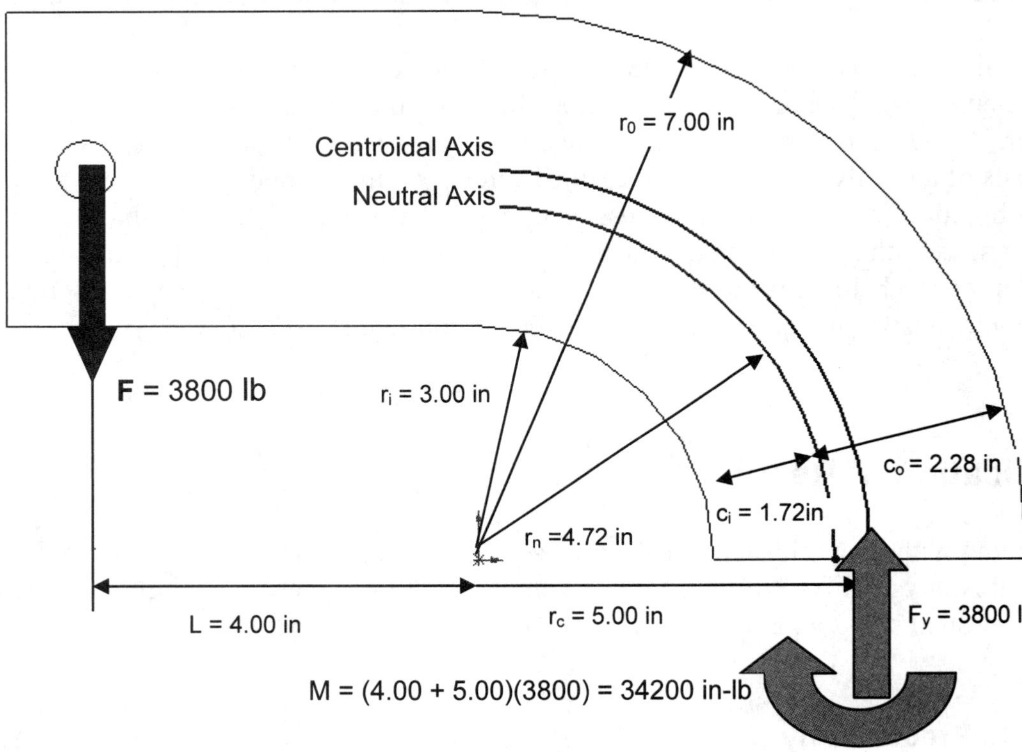

Figure 23 – Geometry associated with calculation of stress in a curved beam.

The reaction force $\mathbf{F_y}$ and moment **M** acting on the cut section are necessary to maintain equilibrium of the upper portion of the curved beam. Equations used to compute the combined bending and axial stresses that result from these reactions are included below. Each equation is of the general form,

Curved beam stress = $\pm$ bending stress $\pm$ axial stress

Where the "±" sign for bending stress depends on what side of the model is being investigated. Bending stress, caused by moment **M**, is compressive on the concave surface of the curved beam. Hence a minus "-" sign is assigned to the bending stress term in equation [1]. However, on the convex side of the beam bending stress causes tension on the beam surface thereby accounting for a "+" sign associated with the first term in equation [2]. Reaction force $\mathbf{F_y}$ acts to produce a compressive stress on the cut section. Therefore, a minus "-" sign is used with the axial stress component in both equations [1] and [2] below. In what direction do both of these stresses act?

Stress at the inside (concave) surface:

$$\sigma_i = \frac{Mc_i}{Aer_i} - \frac{F_y}{A} = \frac{-(34200\text{ in-lb})(1.72\text{ in})}{(3.00\text{ in}^2)(0.28\text{ in})(3.00\text{ in})} - \frac{3800\text{ lb}}{3.00\text{ in}^2} = -24610\text{ psi} \qquad [1]$$

Stress at the outside (convex) surface:

$$\sigma_0 = \frac{Mc_o}{Aer_o} - \frac{F_y}{A} = \frac{(34200\text{ in-lb})(2.28\text{ in})}{(3.00\text{ in}^2)(0.28\text{ in})(7.00\text{ in})} - \frac{3800\text{ lb}}{3.00\text{ in}^2} = 11990\text{ psi} \qquad [2]$$

Comparison with Finite Element Results

In addition to serving as a quick check of results, this section reviews use of the **Probe** tool. Both the bending and axial stresses act normal to the cut surface in Fig. 23. Therefore, it is logical that the Finite Element Analysis stress in the Y-direction (σ_y) should be compared with values computed using equations [1] and [2] above. You are encouraged to produce a plot of stress σ_y on your own. However, abbreviated steps are outlined below if guidance is desired.

1. In the **Simulation** tab, click the **Stress...** icon. Alternatively, right right-click the **Results** folder and from the pull-down menu select **Define Stress Plot...** Either of these actions opens the **Stress Plot** property manager.

2. In the **Display** dialogue box, select **SY: Y Normal Stress** from the pull-down menu. Also in this dialogue box, set the **Units** field to **psi.**

3. Click to un-check ☐ **Deformed Shape**.

4. Click **[OK]** ✓ to close the **Stress Plot** property manager. A new plot named **Stress2 (-Y normal-)** now appears beneath the **Results** folder and a plot of stress σ_y is displayed as shown in Fig. 24. If the plot does not appear, right-click **Stress2 (-Y normal-)** and select **Show** from the pull-down menu.

5. Click the **Plot Settings...** icon to open the **Settings** property manager. Alternatively, right-click **Stress2 (-Y normal-)** and from the pull-down menu select **Settings...**

6. Within the **Settings** property manager, set the **Fringe Options** to **Discrete**.

A plot of normal stress σ_y in the Y-direction should now appear as shown in Fig. 24. The following observations can be made about Fig. 24.

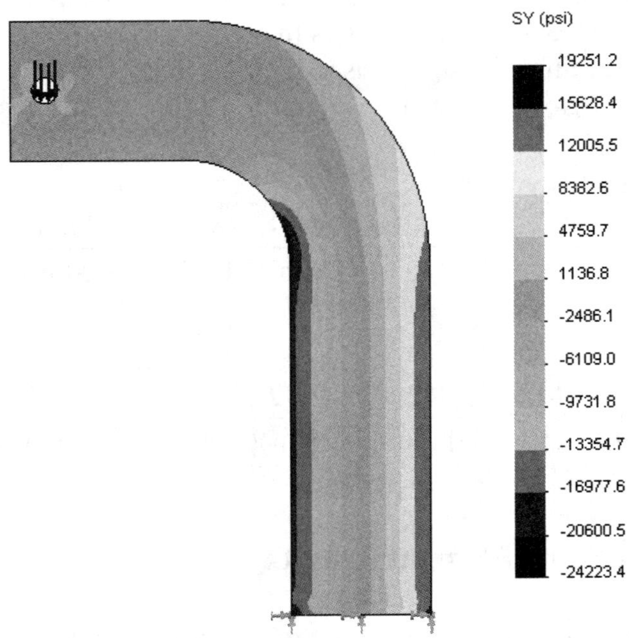

Figure 24 – Plot of **SY: Y Normal Stress** (σ_y) on the curved beam model

OBSERVATIONS:

- Areas of high stress, shown in orange, occur along the right vertical side of the model. Because this region is subject to tensile stress (i.e., positive "+" stress) positive stress magnitudes are expected.

- Compressive, (i.e., negative "-" stress) is shown by dark blue regions located along the left vertical and concave regions of the model. Once again compressive stress should correspond with the user's intuitive sense of stress in that region.

- Low stress regions, corresponding to the neutral axis, or neutral plane, run through the vertical center of the model. Notice the sign change from "+" to "-" in the green color coded region of the stress chart adjacent to the model.

- To see the highest tensile stress (red), it is necessary to zoom in on the lower right-hand corner and right side of the model. Likewise to see the highest compressive stress (dark blue), zoom in on the concave arc of the model.

The model is next prepared to examine stresses at section A-A shown in Fig. 25.

7. Within the **Settings** property manager, set the **Boundary Options** to **Mesh**.

8. Click **[OK]** ✓ to close the **Settings** property manager.

9. Zoom in on the model to where the curved beam section is tangent to the straight, vertical section, shown as $\mathbf{A_i}$ and $\mathbf{A_o}$ in Fig. 25.

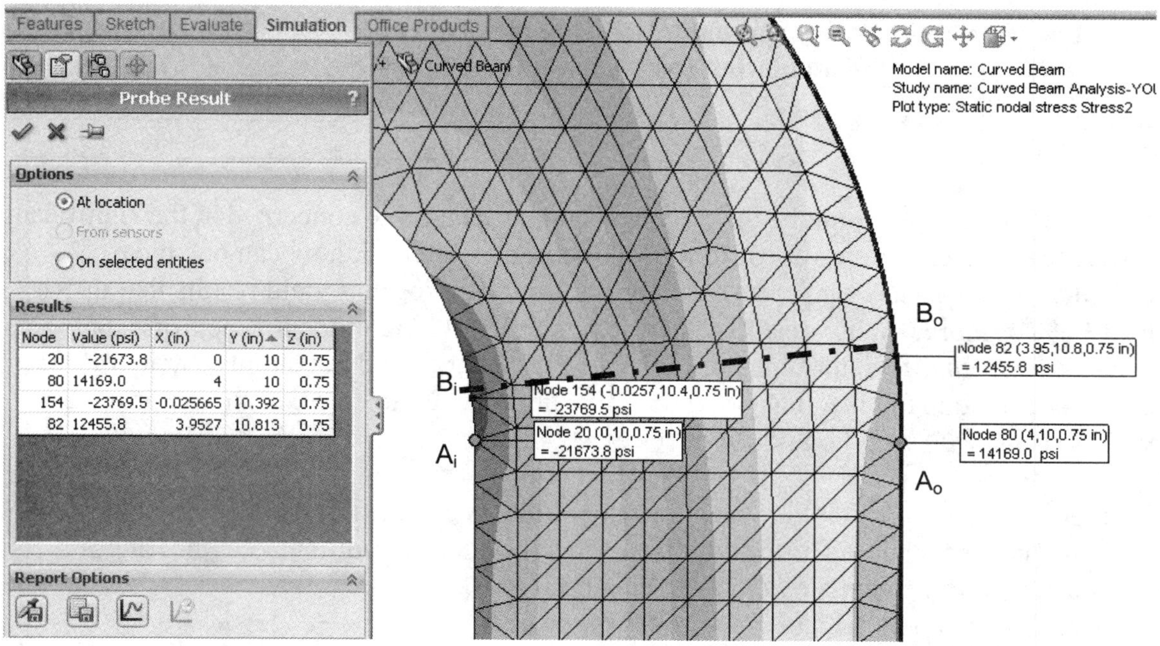

Figure 25 – Use the **Probe** tool to determine stress magnitudes at locations on the concave and convex sides of the curved beam model.

10. On the **Simulation** tab click the **Probe** tool icon or right-click **Stress2 (-Y normal-)** and from the pull-down menu, select **Probe**. The **Probe Result** property manager opens as shown on the left side of Fig. 25.

11. In the **Options** dialogue box, select ⊙ **At location** (if not already selected).

12. Move the cursor over the straight vertical edges on the left and right sides of the model. Each edge is highlighted as the cursor passes over it. Click to select two nodes (one on the left and one on the right) located at the *top* of each line. These nodes are located at the *intersection* between the straight vertical section and the beginning of the curved beam section. Selected nodes correspond to $\mathbf{A_i}$ and $\mathbf{A_o}$ in Fig. 25. If an incorrect node is selected, simply click ⊙ **At location** in the **Options** dialogue box to clear the current selection and repeat the procedure. *Do not close the **Probe Result** property manager at this time.*

The above action records the following data in the **Results** dialogue box: **Node** number, **Value (psi)** of the plotted stress (σ_y), and the **X**, **Y**, **Z** coordinates of the selected node. Also, a small "flag" appears adjacent to each node on the model and repeats data listed in the **Results** table. *It may be necessary to click-and-drag column headings to view values in the **Results** table.*

Table I contains a comparison of results found by using classical equations and Finite Element Analysis at these locations.

Table I – Comparison of stress (σ_y) from classical and finite element methods at Section A-A.

Location	Manual Calculation (psi)	Probe Tool Results (psi)	Percent Difference (%)
Point A_i	-24610	-21673	13.6%
Point A_o	11990	14169	15.4%

As an engineer, you should be disappointed and, in fact, quite concerned at the significant difference between the results of these two methods. After all, how can one have confidence in a design when two seemingly rational approaches yield results that differ by 13.6% or more? When results differ by this order of magnitude it is appropriate to *investigate further* to determine the cause for the disparity and not simply "write off" the differences as due the fact that two alternative approaches are used. Can you provide valid reasons *why* such large differences exist?

Further consideration should reveal the fairly obvious conclusion that St. Venant's principle is once again affecting results. In this instance, a traditional engineering approach would dictate using classical equations for a straight beam in the straight vertical segment of the model below Section A-A, see Fig. 1 (repeated), and a different set of equations in the curved beam portion of the model above Section A-A. However, common sense suggests that there is a *transition region* between these two segments where neither set of classical equations is entirely adequate. In fact, due to the finite size of elements in this region, it is logical to presume that a Finite Element Analysis provides a more accurate solution than do classical equations in this transition region.

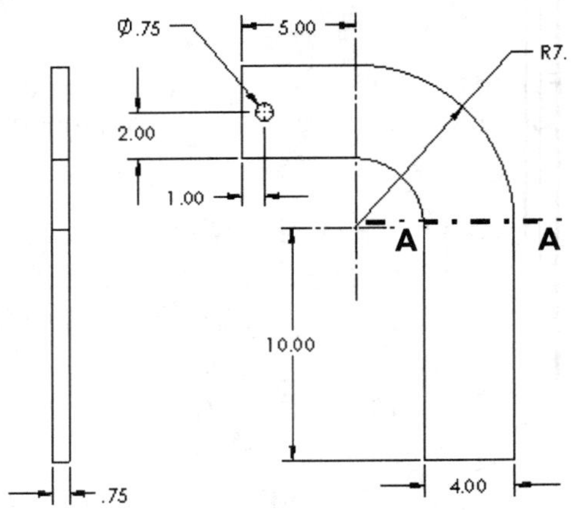

Figure 1 (Repeated) – Basic geometry of the curved beam model.

Given the above observations, we next proceed to sample stress magnitudes at Section **B_i-B_o** in Fig. 25, which is located slightly above the transition region. Proceed as follows.

13. Move the cursor over the curved edges of the model and on the concave side, click to select the *first* node *above* the previously selected node.

14. Next, on the convex side of the model, select the *second* node *above* the previously selected node.

Observe the two new stress magnitudes listed in the **Results** dialogue box and compare them to values listed in Table II below. Nodes $\mathbf{B_i}$ and $\mathbf{B_o}$ thus selected lie on a radial line that forms an approximate angle of 7.5° above the horizontal. Stress values calculated using the classical equations are modified to account for a slight shift of the centroidal axis due to beam curvature and for the change in angle of the axial force. Based on these values, a comparison of classical and FEA results in Table II reveals that values differ by at most 4.0%; a significant improvement over the initial calculations.

Table II – Comparison of stress (σ_y) for classical and finite element methods at Section B_i-B_o.

Location	Manual Calculation (psi)	Probe Tool Results (psi)	Percent Difference (%)
Point $\mathbf{B_i}$	-24515	-23769	3.1%
Point $\mathbf{B_o}$	11940	12455.8	4.1%

15. Click **[OK]** ✓ to close the **Probe Result** property manager.

This concludes the verification of Finite Element results, but note that even better results would be expected at locations further from the transition region.

Assessing Safety Factor for the Curved Beam

SolidWorks Simulation provides a convenient means for the designer to determine and view a plot of Factor of Safety distribution throughout the curved beam model. To use this capability, proceed as follows.

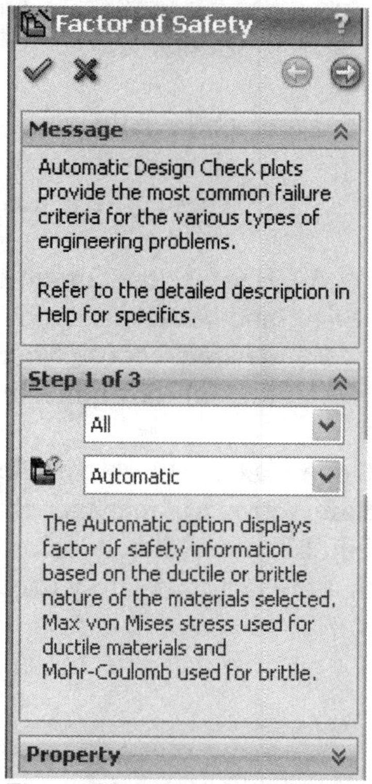

Figure 26 – **Factor of Safety**, Step #1 of safety factor check.

1. In the **Simulation** tab, click the **Factor of Safety** icon . Alternatively, right-click the **Results** folder and from the pull-down menu, select **Define Factor Of Safety Plot…** The **Factor of Safety** property manager opens as shown in Fig. 26 and displays the first step of a three step procedure.

2. Read text in the **Message** dialogue box. This message indicates that the software automatically selects a failure criterion to determine the factor of safety.

3. In the upper pull-down menu of the **Step 1 of 3** dialogue box, select either **All** or **Curved Beam-Split Line1** as the model to be analyzed. Because there is only one part, the result is the same in this case.

Next, in the **Criterion** field, second field from the top, click the pull-down menu o reveal the four failure criteria available for determination of the safety factor.

A brief overview of the four failure criteria is provided below.

- **Max vonMises Stress** – This failure criterion is used for ductile materials (aluminum, steel, brass, bronze, etc.). It is considered the best predictor of actual failure in ductile materials and, as such, provides a good indication of the true safety factor. This criterion is also referred to as the "Distortion Energy Theory" in many design of machine elements textbooks.

- **Max Shear Stress (Tresca)** – This criterion also applies to ductile materials. However, it is a more conservative theory thereby resulting in lower predicted safety factors. As a consequence of its conservative nature, parts designed using this criterion may be somewhat oversized.

- **Mohr-Coulomb Stress** – This failure criterion is applied to the design and analysis of parts made of brittle material (cast iron, concrete, etc.) where the ultimate compressive strength exceeds the ultimate tensile strength ($S_{uc} > S_{ut}$).

- **Max Normal Stress** – Also applicable for brittle materials, this failure criterion does not account for differences between tensile and compressive strengths within SolidWorks Simulation. This theory is also regarded as the least accurate of the methods available.

- Other failure criteria apply for ***shell*** elements made of composite materials. These criteria are not described here.

5. Because the curved beam is made of aluminum and because a good estimate of safety factor is desired, choose **Max von Mises Stress** from the pull-down menu.

Upon making the above selection, the **Factor of Safety** property manager changes to that illustrated in Fig. 27. Immediately below the **Criterion** field notice that the factor of safety check is currently defined as

$$\frac{\sigma_{vonMises}}{\sigma_{Limit}} < 1$$

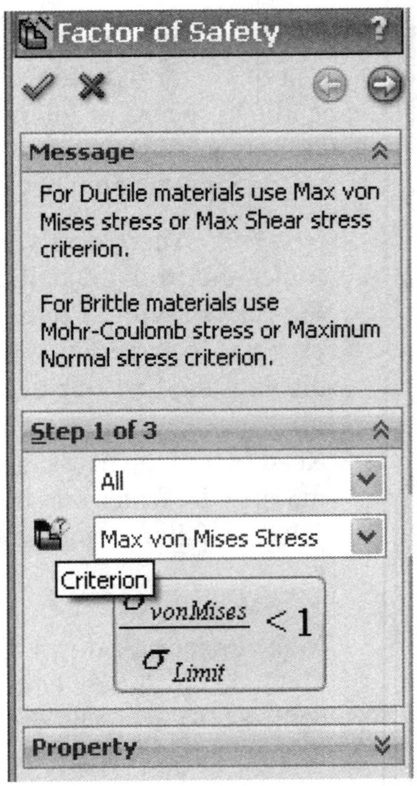

Figure 27 – First **Factor of Safety** property manager. The comparison stress (failure criteria) is selected here.

In other words, the previous equation is currently set to identify locations in the model where the ratio of von Mises stress to the "limiting" value of stress (i.e., the Yield Strength) is < 1.

Thus, the above criterion identifies locations where yielding of the model is *not* predicted because model Yield Strength, the denominator, is greater than the von Mises stress, the numerator. As initially defined, the above ratio is the *inverse* of the traditional safety factor definition, where:

Safety Factor = n = strength/stress

To plot only critical regions of the part, i.e., regions where the Yield Strength is exceeded and the safety factor is < 1, proceed as follows –

6. Advance to the second step by clicking the right facing arrow button at the top of the **Factor of Safety** property manager. The **Step 2 of 3** dialogue box appears as shown in Fig. 28.

7. In the top pull-down menu, select **psi** as the set of **Units** to be used.

8. Under **Set stress limit to**, click to select ◉ **Yield strength** (if not already selected).

9. Do *not* change the **Multiplication factor**.

Notice that the Yield and Ultimate strengths for the model appear at the bottom of this dialogue box.

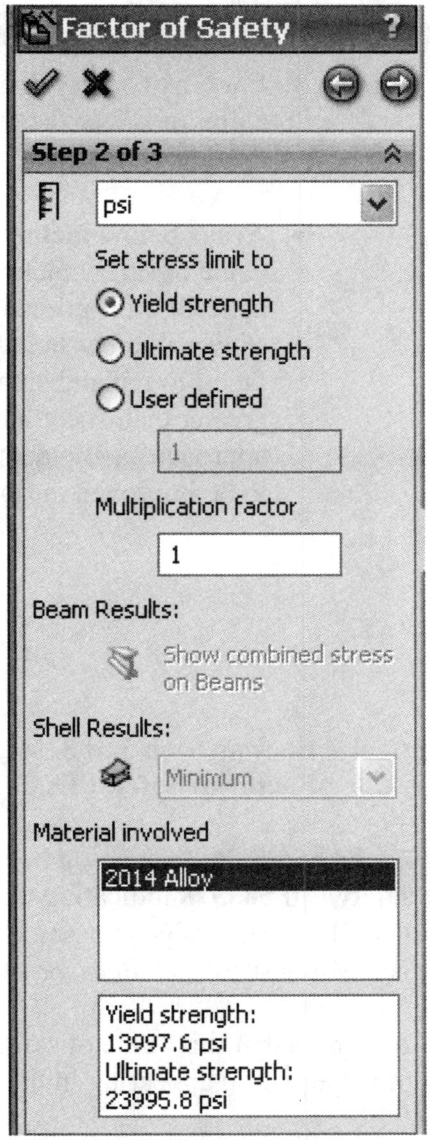

Figure 28 – **Step 2 of 3** in the **Factor of Safety** process.

Design Insight

In the event that a *brittle* material is being analyzed by the Mohr-Coulomb or the Max Normal Stress failure criterion, then it is appropriate to select the O **Ultimate strength** as the failure criterion.

The **User defined** option is provided for cases where a user specified material is not found in the **Material Property** table or SolidWorks material library.

10. Click the right facing arrow button at top of this property manager to proceed to **Step 3 of 3** in the **Factor of Safety** property manager shown in Fig. 29.

Two options are available for displaying the factor of safety. Brief descriptions of each are provided below.

- **Factor of safety distribution** – Produces a plot of safety factor variation throughout the entire part.
- **Areas below factor of safety** – A target value of safety factor is entered in the field beneath this option. The resulting display shows all areas below the specified safety factor in red and areas with a safety factor greater than specified in blue. This approach easily identifies areas that need to be improved during the design process.

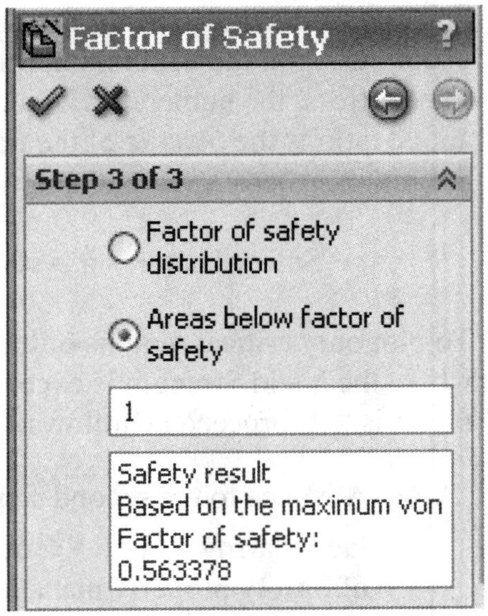

Figure 29 – Redefinition of *Safety Factor* and values to be displayed on the new plot.

11. Beneath **Step 3 of 3**, select ⦿**Areas below factor of safety** and type "**1**" in the **Factor of Safety:** field (if not already "1").

At the bottom of this dialog box the **Safety result** field informs the user that the factor of safety is **0.563378** indicating that the design is *not* safe in some regions of the model. Recall that this value is based on a comparison between Yield Strength and the maximum von Mises stress. *(Values may vary slightly from those shown).*

Also note that this value of safety factor closely matches that computed by the reciprocal of the equation appearing in the first **Factor of Safety** window. That is:

$$\frac{\sigma_{Limit}}{\sigma_{vonMises}} = \frac{13997}{24846} = 0.56335$$

12. Click **[OK]** ✓ to close the **Factor of Safety** property manager. A new plot folder, named, **Factor of Safety1 (- Max von Mises Stress-)**, is listed beneath the **Results** folder. Also, a plot showing regions of the model where the Safety Factor is < 1.0 (red) and where the Safety Factor is > 1.0 (blue) is displayed.

13. Right-click **Factor of Safety1 (-Max von Mises Stress-)**, and from the pull-down menu, select **Chart Options....** The **Chart Options** property manager opens.

14. In the **Display Options** dialogue box, check ☑ **Show min annotation** and click **[OK]** ✓ to close the **Chart Options** property manager.

The preceding step labels the location of minimum Safety Factor on the curved beam as shown in Fig. 30. As expected, this location corresponds to the location of highest stress previously illustrated in Fig. 19.

The figure now on the screen should correspond to Fig. 30. This figure shows regions where the factor of safety is less than 1 (unsafe regions) in red. Regions with a factor of safety greater than 1 (safe regions) are shown in blue. Localized regions, along the right and left vertical edges and extending into the concave region, have a safety factor less than one.

The line of text, circled near the top-left in Fig. 30, provides a "key" to interpret safe and unsafe regions on the model.

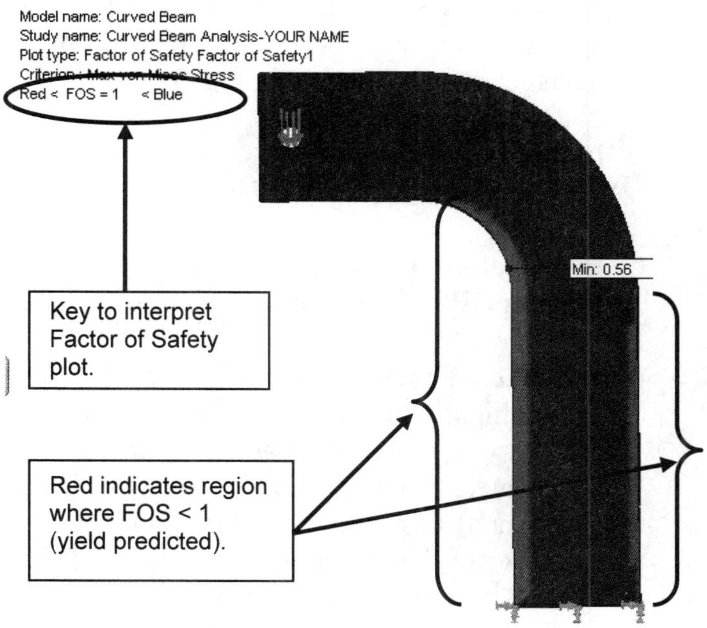

Figure 30 – Curved beam model showing areas where FOS > 1 (safety predicted) and where FOS < 1 (yield predicted).

15. Double-click **Factor of Safety (-Max von Mises Stress-)** and repeat steps 1 through 12 above, but this time set the **Areas below factor of safety** to **2** instead of **1**, in step 11. How does the plot change?

A designer can repeat this procedure for any desired level of safety factor check.

In summary, an important aspect of the von Mises stress is that it can be used to predict whether or not a part might fail based on a comparison of its stress *value* to the magnitude of yield strength. This topic is aligned with the study of theories of failure found in most mechanics of materials and design of machine elements texts.

Analysis Insight

Faced with the above information, a designer would be challenged to redesign the part in any of several ways, depending upon design constraints. For example, it might be possible to change part dimensions to reduce stress magnitudes in the part. Alternatively, if part geometry cannot be changed, a stronger material might be selected or some combination of these or other possible remedies might be applied. Because this aspect of the current example is open-ended, it is not pursued here.

It is always good engineering practice to verify that results obtained correlate well with the given information. One simple way to confirm that results "make sense" is to check whether or not reaction forces are consistent with external loads applied to the finite element model. This section examines how to determine reaction forces at the base of the curved beam model. To accomplish this, proceed as follows.

1. In the SolidWorks Simulation manager, right-click the **Results** folder and from the pull-down menu, select **List Result Force...** The **Result Force** property manager opens as shown in Fig. 31.

2. In the **Options** dialogue box, verify that ⊙ **Reaction Force** is selected.

3. In the **Selection** dialogue box, set **Units** to **English (IPS)**, if not already selected.

4. The **Select Faces, Edges, or Vertices** field is active (highlighted) and awaiting selection of the entity on which reaction forces are to be determined. Rotate the model so that its bottom (restrained) *surface* is visible and click to select it. **Face<1>** appears in the active field. This is the only face where reactions occur.

5. Click the **[Update]** button and the **Reaction Force (lb)** table at the bottom of the property manager is populated with data. Also, X, Y, and Z reaction force components appear at the base of the model.

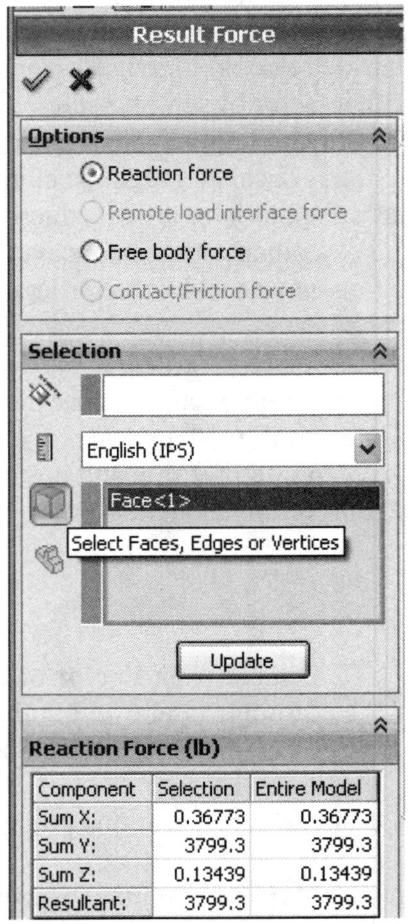

Figure 31 – Data appearing in the **Result Force** property manager.

The **Component** column of this table lists names for the sum of reaction forces in the X, Y, and Z directions and the Resultant reaction. Magnitudes of the X, Y, Z reaction forces listed in the **Selection** column are identical to those in the **Entire Model** column. This result is expected since the entire model is restrained at only this one location.

Results interpretation is as follows:

SumX: 0.36773 (essentially zero) No force applied to model in X-direction.
SumY: 3799.3 (essentially 3800 lb = the applied force)
SumZ: 0.13439 (essentially zero) No force applied to model in Z-direction.
Resultant: 3799.3 (essentially 3800 lb = the applied force)

It should be noted that a *moment* reaction at the base of the curved beam is missing from the **Reaction Force** table. Also, checking the **Reaction Moment (lb-in)** dialogue box, at the bottom of the property manager, reveals no data entries. This outcome does not agree with the usual conventions for reactions associated with a free-body diagram, but it is consistent with our understanding of **Immovable** restraints applied to three-dimensional, solid, tetrahedral elements. The **Immovable** restraint only restricts translations in the X, Y, Z directions at each restrained node. This observation accounts for the fact that there are only three force reactions and no moments in the **Reaction Force** table of Fig. 31. Note, however, that calculated reaction forces do not exactly match the applied forces; slight mathematical errors exist.

6. Click **[OK]** ✓ to close the **Result Force** property manager.

The results above are valid for the **Entire Model**. However, in many instances a model is supported (i.e., restrained) at more than one location. In those instances it is necessary to determine reaction forces at other locations on a model. Performing a reaction check is quite simple and can be viewed as an additional means for users to verify the validity of boundary conditions applied to a model.

Although a surface was selected to examine reaction forces in the above example, it should be evident that other geometric features, such as edges or vertices can also be selected at other restrained locations on a particular model.

Logging Out of the Current Analysis

This concludes an introduction to analysis of the curved beam model. It is suggested that this file not be saved. Proceed as follows.

1. On the Main menu, click **File** followed by choosing **Close** from the pull-down menu.

2. The **SolidWorks** window, Fig. 32, opens and asks, "**Save changes to Curved Beam?**" Select the **[No]** button. This closes the file without saving any changes or results.

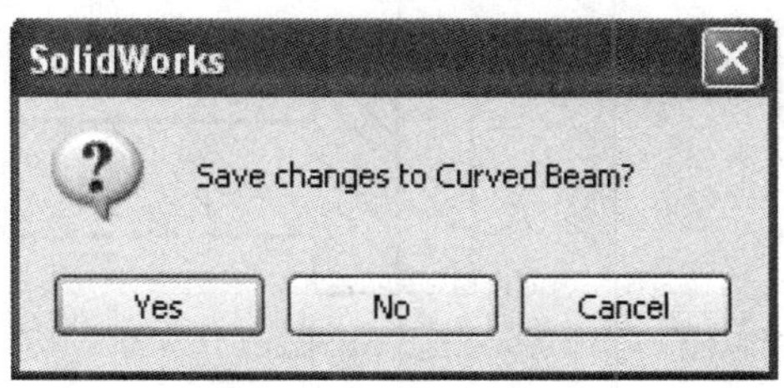

Figure 32 – **SolidWorks** window prompts users to either save changes or not.

EXERCISES

End of chapter exercises are intended to provide additional practice using principles introduced in the current chapter plus capabilities mastered in preceding chapters. Most exercises include multiple parts. In an academic setting, it is likely that parts of problems may be assigned or modified to suit specific course goals.

Designates problems that introduce new concepts. Solution guidance is provided for these problems.

EXERCISE 1 – Curved Beam Stresses in a "C"- Clamp

C-clamps, like that illustrated below, must pass minimum strength requirements before they can be qualified for general purpose use. Clamps are tested by applying equal and opposite loads acting on the gripping faces. Part of the federal test criteria requires that the movable (lower) jaw be extended a certain percentage of the distance of the fully-open state to ensure that column failure of the screw is an integral part of the test. Presuming that the movable jaw of the clamp satisfies the prescribed test criteria, perform a finite element analysis of the C-clamp subject to the following guidelines.

Open file: **C-Clamp 2-1**

- Material: **Cast Carbon Steel** (use S.I. units)
- Mesh: **High Quality** tetrahedral elements
- Fixture: **Fixed** applied to the upper gripping surface.
- External Load: **950 N** applied normal to lower gripping surface.

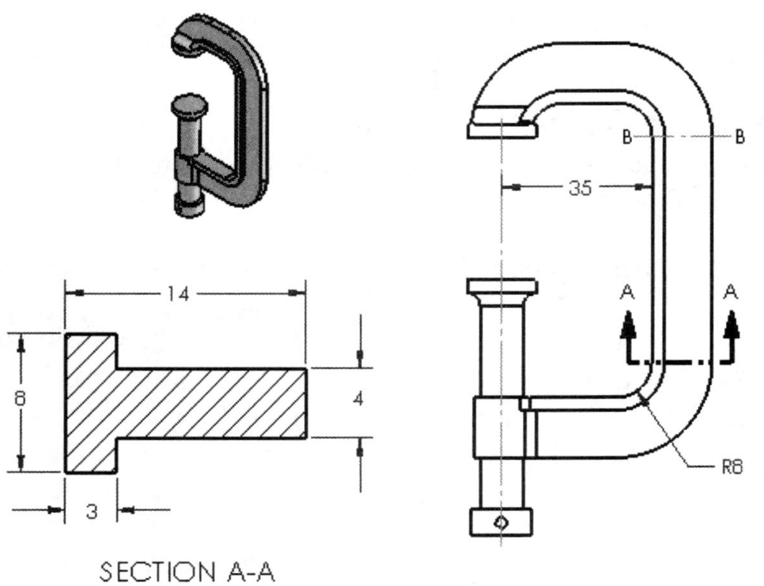

Figure E2-1 – "C"-clamp frame and cross-section dimensions. Stress to be determined at Section A-A.

Determine the following:

a. Use classical equations to compute stress at the inside and outside surfaces of the C-clamp frame at section A-A. Section A-A is located where the straight and curved sections are tangent.

b. Create a stress contour plot of von Mises stress in the frame of the C-Clamp. Include automatic labeling of maximum von Mises stress on this plot.

c. Use the **Probe** feature to produce a graph of the *most appropriate stress* across section A-A. In other words, because values from this plot are to be compared with manual calculations of part (a), it is necessary to choose the corresponding stress from those available within the finite element software. Include a descriptive title and axis labels on this graph. When using the **Probe** feature, begin at the concave (left inside) surface and select nodes across the model continuing to the outside of the "T" cross-section. Use equation [1] to compare percent differences between classical and FEA determination of stresses at the inside and outside surfaces.

$$\% \text{ difference} = \frac{(\text{FEA result - classical result})}{\text{FEA result}} * 100 = \qquad [1]$$

d. Assuming the C-clamp is made of a ductile material, produce a plot showing regions where safety factor < 1.5.

e. Question: Is there justification for using **High** quality elements for analysis of the C-clamp? Justify your answer by providing reasons either "for" or "against" use of **High** quality elements for this model.

EXERCISE 2 – Curved Beam Stresses in Hacksaw Frame

A common, metal-cutting "hacksaw" is shown in Fig. E 2-2. A solid model of the hacksaw is available as file: **Hacksaw 2-2**. The model is simplified to include two 0.125 inch diameter holes that pass through the lower left and lower right ends of the hacksaw "backbone" labeled in Fig. E 2-2. For analysis purposes, the inside surface of the left-hand hole is to be considered **Fixed** (i.e. immovable). Use split lines to create a small "patch" of area on the inside surface of the hole located at the right end of the backbone. On this surface apply a 50 lb force induced by a tensile load in the saw blade that is ordinarily held in place between these two holes. Assume the following.

- Material: **AISI 1020 Steel** (use English units)
- Mesh: **High quality** tetrahedral elements; use default mesh size.
- Units: **English (IPS)**

- Fixture: **Fixed** applied to inside of left hole.
- External Load: **50 lb** applied parallel to the X-direction on the inner surface of right-hand hole (split lines needed; placement of these lines is user defined).

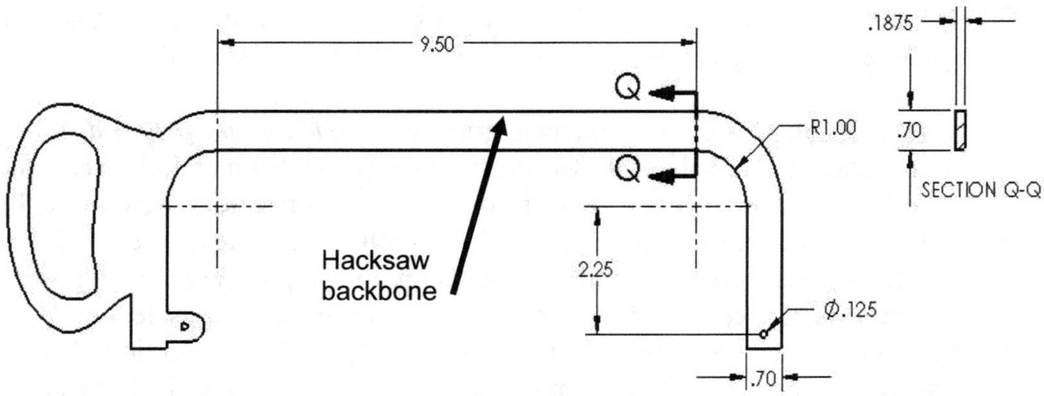

Figure E2-2 – Basic geometry of a hacksaw frame. Stress is to be determined at Section Q-Q.

Determine the following:

a. Use classical equations to compute stress at the inside and outside surfaces of the hacksaw frame at section Q-Q. Section Q-Q is located where the straight and curved sections are tangent.

b. Include a zoomed-in image of the right-hand hole so that the 50 lb applied load can clearly be seen to act between user specified *Split Lines*.

c. Create a stress contour plot of von Mises stress in the saw backbone. Include automatic labeling of maximum von Mises stress on the plot.

d. Use the **Probe** feature to produce a graph of the *most appropriate stress* across section Q-Q, beginning at the inside (concave) surface and continuing to the outside (convex) surface of the backbone cross-section. Use the **Stress Plot** property manager to select the *appropriate stress* for this plot to enable comparison with manual calculations of part (a) above. Include a descriptive title and axis labels on this graph. Also, below the graph, cut-and-paste a copy of the **Probe Results** table showing values used in this comparison. Then use equation [1], repeated below, to compute the percent difference between classical and finite element solutions at the inside and outside surfaces of the saw backbone.

$$\% \text{ difference} = \frac{(\text{FEA result - classical result})}{\text{FEA result}} * 100 = \qquad [1]$$

e. Based on von Mises stress, create a plot showing all regions of the model where Safety Factor < 2.2 and circle these regions on the plot. Include a software applied label indicating the maximum and minimum values of Safety Factor.

f. Question: Is there justification for using **High** quality elements for analysis of the hacksaw backbone? Justify your answer by providing reasons either "for" or "against" using **High** quality elements for this model.

EXERCISE 3 – Stresses in a Curved Anchor Bracket

The curved beam shown in Fig. E 2-3 is subject to a horizontal load applied by means of a pin (not shown) that passes through a hole in its upper end. A solid model of this part is available as file: **Anchor Bracket 2-3**. The lower-left end of the part is attached to a rigid portion of a machine frame (not shown). Thus, because three-dimensional tetrahedral elements are to be used to model this part, the restraint at this location should be considered **Immovable**. Use split lines to create a small "patch" of area on the inside surface of the 16 mm diameter hole. Locate these split lines 24 mm from the right edge of the model. On this surface apply a horizontal force of 8600 N acting in the positive X-direction (to the right). Assume the following.

- Material: **AISI 1010 Steel, hot rolled bar** (use SI units)
- Mesh: **High Quality** tetrahedral elements; use default mesh size.
- Fixture: **Fixed** applied on the inclined surface.
- External Load: **8600 N** in the X-direction applied on the right, inside surface of the 16 mm diameter hole.

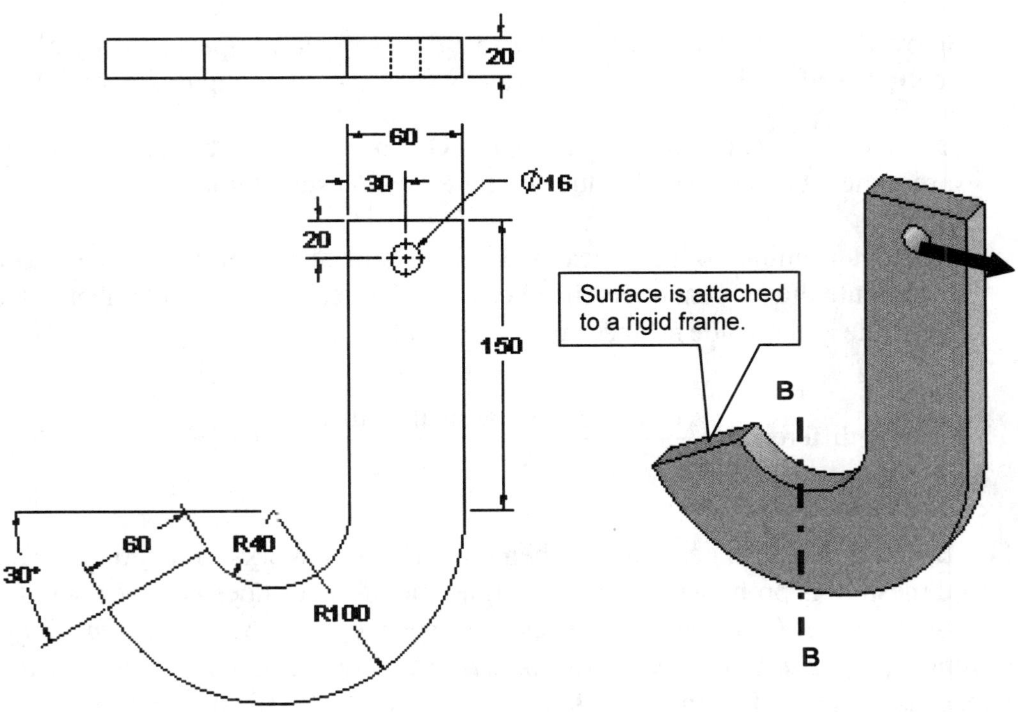

Figure E2-3 Dimensioned view of the Anchor Bracket. Stress is to be determined at Section B-B.

Determine the following:

a. Use classical equations to compute stress at the inside (concave) surface and the outside (convex) surface of the anchor bracket at section B-B. Section B-B passes through the center of curvature of the curved beam and is considered to be a vertical line. Include a labeled free body diagram of the portion of the anchor bracket to the right of section B-B.

b. Include a zoomed-in image of the hole so that the force $F_x = 8600$ N can clearly be seen to act between user specified *Split Lines*.

c. Create a stress contour plot of von Mises stress in the anchor bracket. Include automatic labeling of maximum von Mises stress on the plot.

d. Using von Mises stress, create a plot showing all regions of the model where Safety Factor < 1.0. Indicate regions (if any) where the Safety Factor < 1 occurs by circling their location(s) on the figure and labeling them as FOS < 1. Include a software applied label indicating locations of maximum and minimum values of Safety Factor.

e. Use the **Probe** feature to produce a graph of the *most appropriate stress* across the bracket at section B-B. Begin at the inside (concave) surface and continue to the outside (convex) surface. (See the *"HINT"* at bottom of this page for guidance when making this graph). Use the **Stress Plot** property manager to select the *appropriate stress* for this plot to enable comparison with manual calculations of part (a) above. Add a descriptive title and axis labels to this graph.

   Below the graph or on a separate page either: (a) cut-and-paste a copy of the **Probe Results** table that includes values used for this comparison, or (b) click the **Save** icon , located in the **Report Options** dialogue box, to create an Excel spreadsheet containing all values in the **Probe Results** table.

   After determining both classical and FEA results at section B-B, use equation [1] to compute the percent difference between classical and finite element solutions at the inside and outside surfaces of the bracket.

$$\% \text{ difference} = \frac{(\text{FEA result - classical result})}{\text{FEA result}} * 100 = \qquad [1]$$

HINT: Because the mesh generation scheme within SolidWorks Simulation creates an optimized mesh, it is probable that (a) a straight line of nodes does *not* exist across the model at section B-B (thus, choose the best straight line), and (b) it is also *unlikely* that node points *occur exactly on a vertical centerline through the center of curvature.* For these reasons, and to obtain the best estimate of stress on a vertical line through the curved section, proceed as follows.

- Zoom in on a front view of the model at section B-B.

- On the **Simulation** tab, click the **Probe** icon . This action opens the **Probe Results** property manager.

- On the SolidWorks flyout menu, click the "+" sign to display the complete flyout menu.

- Move the cursor over **Right Plane** in the flyout menu. This action highlights an edge view of the **Right Plane**, which will assist in locating nodes closest to a vertical line at Section B-B. Unfortunately, the line disappears when the cursor is moved, but it is very useful none the less.

╬ EXERCISE 4 – Stresses in a Curved Photoelastic Model (Special Topics: Custom material defined, using a "Hinge" joint for Fixture)

Figure E 2-4 shows a model of curved beam made from a photoelastic material. The beam is subject to an axial load **F**. Beams such as this are commonly used in experimental stress analysis laboratories where photoelastic techniques are studied. Photoelastic material has a unique optical property known as birefringence. Thus, when a photoelastic model is subject to applied loads in a field of polarized light, the light passing through the model undergoes changes of wave length that produce visible "fringes" within the model as shown in Fig. E 2-5. These "fringes" are analogous to, but not equal to, stress contour plots produced when upon completion of a finite element analysis. In this exercise, stresses produced within the curved beam model are examined.

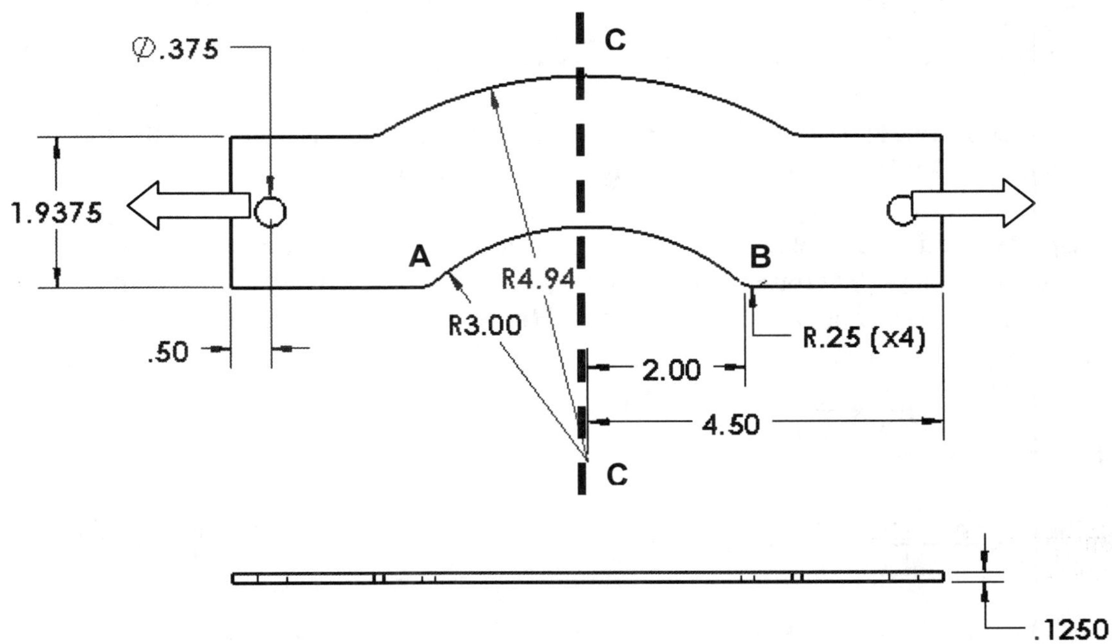

Figure E2-4 – Top view (above) and front (edge) view of a curved beam model.

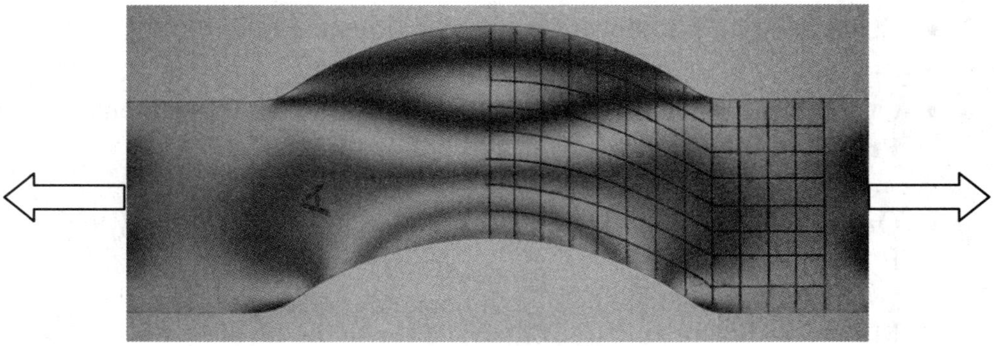

Figure E2-5 – "Fringes" appearing in a photoelstic model subject to a tensile load. A grid is superimposed on the model to facilitate locating specific stress magnitudes and directions.

Create a finite element model of this part that includes custom material specification, fixtures, external loads, a default high quality solid mesh, solution, and results analysis.

Open the file: **Curved Bracket**

- Material: Material properties not found in SolidWorks material library (use custom properties below)
  - **E = 360e3** psi Modulus of Elasticity (use English units)
  - **ν = 0.38** Poisson's ratio
  - S_y = **1200** psi Yield Strength
- Mesh: **High Quality** tetrahedral elements; use default mesh size.
- Fixture: **Hinge Joint** applied at hole on left end of the model.
- External Load: **72** lb in the X-direction applied between split lines on the inner surface of the hole located at the right end of the model..

Two aspects of this exercise are unique. First, properties of the photoelastic material are not available in the SolidWorks material library. And second, fixture at the left hole of the curved bracket is considered to be a **Fixed Hinge** joint. Guidance in the application of these two topics is provided below.

Solution Guidance

<u>**Custom Material Specification**</u> (It is assumed that the user has started a Study in SolidWorks Simulation.)

- Open the **Material** window by right-clicking the **Part** folder and selecting **Apply/Edit Material…**

Simulation Guidance (continued)

- Beneath **Select material source**, choose ⊙ **Custom defined.**
- On the **Properties** tab, located in the right half of the window, select **Units:** as **English (IPS)**.
- Change **Category:** to **Plastic**; change the **Name:** to **Photoelastic material**. The **Description** and **Source:** fields can be left balnk.
- Within the **Property** column of the lower table notice that red, blue, and black colors are used to indicate different **Property** names. Red lettering indicates information *required* for the solution. Blue lettering indicates *desirable, but unnecessary* information. And, property names appearing in black *are not required* for the current solution. Enter the values listed beneath "Material" in the problem statement. Ignore the **Mass density** field, blank fields, and values listed in black type.
- Click **[OK]** to close the **Material** window. A check "✓" appears on the **Curved Bracket** part folder.

<u>**Fixed Hinge Specification**</u> A **Fixed Hinge** joint acts like a door hinge. This joint type allows rotation about a fixed axis on the model, but prevents translation along that axis. For the **Curved Bracket** loaded in tension, using a **Fixed Hinge** at one end of the model prevents translations in the X, Y, Z directions, but allows the model to remain aligned with the external load as the part deforms. Proceed as follows.

- Right-click the **Fixtures** folder and from the pull-down menu select **Fixed Hinge...** The **Fixture** property manager opens as shown in Fig. E 2-6.
- In the **Standard (Fixed Hinge)** dialogue box, the **Cylindrical Faces for Fixture** field is highlighted (light blue).
- Zoom in on the left hole of the model and select its *inner surface*. **Face<1>** appears in the highlighted field, also shown in Fig. E 2-6. This cylindrical surface has an axis perpendicular to the model face.

Figure E2-6 – Specifying a **Fixed Hinge** restraint.

- Click **[OK]** ✓ to close the **Fixture** property manager.

A **Fixed Hinge** restraint allows the model to undergo rotations about the selected hole, but no translations.

Determine the following:

a. Use classical equations to compute stress at the inside (concave) surface and the outside (convex) surface of the curved bracket model at section C-C. Section C-C passes through the center of curvature and is considered to be a horizontal line in the top view. Include a labeled free body diagram of the portion of the model to the right of section C-C.

b. Include a zoomed-in image of the right hole so that the external load, $F_x = 72$ lb, can clearly be seen to act between user specified *Split Lines* on the inner surface of the hole.

c. Create a stress contour plot showing the *most appropriate stress* that should be analyzed acting across section C-C. Include automatic labeling of maximum and minimum stresses on this plot. This stress should correspond to the stress calculated in part (a)

d. Use the **Probe** feature to produce a graph of the *most appropriate stress* across section C-C, beginning at the inside (concave) surface and continuing to the outside (convex) surface of the beam. (See the *"HINT"* at end of this problem for guidance when making this graph). Use the **Stress Plot** property manager to select the *appropriate stress* for this plot to enable comparison with manual calculations of part (a) above. Include a descriptive title and axis labels to this graph.

Below the graph, or on a separate page, either: (a) cut-and-paste a copy of the **Probe Results** table that includes values used for this comparison, or (b) click the **Save** icon 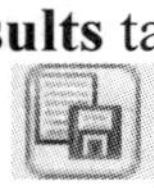, located in the **Report Options** dialogue box. This action creates an Excel spreadsheet containing all values in the **Probe Results** table. This spreadsheet can be inserted onto the page beneath the current graph. In either table, circle the magnitudes of stress on the concave and convex surfaces.

After determining both classical and FEA results at section C-C, use equation [1] (repeated below) to compute the percent difference between these results at the concave and convex surfaces of the model.

$$\% \text{ difference} = \frac{(\text{FEA result - classical result})}{\text{FEA result}} * 100 = \qquad [1]$$

e. On the **Probe** graph created in part (d), label the distance of the neutral axis (neutral plane) from the concave edge of the model at section C-C. Write a brief statement indicating how this value was determined.

f. Return to the plot produced in part (c). This time, use the **Probe** tool to sample stress magnitudes along the concave edge of the model beginning at point **A** and proceeding from node to node until reaching point **B**. Include a graph of these results with your analysis. Add a descriptive title and axis labels to this graph.

g. Is the variation of stress through the middle of the model shown in the graph of part (d) expected? Why? Is the variation of stress shown on the graph of part (f) expected? Why? Is the location of the neutral axis (neutral plane) determined in part (e) located where it is expected to occur on the curved bracket model? Does the neutral axis of a curved member subject to axial load *always* occur at a location *like* that shown in the plot of part (e)? Explain why or why not.

h. Return to the **Results** folder and produce a stress plot of **SI: Stress Intensity**. Compare the general shape of stress contours displayed on this plot with the photoelastic "fringes" shown in Fig. E 2-5. You should notice a similarity between shapes of the stress contours and the photoelastic fringe pattern. These two plots are related, but not identical. Therefore, no direct comparison of stress magnitudes is made here because comparison with photoelastic stress analysis results is beyond the scope of this text.

HINT: Because the mesh generation scheme within SolidWorks Simulation creates an optimized mesh, it is probable that (a) a straight line of nodes does *not* exist across the model at Section C-C, and (b) it is also *unlikely* that node points *occur exactly on a horizontal centerline through the center of curvature.* For these reasons, and to obtain the best estimate of stress on a straight line through the curved section, proceed as follows.

- Zoom in on a top view of the model at section C-C.
- In the Simulation toolbar, click the **Probe** icon . This action opens the **Probe Results** property manager.
- On the SolidWorks flyout menu, click the "+" sign to display the complete flyout menu.
- In the flyout menu, move the cursor over **Right Plane**. This action highlights an edge view of the **Right Plane**. This edge should provide assistance in locating nodes closest to a straight line through section C-C. Unfortunately, the line disappears when the cursor is moved, never the less it is very useful.

Textbook Problems
In addition to the above exercises, it is highly recommended that additional curved beam problems be worked from a design of machine elements or mechanics of materials textbook. Textbook problems provide a great way to discover errors made in formulating a finite element analysis because they typically are well defined problems for which the solution is known. Typical textbook problems, if well defined in advance, make an excellent source of solutions for comparison.

NOTES:

CHAPTER #3

STRESS CONCENTRATION ANALYSIS

This example explores stress in the vicinity of a geometric discontinuity in a part where stress concentration is known to occur. Because geometric discontinuities can assume a variety of shapes, they are often generically referred to as "notches." Stress concentrations and their related stress concentration factors are typically studied in mechanics of materials and/or design of machine elements courses. This example focuses on the validity of Finite Element Analysis (FEA) solutions in the vicinity of these geometric discontinuities and on the effects of mesh size on solution accuracy. However, the general principles learned in this example apply to a wide variety of finite element analysis problems. More specifically, since it is generally accepted that improved finite element solutions result when a smaller mesh size is used, this example examines convergence to a solution through the application of successive mesh refinement.

Because this is the third example, fewer figures and briefer step-by-step procedures are included. In fact, where you already are familiar with procedures and where *no new* procedures are introduced, special instructions encourage users to complete specific tasks on their own. The combination of these two approaches should permit users to work more at their own pace while allowing expanded discussion of new topics.

Learning Objectives

In addition to software capabilities mastered in previous chapters, upon completion of this example, users should be able to:

- Recognize when, how, and why to *defeature* a model.
- Apply *mesh refinement* to a model and understand the influence of mesh density on stress and displacement results.
- Create *multiple copies* of *related studies* quickly and easily within SolidWorks Simulation.
- Check *convergence* to gauge validity of a finite element solution.
- Use multiple *viewports* to compare results of different finite element analyses.

Problem Statement

The rectangular bar illustrated in Fig. 1 is fixed at its left end and is subject to an axial, tensile load **F = 6000** lb applied to the opposite end. A rounded "notch," which causes stress concentration, is located in the center of the member.

Figure 1 – Axially loaded bar with a geometric discontinuity.

Dimensions of the notched bar, shown in Fig. 2, reveal that the member is sufficiently long so that boundary-conditions (i.e., fixtures and external loads) do not significantly affect stresses near the notch. The bar is made of **AISI 1020** steel. Analysis of this model begins below.

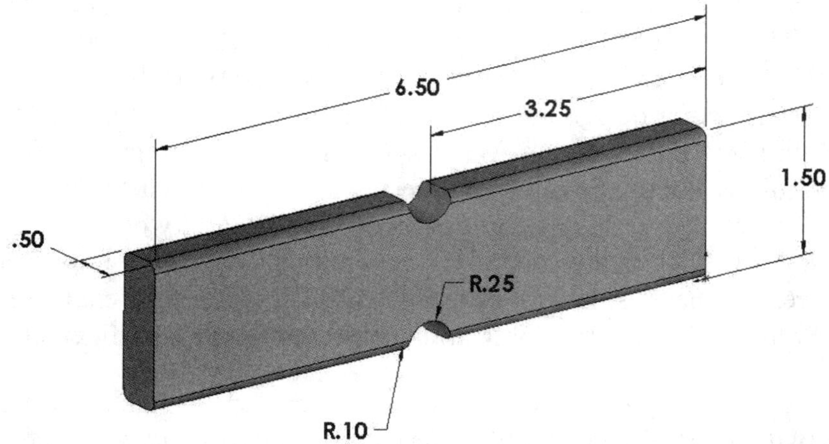

Figure 2 – Dimensioned drawing and a three-dimensional model of a notched bar.

1. Open SolidWorks by making the following selections. (*Note:* "/" is used to separate successive menu selections.)

Start/All Programs/SolidWorks 2009 (or) Click the **SolidWorks** icon on your screen.

2. When SolidWorks is open, select **File / Open…** Then use procedures common to your computer environment to locate and open the SolidWorks Simulation file named **"Notched Bar."**

Create a Static Analysis (Study)

The Study to be created is to be named "**Draft Mesh-DEFAULT Size**." Individuals comfortable with setting up a **Static** analysis using a **Solid Mesh** are encouraged to proceed on their own. Abbreviated steps, 1 through 4 below, are provided for those desiring guidance. *NOTE: This and future chapters make use of right-clicking menu items to make selections. Users who prefer to use SolidWorks Simulation icons, as demonstrated in Chapter #2, are encouraged to do so.*

1. In the main menu, select **Simulation** and from the pull-down menu click to select **Study…** The **Study** property manager opens (not shown).

2. In the **Name** dialogue box, change the name "**Study 1**" by typing "**Draft Mesh-DEFAULT Size**" where the word "DEFAULT" refers to the mesh size used.

3. Verify that a **Static** study is selected, then click **[OK]** ✓. An outline for the study is opened in the Simulation manager tree.

Defeaturing the Model

Before beginning an analysis, it is always a good idea to examine the model to determine whether or not its geometry can be simplified without significantly impacting the analysis. The reason for this is that a simpler model results in a more computationally efficient analysis. Thus, the user must ask, "Is it necessary to include all geometric features on the model in order to obtain a valid solution?" If the answer is "no", then the model can be simplified by *suppressing* (i.e., defeaturing) unimportant features. Typical items that can be suppressed without significantly affecting results are minor geometric features, such as fillets, rounds, and chamfers. *You are cautioned, however, that defeaturing a model can have dire consequences if improper choices are made.* An example of a feature that should *not* be removed is examined in a future example. Defeature the current model as described by two alternate methods included below. It is strongly recommended that both methods be attempted.

Method 1:

1. Depress and *hold* the **Shift** key and move the cursor onto the graphics screen. Then click to select each of the eight rounded surfaces on the model. Some of these surfaces are shown shaded in Fig. 3. If the information "flags" obstruct your view, click ☒ to close them.

2. After selecting all rounds, right-click anywhere in the graphics screen and the pop-up menu shown in Fig. 3 appears. On this menu, select the **Suppress** icon circled in Fig. 3. The suppressed rounds are effectively "removed" from the model as illustrated in Fig. 4

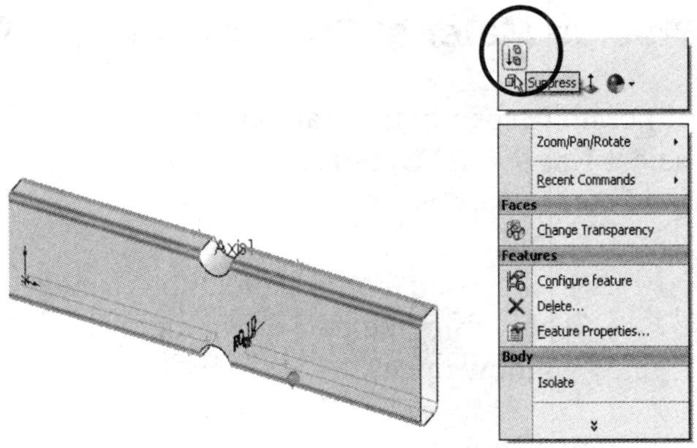

Figure 3 – Rounds selected to be suppressed on the Notched Bar model.

The above procedure works well when only a few geometries are chosen for defeaturing. However, an alternative and somewhat simpler means can be used when the goal is to suppress all rounded edges on this model. Next, use the alternative approach, but first the rounded edges must be returned to the model to enable demonstrating the alternate method. Proceed as follows.

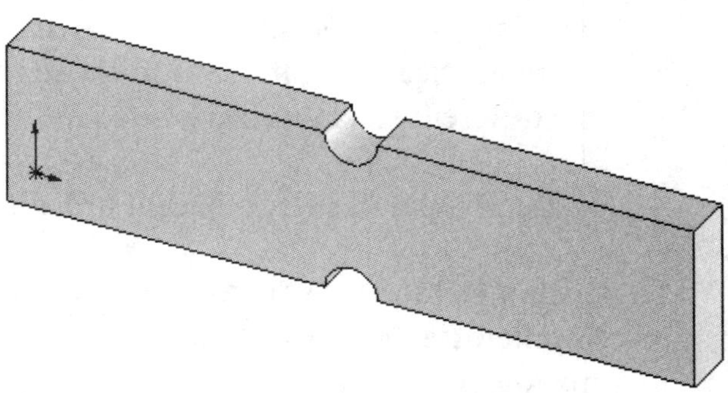

Figure 4 – Notched Bar after defeaturing.

3. In the SolidWorks manager tree, located *above* the SolidWorks Simulation manager at the left side of the graphics screen, locate **Fillet1** and right-click this icon. Above the pop-up menu select the **Unsuppress** icon. Fillets reappear in the model.

Method 2:

4. Once again, locate **Fillet1** in the SolidWorks manager tree and right-click this label. From the box above the pop-up menu, select the **Suppress** icon. All fillets are removed from the model.

> **Analysis Insight:**
> Clearly **Method 2** is the easier of the two methods. However, it requires planning ahead when the SolidWorks model is created. For example, if rounds of the same size were included elsewhere on a more complex model, but if only one set of rounds were to be suppressed, then the SolidWorks part should be created with two different sets of rounds each of which is easily identified by a different name.

Assign Material Properties to the Model

If possible, specify the material for this model on your own. Choose **AISI 1020** steel and select **English (IPS)** units. An abbreviated, step-by-step procedure is provided below if guidance is needed.

1. In the SolidWorks Simulation manager right-click the model name, **Notched Bar**. Then, from the pull-down menu select **Apply/Edit Material…** The **Material** window opens.

2. Select ⦿ **From library files**, then from the pull-down menu select **solidworks materials**.

3. Next, click the "+" sign adjacent to **Steel (32)** and select **AISI 1020** steel from the list of available steels. *Caution: Avoid selecting AISI 1020 Steel, Cold Rolled.* As a parenthetical note, the **(32)** following the listing **Steel (32)** indicates that thirty two different steel types are listed in the materials library.

4. On the **Properties** tab, adjacent to **Units:**, select **English (IPS)**.

5. Click **[OK]** to close the **Material** widow. A check mark "✓" appears on the **Notched Bar** folder and the material designation **(-AISI 1020-)** appears next to this folder.

Apply Fixtures and External Loads

Loads and fixtures acting on this model include an **Immovable** restraint applied on its left-end and a **6000** lb axial force applied normal to its right-end. Practice applying these restraints and loads on your own. After applying restraints and loads, a partial view of the Simulation manager should appear as shown in Fig. 5 and the model should appear as shown in Fig. 6. A step-by-step procedure is provided below if guidance is desired.

1. In the SolidWorks Simulation manager, right-click **Fixtures** and from the pull-down menu, select **Fixed Geometry…** The **Fixture** property manager opens.

2. In the **Standard(Fixed Geometry)** dialogue box, select the **Fixed Geometry** icon. The **Faces, Edges, Vertices for Fixture** field is highlighted (light blue) and is awaiting selection of the surface to be designated **Immovable**.

3. Rotate the model as necessary and select the left end surface of the model. **Immovable** restraints are applied to the left end of the model as seen in Fig. 6.

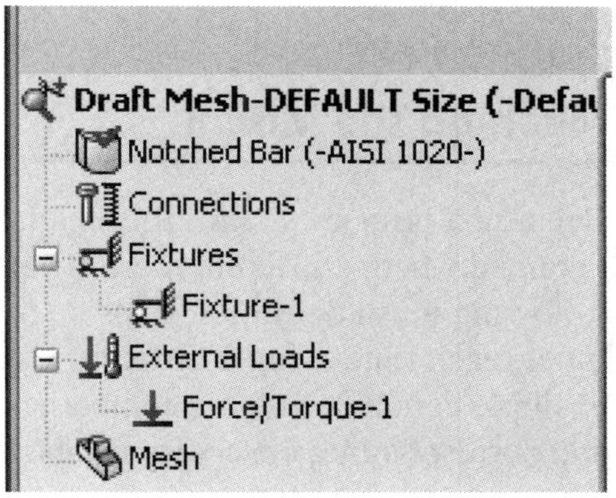

Figure 5 – SolidWorks Simulation manager with **Fixtures** and **External Loads** defined.

4. Click **[OK]** ✓ to close the **Fixture** property manager. **Fixture-1** appears beneath the **Fixtures** folder as seen in Fig. 5.

5. Next, right-click the **External Loads** icon and from the pop-up menu, select **Force…** The **Force/Torque** property manager opens.

6. Within the **Force/Torque** dialogue box, select the **Force** icon (if not already selected) and click to select ⦿ **Normal** as the direction of the force.

7. The **Face and Shell Edges for Normal Force** field is highlighted (light blue) to indicate it is active. Rotate the model and select the right end of the model. Force vectors appear on the right-end as shown in Fig. 6. Ignore force direction at this time.

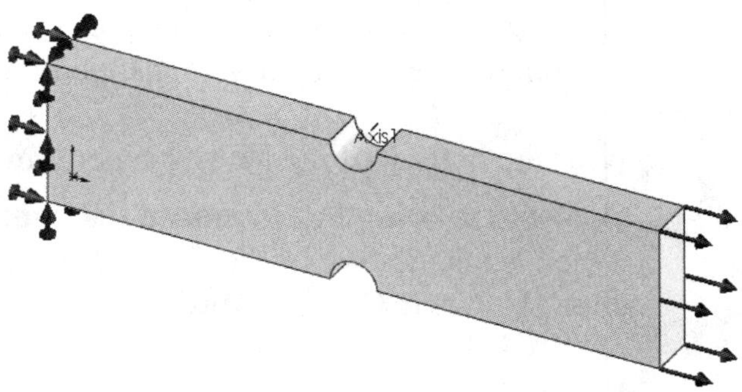

Figure 6 – Notched Bar restrained on its left end and with a **6000** lb force applied normal to its right end.

8. Verify that the **Units** field is set to **English (IPS)**.

9. In the **Force Value** field, type **6000**.

10. Because the default orientation for forces applied normal to a surface is directed *toward* the surface, it is necessary to check ☑ **Reverse direction** to apply a tensile load.

11. Click **[OK]** ✓ to close the **Force/Torque** property manager. **Force/Torque-1** is now listed beneath the **External Loads** folder in Fig. 5. The model should now appear as shown in Fig. 6.

Meshing the Model

Because a primary goal of this example is to examine differences between results obtained when a different mesh *type* or mesh *size* is used, it is suggested that the following mesh definition steps be followed carefully. The model will be meshed five times, each time using a different size or type of mesh or mesh control capability. This example concludes with a comparison of results obtained when using different meshes and corresponding observations about solution accuracy.

Proceed as follows to define the first mesh.

1. Right-click the **Mesh** icon and select **Create Mesh…** The **Mesh** property manager opens as shown in Fig. 7.

2. Check "✓" to open the ☑ **Mesh Parameters** dialogue box and verify that a ⊙ **Standard Mesh** is chosen and that **Unit** is set to **in**. Accept the remaining default settings for mesh size and tolerance. A pointer at the top of this dialogue box should be located approximately in the center of the scale between **Coarse** and **Fine** mesh sizes. This is the default mesh size; do *not* change it.

3. Near the bottom of the **Mesh** property manager, click ⌄ to open the **Advanced** dialogue box, which is also shown in Fig. 7. In this dialogue box, check ☑ **Draft Quality Mesh**.

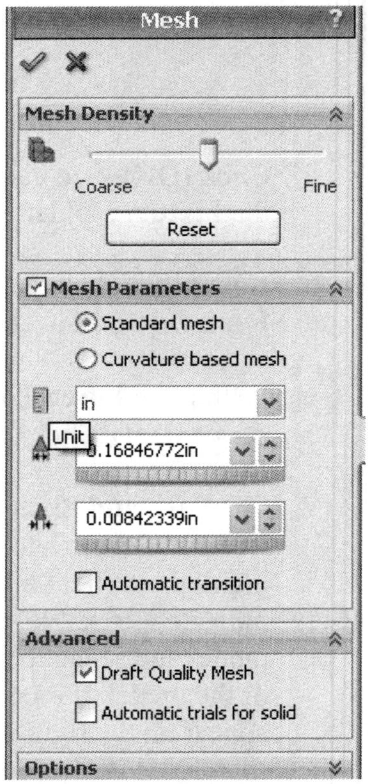

Figure – 7 Default settings for mesh size in the **Mesh** property manager.

4. Verify other system default settings appear as shown in Fig. 7 and click **[OK]** ✓ to close the **Mesh** property manager and mesh the model.

The meshed model appears in Fig. 8.

Figure 9 shows an enlarged view of the notch and the resulting straight-line approximation of the curved notch that results when a **Draft** quality mesh is used. Although rarely used, a draft quality mesh may be useful where quick results are needed for a large, complex model.

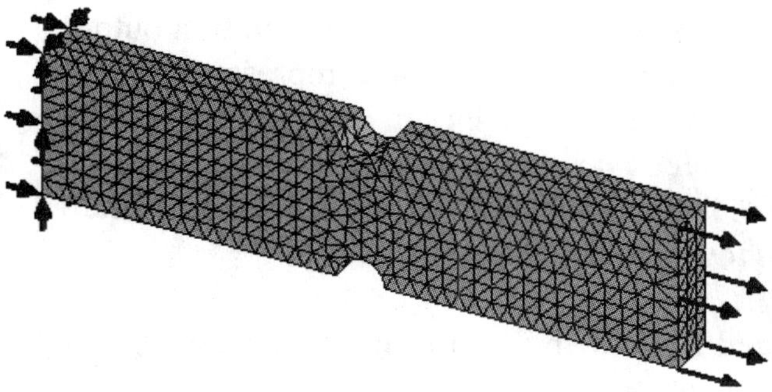

Figure 8 – Draft quality mesh shown on the Notched Bar model.

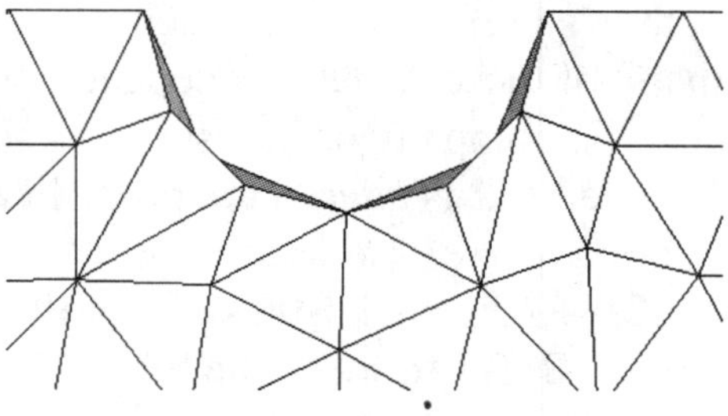

Figure 9 – Close-up view of **Draft** quality mesh reveals straight-line approximation of the curved surface.

Solution

Proceed directly to the solution. You are encouraged to run the **Study** on your own. An abbreviated, procedure is provided below in the event guidance is desired.

1. In the SolidWorks Simulation manager tree, right-click the study name **Draft Mesh-DEFAULT Size (-Default-)** and from the pull-down menu, select **Run**.

The analysis runs and the usual **Results** folders are added at the bottom of the Simulation manager tree. The solution process is complete. Next, proceed to examine the results of this analysis.

Examination of Results

Stress Plots

Recall that this example will be solved five different times, each time using a different mesh size, mesh type, or mesh control technique. Thus, a second goal of this example is to introduce a simple method of creating additional studies that are identical to the first except for different mesh characteristics. For this reason, it is necessary to consider carefully exactly *what results* are to be examined and what characteristics are desired for the *display* of those results. If these two factors are addressed when the *first* set of results is being defined, then similar sets of results can be produced automatically for all subsequent solutions. Proceed as follows to specify the desired plot characteristics used to display the output results.

1. If the **Stress1 (-von Mises-)** plot appears in the graphics area, skip this step. Otherwise, beneath the **Results** folder, double-click on **Stress1 (-vonMises-)** to display the vonMises stress contour plot and the color-coded stress legend.

The following steps are used to specify certain desired characteristics of the current screen image. While some selections are arbitrary, to demonstrate how solution output display can be controlled from one study to the next, other selections represent the author's preferences. In each case a brief justification is given. In practice, however, many of these selections depend upon user preference and/or standard practices within a specific company or industry. As selections below are made, the current image of the Notched Bar is altered to appear like that shown in Fig. 10.

2. Right-click **Stress1 (-vonMises-)** and from the pull-down menu, select **Edit Definition…** The **Stress Plot** property manager opens.

3. In the **Display** dialogue box, set **Units** to **psi**.

4. At the bottom of this property manager, click 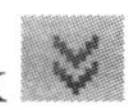 to open the **Property** dialogue box (if not already open).

5. Click to check ☑ **Include title text:** and type **Your Name** and any other information pertinent to this plot. *Justification:* It is important to document the author and context of a Study so that other users of this information know who to contact if questions arise. See arrow in Fig. 10.

6. Click **[OK]** ✓ to close the **Stress Plot** property manager. The information just entered (your name, etc.) appears at the top-left of the graphics screen along with default information about the plot. Briefly examine information included there.

7. Again right-click **Stress1 (-vonMises-)**. From the pull-down menu, select **Chart Options…** The **Chart Options** property manager opens.

8. Beneath **Display Options** click to check ☑ **Show max annotation**. The location of maximum stress is immediately labeled on the plot as shown near the notch in Fig. 10. *Justification:* This choice is made because it is desired to determine the location of maximum stress occurring in the part and whether or not it is near the geometric discontinuity. Rotate the model if the location of maximum stress is unclear.

9. Click **[OK]** ✓ to close the **Chart Options** property manager.

10. Right-click **Stress1 (-vonMises-)** and from the pull-down menu, select **Settings…** The **Settings** property manager opens.

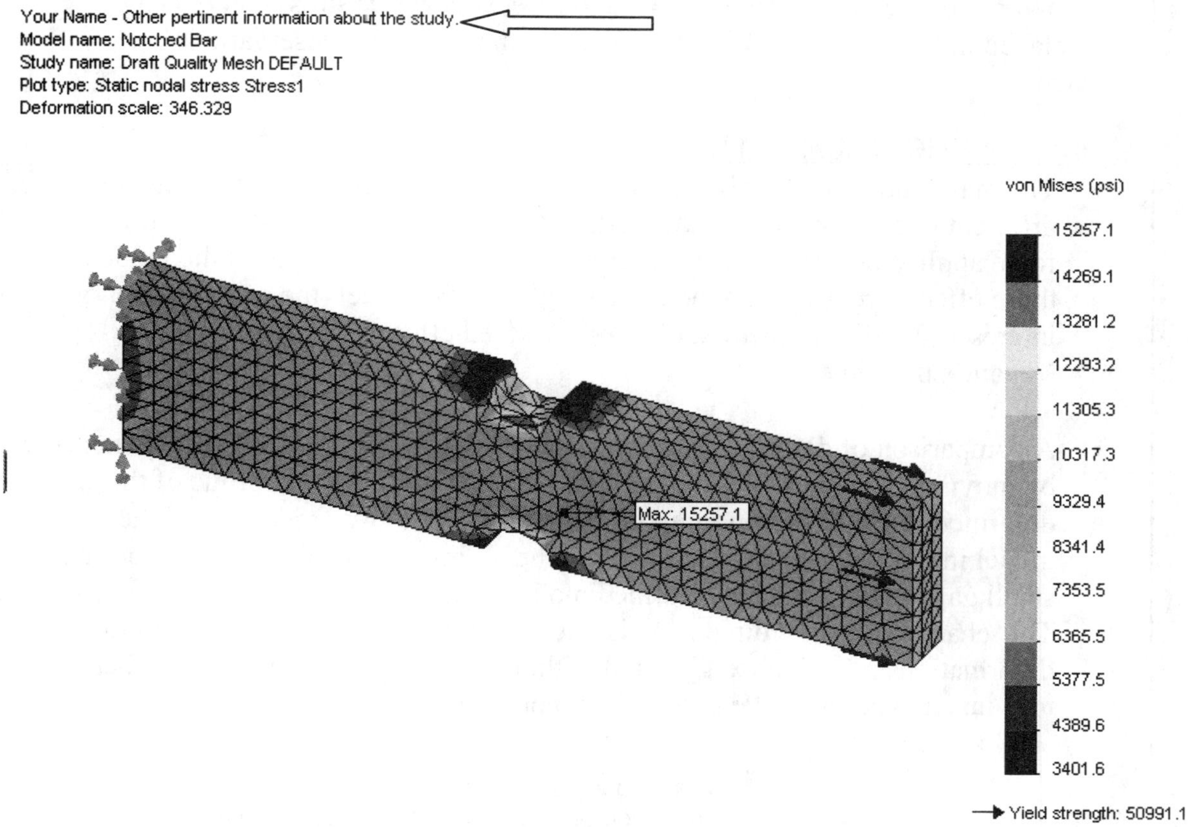

Figure 10 – Trimetric view of the Notched Bar with user specified display options.

11. Beneath **Fringe Options**, select **Discrete**. *Justification:* This option is selected because discrete fringes reproduce better when printed in black, white, and gray tones used in this text. Otherwise, fringe display is a user preference.

12. Beneath **Boundary Options**, select **Mesh**. This option displays the current mesh on the model. *Justification:* Since one goal of this example is to investigate effects of mesh modification upon results, viewing the mesh provides visual feedback about mesh size.

13. Click **[OK]** ✓ to close the **Settings** property manager.

A completed view of the model displaying von Mises stress contours appears in Fig. 10. Note the maximum magnitude of vonMises stress (15,257 psi) determined by this analysis. **Table 1**, near the end of this example, summarizes and compares this value to other results obtained when different mesh sizes and mesh types are applied to the model.

Analysis Insight

Two views of the Notched Bar showing discrete vonMises stress contours are displayed in Figs. 11 and 12. For these plots, the following observations are made.

OBSERVATIONS for Fig. 11:

- The magnitude and distribution of stress at left and right ends of the model are different due to the **Immovable** restraint applied at the left end and uniform force applied normal to the right-end. However, due to length of the model, these effects are negligible near the middle of the model (the area of primary interest). This is another example of localized effects explained by St. Venant's principle.

- A comparison of deformed and *un*-deformed shapes of the model can be made by moving the cursor over the model. This action causes an outline of the *un*-deformed shape to be superimposed on the model. In a front view of the model in Fig. 11, a slight narrowing in the Y-direction is observed by noting a small gap between the un-deformed model outline and the stress contour plot. This change of lateral dimension is due to Poisson's ratio effect. Recall that deformations are often exaggerated within SolidWorks Simulation to enhance user understanding of the physical phenomenon.

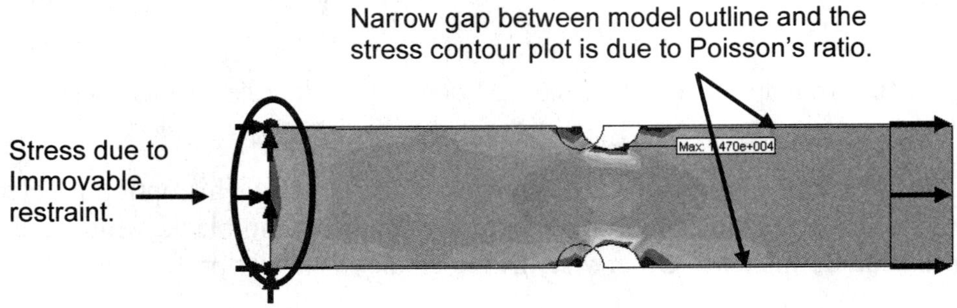

Figure 11 – vonMises stress contours and comparison of deformed and un-deformed models of the Notched Bar. The **Mesh** is not shown on this plot so that Poisson's effect is more easily seen.

Analysis Insight (continued)

OBSERVATIONS for Fig. 12:

- Superimposing the current mesh onto the model reveals slight differences between element geometry near the top and bottom notches. Carefully observe these differences on Fig. 12 or on your screen.

- Stress *distribution* adjacent to notches located at the top and bottom of the bar is different. This difference may be due to somewhat different mesh shapes in these two areas of the model.

NOTE: Because the meshing process is automated and because it "starts form scratch" and seeks an optimum mesh each time a part is meshed, it is possible that a user obtained mesh might differ from that shown in Fig. 12.

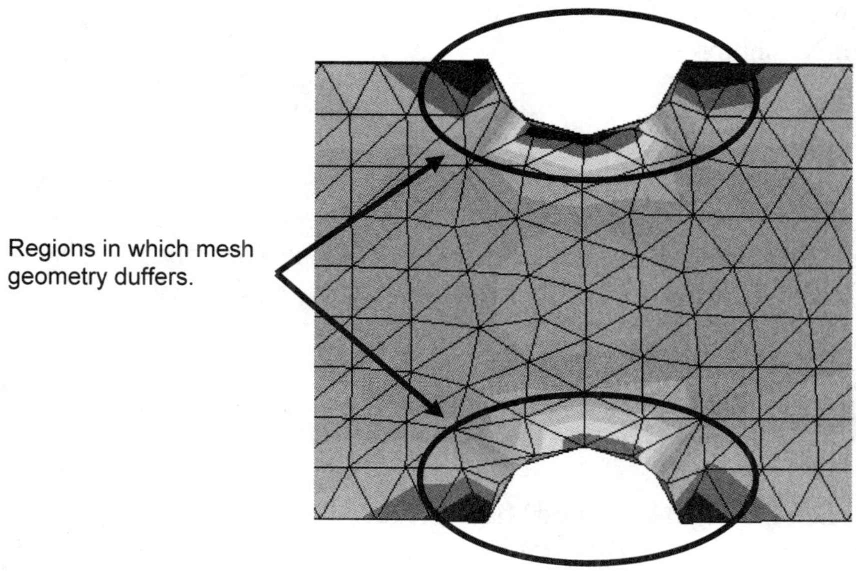

Figure 12 – Close-up view of **Draft** quality mesh in the vicinity of the two notches. Carefully observe slight differences in mesh geometry and distribution of vonMises stress.

Creating a Copy of a Plot

Due to the *axial* tensile force applied to the Notched Bar in the X-direction, it is logical to examine stresses in the X-direction (i.e., σ_x). To do so requires definition of another **Stress Plot** similar to that defined for the vonMises stress plot displayed above. However, repeating all steps required to produce a plot with the *same* characteristics is somewhat tedious and time consuming. Therefore, use the following shortcut to create a *copy* of the current graph and all its display settings.

1. In the Simulation manager tree click-and-drag the **Stress1 (-vonMises-)** folder upward and drop it onto the **Results** folder as illustrated in Fig. 13.

   A new copy of the contents of the **Stress1 (-vonMises-)** folder appears at the bottom of the **Results** list and is labeled **Copy [1] Stress1 (-vonMises-)** (shown at the arrow in Fig. 13). This new folder contains an exact duplicate of all commands previously used to define **Stress1 (-von Mises-)**. The following steps outline how to modify this *copied* folder to contain a plot of σ_x.

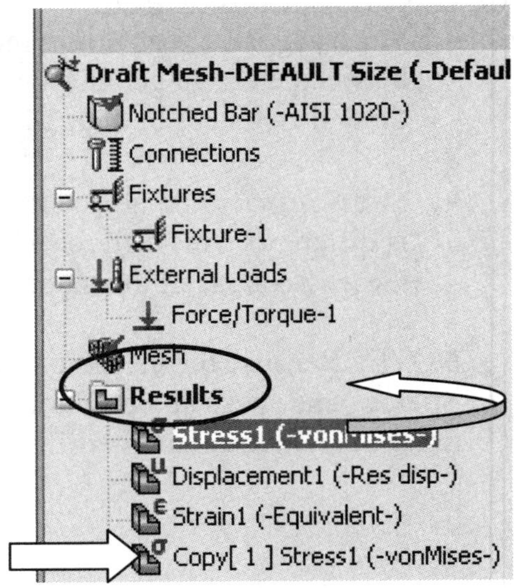

Figure 13 – Making an exact copy of a plot folder.

2. Click-*pause*-click on the name **Copy[1] Stress1 (-vonMises-)** and type a new descriptive name for the new plot. Since this new folder is to contain σ_x, type: "**Sigma-X**" and press **[Enter]**.

The *changed name* now appears as **Sigma-X (-vonMises-)**. This name, of course, makes no sense since these names represent two different stresses. The reason for this is that, although the folder *name* was changed, the copied contents (namely vonMises stress) still reside in the folder. However, this is easily corrected by the following steps.

3. Right-click **Sigma-X (-vonMises-)** and the pop-up menu at right displays possible options. Select **Show** and the existing vonMises stress plot is displayed again. Do nothing with this plot.

4. Right-click the **Sigma-X (-vonMises-)** folder a second time. This time the traditional pull-down menu appears. A partial view of this menu is shown in Fig. 14. From this menu select **Edit Definition…** and the **Stress Plot** property manager opens.

5. In the dialogue box beneath **Display**, open the **Component** pull-down menu and from the list of possible stresses select **SX: X Normal stress**.

6. Click **[OK]** ✓ to close the **Stress Plot** property manager.

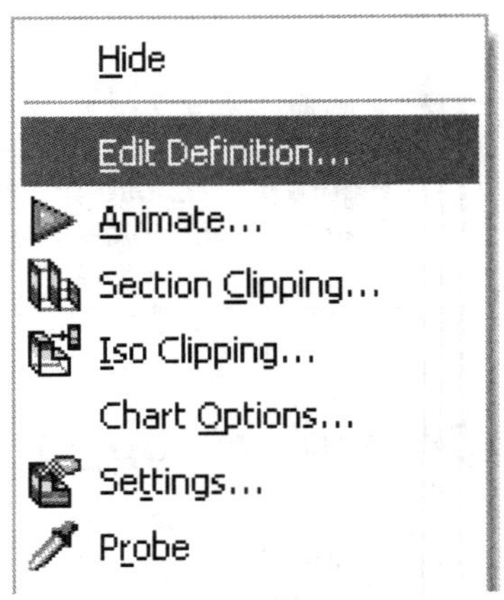

Figure 14 – Partial view of pull-down menu.

The *correct* name for the stress now appears in the SolidWorks Simulation manager tree as **Sigma-X (-X normal-)**. This name is a combination of the name you typed to identify the stress plus a system applied label to identify σ_X.

7. A plot of **Sigma-X (-X normal-)** should appear on the screen as seen in Fig 15. If not, right-click **Sigma-X (-X normal-)** and select **Show**.

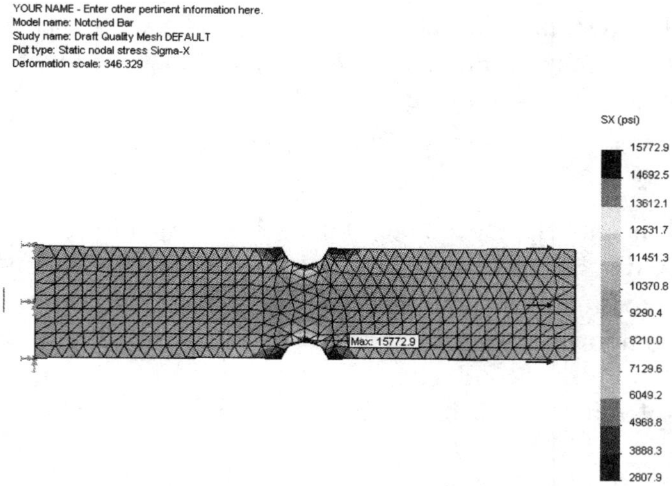

Figure 15 – Graphic display of normal stress in the X-direction (σ_X).

Analysis Insight

<u>OBSERVATIONS for Fig. 15</u>:

- Maximum stress in the X-direction σ_X = 15,773 psi is larger than the previously viewed vonMises stress σ' = 15,257 psi.
- All display settings established for **Stress1 (-vonMises-)** are replicated in the **Sigma-X (-X normal-)** plot folder, (i.e., discrete fringes are shown, your name and a brief description appear at top-left of the graphics screen, the maximum stress magnitude and its location are labeled on the plot, and the mesh is superimposed on the model). NOTE: If the description appearing next to your name in the top line is no longer valid, it can be changed; see steps 2 through 5 of the previous section.

Displacement Plot

Another goal for this example is to determine when an analysis converges to a solution. Although both stress and displacement can be used to make this determination, it turns out that displacement plots typically yield better information about solution convergence than do stress contour plots. Based on your reading of the Introduction to this text, do you understand the reason for this? This question is answered later in this example. Based on this discussion, a **Displacement** plot is created next.

1. Double-click the **Displacement1 (-Res disp-)** folder. The default displacement plot named **Displacement1 (-Res disp-)**, which is short for "resultant displacement," is displayed.

The resultant displacement image, **(-Res disp-)**, is simply a plot of the square root of the sum of the squares of the X, Y, and Z displacement components at any point within the model as given by equation [1] below.

$$Resultant\ Displacement = \sqrt{X^2 + Y^2 + Z^2} \qquad [1]$$

It is entirely acceptable to use **(-Res disp-)** for this analysis. However, we next select the X-displacement to be displayed for two reasons. First, the X-displacement is in the direction of the applied load and therefore it accounts for the primary displacement component (Y and Z displacements due to Poisson ratio effects are *very* small relative to X). And, second, choosing the X-displacement provides an opportunity to demonstrate selection of a different displacement component as outlined in the following steps.

2. Right-click **Displacement1 (-Res disp-)**, and from the pull-down menu select **Edit Definition…** The **Displacement Plot** property manager opens as shown in Fig. 16.

3. In the **Display** dialogue box, open the **Component** pull-down menu and select **UX: X Displacement** to display the X-component of displacement.

4. Verify that **Units** are set to inches **in**.

5. Click **[OK]** ✓ to close the **Displacement Plot** property manager.

The X-displacement image is displayed using system default settings. Below, two cosmetic changes are made to this plot.

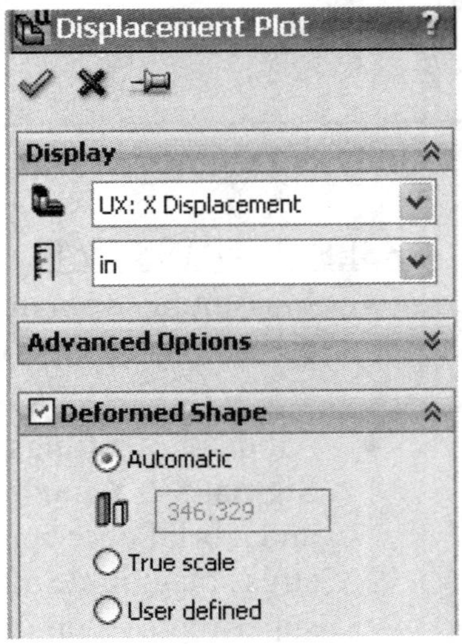

Figure 16 – Selecting the X-component of displacement for display.

6. Right-click **Displacement1 (-X disp-)** and from the pull-down menu, select **Settings…** The **Settings** property manager opens as shown in Fig. 17.

7. Beneath **Fringe options** select **Discrete** for the type of fringe display and beneath **Boundary options** select **Model** (if not already selected) to turn on a black outline of the model. A mesh display is not needed here.

Figure 17 – Display options specified in the **Settings** property manager.

8. Click **[OK]** ✓ to close the **Settings** property manager and a plot of **UX: X Displacement** is displayed like that shown in Fig. 18.

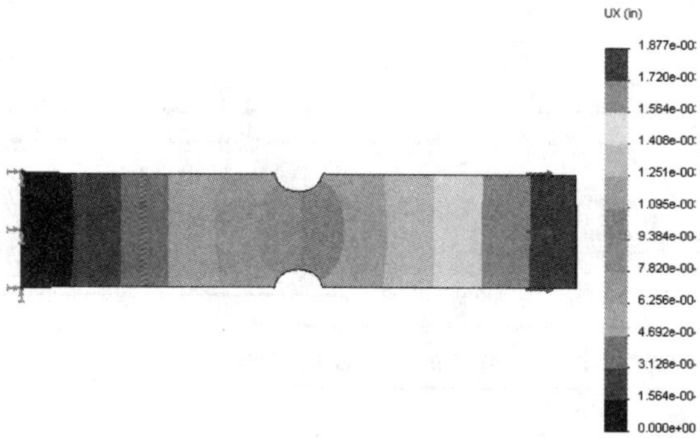

Figure 18 – Displacement plot modified to show **UX: X Displacement** using an outlined model and discrete fringes.

Recall that default plots show exaggerated displacements. Thus, if it is desired to view *true* displacements, right-click **Displacement1 (-X disp-)** and from the pull-down menu select **Edit Definition…** The **Displacement Plot** property manager, shown in Fig. 16, opens and beneath **Deformed Shape** click to select ⦿ **True scale** and click the **[OK]** ✓. This action establishes a 1:1 scale for the displacement plot. Try this; then before proceeding, change back to the ⦿ **Automatic** default setting.

9. Click **[OK]** ✓ to close the **Displacement** property manager.

Because both stress and displacement plots are defined above, it is possible to produce additional nearly identical *copies* of the entire Study. A copy of this Study can be created in which everything remains the same except for mesh type and size. Upon completion of additional studies using different mesh types and sizes, the stress and displacement results from all studies is compared. Proceed as follows to define these new studies. Two different ways of creating *copies* of a Study are illustrated.

Creating New Studies

Basic Parts of the Graphical User Interface

Before outlining one method of duplicating a Study, the names used to identify various parts of the graphical user interface are reviewed. Also, a new part of the graphical user interface is introduced. Review of these parts of the screen image is essential because several names are quite similar. Refer to Fig. 19 while reading the descriptions below.

- SolidWorks Feature Manager Tree – Users familiar with SolidWorks should already be familiar with the Feature manager tree. It is located to the left of the graphics screen near the top of the manager tree. See label on Fig. 19. Its name derives from the fact that various features of a model, such as sketches, holes, fillets, extrusions, mates, etc. are listed in this portion of the manager tree.
- Simulation Manager Tree (also referred to as the Simulation manager) – The Simulation manager tree refers to the finite element portion of a Study. It also

appears at the left side of the screen and is located just below the SolidWorks Feature manager. Both these entities are referred to as manager "trees" because they contain a list of items added to the model as the analysis grows in size.

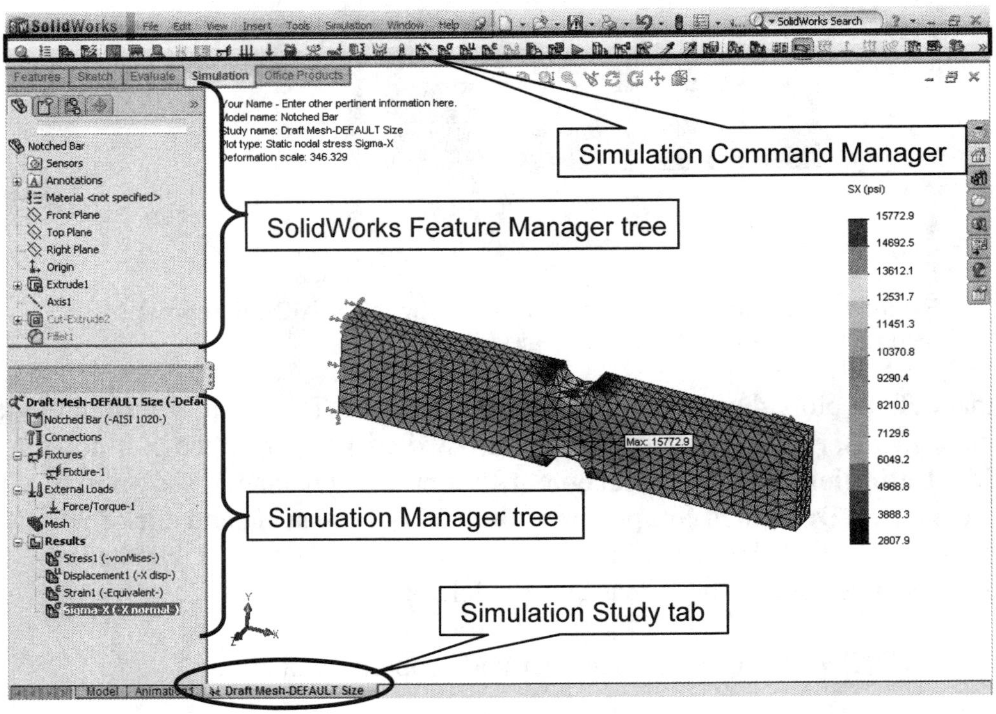

Figure 19 – Identification of various portions of the graphical user interface.

- Simulation Command Manager (also simply referred to as the **Simulation** tab) – This command manager contains icons (symbols for commands) used to develop the finite element portion of a Study. Command manager icons appear boxed across the top of the screen shown in Fig. 19. Icons located in the Simulation Command manager were used extensively in Chapter 2.

- Simulation Study Tab – This *new* tab has always been present, but is not referred to until now. It is located beneath the graphics screen and is circled in Fig. 19. The tab is identified by the name of the current study, **Draft Mesh-DEFAULT Size**, and contains all information used to define the current Study. This information includes items such as **Material** specification, **Fixtures, External Loads**, and the **Mesh** that are currently displayed in the Simulation manager tree.

The following section outlines one method for copying the contents from one Simulation Study tab to create a new study.

Study Using High Quality Elements and COARSE Mesh Size

The main reason so much emphasis was placed upon refining plots for the draft quality mesh applied to the notched bar is that all those settings can be copied as we proceed to examine other mesh types and sizes applied to the same part. Begin by copying the current Study as outlined below.

1. At bottom of the screen, right-click to select the Simulation Study *tab* named **Draft Mesh-DEFAULT Size**. A pop-up menu opens as shown in Fig. 20.

2. In the pop-up menu, select **Create New Simulation Study**. The **Study** property manager opens.

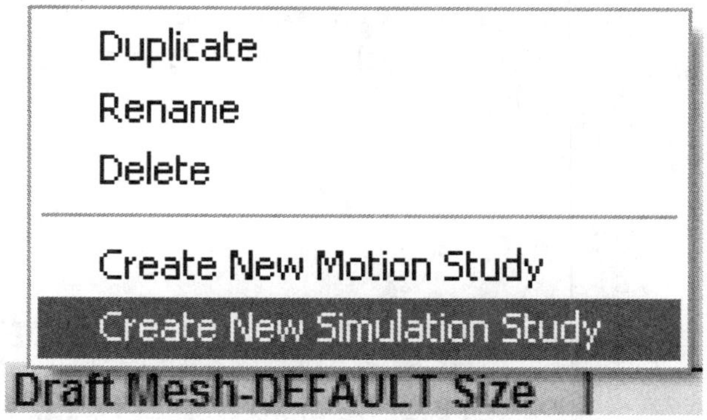

Figure 20 – Pop-up menu revealed by right-clicking on the current Study name.

3. In the **Study** property manager verify that **Static** is selected as the Study **Type**, and click **[OK]** ✓ to close the **Study** property manager.

4. A new Simulation Study *tab* named **Study 1** appears at the bottom of the screen and the outline for that new Study, named **Study 1 (-Default-)**, appears in the Simulation manager tree.

Observe that all of the folders (**Notched Bar**, **Connections**, **Fixtures**, **External Loads**, and **Mesh** are empty, (i.e., undefined). The following steps outline the procedure to copy most of these items from the original Study into this new Study. Proceed as follows.

5. At bottom of the screen, return to the Study named **Draft Mesh-DEFAULT Size** by clicking its tab on the Simulation Study tab.

6. Within the Simulation manager tree, click-and-drag the folder named **Notched Bar (-AISI 1020-)** *from* the **Draft Mesh-DEFAULT Size** Study onto the **Study 1** tab as illustrated in Fig. 21. Notice a check mark "✓" on the new **Notched Bar** folder.

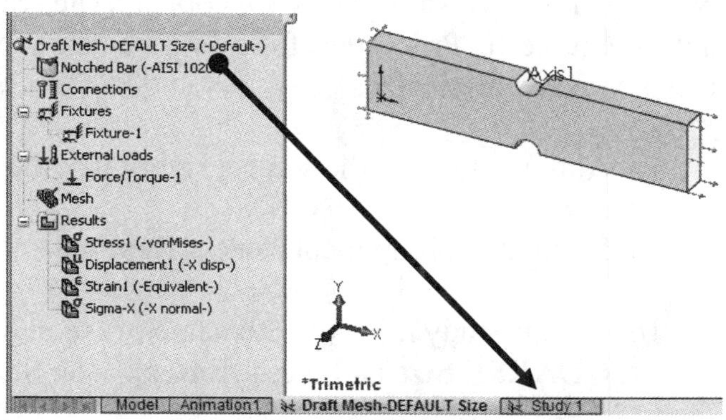

Figure 21 – Copying **Material** properties from one Study to another using the *click-and-drag* technique.

7. Return to the Study named **Draft Mesh-DEFAULT Size** by clicking its tab on the Simulation Study tab.

8. This time, click-and-drag the **Fixtures** folder from the **Draft Mesh-DEFAULT Size** Study onto the **Study 1** tab as illustrated in Fig. 22. Notice that both the **Fixtures** folder and its contents, namely **Fixture-1**, appear in the new study.

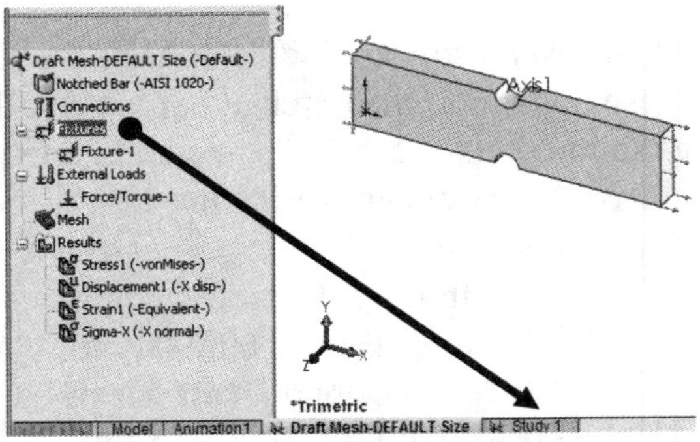

Figure 22 – Copying the **Fixtures** folder from one Study to another using the *click-and-drag* technique.

9. Again click the **Draft Mesh-DEFAULT Size** tab, but this time click-and-drag the **External Loads** folder onto the **Study 1** tab. The words **Force/Torque-1** should be listed beneath the **External Loads** folder. *This move is not illustrated in a figure.*

10. Finally, repeat the click-and-drag procedure by copying the **Results** folder from the **Draft Mesh-DEFAULT Size** Simulation manager tree to the **Study 1** tab.

11. If vectors representing **Fixture-1** or **Force/Torque-1** do not appear on the model, right-click each folder and from the pull-down menu select **Show All**.

12. To verify that data from the previous Study has been copied correctly, right-click the **Force/Torque-1** icon and from the pop-up menu, select **Edit Definition...** Observe the force magnitude of 6000 lb is displayed in the **Force/Torque** property manager.

13. Click **X** to close the **Force/Torque** window.

Notice that the **Mesh** folder is *not* copied. The reason for this is that each new study uses a different mesh. Proceed as follows to re-name the new Study and to define a different mesh type and mesh size.

14. At the bottom of the screen, right-click the **Study-1** tab.

15. From the pop-up menu, select **Rename**.

16. On the Study *tab*, type the name of the new Study as: **High Quality Mesh-COARSE Size** and press **[Enter]**. The Study name is updated on the tab.

Proceed as follows to create the new mesh.

17. Right-click the **Mesh** icon and select **Create Mesh…** The **Mesh** property manager opens.

18. In the **Mesh** property manager, check ☑ **Mesh Parameters** to open this dialogue box. Note the current mesh size (0.16846772 in).

19. Next, within the **Mesh Density** dialogue box, click-and-*drag* the mesh size slide-control to **Coarse** at the far left-end of the scale. Mesh size is now (0.33693543 in), which is twice as large as the default mesh indicated with the pointer at the middle of the scale.

20. At the bottom of the **Mesh** property manager, select to open the **Advanced** dialogue box. If necessary, click to clear the check mark adjacent to ☐ **Draft Quality Mesh**. This action changes mesh quality from **Draft** quality to **High** quality as evidenced by the change of notation that shows **Jacobian points** are now set to **4 points**. This subtle message is not easily interpreted by new users, but it signifies that a **High** quality mesh is now active. All other settings in this property manager remain unchanged.

Again observe the **Mesh Parameters** dialogue box and notice that changing the mesh *type* from **Draft** quality to **High** quality does not change the mesh *size*. The coarse mesh size is still 0.33693543 in. Using a **High** quality mesh simply adds mid-side nodes to each side of the tetrahedral element, thereby making it better able to model curved surfaces. This added ability to model curvature makes **High** order elements more *flexible* (i.e. less stiff) than **Draft** quality elements. The effects of this change are examined later in this example.

21. Click **[OK]** ✓ to close the **Mesh** property manager. Re-meshing of the model occurs automatically.

The Solution is next run as follows.

22. At top of the Simulation manager tree, right-click **High Quality Mesh-COARSE Size (-Default-)** and from the pull-down menu, select **Run**. Aside: Note the speed with which this solution is completed.

Briefly examine contents of the **Results** folder to observe maximum stress magnitudes shown on **Stress1 (-vonMises-)**, and **Sigma-X (-X normal-)** plots. Also note the maximum displacement shown on **Displacement1 (-X disp-)** plot. Because the **Results** folder was *copied* from the previous study, notice that all plots are displayed in the previously selected format. No further work is required to adjust each plot.

A plot of **Sigma-X (-X normal-)** is included in Fig. 23. This figure shows the **COARSE** size **High** quality mesh used for the current study. Compare it to the **DEFAULT** size

Draft quality mesh shown in Fig. 15. Which has more nodes and elements? Which is more accurate? These questions are answered at the conclusion of this example.

OBSERVATIONS:

- Both the vonMises stress and normal stress in the X-direction (σ_x) are larger for the **High** quality coarse size mesh than predicted by the **Draft** quality default size mesh.

- The magnitude of the X-displacement is also larger for the **High** quality coarse mesh than that predicted using a **Draft** quality mesh of default size. Recall an earlier statement that **High** quality elements are not as "stiff" as **Draft** quality elements. This lower mesh stiffness results in larger deflections as will be observed again later in this example.

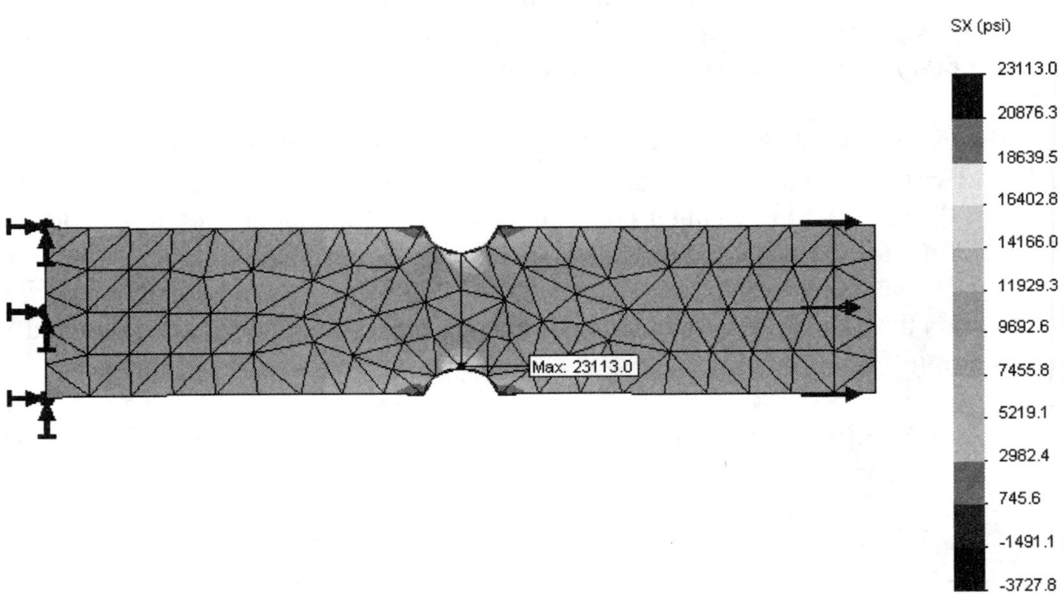

Figure 23 – A high quality, coarse mesh displayed on the Notched Bar model.

Study Using High Quality Elements and DEFAULT Mesh Size

In this section the Notched Bar example is solved again, but this time using a High quality **Default** size mesh (i.e., a smaller mesh than the coarse mesh). Because this new solution is basically a repeat of the section above, complete, but abbreviated instructions are provided below. Practice performing these steps on your own.

1. At bottom of the screen, right-click the Simulation Study *tab* named **High Quality Mesh-COARSE Size**. A pop-up menu opens as shown in Fig. 24.

2. In the pop-up menu, select **Create New Simulation Study**. The **Study** property manager opens.

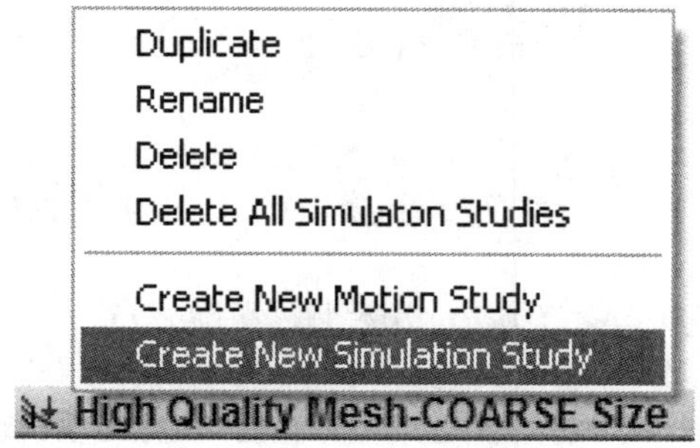

Figure 24 – Pop-up menu revealed by right-clicking on the current Study name.

3. In the **Study** property manager verify that **Static** is selected as the Study **Type**, and click **[OK]** ✓ to close the **Study** property manager.

4. A new Simulation Study *tab* named **Study 1** appears at the bottom of the screen and the outline for that new Study, named **Study 1 (-Default-)**, appears in the Simulation manager tree.

5. Once again note that all of the folders (**Notched Bar**, **Connections**, **Fixtures**, **External Loads**, and **Mesh** within this new Study are empty, (i.e., undefined). The following steps outline the procedure to copy selected items from the original Study into this new Study. Try this on your own, or follow the abbreviated steps below.

6. At bottom of the screen, return to the Study named **High Quality Mesh-COARSE Size** by clicking its tab.

7. Within the Simulation manager tree, click-and-drag the folder named **Notched Bar (-AISI 1020-)** *from* the **High Quality Mesh-COARSE Size** Study onto the **Study 1** tab as illustrated in Fig. 25. This action copies **Material** properties to the new study. Notice a check mark "✓" appears on the new **Notched Bar (-AISI 1020-)** folder.

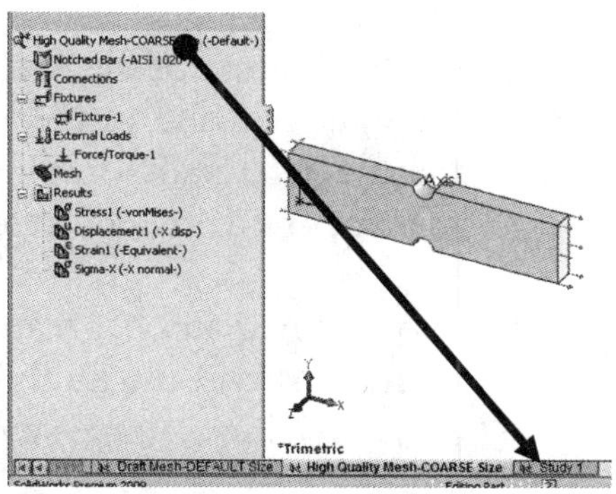

Figure 25 – Copying **Material** properties from one Study to another using the *click-and-drag* technique.

8. Repeat steps 6 and 7, but this time click-and-drag the **Fixtures** folder from the **High Quality Mesh-COARSE Size** Study onto the **Study 1** tab. Both the **Fixtures** folder and its contents, namely **Fixture-1**, should now appear in the **Study 1** Simulation manager tree.

9. Again click the **High Quality Mesh-COARSE Size** tab, but this time click-and-drag the **External Loads** folder onto the **Study 1** tab. Observe that **Force/ Torque-1** should appear beneath the **External Loads** folder on the **Study 1** tab.

10. Finally, repeat the click-and-drag procedure to copy the **Results** folder from the **High Quality Mesh-COARSE Size** Simulation manager tree to the **Study 1** tab.

*Do NOT copy the **Mesh** folder!*

11. If vectors representing **Fixture-1** or **Force/Torque-1** do not appear on the model, right-click each folder and from the pull-down menu select **Show All**.

12. At the bottom of the screen, right-click the **Study-1** tab and from the pop-up menu, select **Rename**.

13. On the Study *tab*, type the name of the new Study as: **High Quality Mesh-DEFAULT Size** and press **[Enter]**. The Study name is updated on the tab.

Proceed as follows to create the new mesh.

14. Right-click the **Mesh** icon and select **Create Mesh…** The **Mesh** property manager opens.

15. In the **Mesh** property manager, check ☑ **Mesh Parameters** to open this dialogue box. The current default mesh size should be 0.16846772 in. If any other value appears, click the **[Reset]** button below the sliding pointer scale to reset the default mesh size to the mid-scale value; slight round-off may occur.

16. At the bottom of the **Mesh** property manager, select ≫ to open the **Advanced** dialogue box and verify that **Jacobian points** is set to **4 points**. This signifies that a **High** quality mesh is now active. All other settings in this property manager remain unchanged.

17. To discover another feature of the software, in the **Options** dialogue box, check ☑ **Run (solve) the analysis**. Checking this box causes the model to be meshed *and* solved in a single step.

18. Click **[OK]** ✓ to close the **Mesh** property manager. The model is re-meshed and the Solution is run automatically. Aside: Note the speed with which this solution is completed.

Briefly examine maximum magnitudes on plots of **Stress1 (-vonMises-)**, **Sigma-X (-X normal-)**, and **Displacement1 (-X disp-)** in the **Results** folders. Because of the smaller mesh size, all values should *exceed* those of the previous Study.

Study Using High Quality Elements and FINE Mesh Size

Next, solve the Notched Bar example for the fourth time. But, this time use a Fine size high quality mesh. The solution process parallels that of the preceding section with the exception that a new descriptive name is assigned to the study (include the word **"FINE"** to identify the new mesh size) and reset mesh size to **Fine** when re-meshing the model. Because this new solution is a repeat of the previous two solutions, try to solve it on your own. However, if guidance is desired, follow the abbreviated procedure in the preceding section.

Notice the significant increase of Meshing and Solution time required for the fine mesh (approximately 20 to 40 seconds). Complete this Study by examining results and comparing stress and displacement magnitudes with prior results. An image of the solution appears in Fig. 26.

Study Using High Quality Elements and MESH CONTROL

Perhaps the *most important* approach to refining mesh size is that of applying *mesh control*, which is investigated in this section. By this point in the example it is evident that a smaller mesh results in improved approximations of stress in a model. However, the approach of progressively using smaller and smaller mesh size throughout the entire

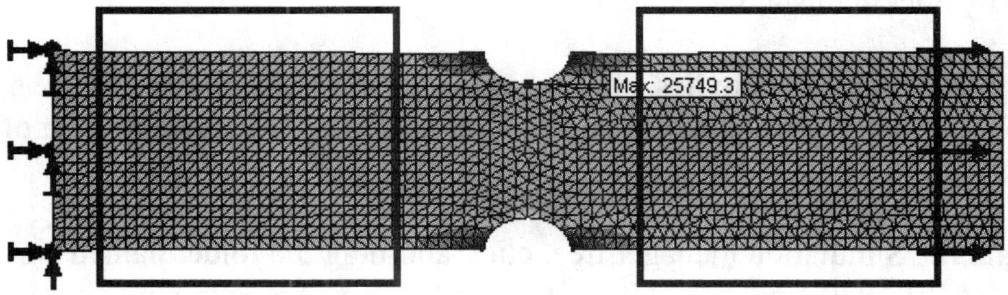

Figure 26 – "Boxed" areas denote regions where *inefficient* use is made of a **Fine** size mesh because stress is uniform (constant) or nearly uniform in these regions of the model.

model (i.e., use of a global mesh size) results in significant inefficiencies during the solution process. For example, when the **Fine** mesh of the previous section is used, consider the large number of equations solved in regions of the model where stress is nearly uniform as illustrated by the "boxed" regions shown in Fig. 26.

However, use of *mesh control* allows the user to control element size on selected entities of the model, such as **Faces**, **Edges**, **Vertices**, or **Reference Points**. Controlling mesh size makes it possible to specify a smaller mesh only in selected regions of high stress gradient, such as near the notch, while simultaneously using a significantly larger mesh size in regions where stress distribution is relatively uniform. Locating local regions of high stress at the start of an analysis is easily accomplished by using a default mesh. This fact was observed earlier in this example when high stress magnitudes were found in the vicinity of the "notch." The procedure below outlines steps for applying mesh control to selected parts of the model.

As in the preceding section, the Notched Bar example is solved again. But, this time a High quality **Default** size mesh is used except in the region around the "notch." Because use of mesh control introduces new software capabilities not used above, all steps in this procedure are outlined below. Users are encouraged to copy all parts of the previous study to a new Simulation Study tab, named **Study 1**, on their own. If guidance is desired, previously used steps are repeated in abbreviated form below. Follow steps 1 through 11.

1. At bottom of the screen, right-click the Simulation Study *tab* named **High Quality Mesh-FINE Size** and in the pop-up menu choose **Create New Simulation Study**. The **Study** property manager opens.

2. In the **Study** property manager verify that **Static** is selected as the Study **Type**, and click **[OK]** ✓. A new Simulation Study *tab* named **Study 1** appears at the bottom of the screen. *NOTE: A new Study name can be typed in the* ***Name*** *dialogue box at this time. The name "****Study 1****" is only used to shorten written reference to it in the steps below.*

3. At bottom of the screen, return to the Study named **High Quality Mesh-FINE Size** by clicking its tab.

NOTE: Any of the previous studies can be used as the starting point because the **Material, Fixtures, External Loads,** and **Results** folders are identical in each of the previous studies.

4. Within the Simulation manager tree, click-and-drag the folder named **Notched Bar (-AISI 1020-)** *from* the **High Quality Mesh-FINE Size** Study onto the **Study 1** tab.

5. Repeat steps 4 and 5, but this time click-and-drag the **Fixtures** folder onto the **Study 1** tab.

6. Repeat the click-and-drag procedure to copy the **External Loads** folder onto the **Study 1** tab.

7. Finally, repeat the click-and-drag procedure to copy the **Results** folder from the **High Quality Mesh-FINE Size** Simulation manager tree to the **Study 1** tab.

8. If vectors representing **Fixture-1** or **Force/Torque-1** do not appear on the model, right-click each folder and from the pull-down menu select **Show All**.

Do NOT copy the ***Mesh*** *folder!*

9. At the bottom of the screen, right-click the **Study-1** tab and from the pop-up menu, select **Rename**.

10. On the Study *tab*, type the name of the new Study as: **High Quality Mesh-MESH CONTROL** and press **[Enter]**. The Study name is updated on the tab.

The following steps introduce use of *mesh control.*

11. Right-click the **Mesh** folder and from the pull-down menu, select **Apply Mesh Control...** The **Mesh Control** property manager opens as illustrated in Fig. 27.

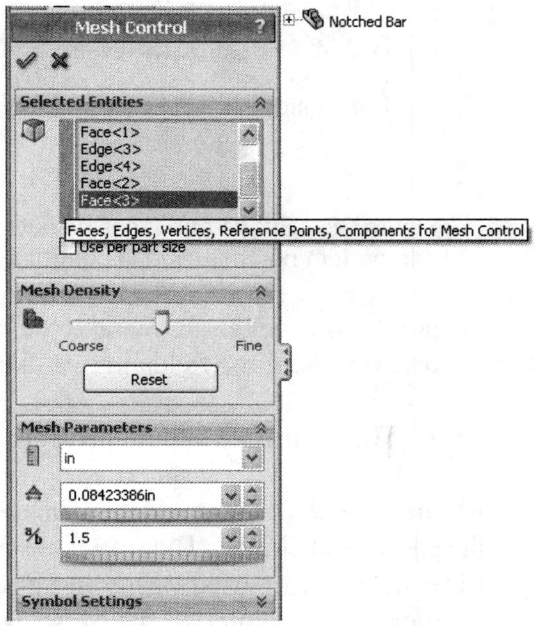

Figure 27 – Selections made in the **Mesh Control** property manager.

As noted above, an advantage of using mesh control is that it can be applied to local regions on a model. In the following steps, portions of the model in the vicinity of the stress concentration are selected.

12. In the **Selected Entities** dialogue box, the **Faces, Edges, Vertices, Reference Points, Components for Mesh Control** field is highlighted (light blue) indicating it is active.

13. Move the cursor onto the model and *at both the top and bottom notches*, select the two curved **Edges** and one **Face** at each notch as illustrated in Fig. 28. **Edge<1>**, **Edge<2>**, **Edge<3>**, **Edge<4>**, and **Face<1>**, **Face<2>** appear in the highlighted field of Fig. 27 in the order selected by the user.

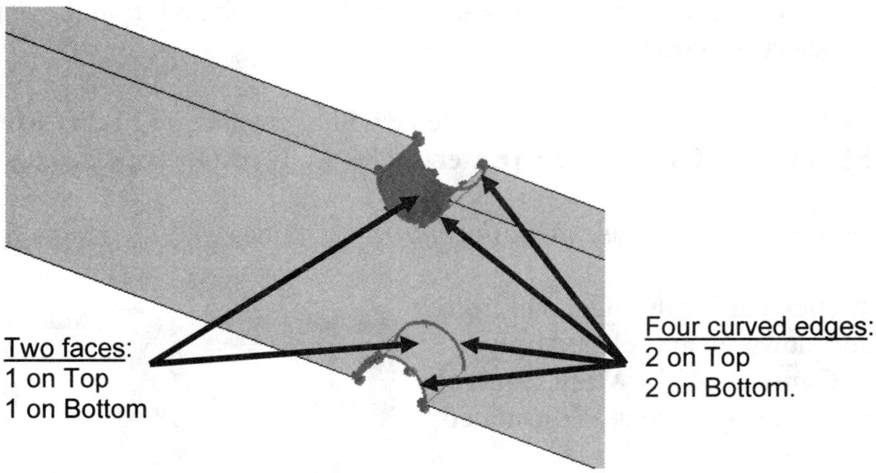

Figure 28 – Edges and faces selected for application of **mesh control** at top and bottom notches. Mesh control symbols appear on the selected entities.

At this point, no changes are made to default values in the **Mesh Parameters** dialogue box. However, the three fields in this dialogue box are explained below.

Unit: The **Unit** field should be set to **in**.

Element Size: A system determined element size is applied to the edges and notch faces selected above. The initial element size (0.08423386 in) corresponds to the **Fine** mesh setting used earlier in this example. This statement is true despite the location of the pointer on the **Mesh Density** slider-scale. Stated another way, the software sets the default mesh size in the mesh control region to half of the default mesh size of the remainder of the model. *Do not change the slider setting.*

Ratio: **a/b** = **1.5** This value controls the increase of element size from one layer of elements to the next as elements radiate away from the selected entities. If "E" = default element size, then subsequent layers of elements increase in size according to the progression: E, E*(a/b), $E*(a/b)^2$, . . . $E*(a/b)^n$ until $E \geq$ the default element size for the remainder of the model.

Steps below complete the mesh definition.

14. Click **[OK]** ✓ to close the **Mesh Control** property manager.

Unlike previous Studies, notice that the new mesh does not immediately appear on the model. Proceed as follows to update the mesh and run the solution.

15. Right-click the **Mesh** folder and from the pull-down menu, select **Mesh and Run**. Aside: Note the faster speed with which this solution is completed.

The model is re-meshed and an enlarged view of the mesh in the vicinity of the notches is shown in Fig. 29. Also notice that a **Mesh Controls** icon and a **Control-1** icon appear below the **Mesh** folder in the Simulation manager tree.

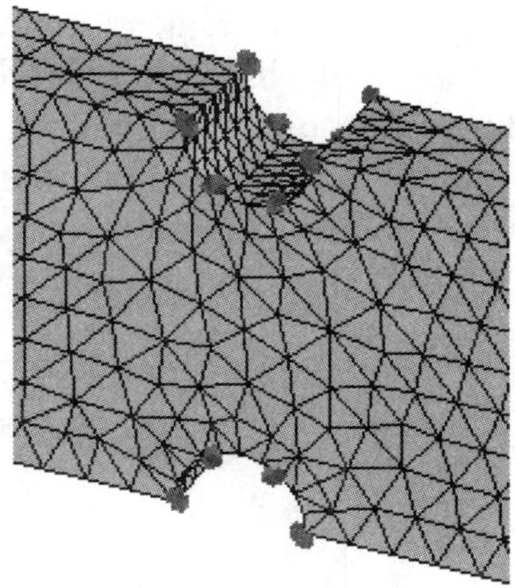

Figure 29 – View of mesh size altered by application of **Mesh Control** in the vicinity of the notches.

Examine results shown on plots in the **Results** folder. Then proceed to gain greater insight into factors affecting **Mesh Control** by making the changes outlined below.

16. In the Simulation manager tree, right-click the **Control-1** icon and from the pull-down menu select **Edit Definition…** The **Mesh Control** property manager opens as previously shown in Fig. 27. Notice that previously selected edges and faces remain unchanged.

17. In the **Mesh Parameters** dialogue box change the **a/b Ratio** value to **1.2**.

This action results in a decrease of size changes from one element layer to the next. Simultaneously the number of layers between the smallest elements and default size elements, used for the remainder of the model, increases as is illustrated in Fig. 30.

18. Click **[OK]** ✓ to close the **Mesh Control** property manager.

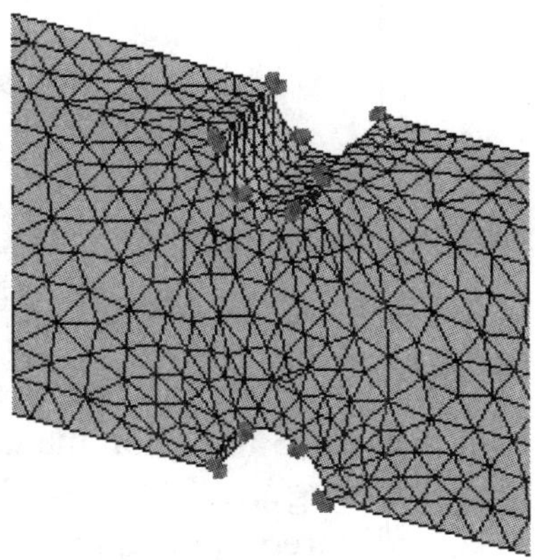

Figure 30 – **Mesh Control** using a smaller **Ratio a/b = 1.2** results in a more gradual transition from small to large mesh size.

In the Simulation manager tree, Fig. 31, observe the *Error* symbols adjacent to the Study name **High Quality Mesh-MESH CONTROL (-Default-)** and the **Mesh** folder. Also, a *Warning* symbol appears adjacent to the **Results** folder. Descriptions of the three warning and/or error symbols used in SolidWorks Simulation are included below.

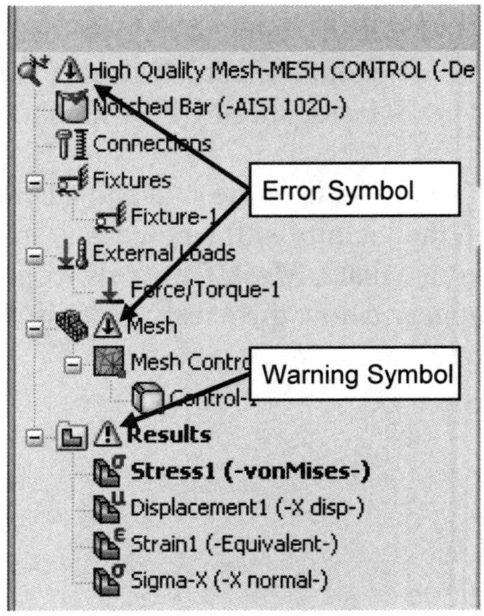

Figure 31 - SolidWorks Simulation Manager tree showing two errors and a warning.

Icon	Description
	This icon indicates an error in the Study. In this example, it appears adjacent to the Study name near the top of the Simulation manager tree and adjacent to the **Mesh** folder.
	This icon indicates an error with a feature. It appears adjacent to the incorrect feature name in the SolidWorks Simulation manager tree.
	This icon indicates a warning concerning a feature. It appears on the specific feature or on the **Results** folders if it is invalid.

To determine the source of these warnings, proceed as follows.

19. Right-click the **High Quality Mesh-MESH CONTROL (-Default-)** Study name in the Simulation manager tree and from the pull-down menu, select **What's wrong?...** The **What's Wrong** window opens, as shown in Fig. 32, and displays all three errors and warnings.

Read all statements adjacent to each error or warning in the **What's Wrong** window shown in Fig. 32. Because all error/warning statements are caused by the same irregularity, they are dealt with in a brief paragraph beneath Fig. 32.

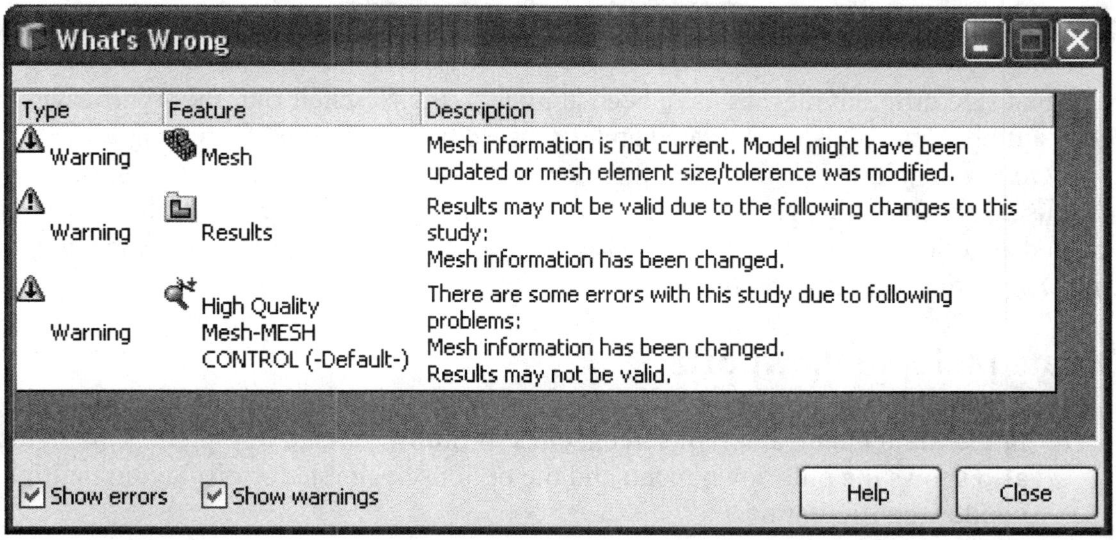

Figure 32 – Error and warning descriptions associated with the current study.

It was previously noticed (step 16) that, after the **Mesh** property manager was closed, the current model was not automatically meshed. Instead, it was necessary to select ☑ **Mesh and Run**. A consequence of this action is that, not only was the model meshed, but also a finite element solution was performed based on the initial mesh. That mesh had a **Ratio a/b = 1.5**. Then, to demonstrate a more gradual transition of mesh size in the vicinity of the notch, a new **Ratio** of **a/b = 1.2** was specified. This action changed the previous mesh, thereby rendering the previous Solution invalid for the new mesh. In brief, the statement: "**Mesh information has been changed**." which is found in all three statements in the **What's Wrong** window, warns the user that a *new* Solution, which is based on the *new* mesh, must be run in order to obtain results applicable to the revised mesh.

Based on the above observation it is only necessary to run a new Solution, corresponding to the new mesh, to eliminate the errors reported in Fig. 32. Proceed as follows.

20. Right-click on the **Mesh** folder and from the pull-down menu, select **Mesh and Run**. Once again notice the faster speed with which this solution is completed.

The model is re-meshed automatically and a new solution is run. This new Solution corresponds to the revised mesh, previously shown in Fig. 30

Summary

By using *mesh control*, a small mesh is created in areas of high stress gradient while a larger mesh is used in other regions of the model. Thus, mesh control results in efficient use of computational facilities, yet yields improved results in regions of discontinuity selected by the user.

Results Analysis

Now that five different meshes have been applied to the Notched Bar, the significance of the resulting solutions is investigated and discussed below. Begin by creating a *simultaneous* display of results from the four Studies for which high quality elements were used, but for which *global* element size was changed. To open multiple viewports, proceed as follows. *SolidWorks users may be familiar with this software feature and are encouraged to proceed on their own.*

Create Multiple Viewports

1. In the Main menu, at top of screen, click **Window**, circled in Fig. 33. This figure also shows the pull-down menu and the options available for displaying multiple window configurations.

2. Move the cursor onto **Viewport** and from the second-level pull-down menu, select **Four View**.

The graphics area immediately displays four views of the current screen image. This image is altered in the following steps.

Various plots can be displayed in these viewports in keeping with user preferences.

However, to facilitate discussion, it is suggested that the following order be used. Begin by placing a plot of vonMises stress found using the **Draft** quality mesh in the upper left-hand viewport. The following steps outline this procedure.

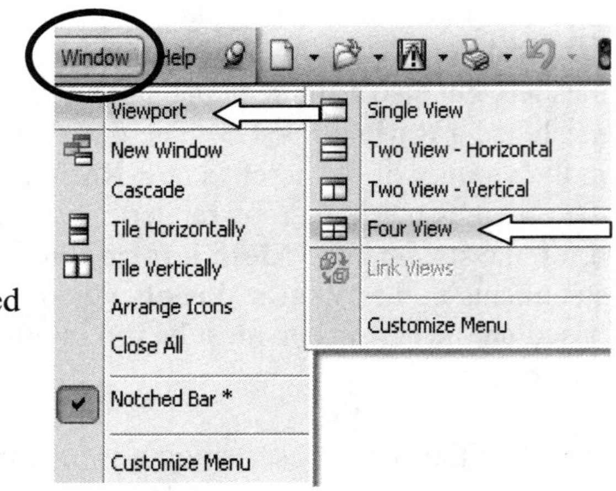

Figure 33 – Menu selections used to open multiple viewports.

3. Click anywhere in the upper left-hand viewport (labeled "**A**" in Fig. 34). This action activates the viewport.

4. On the Simulation Study tab, at bottom of screen, select the tab labeled **Draft Mesh-DEFAULT Size**. This action displays a listing of the Study contents in the Simulation manager tree. If necessary, click ◀ to shift tabs to the right.

5. Next, click "+" adjacent to the **Results** folder to display its contents (if not already displayed).

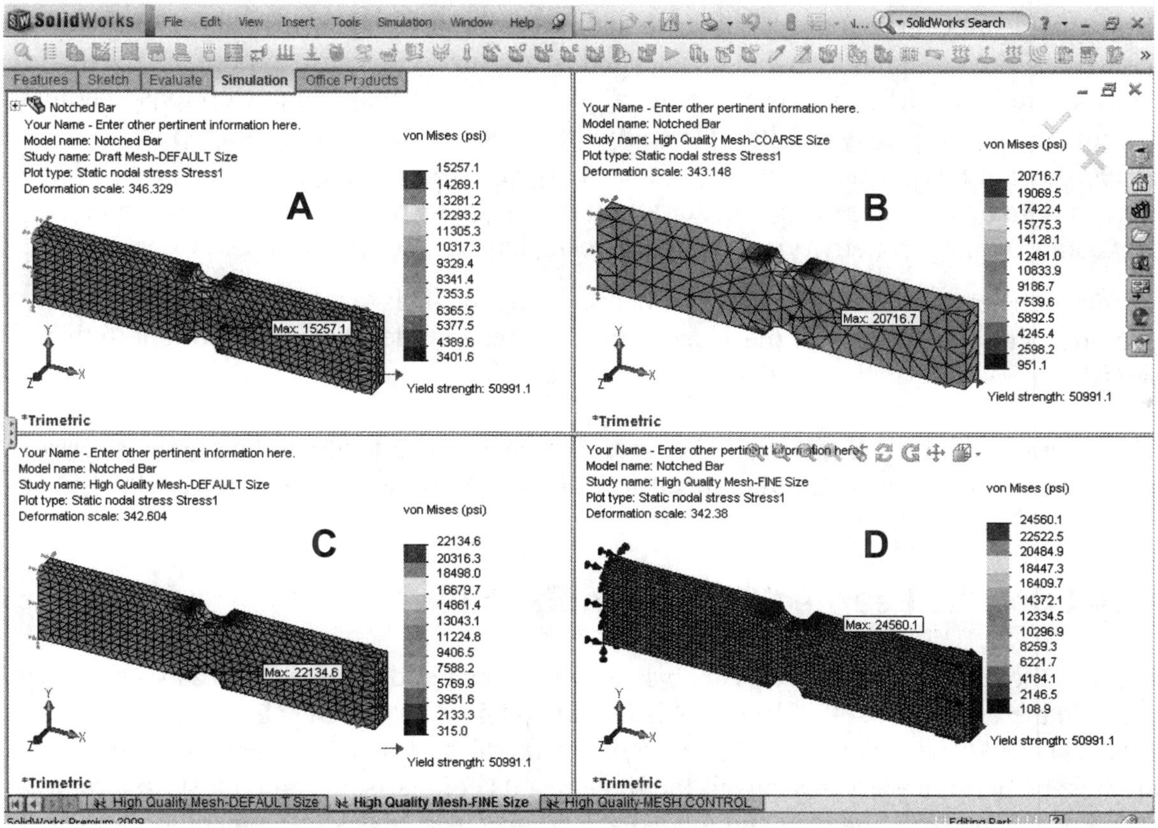

Figure 34 – Multiple viewports facilitate comparison of results from multiple different studies or different aspects of a model within a single study.

6. Finally double-click **Stress1 (-vonMises-)** and the contents of that plot are displayed in viewport "**A**" as illustrated in Fig. 34. See NOTES below.

> <u>NOTE 1</u>: Do not be concerned if your *view* of the model differs from that shown. Desired views can be adjusted later based upon user preferences. In fact, notice that the default view orientation corresponds to Top, Isometric, Right-side, and Front views of the model in a clockwise direction beginning at the top-left of the screen.
>
> <u>NOTE 2</u>: Viewport labels **A, B, C, D** are added to the textbook image to facilitate discussion. These letters do not appear on the SolidWorks screen image.

7. Click in viewport **B** and repeat steps 4 to 6 for the von Mises stress plot of the **High Quality Mesh-COARSE Size**.

8. Click in viewport **C** and repeat steps 4 to 6 for the von Mises stress plot of the **High Quality Mesh-DEFAULT Size**.

9. Finally, click in viewport **D** and repeat steps 4 to 6 for the von Mises stress plot of the **High Quality Mesh-FINE Size** study. This display takes longer to appear due to more data associated with the fine mesh.

Now that results of the four global element size studies are displayed in individual viewports, the screen images can be adjusted according to user preferences. Click in the viewport to be modified and use traditional pan, zoom, rotate, and view options to adjust the image to best display results. Typically the choice of view depends upon those aspects that are of primary importance to a study. For example, a close-up view of the notch might be used to replace one, or all, of the views shown in Fig. 34. Viewports **A**, **B**, **C**, and **D** show trimetric views of each meshed model. To obtain these views, click inside each viewport and select the Trimetric icon. This view is selected because it provides a good overview of mesh size and stress magnitudes that are important to this analysis.

Your graphics screen should look *similar* to Fig. 34. The left side of the graphics screen is minimized to focus attention on results. *Close the Study without saving results.*

What Can Be Learned From This Example?

Most of the primary goals of this analysis were encountered and mastered as you worked through the example itself. Those goals included: knowing 'when,' 'how,' and 'why' a model should be *defeatured*; using the *copy* feature to quickly create new plots and new studies; using multiple *viewports* to facilitate results comparisons; and, most important, using *global mesh refinement* and *local mesh control* as analysis refinement tools. The importance of each capability as part of an overall Finite Element Analysis (FEA) is discussed further in the "Analysis Insight" section below.

Other Uses of the Copy Feature

The *copy* feature within SolidWorks Simulation is not limited to creating new studies in which a change of mesh size is the only analysis variable. In fact, any variable of a finite element analysis can be the central focus in a multiple solution study. For example, other variables that could be altered during a repetitive analysis include, but are not limited to: material properties, loads, fixtures, or modifications to the model geometry itself.

Analysis Insight

The importance of mesh refinement and mesh control as part of a complete finite element analysis cannot be overstated! A single solution to a finite element analysis provides only one snapshot of what a possible solution to a problem might be. A primary reason for performing multiple analyses is to determine whether or not a study is converging to an acceptable solution.

Analysis Insight (continued)

To determine *convergence*, it is possible to examine either stress results or displacement results. From the Introduction to this text, recall that displacements are the primary unknowns in a finite element analysis. From displacements the strains are calculated, and finally, from the strains the stresses are computed. Because displacements are the first link in the solution chain, they are usually a better indicator of convergence to a solution as element size is altered. For the sake of brevity, only vonMises stress results and X-displacement results corresponding to *global* mesh size variation are compared below when testing for convergence.

To relate this discussion to the Notched Bar, **Table 1** summarizes results of all analyses developed in this example. Von Mises stress data and displacement data in **Table 1** are obtained from Fig. 34 and mesh control plots created throughout this study. Information about the number of nodes and elements in each mesh is obtained by right-clicking each **Mesh** folder and selecting **Details…** This procedure was demonstrated in Chapter 1.

In **Table 1**, focus your attention solely on the von Mises stress results column corresponding to the **High** quality mesh contained in the middle three rows of the table. These three rows show how stress magnitude increases as mesh size varies from 'coarse' to 'default' to 'fine.' Casual observation of magnitudes listed in the von Mises stress column reveals an increase of stress as the number of elements increases. This result is expected due to the ability of smaller elements to better delineate stress magnitudes in increasingly smaller regions of high stress gradient. This finding might lead one to expect that as element size gets smaller and smaller, the stress values will continue to grow larger and larger. However, in a properly constructed study quite the opposite is true! In an analysis that is *converging* to a solution, stress results tend to *level off* to some limiting value where that limiting value should represent the best approximation to stress in the model. This is the reason that *multiple* solutions should be a standard part of every finite element analysis (i.e., to determine *convergence* to a solution).

TABLE 1 – Summary of Results from the Notched-Bar Study

Mesh	No. Nodes	No. Elements	vonMises Stress (psi)	Sigma-X (psi)	Displacement X-Direction (in)
DRAFT Quality (Default size)	1,610	6,471	15,257	15,773	0.001877
HIGH Quality (Coarse size)	1,854	1,001	20,717	23,113	0.001894
HIGH Quality (Default size)	10,662	6,471	22,135	23,464	0.001897
HIGH Quality (Fine size)	81,160	54,927	24,560	25,749	0.001898
HIGH Quality (Mesh Control)	12,097	7,354	24,245	25,281	0.001898

Analysis Insight (continued)

If the von Mises stress values are plotted against an increasing number of elements, the graph in Fig. 35 is obtained. Results depicted in Fig. 35 show a slight, as opposed to a rapid, increase of stress corresponding to a doubling of the number of elements from point to point along the abscissa. This trend, while not totally definitive, indicates stress values may be reaching a limiting value.

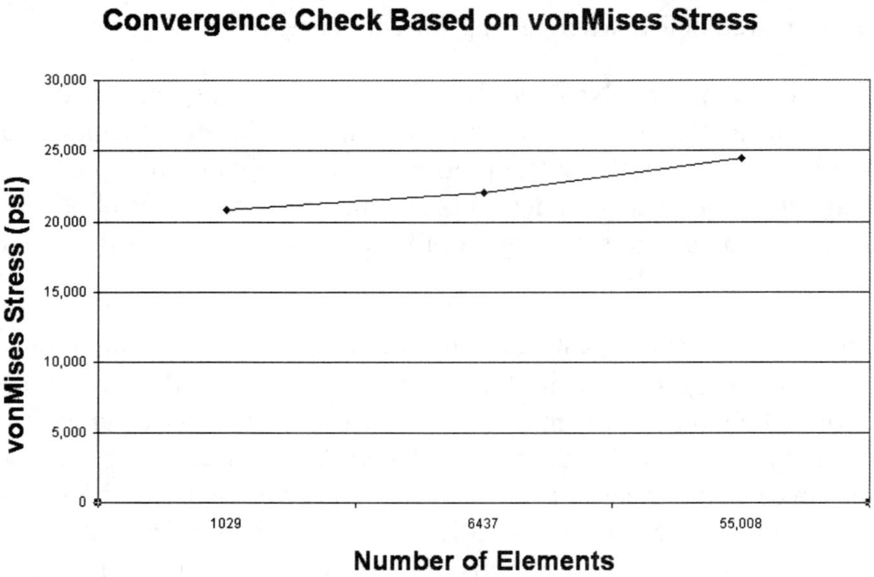

Figure 35 – Convergence check using vonMises stress as a measure.

Displacement versus the number of elements is examined next to determine whether or not it provides a better indication of convergence to a solution than does the von Mises stress. Data in the displacement column of **Table 1** reveals an upward trend as the number of elements increases (i.e., as global mesh size gets smaller).

When plotted, displacement versus number of elements yields the graph shown in Fig. 36. In addition to straight line segments drawn through the data points, a higher-order curve fit was applied to the data resulting in the curved line shown. In either case, the "leveling off" of results (i.e., convergence to a maximum displacement value) is indicative that the solution is converging.

Analysis Insight (continued)

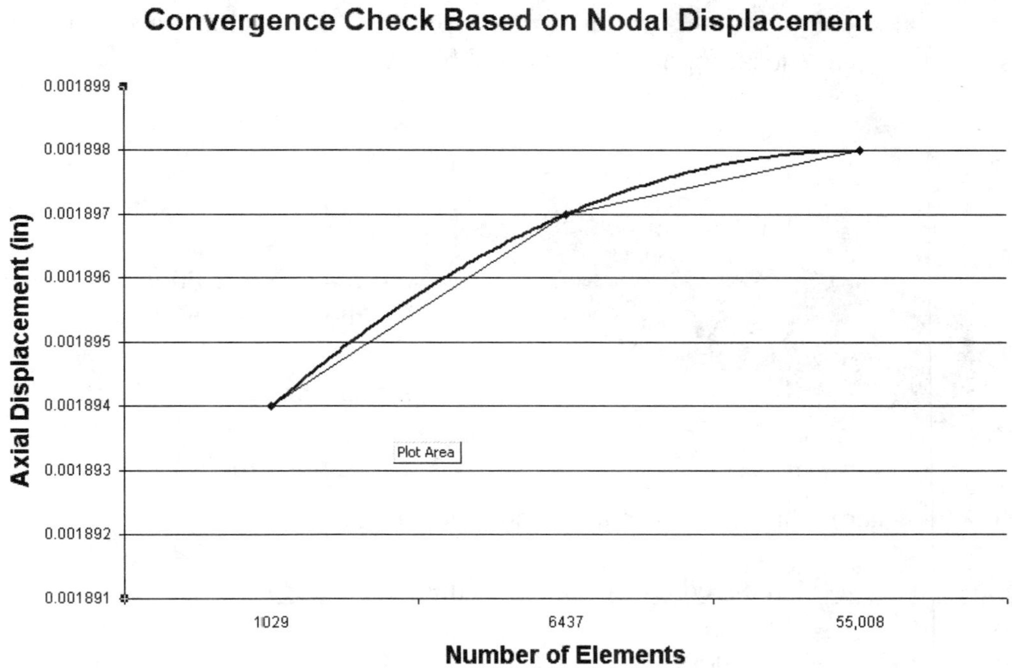

Figure 36 – Convergence check using displacement as a measure.

Summary:
The *need* to conduct more than a single finite element analysis is demonstrated in this example. The *reason* for conducting more than one analysis is to determine whether or not an analysis is approaching a limiting value. This is known as a convergence check.

Aside #1:
Results of the **Draft** quality mesh are *excluded* from the above discussion because it is most revealing to compare results obtained using the same *type* of mesh. All other meshes were **High** quality

Aside #2:
Comparison of displacement results for **Draft** quality and **High** quality meshes of the *same* size, shown in **Table 1**, confirms that a **Draft** quality mesh is stiffer than a **High** quality mesh because smaller displacements result for the **Draft** quality mesh.

Aside #3:
Despite the emphasis on *global* mesh size refinement in this example, perhaps the most important means for controlling mesh size is use of *mesh control*. Mesh control can be applied on a *local* basis and provides accurate results at significantly lower computational overhead. For example, comparing values in **Table 1**, the mesh control approach uses approximately 6.7 times fewer nodes and elements than does a globally **Fine** mesh, yet von Mises stress results differ by less than 1.3%.

Comparison of Classical and FEA Results

The importance of checking finite element results is emphasized throughout this text. Therefore, in keeping with this premise, it is appropriate to conclude this example with a classical analytical check. Figure 2 is repeated below.

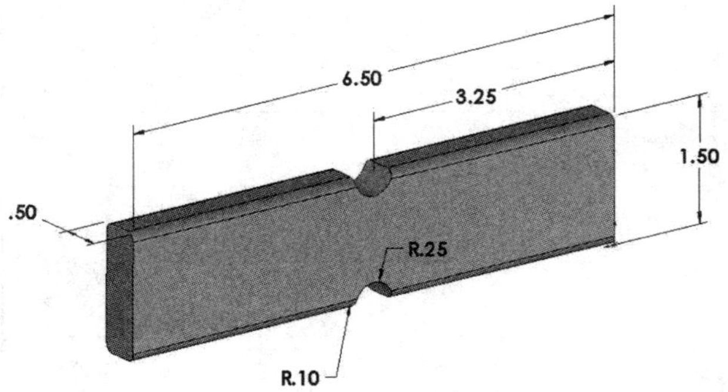

R = notch radius = 0.25 in.

h = height (top to bottom) = 1.50 in

d = h – 2*R = 1.00 in (dimension at the reduced cross-section)

t = bar thickness = 0.50 in

F = applied force = 6000 lb

Figure 2 (repeated) – Dimensioned image of notched bar.

Nominal stress at the reduced cross-section in the Notched Bar:

$$\sigma = \frac{F}{A} = \frac{F}{d*t} = \frac{6000}{1*0.5} = 12000\ psi$$

Geometric stress concentration factor: where: R/d = 0.25/1.00 = 0.25
h/d = 1.50/1.00 = 1.50

K_t = 2.1 (approximate) ← From stress concentration factor chart found in a standard machine design textbook.

Maximum stress in the Notched Bar:

$\sigma_{max} = K_t * \sigma = 2.1 * 12000 = 25200$ psi

Percent difference:

% Difference = [(SolidWorks Simulation – Classic)/ (SolidWorks Simulation)] * 100

% Difference = [(25749 – 25200)/(25749] * 100 = 2.13%

Note that Sigma-X (σ_x) is used for comparison purposes since the classical equations for stress concentration depend upon axial stress as opposed to vonMises stress. The above calculations provide a good check of finite element results. Note that resultant stress $(\sigma_x)_{Max}$ predicted by the mesh control model yields a 0.32 % difference.

EXERCISES

End of chapter exercises are intended to provide additional practice using principles introduced in the current chapter plus capabilities mastered in preceding chapters. Most exercises include multiple parts. In an academic setting, it is likely that parts of problems will be assigned or modified to suit specific course goals.

╬ ***Designates problems that introduce new concepts. Solution guidance is provided for these problems.***

EXERCISE 1 – Effect of Mesh Size at Hole Location

A rectangular bar with a centrally drilled hole is illustrated in Fig. E 3-1. The bar is supported **(Fixed/immovable)** at its left-end and subject to an axial, tensile force of 370 kN applied normal to its opposite end. The bar is made from 2018 aluminum alloy. Open the file: **Plate With Hole 3-1**.

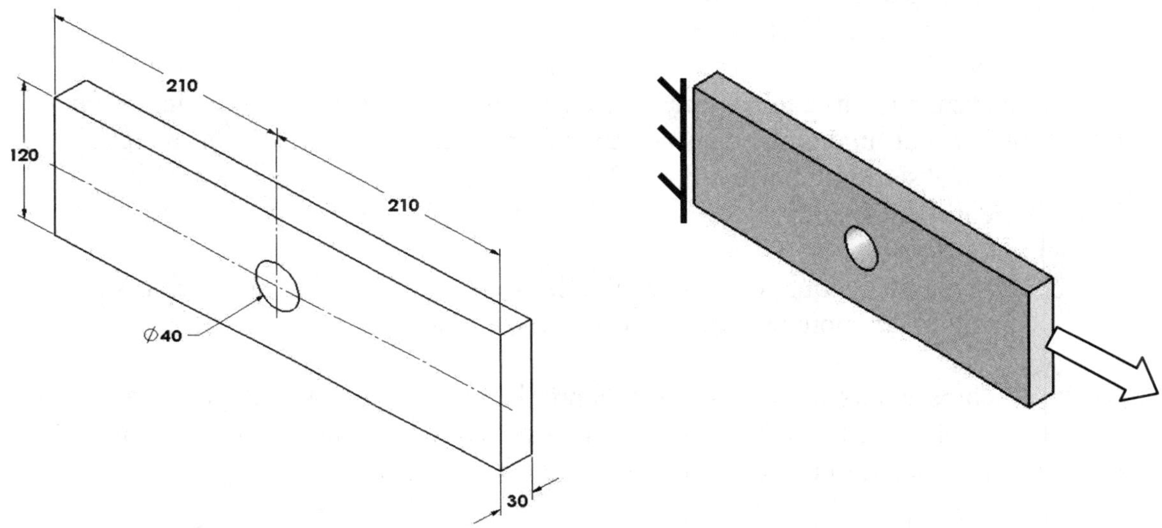

Figure E3-1 – Aluminum bar with central hole subject to an axial force. A geometric discontinuity is present in the form of the 40 mm diameter hole.

- Material: **2018 Alloy** aluminum (Use S.I. units)
- Mesh: **High Quality** tetrahedral elements. Use three different meshes as specified in parts (a, c, and d) below.
- Fixture: **Fixed** (Immovable) applied to left end.
- External Load: **370 kN** applied normal to the right-end causing tension in the bar.

Develop a finite element model that includes: material specification, fixtures, external loads, mesh generation, and solution as specified below. For this analysis use high quality meshes of the sources specified below and perform the following:

Determine the following:

a. Using a *default* size mesh, create a contour plot of the *most appropriate stress* to permit comparison of stress magnitude adjacent to the hole with that predicted by classical equations for stress computed at the same location. See part (e) for calculation of classical results. Include fixtures, external load, and the mesh on this plot.

b. Use the **Probe** feature to produce a graph of the *most appropriate stress* from the top (or bottom) edge of the bar to the edge of the central hole. Because a straight path may not be available, choose both corner and mid-side nodes in as straight a line as possible.

c. Repeat part (b) after resetting the mesh size to *fine*. Use the copy feature to save time creating this study.

d. Repeat part (b) a third time after resetting the mesh size by applying *mesh control* around both edges and the inner surface of the hole. Use a mesh control setting: **Ratio a/b** = **1.2**. Also use the copy feature to save time creating this study.

e. Use classical equations and available stress concentration factor charts to manually compute maximum stress at the hole.

f. Compare maximum stress results predicted using the three different meshes with that predicted by classical stress equations. Compute the percent difference for each comparison using equation [1].

$$\%\ \text{difference} = \frac{(\text{FEA result - classical result})}{\text{FEA result}} * 100 = \qquad [1]$$

g. Comment upon which FEA results are in best agreement with predictions of the classical equations? Which method of mesh refinement is usually preferred and why?

h. Based upon results for the maximum *appropriate stress* in the model, is the material Yield Strength exceeded? If "yes," what does theory predict will be the outcome in a ductile material such as Aluminum used in this example?

EXERCISE 2 - Effect of Mesh Size at Shaft Fillet

A cylindrical rod changes diameter at the fillet shown in the Fig. E3-2. It is well known that generous fillets are beneficial in reducing stress concentration at changes of cross-section. This is particularly important because the bar in question is made from a relatively brittle material, gray cast iron, and the fillet radius is not very large. As such, the rod is subject to significant effects of stress concentration at the geometric discontinuity. Consider the rod supported **(Immovable/Fixed)** at its left-end and subject to a 1,200 lb tensile force applied to its opposite end.

Open the file: **Shaft with Fillet 3-2**.

- Material: **Gray Cast Iron** (Use English units)
- Mesh: **High Quality** tetrahedral elements. Use three different meshes as specified below.
- Fixture: **Fixed** applied to left end of shaft.
- External Load: 1,200 lb applied normal to the right-end causing tension in the bar.

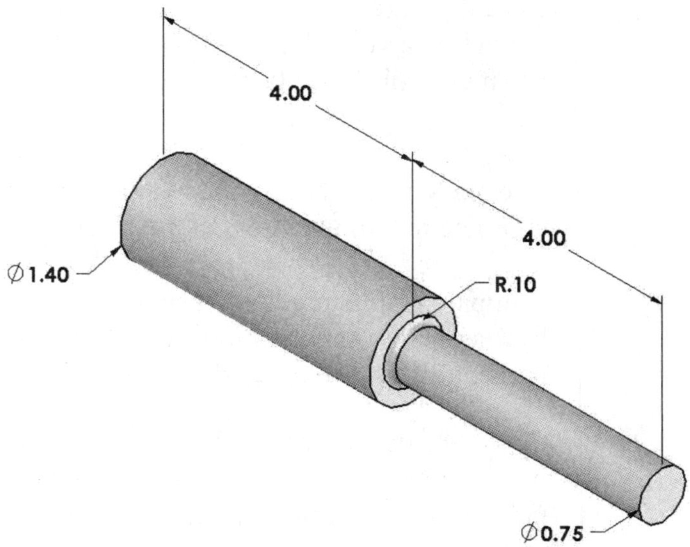

Figure E3-2 – Gray Cast Iron cylindrical rod subject to an axial tensile load of 1,200 lb.

Determine the following:
Develop a finite element model that includes: material specification, fixtures, applied external load, mesh generation (as specified below), and solution.

NOTE: This example is one where it is *not* appropriate to defeature the model because deleting the fillet radius would cause a dramatic increase of stress at the change of shaft diameter. In fact, a sharp fillet would probably result in stress values continuing to increase as the mesh size gets smaller. This is an example of a solution where *divergence* from a solution rather than *convergence* to a solution would occur.

a. Develop a finite element model using a default size, high quality mesh. For this mesh, perform the following:

   - Create a stress contour plot of the *most appropriate stress* to permit comparison of stress magnitude in the vicinity of the fillet with that predicted by classical stress equations computed at the same location. Include a mesh on this plot.

- Use the **Probe** feature to produce a graph of the *most appropriate stress* commencing approximately ½ in to the right of the fillet and progressing, in as near a straight-line as possible, through the fillet area up to the outside diameter of the left segment (large diameter segment) of the shaft. Choose both corner and mid-side nodes.

b. Repeat part (a) after resetting the mesh size to fine. Use the copy feature to save time creating this study.

c. Repeat part (a) again beginning with the default size mesh. Use the copy feature to save time creating this study. Then, alter the mesh by applying mesh control on the fillet. Use a mesh control ratio setting of: **Ratio a/b** = **1.2**.

d. Use classical equations and available stress concentration factor charts to compute maximum stress at the fillet.

e. Compare results predicted using the three different meshes with that predicted by classical stress equations; clearly label each calculation. Compute the percent difference for each comparison using equation [1] (repeated).

$$\% \text{ difference} = \frac{(\text{FEA result - classical result})}{\text{FEA result}} * 100 = \qquad [1]$$

f. Determine the Safety Factor, or lack thereof at the change of cross-section (i.e., at the fillet). Create a plot showing regions (if any) of the model with Safety Factor less than two. Note: Cast iron, being a brittle material, has an ultimate strength rather than a yield strength. Account for this fact when determining safety factor.

g. Comment upon which FEA results are in best agreement with predictions of the classical equations? Based on your comparison, which method of mesh refinement is preferred and why?

h. For users conversant with modifying solid models in SolidWorks, proceed to alter the fillet radius at the change of cross-section to a radius equal to half the difference of the two shaft sizes [r = (D – d)/2] and repeat parts assigned by your instructor. Report the amount by which it is possible to reduce stress at the fillet.

⩩ EXERCISE 3 - Stress in a Lawn Mower Blade due to Centrifugal Force (Special Topics: Custom Material, Centrifugal Force, Soft Spring Supports)

Dimensions of a typical steel lawn mower blade are shown in Fig. E3-3. The density used for steel is 0.282 lb/in^3. For simplicity, the blade is modeled as having a uniform cross section with a centrally drilled 0.50 inch diameter hole. The goal is to determine maximum stress in the blade in the vicinity of the central hole. The blade rotates at 3000 rpm and, hence, is subject to centrifugal force. Due to the highly variable nature of "mowing forces" acting on the blade (caused by different grass heights), mowing forces are to be neglected.

Develop a finite element model that includes: material specification, applied centrifugal force, mesh generation, and solution. Solution guidance is provided relative to the application of a *centrifugal load* and the need for *soft spring* supports.

Open the file: **Lawn Mower Blade**

- Material: Steel properties not found in the Material table (use properties below).
  Elastic Modulus: **30 000 000** psi
  Poisson's Ratio: **0.292**
  Density: **0.282** lb/in^3
  Yield strength: **60 000** psi

- Mesh: **High Quality** tetrahedral elements; use the default size mesh.

- Fixture: **Soft Spring** See Solution Guidance section below for application details.

- External Load: None. Load is due to internal centrifugal forces cause by 2800 rpm.

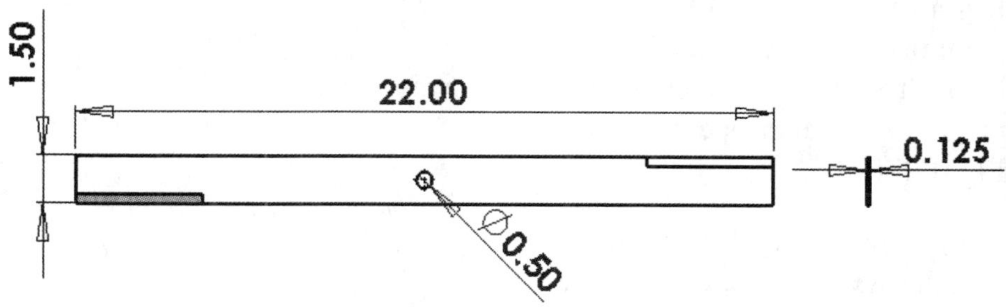

Figure E3-3 – Basic dimensions of a typical lawn mower blade.

Three aspects of the current exercise are unique. First, the blade made from a custom material that is not available in the SolidWorks material library. Second, a centrifugal force is applied to load the model. Centrifugal force is not an *external* force. Instead it is a load caused by high speed rotation. Guidance on these two topics is provided below. Third, no **Fixtures** are applied to this model. Therefore, **Soft Springs** must be applied to maintain equilibrium. (See Chapter #1, pg. 1-36 at top bullet; to bottom of pg. 1-37).

Solution Guidance

Custom Material Specification (It is assumed that the user has started a Study in SolidWorks Simulation.)

- Open the **Material** window by right-clicking the **Part** folder and selecting **Apply/Edit Material…**
- Beneath **Select material source**, choose ⊙ **Custom defined**.
- On the **Properties** tab, located in the right half of the window, select **Units:** as **English (IPS)**.
- Change **Category:** to **Mower Blade** and in the **Description** field, type **Custom Steel**.
- Within the left column of the lower table notice that red, blue, and black colors are used to indicate different **Property** names. Red lettering indicates information *required* for the solution. Blue lettering indicates *desirable, but unnecessary* information. And, property names appearing in black *are not required* for the current solution. Enter the values listed beneath "Material" in the problem statement. Ignore blank fields and values listed in black type.
- Click **[OK]** to close the **Material** window. A check "✓" appears on the **Lawn Mower Blade** part folder.

Centrifugal Force Specification

- Right-click **External Loads** and from the pull-down menu select **Centrifugal…** The **Centrifugal** property manager opens as shown in Fig. E3-4.
- In the **Selected Reference** dialogue box the **Axis, Edge, Cylindrical Face for Direction** field is highlighted (light blue). Select the *inside* cylindrical *surface* of the hole.

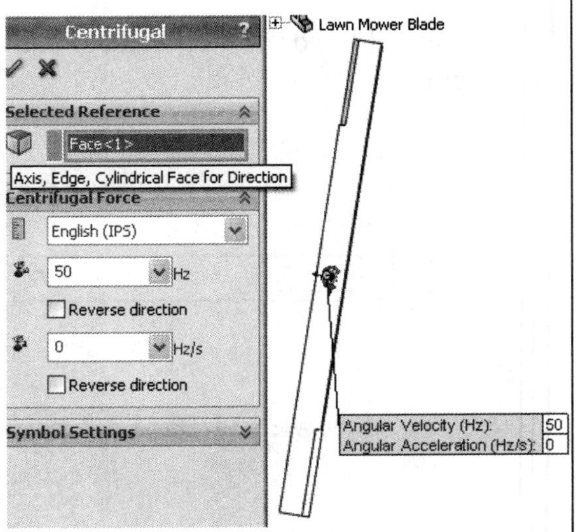

Figure E3-4 – Specifying a **Centrifugal** force on a mower blade rotating at 3000 RPM.

- Convert the blade rotation speed of 3000 rpm to **Hz** (i.e., cycles/second or rpm/sec).

Solution Guidance (continued)

- In the **Centrifugal Force** dialogue box, verify that **Unit** is set to **English (IPS)** and in the **Angular Velocity** dialogue box, type the rotational speed calculated in the previous step. After typing this value, a red arrow appears at the hole to indicate the direction of rotation. If rotation is not in the direction of the cutting edges of the blade (sides with tapered edges), then check ☑ **Reverse Direction**.

- Click **[OK]** ✓ to close the **Centrifugal** property manager.

<u>**Rigid Body Motion Prevention (Soft Springs)**</u>

As noted above, **Soft Springs** must be applied to the model prior to running the solution. The lawn mower blade of this exercise is analogous to the Yoshida Buckling model of Chapter 1. Therefore, follow the procedures for applying **Soft Springs** beginning on top of page 1-35 and apply them to this example.

Determine the following:

Develop a finite element model that includes: material specification, soft springs, applied external load (centrifugal force), mesh generation, and solution.

a. After running the solution and obtaining the **Results** folder, edit the **Stress1 (-vonMises-)** plot by doing the following.
   - Turn off the ☐ **Deformed Shape**. You will know when the deformed shape is turned off because the centrifugal force arrow will again appear at the central hole.
   - Display **Discrete** fringes on the model
   - Display the **Mesh** on the model
   - Turn on ☑ **Show max annotation**
   - Next, *copy* the **Stress1 (-vonMises-)** plot. Then change the copied plot to display **P1: 1st Principal Stress**. Also, re-name this plot to reflect its true identity. Zoom in on the central hole and create a plot of the σ_1 stress contours.
   - Repeat the preceding step, except create a plot of **SX: X Normal Stress**.

b. Zoom in on the central hole of the mower blade that displays a plot of **P1: First Principal Stress**. Then, use the **Probe** tool to select all corner and mid-side nodes beginning at the top or bottom inner edge of the hole and proceeding outward to the *nearest* side of the blade. When selecting nodes, traverse the model in the straightest line possible. Create a graph of this data. Alter the graph title and axes labels to better describe information contained on the graph.

c. Repeat step (b) to produce a graph showing the variation of **SX: X Normal Stress** at the same location on the model.

d. Manually calculate the nominal tensile stress at the center of the blade caused by blade rotation. Include the labeled free-body diagram used as the basis of this calculation. Also, show the calculation used to determine maximum stress at the hole location. Include a reference to the stress concentration factor chart used to make this calculation. Label each calculation. Simplify the analysis as follows. *HINT:* For the manual calculation *only*, create a free-body diagram of half of the mower blade as shown in Fig. E3-5. Assume half of the blade mass is located at the center of mass "**G.**"

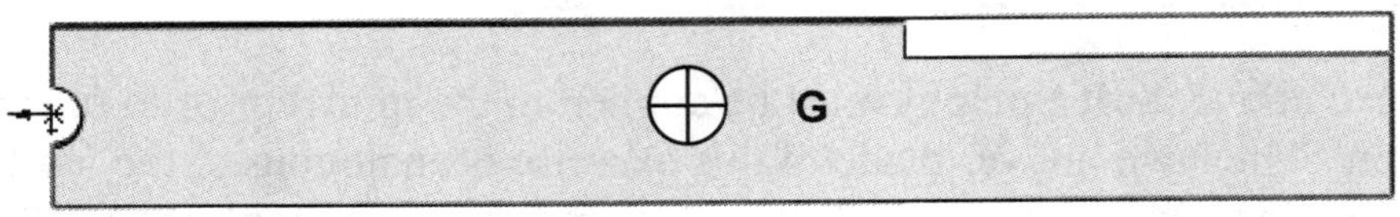

Figure E3-5 – Suggested model to be used as a free-body diagram for manual calculations *only*. Do *not* use the above model for finite element analysis.

e. Use equation [1], repeated below, to compare percent differences between manually calculated maximum stress values and **P1: First Principal Stress** and **SX: X Normal Stress** calculated using the finite element approach. Which of these stresses is in best agreement with finite element results? Why?

$$\% \text{ difference} = \frac{(\text{FEA result - classical result})}{\text{FEA result}} * 100 = \qquad [1]$$

Textbook Problems
In addition to the above exercises, it is highly recommended that additional problems involving stress concentration and/or significant changes of part geometry be worked from a design of machine elements or mechanics of materials textbook. Textbook problems provide a great way to discover errors made in formulating a finite element analysis because they typically are well defined problems for which the solution is known. Typical textbook problems, if well defined in advance, make an excellent source of solutions for comparison.

CHAPTER #4

THIN AND THICK WALL PRESSURE VESSELS

This chapter investigates modeling of thin and thick wall pressure vessels. More importantly, however, the use of *shell* elements is introduced and guidelines are provided regarding their use as opposed to *solid* tetrahedral elements. When taken alone, thin and thick wall pressure vessel problems are solvable in rather a straight forward manner by using classical stress equations. Therefore, advantages of the Finite Element Analysis (FEA) approach are realized most when investigating stresses in more geometrically complex regions of a pressure vessel. These regions include, but are not limited to, locations of pipe connections, saddles, or other flanges or support structures associated with pressure vessel design and installation. Many of these special situations can be handled by application of principles outlined in preceding chapters. Thus, the two examples of this chapter focus on introducing additional capabilities of the finite element software rather than on pressure vessels per se'.

Learning Objectives

Upon completion of this example, users should be able to:

- Convert a solid model to a part modeled using *shell* elements, and use a *shell* mesh to model thin-wall parts (whether or not the part is a pressure vessel).
- Change *system default* settings to simplify analyses with common characteristics.
- Recognize part *symmetry* and use it to reduce solution size and computation time. Know when and how to apply *symmetrical restraints*.
- Apply *section clipping* to enhance viewing of results.
- Apply uniform *pressure* loading.

THIN-WALL PRESSURE VESSEL

Thin-wall pressure vessels are found in many common applications. Included among them are carbonated beverage containers (aluminum cans and plastic bottles), aerosol cans used to dispense everything from hair spray to paint, hydraulic cylinders, steam boilers, and tall water tower tanks that provide pressure to public water systems.

Problem Statement

This example is based on a thin-wall cylindrical pressure vessel closed on both ends with hemispherical heads as illustrated in Figs.1(a) and (b). Wall thickness t = 3 mm and inside diameter of the cylinder d_i = 144 mm. The vessel is made of **AISI 1045** cold drawn steel and is subject to an internal pressure **P = 1.4 MPa**. Other dimensions are included in Fig. 1(a). A typical application for a similar vessel is shown in Fig. 1(b).

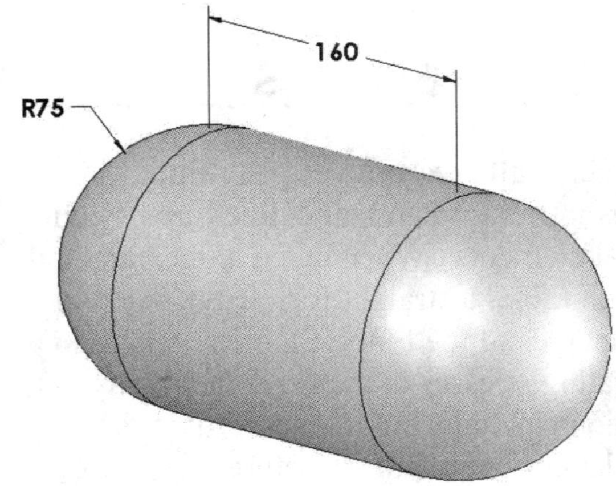

Figure 1(a) – Basic dimensions of a thin-wall pressure vessel closed with hemispherical ends.

Figure 1(b) – Pressurized cylindrical fuel tank at construction site during winter.

The dividing line between thin and thick wall pressure vessels is defined differently in various machine design[1] and mechanics of materials texts. If wall thickness "t" falls in the range where $t \leq r_i/20$ to $t \leq r_i/5$, (where, r_i = cylinder inside radius) then the cylinder is considered a thin-wall pressure vessel. This determination must be made at the outset of any pressure vessel problem because choice of the appropriate set of classical equations depends upon whether wall thickness is classified as "thin" or "thick." By either definition above, the current model can be considered a thin-wall pressure vessel since the minimum criteria yields: $t = 3$ mm $\leq$ (72 mm)/20. Another assumption applied to thin-wall pressure vessels is that magnitude of the tangential stress (σ_t), also known as "hoop" stress or "circumferential" stress, is assumed *uniform* through the wall thickness.

Primary stresses in the pressure vessel walls are given by:

Tangential stress: $$\sigma_t = \frac{p * d_i}{2 * t} = \frac{(1.4e6 \frac{N}{m^2})(0.144 \cancel{m})}{2(0.003 \cancel{m})} = 33.6e6 \text{ Pa} \qquad [1]$$

Longitudinal stress: $$\sigma_\ell = \frac{p * d_i}{4 * t} = \frac{1}{2}\sigma_t = \frac{1}{2}(33.6e6 \text{ Pa}) = 16.8e6 \text{ Pa} \qquad [2]$$

(for a closed-end cylinder)

Where: p = pressure (N/m^2) = 1.4 MPa
t = wall thickness (m) = 0.003 m
d_i = inside diameter (m) = 0.150 m – 2*0.003 m = 0.144 m

These two stresses are perpendicular to sides of a stress element aligned with and perpendicular to the longitudinal axis of the cylinder shown in Fig. 2. Because no shear stresses act on sides of the element shown in Fig. 2, σ_t and σ_ℓ are principal stresses.

[1] Budynas, R.G., Nisbett, J.K., Shigley's Mechanical Engineering Design, use: $t \leq r_i/20$.
Collins, J.A., Mechanical Design of Machine Elements, uses: $t \leq 10\% * d = (.1)(2*r) = r_i/5$.

Finally, all stresses on the hemispherical ends are tangential stresses, but their magnitude is half of that in the cylindrical portion of the vessel.

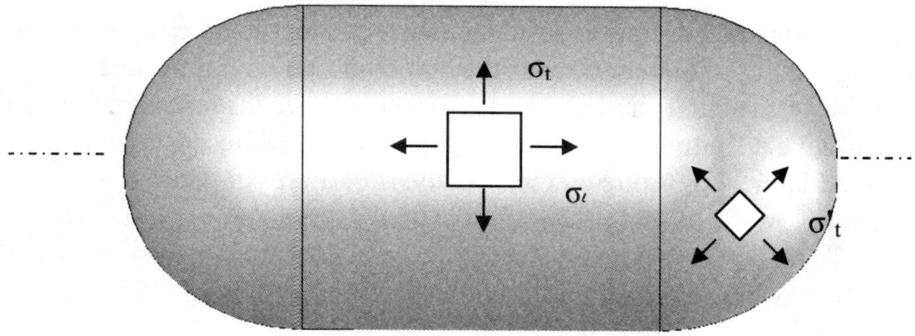

Figure 2 – Stress elements showing orientation of σ_t and σ_ℓ on the pressure vessel surface and on the hemispherical end. ($\sigma'_t = \frac{1}{2}\,\sigma_t$)

Due to St. Venant's principle, normal stresses depicted in Fig. 2 are only valid at locations well removed from the junction between the cylindrical section and the hemispherical ends where end-conditions exist. Thus, to permit comparison with results of equations [1] and [2], the following finite element analysis focuses on stresses near the mid-section of the cylinder and on the hemispherical heads.

The next decision to be made is whether to use *solid* or *shell* elements for the finite element model. The guideline for this decision is quite different than that applied above to determine what set of classical equations should be used. For the current model, it is possible to use either *solid* or *shell* elements. Both would produce valid results. However, the selection of element type has a significant influence on the number of elements in a model, and hence upon solution time and memory requirements. Draft and high quality shell elements are pictured in Figs. 3 (a) and (b).

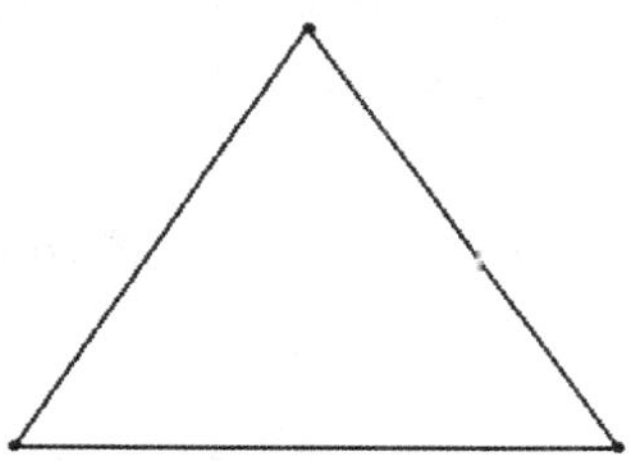

Figure 3 (a) – First-order (draft quality) triangular shell element.

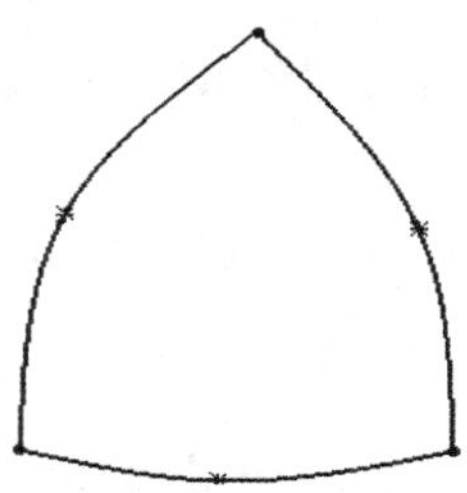

Figure 3 (b) – Second-order shell element includes three additional mid-side nodes.

Shell elements are typically used for sheet metal and other thin parts. The principle used to decide what element type to use is that *shell* elements are applied when the thickness to span ratio is less than 0.05. For the current model, if the cylinder were laid out flat, the wall thickness (3 mm) divided by the cylinder circumference ($\pi d_i^2/4 = \pi(144)^2/4 = 16286$ mm) yields: 3 mm/16286 mm = 0.0018 which is < 0.05. "Span ratio" is not well defined within SolidWorks. However, a simpler guideline to decide what element type to use is that *solid* elements are applied when two (default size) elements fit nicely across the thickness of the part (i.e., across the part's minimum dimension).

Shell elements look somewhat similar to solid elements except they are represented graphically as a single layer of elements, as if they were drawn on a thin sheet of paper. Later images will illustrate actual shell elements. However, because parts modeled using shell elements must have a finite thickness, a corresponding thickness is assigned to shell elements as described later. The finite element analysis of a pressure vessel using shell elements is outlined below.

1. Open SolidWorks by making the following selections. (*Note:* "/" is used to separate successive menu selections.)

Start/All Programs/SolidWorks 2009 (or) Click the **SolidWorks** icon on your screen.

2. From the main menu within SolidWorks select **File / Open**. Then proceed to where your files are saved and open the SolidWorks Simulation file named **Thin Wall Pressure Vessel**. *It is strongly suggested that this model file be used for the current example rather than a user created pressure vessel model.*

Understanding System Default Settings

This section digresses from the problem solution to investigate methods of changing system default settings. Changing system default settings at the start of a Study can be advantageous because it can save time throughout the remainder of an analysis. For example, earlier problems required frequent specification of items such as mesh quality, units, and other attributes of an analysis. However, if these attributes are specified one time at the start of an analysis, they remain constant throughout the remainder of the problem. To practice altering some of these parameters, proceed as follows.

1. In the main menu, at top of screen, click **Simulation** to open a pop-up menu.

2. Near the bottom of this menu, select **Options...** The **Systems Options – General** window opens as shown in Fig. 4.

In this window, the **Systems Options** tab is initially selected as illustrated in Fig. 4. In the list at left of this window, the word **General** is highlighted to denote what settings are currently displayed. Because the current study focuses on use of a shell mesh, in the right half of this window, observe the default color scheme used to denote the bottom surface of shell elements. The text **Shell bottom face color** appears next to the system default color, orange, indicated adjacent to the arrow in Fig. 4. Before proceeding, observe other system default settings in this window. In particular, note that items such as ☑ **Show errors**, and ☑ **Show warnings** are checked. These two items were observed in the example of the previous chapter. Also, notice that ☑ **Show yield strength marker for vonMises plots** is checked thereby establishing it as a default display item on von Mises stress plots. Recall that this feature was used in the curved beam analysis of Chapter 2.

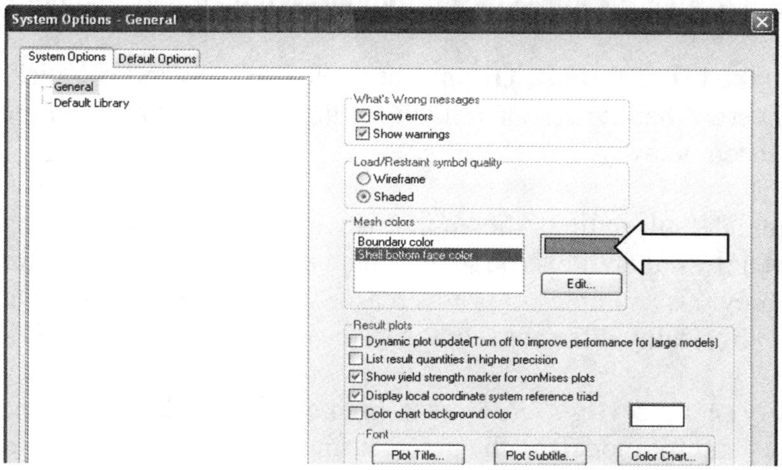

Figure 4 – Default settings beneath the **System Options** tab. Default color of the bottom surface of a shell mesh is shown here.

3. Next click the **Default Options** tab. Within this tab **Units** is highlighted (gray) to indicate it is selected in the list at the upper-left of the window. Only the right-half of this window is illustrated in Fig. 5. Within this window, the settings should appear as listed below. Note that SI units are default within SolidWorks Simulation; if not, change to the settings shown.

   - Beneath **Unit System**, set default units to ⊙ **SI [MKS]**, if not already selected.
   - Beneath **Units**, the unit of **Length/ Displacement**: should be set to **m** (meters).
   - Adjacent to **Pressure/Stress:**, default units should be set to **N/m^2**. Other units do not pertain to this analysis and can be ignored.

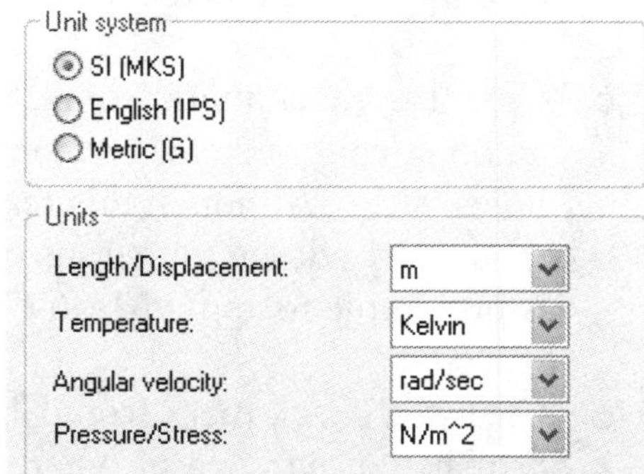

Figure 5 – Selecting units to be applied throughout the analysis.

Specifying units as outlined above establishes a common set of units for an entire analysis. If, for example, your company or future employer uses English units exclusively, it would be a time-saver to reset default units accordingly. This could have been done for English unit examples worked in Chapters 1 and 2.

4. Return to the list of **Default Options** tab at the left of this window and click to select **Load/Fixture**, the **Default Options – Load/Fixture** window is displayed.

Brief examination of the right-half of the window (not shown) reveals that the **Symbol size** and **Symbol colors** for various types of loads and restraints can be specified here. Although nothing is changed in this window, color-blind users may find it beneficial to alter default **Symbol colors** to suit their personal preferences.

5. Next, from the list of **Default Options** at the left of the window, click to select **Mesh** and verify that the system default settings in the right half of the window appear as listed below.

Knowing the system default settings shown in this window and understanding that they remain unchanged unless altered by you, makes unnecessary many of the often repeated steps included in previous examples. For this reason, a brief explanation of each setting is included below. Reset any different settings to the default values listed below.

- **Mesh Quality** set to ⊙ **High**. *Reason*: A high quality mesh is recommended for most analyses and for models with curved surfaces. A draft quality mesh is typically only used for an initial study where quick, approximate results are adequate.

- **Jacobian check** set to **[4 points]**. *Reason*: This option sets the number of integration points used when checking distortion levels in tetrahedral elements. The **4 points** selection is adequate for most analyses. Although **4** is the standard value, **6** points are automatically used for a shell mesh. Thus no change is necessary.

- **Mesher type** set to ⊙ **Standard**. *Reason*: The **Standard** mesher is faster and produces good results for most models. It is faster than the **Curvature based** meshing scheme listed at the bottom of this box.

- Clear the check mark from ☐ **Automatic transition**. *Reason*: This option automatically reduces element size at *every* change of geometry (fillets, rounds, holes, etc.). Although this feature is nice, it unnecessarily complicates complex models by adding numerous nodes and elements in regions of little or no interest. It is preferable to apply **Mesh Control** (Chapter 3) only in regions of interest.

- Clear the check mark from ☐ **Automatic trials for solids**. *Reason*: This option is primarily used in cases where meshing difficulty is encountered. It is not demonstrated in this text.

- Clear the check mark from ☐ **Remesh failed parts with incompatible mesh**. *Reason*: This option is used where meshing difficulty occurs between bonded, solid parts by attempting to use incompatible mesh types. These instances are not encountered in this text.

- Check to select ☑ **Automatic shell surface re-alignment for non-composite shells**. *Reason*: This option causes the software to automatically reorient top and bottom surfaces of shell elements so that they are consistent within a model.

Ignore remaining options within this window.

6. Next, from the **Default Options** list, select **Results**. Verify that the **Default solver** is set as ⦿ **FFEPlus**. *Reason:* **FFEPlus** is the fastest solver available in SolidWorks Simulation.

7. Other options in this window direct analysis results to system default folders within SolidWorks. Unless other guidelines for file storage exist within your organization (university or company), use the default settings and ignore other settings in this window.

8. Return to the **Default Options** list and select **Plot**. The **Default Options - Plot** window opens. The right-half of this window is shown in Fig. 6.

9. Within this window, set **Fringe options:** to **Discrete**. This is a user preference, but is typically selected as **Discrete** in this text due to enhanced image characteristics when printed in black, white, and gray tones.

10. Adjacent to **Boundary options:** select **Model** to show a black outline of the model. *Reason:* This option helps identify model boundaries when stress contour plots are viewed on complex shapes or where "clipping" is used. This selection is also a user preference.

11. Another user preference is whether or not to display results on the deformed or undeformed shape of the model. Although this text typically elects display of the undeformed model, accept the default choice ⦿ **Show results on deformed shape**. Changes will be made on a case by case basis.

Familiarize yourself with other settings within this window. Other settings should remain set to system defaults.

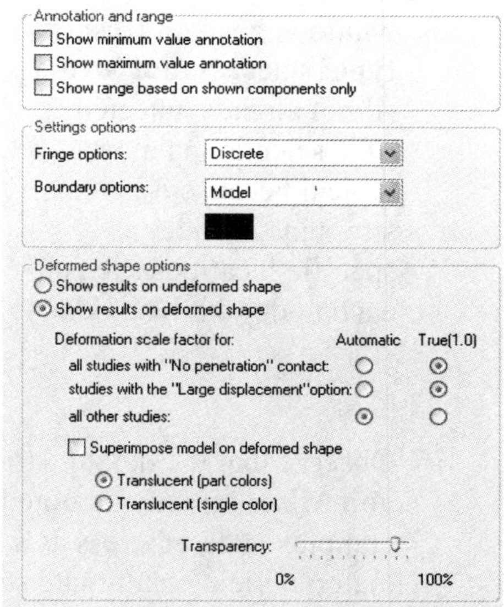

Figure 6 – The **Plot** window is used to specify display options for all plots.

12. Next, in the **Default Options** list, click **Color Chart** and briefly observe items the user can control regarding display characteristics of the color chart including its placement on the screen, its size, and the format of numbers listed adjacent to the chart. In the **Number format** box, select **Scientific(e)** and set **No. of decimal places:** to **3**. Make no other changes to default settings.

A nice feature about using the above capabilities is that each and every plot in the current and future studies can be produced with the same set of user selected settings. Pre-setting these parameters for all plots saves considerable time when a consistent set of plot characteristics is desired. However, using these capabilities does not preclude a user from altering characteristics of a particular plot at any point during a Study.

We next investigate default settings of all plots created during a Study.

13. Click the "+" sign adjacent to **Default Plots** (if not already selected) and a listing of system default plots appears as shown on the left-side of Fig. 7.

14. At the left of the screen, below the **Static Study Results** folder, click to highlight the <u>*name*</u> **Plot1**. As of this writing, selecting the icon adjacent to **Plot1** does not activate this selection. The right half of the screen image, shown in Fig. 7, appears.

15. In the right-half of the window, beneath **Results type:** select **Nodal Stress** (if not already selected). This selection is most typical because it gives stress magnitudes at specific locations (i.e., at each node) on the model.

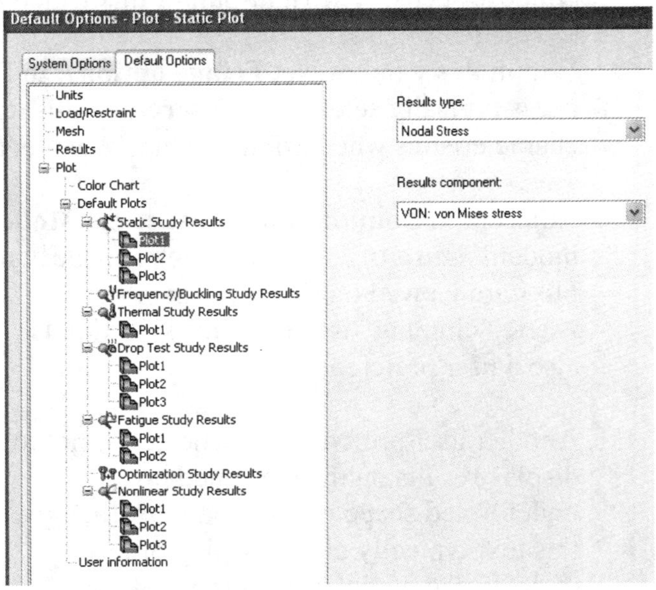

Figure 7 – Individual plots are pre-defined to indicate items and components to be plotted.

16. Observe that the default stress plot listed beneath **Results component:** is **VON: von Mises stress**. As noted in Chapter 2, von Mises stress represents the most complex state of stress as a single value. As such, its value is easily compared to material yield or ultimate strength to give an indication of the safety, or lack thereof, in a part. This reason alone justifies it as worthy of being designated a default plot.
17. Return to the list of plots at the left of the screen and click the *name* **Plot2**. In the right-half of the screen observe **Displacement** as the **Results type:** and **URES: Resultant Displacement** for the **Results component:**.

18. Finally, click the *name* **Plot3** and observe the default definition of this plot is **Elemental Strain** as the **Results type:** and **ESTRN: Equivalent Strain** in the **Results component:** field.

Contents of the three default plot folders are based on the assumption that most users are interested in magnitudes of vonMises stress, model displacement, and strain in the model. Although this is a logical assumption, this text focuses primarily on stress results.

If additional default plots are desired, they can be added now or in the future. To demonstrate how to add an additional default plot, proceed as follows.

19. Right-click **Static Study Results** and from the pop-up menu, select **Add New Plot** as shown in Fig. 8. Immediately **Plot4** is added to the bottom of the current list.

    Define the contents of this new plot as follows.

20. In the right-side of the window, beneath **Results type:**, select **Nodal Stress** from the pull-down menu (if not already selected).

21. Beneath **Results component:**, select **P1: 1st Principal Stress**.

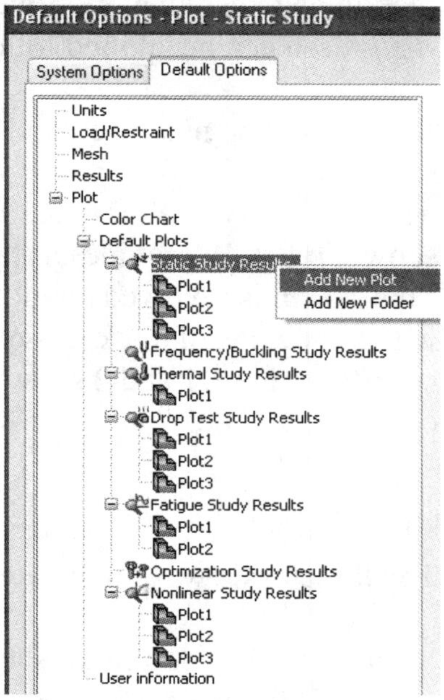

Figure 8 – Adding a new plot and including user information on all printed plots.

OBSERVATION:
Because the current Study involves analysis of stresses in the walls of a cylindrical pressure vessel, it is known in advance that tangential and longitudinal stresses will result. Further, it is well known that tangential stress (σ_t) and longitudinal stress (σ_ℓ) correspond to the first and second principal stresses (σ_1 and σ_2) respectively. Therefore, *if* a user were dealing with pressure vessel analysis on a routine basis, it might make sense to add plots of the first and second principal stresses to the *default* set of plots produced at the conclusion of every study. However, since that is not the case for future examples included in this text, **Plot4** is deleted in the following step.

22. Right-click **Plot4** and from the pop-up menu, select **Delete**.

The above overview should provide sufficient insight so that users can access the **Default Options** window at the start of a Study to define characteristics they wish to apply. This action can save considerable time when common settings are used throughout a study.

23. Click the **[OK]** button to close the **Default Options** window.

CAUTION: As of this writing (SolidWorks Simulation 2009, Service Pack 2.2) *only some* of the features above function as described. Many other changes to default settings do not take effect despite their being altered in the **Default Options** window.

Creating a Static Analysis Using Shell Elements

Because *shell* elements require special preparation of the model within SolidWorks, this section begins with a brief overview of the basic methods of creating models to which a *shell* mesh can be applied followed by a walk-through of the actual steps.

The process begins by creating the part model within SolidWorks. For the thin wall pressure vessel, the line sketch, shown in Fig. 9, provides a starting point. This sketch is revolved about the X-axis at which time a wall thickness of 3 mm is specified. Figs. 1 and 2 show the completed model.

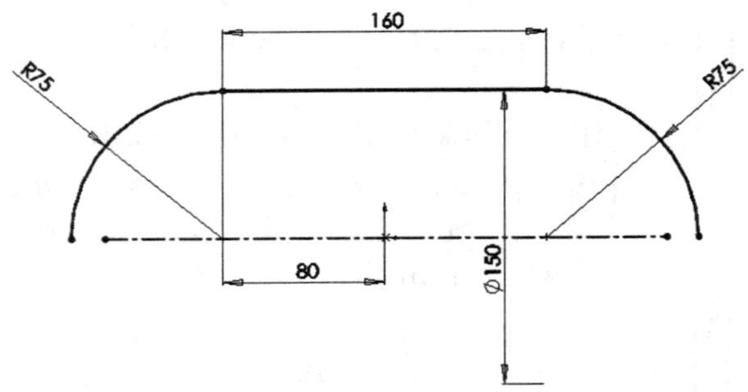

Figure 9 – Line sketch used to generate the solid model.

The three basic ways to create a *shell* model are described briefly below.

a. First, by definition sheet metal parts are considered 'thin' by their very nature. These parts are automatically modeled as *shell* elements as demonstrated in several end-of-chapter problems.

b. Second, solid models can be converted to *shell* elements by defining a "mid-surface" located between the inner and outer surfaces of a solid model. This method illustrated in the current example.

c. Finally, a solid body can be converted to a sheet metal part and then to a shell model. This approach is best adapted to moderately thick parts that contain multiple bends between adjacent surfaces. This method is relatively straight forward and interested users are referred to Simulation **Help** for information.

Despite the numerous references to "sheet metal" above, this does *not* imply that parts must be made of sheet metal. Consider for example children's toys or power-tool carrying cases made of plastic. Due to their thin walls, these items can be modeled as sheet metal parts. Thus, do not let the words, "sheet metal," be misleading; they refer to how the part is modeled in SolidWorks rather than the material of which a part is made. Caution is advised, however, because a shell mesh does not apply to thin models made of *composite* materials. The reason for this is because a composite material, by its very nature, implies it is made of multiple different materials. Further, these materials are typically fabricated in multiple layers, and hence their properties are not uniform throughout their thickness.

Converting a Solid Model to a Shell Model

The model on your screen should appear similar to Fig. 10. Notice that the process for converting from a solid model to a shell model begins within SolidWorks, not in the Simulation portion of the program.

However, before converting the solid model into a shell model, the model is simplified by making use of *symmetry*. The thin-wall, cylindrical pressure vessel pictured in Fig. 10 is clearly a theoretical, "textbook" model. The rationale for this statement is quite obvious because no visible means of support are shown for the model as are no openings to permit fluids to enter or exit the container. However, this somewhat artificial geometry permits examination of methods to treat *symmetry* when it occurs in a problem.

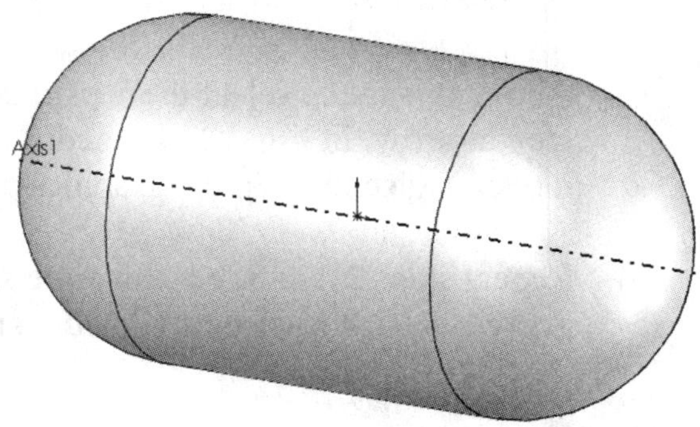

Figure 10 – Thin wall pressure vessel. Only one axis of symmetry is shown.

Because vessel geometry is symmetrical *and* because the internal pressure is uniform (symmetric loading), it is possible to analyze only a portion of the model. Figure 11 reveals that the current model was intentionally centered about the coordinate system origin when it was built. The front, right, and top sketch planes, included in Fig. 11, aid in visualizing that the model can be divided into eight symmetrical pieces. Model symmetry can be used to save computer memory and computation time. Because this is a rather simple model, significant savings are not realized. However, consider the computational savings realized if symmetry is used to model a complete aircraft fuselage (a pressure vessel when in flight). The curent example demonstrates how symmetry can and should be used in other finite element solutions. Also, *symmetry* boundary conditions are introduced below.

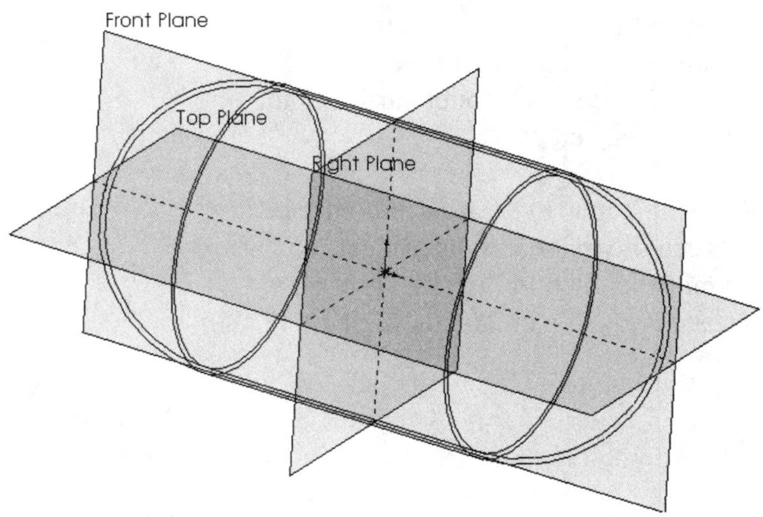

Figure 11 – Front, right, and top sketch planes introduced to show division of the model into symmetrical portions.

1. If **Axis1** does not appear on the model, from the main menu select **View**. Then, from the pop-up menu, select **Axes**. **Axis1** should appear on the model as shown in Fig. 10.

2. Near the bottom of the SolidWorks Feature manager tree, right-click the grayed-out **1/4 Symmetry Model**. This action causes the pop-up menu, shown in Fig.12, to open.

3. Above this menu select the **Unsuppress** icon at arrow in Fig. 12. Immediately ¼ of the model is displayed in the graphics area.

4. Repeat steps 2 and 3, but this time select the grayed-out **1/8 Symmetry Model** and **Unsuppress** it.

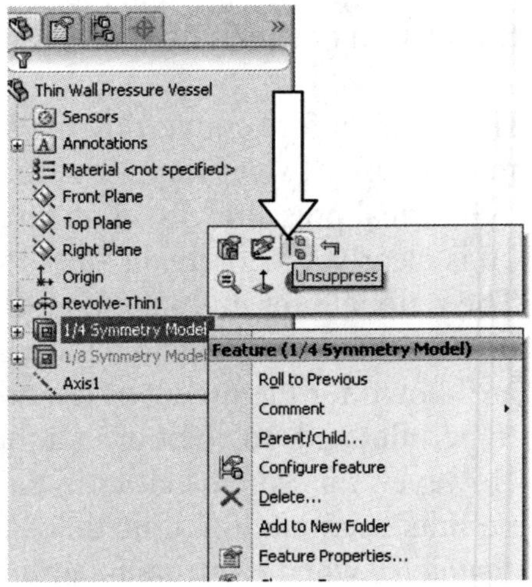

Figure 12 – **Unsupressing portions** of the symmetrical model in the SolidWorks feature manager.

The portion of the model selected for analysis should appear as shown in Fig. 13. Note that virtually any fraction of the model could be selected, but the ⅛ model is useful for reasons described later.

Also, notice how the use of descriptive names in the SolidWorks feature manager facilitated identification and selection of desired model attributes in the preceding steps.

The next step is to create a mid-surface between the inner and outer faces of the model shown in Fig. 13. That new surface is used to create the shell mesh.

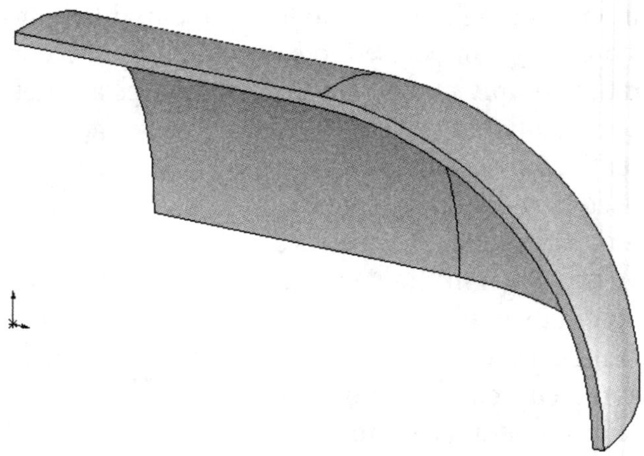

Figure 13 – A ⅛ model of the thin-wall pressure vessel. Symmetry is used to reduce analysis time and computer memory requirements.

5. From the main menu, select **Insert** and from the next two pull-down menus, select **Surface ▶** followed by **Offset...** The **Offset Surface** property manager opens.

6. Placing the cursor in the light blue field of the **Offset parameters** dialogue box reveals the message, **Surface or Faces to Offset**.

7. Move the cursor onto the *inner surface* of the model and right-click. In the pop-up menu, choose **Select Tangency** and immediately a ghost image of an offset surface appears inside the model, see Fig. 14. Also, **Face<1>** and **Face<2>** appear in the highlighted field. **Face<1>** and **Face<2>** refer to the cylindrical and hemispherical surfaces that are tangent to one another.

8. If the offset surface is not clearly visible, increase the **Offset Distance** by typing **10** or **15** mm in the box located at the bottom of the **Offset parameters** dialogue box.

It is also acceptable to select outside surfaces of the model. The only difference is that the offset surface appears on the outside of the model and locations of the surface in the steps below will be reversed.

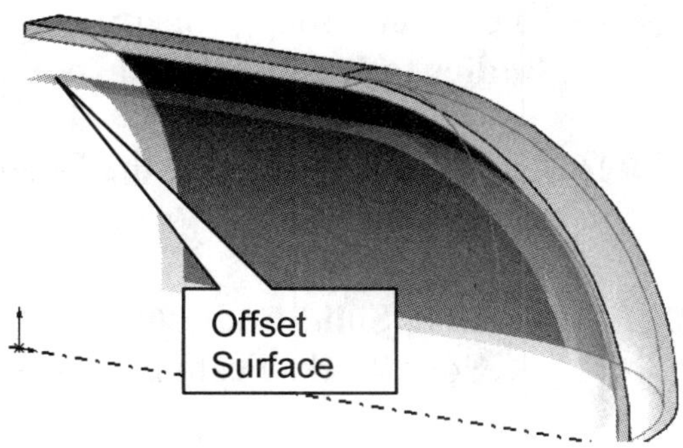

Figure 14 – An **Offset Surface** appears inside the pressure vessel model.

9. Because the shell is to be placed at the mid-surface of the model, in the **Offset Distance** field, shown in Fig. 15, type **1.5** mm**,** which is half of the 3 mm wall thickness.

10. To visualize where the offset surface is located zoom in on any segment of the wall *edge* and toggle (i.e., multiple click) the **Flip Offset Direction** button. When the surface appears midway between the inside and outside walls it is correct. NOTE: Due to its light color, the mid-surface may be difficult/impossible to see when located between the surfaces.

11. Click **[OK]** to close the **Offset Surface** property manager.

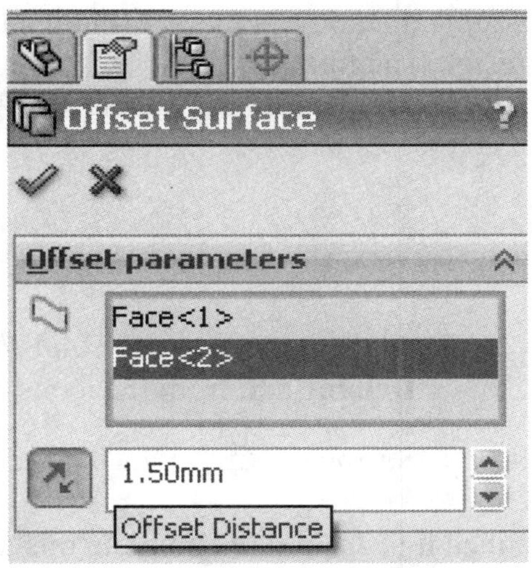

Figure 15 – Selecting offset surfaces and specifying the **Offset Distance**.

12. Move the cursor into the SolidWorks Feature manager and click the "+" sign adjacent to **Solid Bodies(1)**. This reveals the **1/8 Symmetry Model** as the original solid body.

13. Immediately below the above selection, click the "+" sign adjacent to **Surface Bodies(1)**. This action reveals **Surface-Offset1**, which was created in the steps above.

Caution: In the following step do *NOT* select the **1/8 Symmetry Model** located at the bottom of the SolidWorks Feature manager tree.

14. Next, return to **Solid Bodies(1)** and beneath it right-click on **1/8 Symmetry Model**. This action opens a pull-down menu. In the menu select 

15. The **Delete Body** property manager opens and shows **1/8 Symmetry Model** in the **Bodies to Delete** dialogue box.

16. Click **[OK]** ✓ to close the **Delete Body** property manager and the following things occur:

- Both **Solid Bodies(1)** and **1/8 Symmetry Model** are removed from the SolidWorks Feature manager tree.
- The model appears as a thin surface (i.e., a *shell*) shown in Fig. 16.
- ☒ **Body-Delete1** appears at the bottom of the Feature manager tee.

The preceding steps appear to delete the **Solid Bodies(1)** folder and its contents from the Feature manager tree. However, **Delete Body** is simply a feature in the tree and it can be restored as follows.

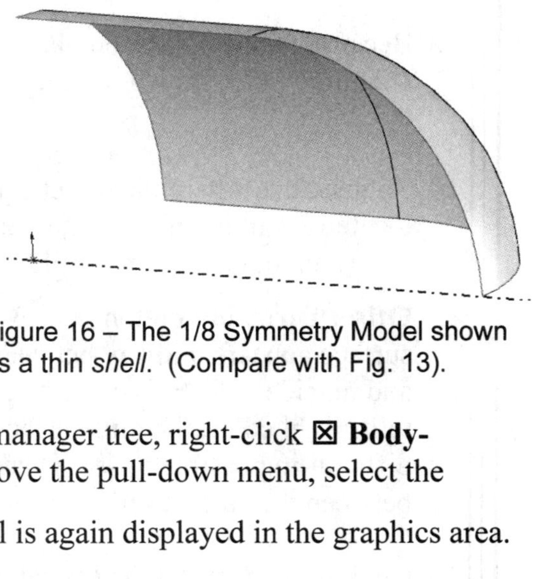

Figure 16 – The 1/8 Symmetry Model shown as a thin *shell*. (Compare with Fig. 13).

17. At the bottom of the SolidWorks Feature manager tree, right-click ☒ **Body-Delete1** and from the icons located just above the pull-down menu, select the **Suppress**  icon. The solid body model is again displayed in the graphics area.

Since it is desired to complete this analysis using a shell model, undo the preceding step as follows.

18. Once again right-click ☒ **Body-Delete1** and from the icons located just above the pull-down menu, select the **Unsuppress**  icon and the shell model reappears in the graphics area.

This concludes one of the three different procedures for converting a solid model to a shell model. The next section outlines the remainder of the shell analysis process.

Open a New Simulation Study

1. In the main menu, select **Simulation** and from the pull-down menu choose **Study...** Alternatively, on the **Simulation** tab, click the **New Study** icon. The **Study** property manager opens, Fig. 17.

2. In the **Name** dialogue box, type **Pressure Vessel-Shell Study** as a descriptive name for the Study.

3. Verify that the **Type** dialogue box is set to **Static**.

4. Click **[OK]** ✓ to close the **Study** property manager.

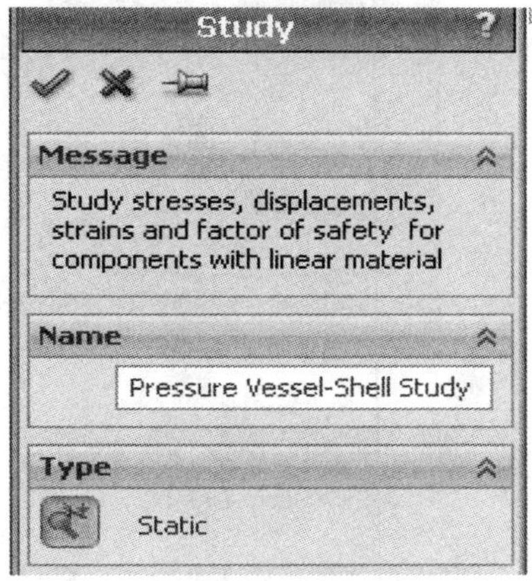

Figure 17 – **Study** property manager showing Study **Name** and Study **Type** **(Static)**.

Assigning Material Properties

1. In the Simulation manager tree, right-click the **Thin Wall Pressure Vessel (-Thickness: not defined-)** icon and from the pull-down menu select **Apply/Edit Material...** The **Material** window opens. Observe that the part icon appears as a thin surface rather than the original solid part.

2. Beneath **Select material source**, choose ⦿ **From library files:** and from the pull-down menu select **solidworks materials**.

3. Click the "+" sign adjacent to **Steel (32)** and from the list of materials, select **AISI 1045 Steel, cold drawn.** Before closing the **Material** window, check **Units:** beneath the **Properties** tab. **Units:** *should* be set to **SI**. Recall changing default units to **SI** at the beginning of this example. *If necessary, change **Units:** to **SI**.*

4. Click **[OK]** to close the **Material** window. A "✓" appears on the surface icon.

Defining Shell Thickness

The software recognizes that the pressure vessel is modeled as a "thin" part due to the **Revolve-Thin1** command circled in the SolidWorks Feature manager, Fig. 18. Also recall that wall thickness was specified when creating the SolidWorks model. However, because the solid model was converted to a shell model, the software allows the user to specify thickness again in the event that a different thickness is desired for the analysis. To specify shell thickness, proceed as follows.

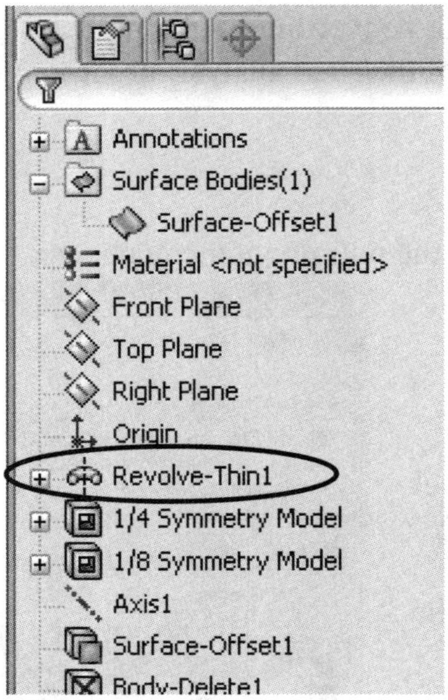

Figure 18 – SolidWorks Feature Manager tree.

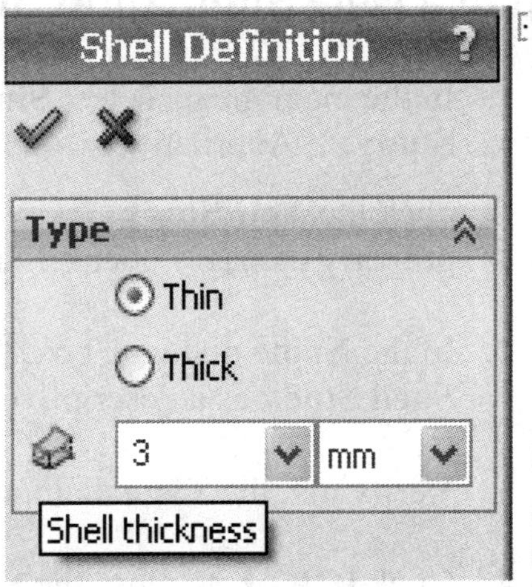

Figure 19 – Shell thickness is specified in the **Shell Definition** property manager.

1. Right-click **Thin Wall Pressure Vessel (-Thickness: not defined/Material: AISI 1045 Steel, cold drawn-)**. *It is unlikely that the entire name appears on the screen due to the narrow width of the manager tree.)* From the pop-up menu select **Edit Definition…** The **Shell Definition** property manager opens as shown in Fig. 19.

2. In the **Type** dialogue box, select ⊙ **Thin**.

3. Verify **Units** are set to **mm** and type **3** into the **Shell Thickness** box in Fig. 19.

4. Click **[OK]** ✓ to close the **Shell Definition** property manager.

Assigning Fixtures and External Loads

Symmetry Restraints Applied

As noted earlier, the pressure vessel is a symmetrical model as far as both geometry and loading are concerned. This section introduces symmetrical loading and fixture boundary conditions as outlined next. What is different, however, is that shell elements restrict both *translation* and *rotation* at node locations. This is unlike solid tetrahedral elements that restricted only *translations* at node locations. The next step is to define restraints and loads applied to the model.

1. Right-click the **Fixtures** folder and from the pull-down menu select **Fixed Geometry…** The **Fixture** property manager opens in Fig. 20.

Before proceeding to the next step, observe movement of the animated model in the **Example** dialogue box. The effect of **Fixed** restraints is clearly depicted along two edges of the generic model.

2. Open the **Advanced** dialogue box and from the list of options, select **Use Reference Geometry**, circled in Fig. 20.

Once again observe movement of the generic model in the **Example** dialogue box. This animation illustrates translations that can be specified in the X, Y, and Z directions. However, before defining restraints, it is necessary to identify the edges on which the restraints are to be applied.

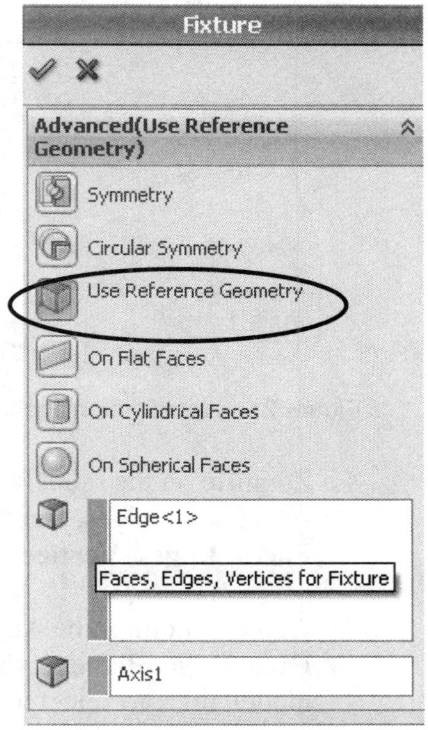

Figure 20 – The **Advanced** dialogue box is used to select edges for symmetry restraints.

> **Aside:**
> The user might wonder why **Symmetry** or **Circular Symmetry** was not selected from the list of options in the **Advanced** property manager. Some general guidance is provided below.
>
> a. **For Solid Models** – Every face that is coincident with a plane of symmetry should be prevented from movement in its normal direction.
>
> b. **For Shell Models** – Every edge that coincides with a plane of symmetry should be prevented from translating in the normal direction and from rotating in the other two perpendicular directions.

Neither the **Symmetry** nor the **Circular Symmetry** options provide the ability to model symmetry for the current Shell model. For this reason the general guideline listed in item (b) above is applied to the 1/8 Symmetry model.

Refer to the partial view of the **Advanced** dialogue box, shown in Fig. 20, and the part model in Fig. 21 while implementing the following steps.

3. Near the bottom of the **Advanced** dialogue box the **Faces, Edges, Vertices for Fixture** field is highlighted (light blue) to indicate it is active and awaiting user selection of edges to which symmetry restraints are to be applied.

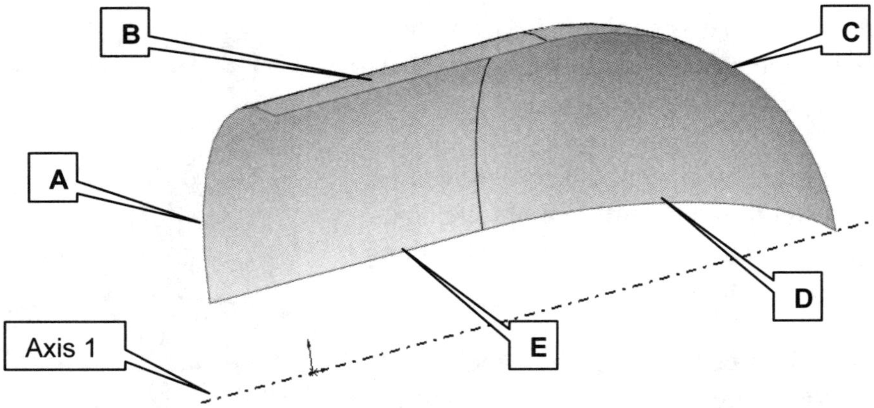

Figure 21 - Identification of shell edges to which symmetry restraints are applied.

4. Zoom-in on the model to select the ¼ circular edge, labeled **A** in Fig. 21. Do *not* select other edges, faces, or vertices. The selected edge, **Edge<1>** appears in the **Faces, Edges, Vertices for Fixture** field and is highlighted on the model.

5. At the bottom of the **Advanced** dialogue box click to activate (light blue) the **Face, Edge, Plane, Axis for Direction** field. Then, if **Axis1** is visible on the model, click to select it. Otherwise, click the "+" to open the SolidWorks flyout menu and from the menu, select **Axis1**. **Axis1** now appears in the active field. This step establishes **Axis1**as an axis of symmetry along the length of the model.

Next, apply the principle stated in item (b) of the previous page, which states: *"Every edge that coincides with a plane of symmetry should be prevented from translating in the normal direction and from rotating in the other two perpendicular directions."* To do this, proceed as follows.

6. In the Simulation manager tree, scroll down to the **Translations** dialogue box shown in Fig. 22. Then select the **Axial** icon. Ensure that **0** appears in the value box. This selection sets to zero model translation along **Axis1**.

7. Next scroll down to the **Rotation** dialogue box and set both **Radial** and **Circumferential** rotations to zero, (i.e., rotation in either of these directions is prevented).

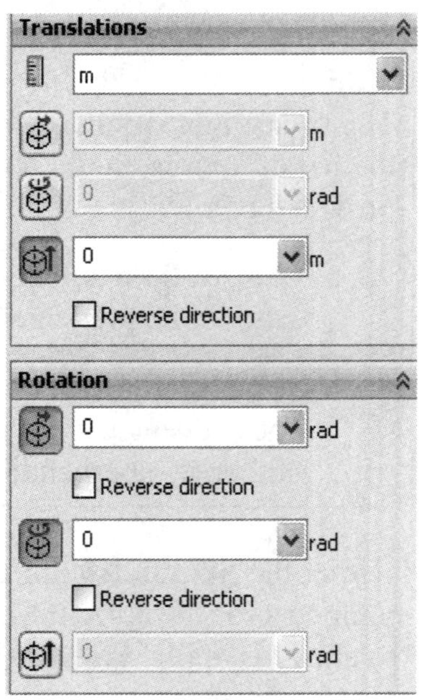

Figure 22 – Displacements set to zero on model edges.

8. Click **[OK]** ✓ to close the **Fixture** property manager.

Next, repeat the above procedure, but select all edges **B**, **C**, **D**, and **E** of Fig. 21and apply appropriate restraints. Try this on your own, or follow the steps outlined below.

9. Right-click the **Fixtures** folder and from the pull-down menu select **Fixed Geometry…** The **Fixture** property manager opens.

10. Open the **Advanced** dialogue box and from the list of options, select **Use Reference Geometry**, circled in Fig. 20. Also, the **Faces, Edges, Vertices for Fixture** field is highlighted (light blue) to indicate it is active.

11. On the model, select edges **B**, **C**, **D**, and **E** labeled in Fig. 21. **Edge<1>** through **Edge<4>** appear in the **Faces, Edges, Vertices for Fixture** field and are highlighted on the model. Refer to Fig. 23.

12. At the bottom of the **Advanced** dialogue box click to activate (light blue) the **Face, Edge, Plane, Axis for Direction** field. Then, click the "+" to open the SolidWorks flyout menu and from the menu, select **Axis1**. **Axis1** now appears in the active field.

13. Set the **Translations** and **Rotation** restraints as shown in Fig. 23. Make certain that translation and rotation values are set to zero (**0**).

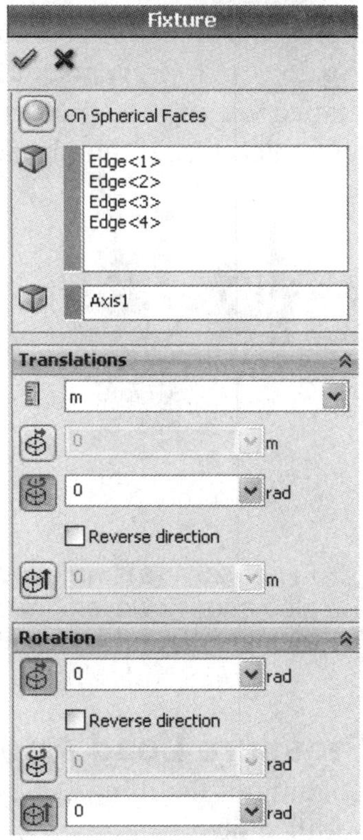

Figure 23 – **Translations** and **Rotation** settings for edges **B**, **C**, **D**, and **E.**

14. Click **[OK]** ✓ to close the **Fixture** property manager.

The resulting symmetry restraints are shown on the model in Fig. 24.

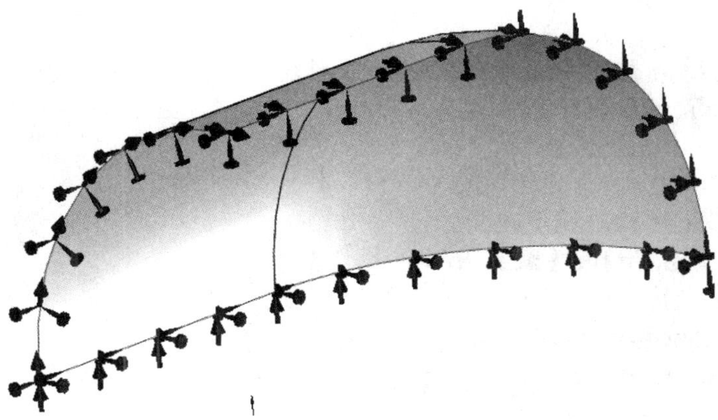

Figure 24 – An internal view of the model showing **Symmetry** restraints applied to all cut edges.

Carefully observe the symbols used to indicate symmetry boundary conditions. All previous examples used solid tetrahedral elements for which **Immovable** restraints were appropriate. **Immovable** restraints prevent translations in the three coordinate directions X, Y, Z and are pictured in Fig. 25 (a). When fully restrained, shell elements restrict three translations in X, Y, Z directions *plus* they prevent rotations specified above. **Fixed** restraints are illustrated in Fig. 25 (b) where the added "disk" on the tail of each vector represents an added rotational restraint. Finally, the **Symmetry** restraint is pictured in Fig.25 (c). It prevents translation in a direction normal to the restrained face (arrow shaped vector) *and* prevents rotation about the other two axes associated with the restrained face ("thumb-tack" appearance vectors). See the restrained model in Fig. 24.

(a) (b) (c)

Figure 25 – (a) **Immovable** restraint symbol; (b) **Fixed** restraint symbol only applies to shell elements, however it need not always be used; (c) **Symmetry** restraint applied to shell elements on cut surfaces of the thin-wall pressure vessel.

Pressure Load Applied

Loading of the thin-wall cylinder is completed by the addition of an internal pressure as outlined next.

1. Right-click the **External Loads** folder and from the pull-down menu select **Pressure…** The **Pressure** property manager opens.

2. In the **Type** dialogue box, choose ◉**Normal to selected face** (if not already selected).

3. The **Faces for Pressure** field is highlighted (light blue) to indicate it is active. Select the *inside* surfaces of both the cylindrical and hemispherical portions of the model. **Face<1>** and **Face<2>** should appear in the **Faces for Pressure** field and both surfaces appear highlighted to indicate their selection.

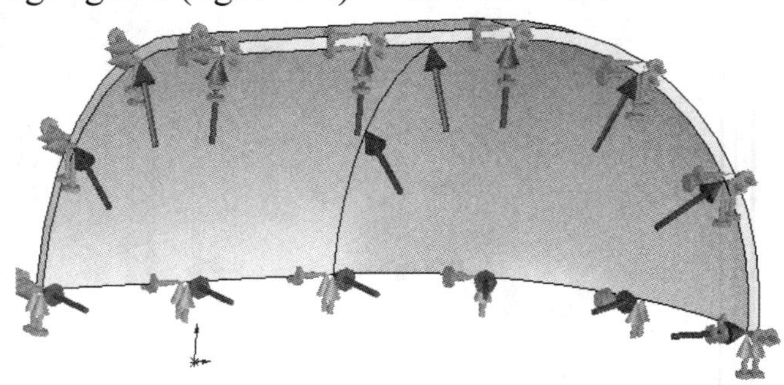

Figure 26 – Uniform pressure distribution acting on internal surfaces of the model.

4. Within the **Pressure Value** dialogue box, verify that **Units** are set to **N/m^2** and beneath this field, in the **Pressure Value** field, type **1.4e6** for the applied internal pressure. Units of **N/m^2** appear adjacent to this field.

Arrows should appear along all edges of the model as shown in Fig. 26. If the pressure arrows are not directed *toward the inner surface*, check **Reverse direction**.

5. Click **[OK]** ✓ to close the **Pressure** property manager.

Because the 1/8 model is selected, symmetry restraints are applied to restrict model translations and rotations in the appropriate directions. Therefore, no additional restraints need be applied. However, if the model were not fully restrained, a warning would appear during the Solution and additional restraints to prevent "rigid body motion" would need to be applied. The need for rigid body restraint is demonstrated in the next section.

Meshing the Model

Because the software recognizes the model is a thin shell, the meshing process outlined below is considerably shortened.

1. In the Simulation manager tree, right-click the **Mesh** folder and from the pull-down menu select **Create Mesh...** The **Mesh** property manager opens.

2. Accept the default mesh size and click **[OK]** ✓ to close the **Mesh** property manager.

Meshing proceeds automatically and Fig. 27 shows an image of the thin-wall pressure vessel displayed with a *shell* mesh and all applied loads and fixtures. Notice that the model appears as a "paper-thin" shell.

Consistent with system default conventions adopted at the beginning of this example, the color orange represents the "bottom" surface of the shell elements. If the inner surface of the model is considered as the "bottom," and if this surface is not orange, then surfaces appearing orange on your model may have to be "flipped" (i.e., reversed). Do this only if necessary using the following steps.

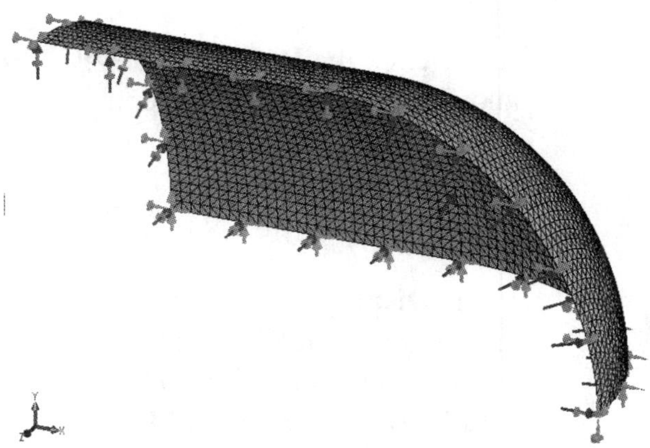

Figure 27 – A **Shell** mesh applied to the mid-surface of the pressure vessel model. Note that "top" and "bottom" surface designations are reversed.

3. While pressing the **[Shift]** key, click to select both the cylindrical *and* hemispherical surfaces on either the inside or outside of the model.

4. Right-click the **Mesh** icon and from the pull-down menu select **Flip Shell Elements**. This action should reverse locations of the top and bottom surfaces.

NOTE: It may be necessary to repeat step 4 to cause the desired changes to take effect.

Colors of the top and bottom surfaces should now reverse, (orange moves to the inside [bottom] and gray is switched to the outside [top] surface). The last two steps are not mandatory. They simply illustrate how the model can be altered to conform to the user's preference. The model is now complete and ready to be solved as outlined below.

Solution

1. Right-click **Pressure Vessel-Shell Study (-Default-)** and from the pull-down menu select **Run**.

After the Solution is complete, the three system default plots, **Stress1 (-vonMises-)**, **Displacement1 (-Res disp-)**, and **Strain1 (-Equivalent-)** are listed at the bottom of the Simulation manager tree.

Results Analysis

Because the emphasis of this example is on mastering basic techniques for working with shell elements, the review of final results is rather brief. Thus, a quick look at results of this analysis should confirm the accuracy of this approach. Only stress results are examined below.

1. Right-click the **Results** folder and from the pull-down menu select **Define Stress Plot...** The **Stress Plot** property manager opens.

2. In the **Display** dialogue box, click to open the **Component** pull-down menu and from the list of stresses, select **P1: 1st Principal Stress.**

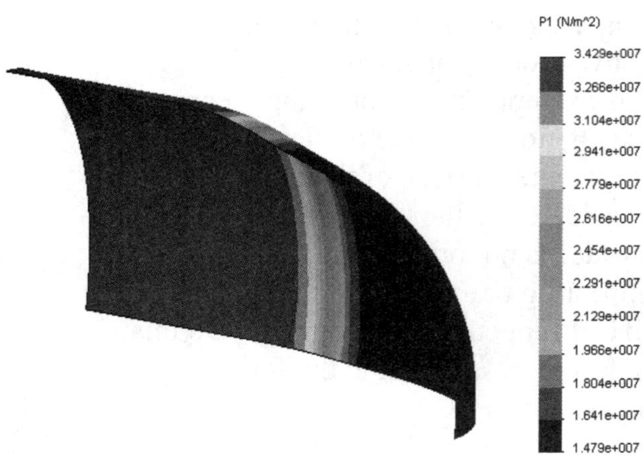

Figure 28 – First principal stress distribution over the thin-wall pressure vessel.

3. Click **[OK]** ✓ to close the **Stress Plot** property manager and a plot of 1st principal stress, like that shown in Fig. 28, appears in the graphics area. Also, **Stress2 (-1st principal-)** is added beneath the **Results** folder.

For convenience in viewing results, turn off the load and restraint symbols. Try this on your own. If difficulty is encountered, proceed as follows.

4. Right-click the **Fixtures** folder and from the pop-up menu select **Hide All.**

5. Repeat step 4 for the **External Loads** folder.

6. Return to the **Stress2 (-1st principal-)** folder. The plot should now appear similar to Fig. 28.

Unlike solid, tetrahedral elements for which stress variation is shown throughout the thickness of the model, (i.e., variation of stress from the inside to the outside surface), results plotted for *shell* elements correspond to either the top *or* the bottom surface. Below we investigate what surface the 1st principal stress is shown on and then compare it to stress on the opposite side of the shell. Proceed as follows.

7. Right-click **Stress2 (-1st principal-)** and from the pull-down menu select **Edit Definition...** The **Stress Plot** property manager opens.

8. In the bottom field of the **Display** dialogue box observe that **Top** is indicated as the **Shell Face** on which the current plot is shown. See Fig. 29.

9. Click **[OK]** ✓ to close the **Stress Plot** property.

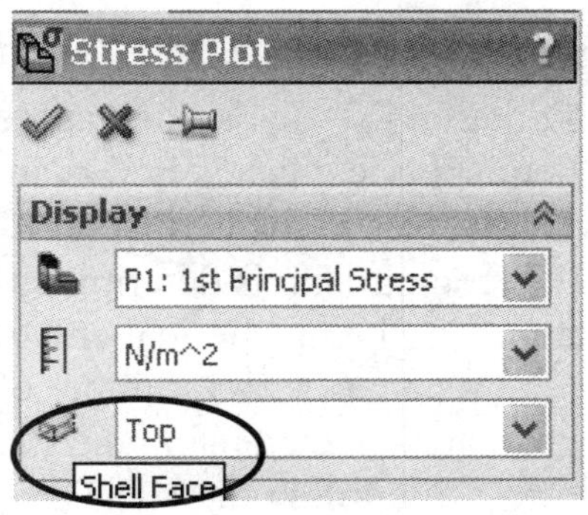

Figure 29 – Designating the **Shell Face** on which the stress plot is displayed.

At the bottom of the Simulation manager tree, click-pause-click on the name **Stress2 (1st principal-)** and type: **1st Principal Stress-TOP** and press **[Enter]**. This name identifies the current plot as shown in Fig. 30.

10. Next, click on the **Results** folder and from the pull-down menu, select **Define Stress Plot...** The **Stress Plot** property manager opens.

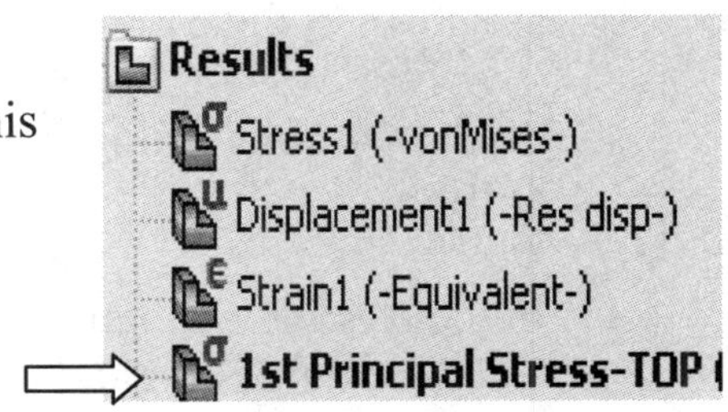

Figure 30 – Re-naming the stress plot using a descriptive name.

11. In the **Display** dialogue box, click to open the **Component** pull-down menu and from the list of stresses, select **P1: 1st Principal Stress**.

12. In the bottom field of the **Display** dialogue click to open the pull-down menu and select **Bottom** as the **Shell Face** on which a new plot is shown.

13. Click **[OK]** ✓ to close the **Stress Plot** property.

On your own, change the name of the plot just created to **1st Principal Stress-BOTTOM**. Refer to step 10 above if guidance is needed.

14. Next, alternatively double-click on **1st Principal Stress-TOP** and then **1st Principal Stress-BOTTOM** to display the plots and to compare the two *different* maximum values of σ_1 shown on each surface.

Taking the maximum value for $\sigma_1 = \sigma_t$ = 3.49947e+007 N/m^2 (numbers may vary) from the **1st Principal Stress-BOTTOM** plot and comparing it with the value calculated using equation [1] for stress in a thin wall pressure vessel $\sigma_t = 3.36e7$ N/m^2, the following percent difference is determined (values rounded).

$$\% \text{ difference} = \left[\frac{\text{FEA result} - \text{classical result}}{\text{FEA result}}\right]100 = \left[\frac{3.4995e7 - 3.36e7}{3.4995e7}\right]100 = 3.98\% \quad [3]$$

Equation [3] yields good agreement. Next, recalling that tangential stress in the hemispherical heads is ½ σ_t in the cylindrical portion, the following comparison is made for stresses in the hemispherical head. The value of stress for this comparison is determined in two different ways. First, the entire hemispherical end of the vessel is selected and second, an arbitrary number of points on the hemispherical head are selected using the **Probe** tool. Try this on your own. The following steps provide guidance if desired.

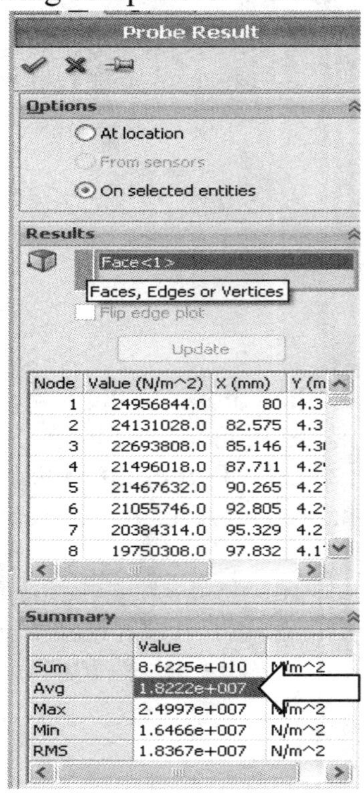

Figure 31 – **Probe Results** on the *entire* hemispherical end of the pressure vessel.

15. Right-click **1st Principal Stress-BOTTOM (-1st principal-)** and from the pull-down menu, select **Probe**. The **Probe Result** property manager opens as shown in Fig.31.

16. In the **Options** dialogue box choose ⊙ **On selected entities**.

17. In the **Results** dialogue box the **Faces, Edges or Vertices** field is highlighted (light blue). Move the cursor onto the hemispherical end of the model and click to select it. **Face<1>** appears in the **Faces, Edges or Vertices** field.

18. Near the middle of the **Results** dialogue box, click the **[Update]** button and immediately the table is populated with stress magnitudes at all nodes on the hemispherical surface.

19. In the **Summary** dialogue box, near bottom of the property manager, observe the average (**Avg**) value of stress on this surface is 1.8222e+007 N/m^2., Fig. 31 (numbers may vary). Be aware that this value includes a portion of the higher stresses near the hemispherical to cylindrical transition region on the model.

The value of stress determined using classical equations is determined by taking half of the value of $(\sigma_t)_{hemispherical} = ½ * (\sigma_t)_{cylinder} = ½ * 3.36e7$ Pa = 1.68e7 N/m^2. The percent difference between finite element and classical results yields the following comparison for stress magnitude in the hemispherical end.

$$\%\text{ difference} = \left[\frac{\text{FEA result} - \text{ classical result}}{\text{FEA result}}\right]100 = \left[\frac{1.822e7 - 1.68e7}{1.822e7}\right]100 = 7.79\% \quad [4]$$

The relatively high percent difference in equation [4] is due, in part, to stress variation at the transition between cylindrical and hemispherical regions. An alternate way to determine stress in the hemispherical end (or anywhere on any model) is described next.

20. In the **Probe Result** property manager, return to the **Options** dialogue box and select ⊙ **At location**. The format of the **Probe Result** property manager changes and all values are cleared from the tables.

21. Move the cursor onto the hemispherical end of the model and click to select several nodes at points in the dark blue color-coded area as shown in Fig. 32. Select points well away from the junction between the hemispherical and cylindrical surfaces.

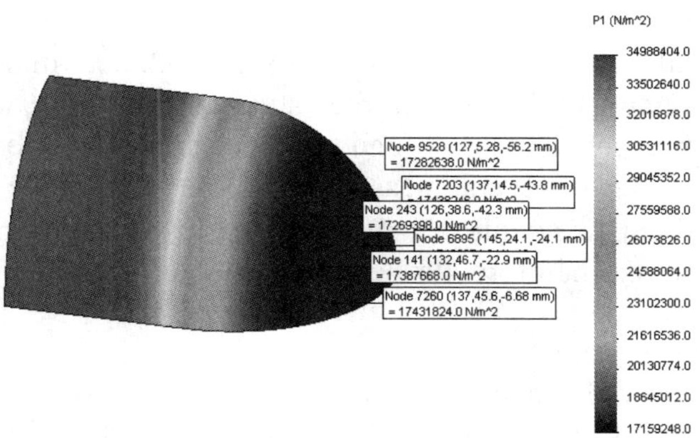

Figure 32 – Randomly selected nodes used determine an average value of stress on the “bottom” surface of the hemispherical end.

Manually compute the average stress based on values listed in the **Results** dialogue box (not shown). The percent difference between Finite Element and classical equations is shown in equation [5]. Not surprisingly the percent difference is reduced because higher stress magnitudes near the transition region are excluded from this calculation. (Results will vary.)

$$\% \text{ difference} = \left[\frac{\text{FEA result} - \text{classical result}}{\text{FEA result}} \right] 100 = \left[\frac{1.67e7 - 1.68e7}{1.67e7} \right] 100 = 0.59\% \qquad [5]$$

22. Click **[OK]** ✓ to close the **Probe Result** property manager.

The percent difference between results is significantly reduced by selecting locations well removed from the transition region. This is yet another example of St. Venant's principle.

Next, display the value of second principal stress and compare it against the value computed for longitudinal stress calculated using classical equations; see equation [2] on page 4-2. Try creating a plot of second principal stress on the bottom surface on your own. If guidance is needed, proceed as follows.

23. Right-click the **Results** folder and from the pull-down menu select **Define Stress Plot…** The **Stress Plot** property manager opens.

24. In the **Display** dialogue box, click to open the **Component** pull-down menu and from the list of stresses, select **P2: 2nd Principal Stress.**

25. In the **Shell Face** pull-down menu, verify that the **Bottom** surface is selected; if not select it. Also, verify that **UnitS** is set to **N/m^2**.

26. Click **[OK]** ✓ to close the **Stress Plot** property manager and a plot of 2nd principal stress appears in the graphics area.

Using the **Probe** tool and the procedure illustrated for Fig. 32, determine an average value for stress corresponding to the yellow/green areas at the mid-section of the cylinder. This stress corresponds to the second principal stress on the bottom (inside) surface. Based on an average of several measurements, the stress value is $\sigma_2 = \sigma_\ell =$ 1.745e7 N/m^2. As expected, this value of longitudinal stress is approximately equal to half of the tangential stress. Therefore, further exploration of this stress is not pursued here.

Notice that σ_1 and σ_2 observed above occur on the *bottom* (i.e., inside) surface of the model. To illustrate that a slightly different state of stress occurs on the *top* (i.e., outside) surface of the model, return to **1st Principal Stress-TOP (-1st principal-)** to investigate stress magnitudes on that surface.

27. Double-click **1st Principal Stress-TOP (-1st principal-)** to again display the plot of σ_1.

The maximum value of σ_1 displayed on the current plot is for stress on the *top* (outside) surface of the model. This value should be approximately: $(\sigma_1)_{Max}$ = 3.5115e+007 N/m^2. Next, examine maximum stresses on the bottom (inside) surface.

28. First, display the plot by double-clicking on **1st Principal Stress-BOTTOM**.

29. At the top of the color-coded stress scale note $(\sigma_1)_{Max}$ = 3.4995e+007 N/m^2.

30. Click **[OK]** ✓ to close the **Stress Plot** property manager.

Analysis Insight

Stress magnitude of σ_1 on the bottom (i.e., inner surface) of the pressure vessel shows the following value: $(\sigma_1)_{Max}$ = 3.5115e+007 N/m^2 while that on the top (i.e., outer surface) is $(\sigma_1)_{Max}$ = 3.4995e+007 N/m^2. Based on different results occurring on these two surfaces, two observations are made.

- First, circumferential stress on the outside surface of the pressure vessel is greater than that observed on the inner surface.
- Second, unlike stresses on different surfaces of a solid model that can be observed by rotating the model, stresses on top and bottom surfaces of shell elements can only be observed by altering the **Stress Plot** definition of the surface observed.

At this point the *shell* element example is concluded. Before analyzing the thick-wall pressure vessel, select **File / Close**. When prompted to "**Save changes to Thin Wall Pressure Vessel**," select **[No]** to exit the thin-wall pressure vessel example without saving results.

THICK WALL PRESSURE VESSEL

In the second-half of the current chapter, analysis of a thick-wall pressure vessel is performed. Thick-wall pressure vessels are found in numerous applications including high pressure piping, gun and cannon barrels, some hydraulic cylinders, and related uses. Thick-wall pressure vessels are classified as such in applications where wall thickness "t" exceeds $t > r_i/20$, where r_i = inside radius. For these applications, assumptions related to thin-wall pressure vessels are no longer valid. Primary among these differences are: (a) radial stress, which is neglected in thin-wall formulations, is known to vary through the thickness of a thick-wall vessel; and (b) tangential (a.k.a., hoop or circumferential) stress also varies through the wall thickness. Much of thick-wall cylinder theory is also relevant to analysis of press and shrink fits, which are investigated in the next chapter.

Problem Statement

Thick-Wall Pressure Vessel

This example is based on a thick-wall cylindrical pressure vessel that is closed on one end, but attached to a rigid pipe connection at the opposite end as illustrated in Fig. 33. This vessel is made of Alloy Steel and is subject to an internal pressure P_i = 16.0 MPa and an external pressure that approximates standard atmospheric pressure P_o = 0.101 MPa. Cylinder dimensions, necessary to apply classical stress equations, are also included in Fig. 33. The goal is to determine tangential and radial stress variation through the cylindrical walls of the pressure vessel.

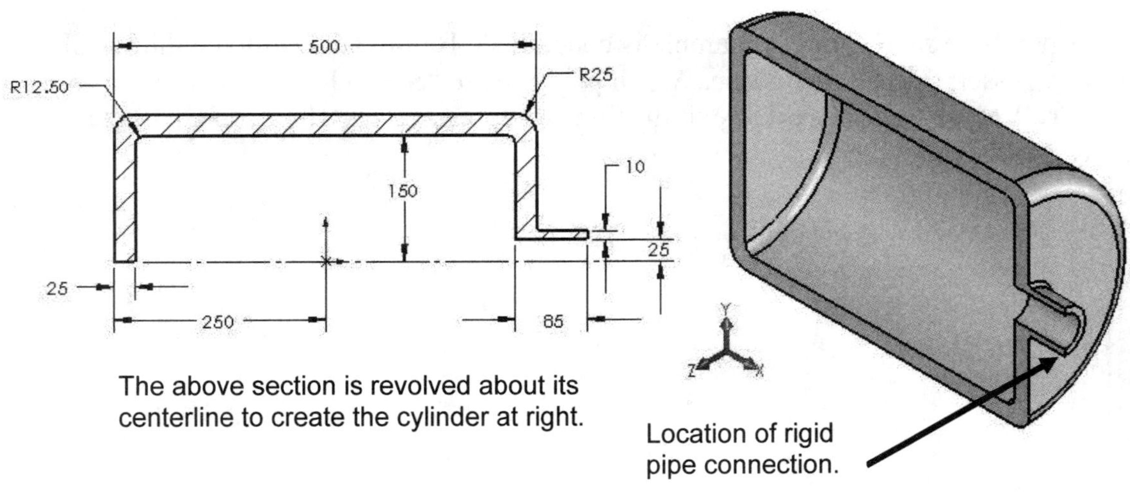

Figure 33 – Basic dimensions and geometry of the thick-wall pressure vessel.

1. Open SolidWorks by making the following selections. (*Note:* "/" is used to separate successive menu selections.) *Skip to step 2 if SolidWorks is already open.*

Start/All Programs/SolidWorks 2009 (or) Click the **SolidWorks** icon on your screen.

2. From the SolidWorks main menu, select **File / Open**. Then use procedures common to your computer environment to open the SolidWorks Simulation file named **Thick Wall Pressure Vessel**.

Defining the Study

Because tetrahedral elements are used to create a solid model of the pressure vessel, the majority of procedural steps employed to create this study are familiar to users who have worked the preceding examples. However, all necessary steps are included. This study again uses symmetry restraints, but of a different type, and also introduces new methods for viewing results.

1. In the main menu, click **Simulation** and from the pull-down menu, select **Study…** The **Study** property manager opens.

2. In the **Name** field, type: **Thick Wall Pressure Vessel**.

3. Select a **Static** study and click **[OK]** ✓ to close the **Study** property manager. An outline of the new study appears in the SolidWorks Simulation manager.

Unlike the 1/8 model used for the thin-wall pressure vessel, a 1/2 model is selected for the thick-wall example. Notice also that complete geometric symmetry does not exist for this model (left and right ends of the model differ). Prior to commencing a finite element analysis, the model is defeatured and half of the model is suppressed. For purposes of illustration, the small fillet at the pipe connection is selected to be defeatured. Proceed as follows.

4. Near the bottom of the SolidWorks Feature manager, right-click **Pipe Connector Fillet** and select the **Suppress**  icon. The fillet is removed at the junction between the cylinder and pipe extension as illustrated in Fig. 34.

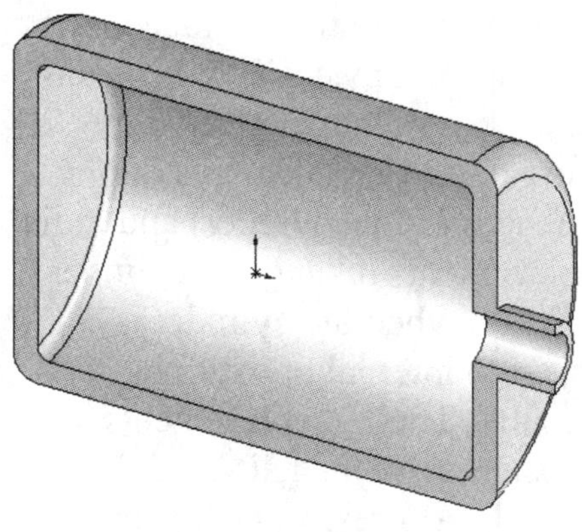

Figure 34 – Half-section of the thick-wall pressure vessel after defeaturing.

5. Also near the bottom of the SolidWorks Feature manager, right-click **Half-Model of Cylinder** and from the pop-up menu, select the **Unsuppress** icon.

The model changes to the half-cylinder shown in Fig. 34. Notice how assigning descriptive names to folders facilitates identifying their function. Prior to renaming the **Half-Model of Cylinder** folder, its generic name was "Cut-Extrude2."

Assign Material Properties

1. Right-click the **Thick Wall Pressure Vessel** folder *(not the Study name)* and from the pull-down menu, select **Apply/Edit Material...** The **Material** window opens.

2. Because users should be familiar with this window, on your own select ⊙ **From library files:** and choose **Alloy Steel (SS)**. Verify that units are set to **SI**, then click **[OK]** to close the window. A check mark "✓" appears of the **Thick Wall Pressure Vessel** icon.

Define Fixtures and External Loads

1. Right-click **Fixtures** and from the pull-down menu choose **Fixed Geometry...** The **Fixture** property manager opens.

2. Click to open the **Advanced** dialog box and from the list of options select **Symmetry**. Next, select the cut surface highlighted in Fig. 35. **Face<1>** appears in the **Planar Faces for Fixture** field.

3. Click **[OK]** ✓ to close the **Fixture** property manager.

Restraint symbols appear on the model normal to the cut face in the Z-direction. Physically this means that existing symmetry restraints permit axial displacements (along the length of the cylinder) and radial displacements (change of cylinder diameter) when the cylinder is subject to internal or external pressure. These displacements are consistent with the half-model selected. At present, however, both X and Y displacements of the model are still possible because the model is not fully restrained.

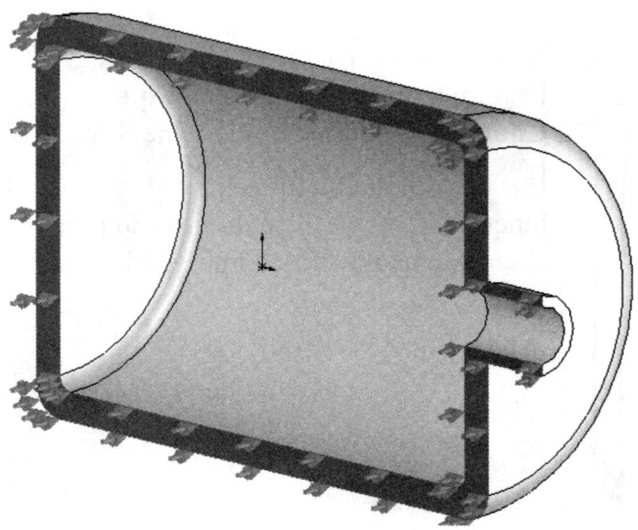

Figure 35 – Half-model of pressure vessel with symmetry restraints applied in the Z-direction.

Because symmetry restraints only restrain the model in the Z-direction, it is necessary to apply additional restraints in the X and Y directions to prevent what is known as "rigid body" motion. The type of restraints selected depends heavily upon the nature of actual operating conditions. Because the right end of the pipe connection is considered attached to a rigid (i.e., immovable) pipe extension, not shown, the remaining restraints are applied at that location. Fortunately, this immovable restraint does not interfere with finite element results in the thick-wall portion of the pressure vessel.

Analysis Insight
Although not part of this example, consider the following two scenarios:

A different set of fixtures results if, in addition to being attached to a rigid pipe at its right end, the left end of the cylinder is mounted against a fixed surface (e.g., a wall or support bracket). That additional restraint would alter stress distribution within the cylinder because longitudinal deformation of the model is prevented at both ends.

Consider yet one additional design/analysis scenario in which the model, restrained as described in the preceding paragraph, is subsequently subjected to a significant temperature change. This condition would add temperature induced deformation (expansion or contraction) associated with the coefficient of thermal expansion for the model material. This scenario would require a separate thermal analysis to determine deformations and stresses caused by a temperature change.

Continue to define remaining restraints and loads in the following steps.

4. Right click the **Fixtures** folder and from the pull-down menu select **Fixed Geometry...** The **Fixture** property manager opens.

5. Within the **Standard (Fixed Geometry)** dialogue box, select **Fixed Geometry**.

6. Zoom in on the right-end of the pipe extension, shown in Fig. 36, and click to select this surface. Immovable restraint symbols in the X, Y, and Z directions are added to the model and **Face<1>** appears in the **Faces, Edges, Vertices for Fixture** dialogue box.

7. Click **[OK]** ✓ to close the **Fixture** property manager. The model is now fully restrained in all directions.

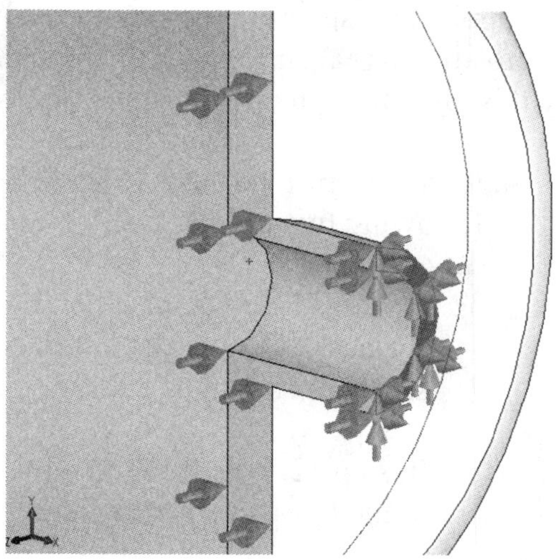

Figure 36 – The **Fixed/Immovable** restraint is added to the attachment surface associated with a rigid pipe connection.

The next step is to apply an internal pressure $P_i = 16.0$ MPa to all internal surfaces of the pressure vessel. Proceed as follows.

8. Right-click **External Loads** and from the pull-down menu select **Pressure...** The **Pressure** property manager opens.

9. In the **Type** dialogue box, select ⦿**Normal to selected face**.

10. The **Faces for Pressure** field is highlighted (light blue) to indicate it is active and awaiting user input.

11. Move cursor onto the model and click to select *all interior* surfaces (both cylinder ends, both internal fillets, and cylindrical surfaces of the cylinder and the pipe extension). A total of six faces **(Face<1>, Face <2>, ... Face<6>)** should be listed in the **Faces for Pressure** field.

12. Beneath **Pressure Value**, verify that **Units** are set to **N/m^2** and type **16.0e6** in the **Pressure Value** field.

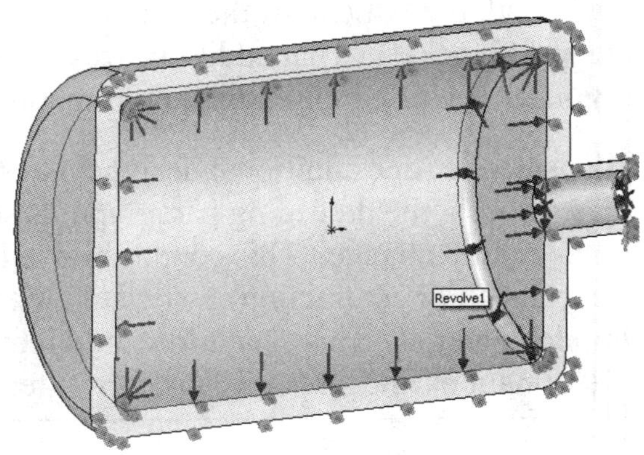

Figure 37 – Internal pressure applied to six faces within the thick-wall pressure vessel.

13. Click **[OK]** ✓ to close the **Pressure** property manager. The model should appear as shown in Fig. 37.

Next apply atmospheric pressure $P_o = 0.101$ MPa to all external surfaces of the model. Try this on your own or follow steps below.

14. Repeat steps 8 through 13 with the following two exceptions.

    a. In step 11, select *all exterior* surfaces. Once again, a total of six faces should be chosen.

    b. In step 12, type **0.101e6** N/m^2 in the **Pressure Value** field.

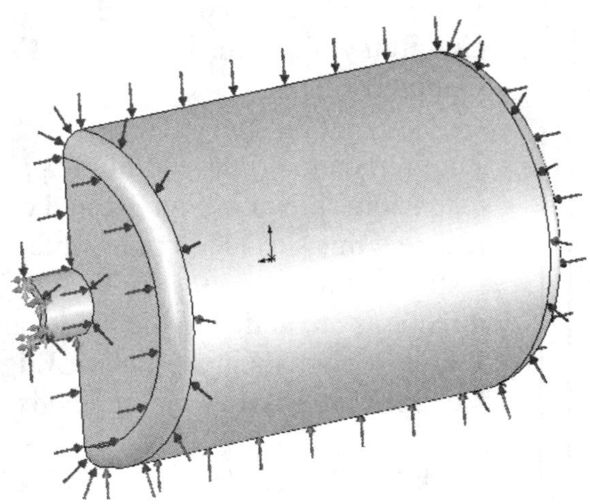

Figure 38 – Atmospheric pressure applied to exterior of the thick-wall pressure vessel.

Upon completion of steps 14 (a) and (b), a view of the exterior of the pressure vessel should appear as shown in Fig. 38.

Mesh the Model

1. Right-click the **Mesh** folder and from the pull-down menu select **Create Mesh…** The **Mesh** property manager opens.

2. In the **Mesh Density** dialogue box accept the default mesh size (slider pointer located at middle of the **Coarse/Fine** indicator scale). Also, in the **Mesh Parameters** dialogue box, verify that **Units** are expressed in **mm**. If not, change them using the pull-down menu.

3. Near bottom of the property manager, click  to open the **Advanced** dialogue box.

4. Within this dialogue box verify that default settings appear as **Jacobian points** set to **4 points**.

5. Click **[OK]** ✓ to close the **Mesh** property manager.

The meshed model along with its boundary conditions is shown in Fig. 39.

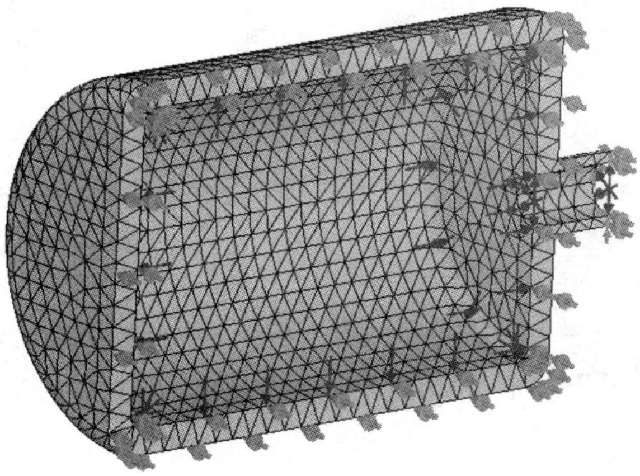

Figure 39 – Default mesh size applied to the thick-wall pressure vessel.

Analysis Insight

Examination of mesh size on the *cut surface* of the pressure vessel in Fig. 39 reveals that a single element spans the entire wall thickness. However, near the beginning of this chapter, a general guideline for determining when *solid* elements can be used stated that, "…the minimum number of elements recommended across the thickness of a part (i.e., across the part's minimum dimension) should be *at least two elements."* Given this guideline, it is appropriate to reduce element size so that at least two elements span the thickness of the pressure vessel wall. This change is easily made by returning to the **Mesh** property manager and adjusting mesh size as outlined next.

6. Right-click the **Mesh** folder and from the pull-down menu select **Create Mesh…** The **Mesh** property manager opens

7. In the **Mesh Density** dialogue box click-and-*drag* the pointer on the **Mesh Factor** sliding-scale from its default, mid-range position, to the **Fine** position.

8. Click **[OK]** ✓ to close the **Mesh** property manager and initiate re-meshing the model. Note the increased time required to mesh the model. The model now appears as shown in Fig. 40 with two elements across the wall thickness.

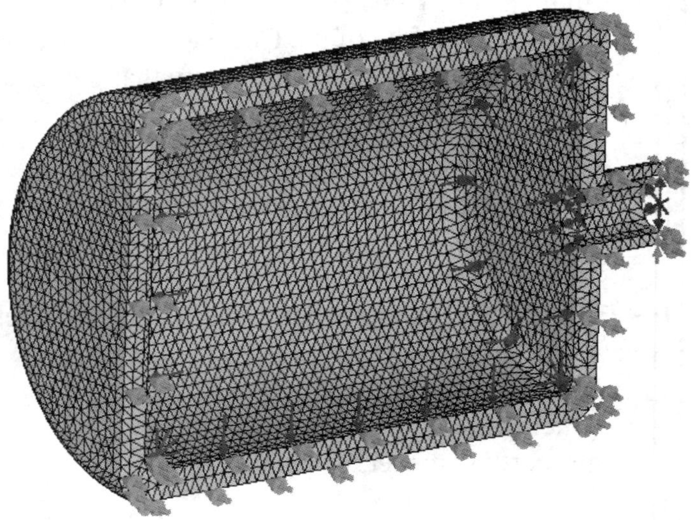

Figure 40 – Pressure vessel showing mesh size reduced to half of the default mesh size so at least two elements span the cylinder wall thickness.

Analysis Insight

Based on the stress concentration example of Chapter 3, where variation of mesh size was investigated, it was found that moving the pointer on the mesh size slider-scale to either the left or right extreme positions had the effect of doubling or halving the default mesh size.

The default mesh size for the model shown in Fig. 39 is **20.060353 mm**. Thus, changing element size to **Fine** reduces its nominal size to **10.0302 mm**, or exactly half the previous size. As a consequence, two elements now span the thick-wall portion of the pressure vessel as illustrated in Fig. 40.

Although two elements span the thick-wall portion of the model, only one element spans the thickness in the pipe connector neck. Zoom in and examine the neck area. This outcome might be considered acceptable because tangential and radial stresses in the thick-wall portion of the pressure vessel are of primary importance in this study.

When compared to the original model, however, a dramatic increase in the number of nodes and elements is observed for the re-meshed model. These changes are summarized in Table 1.

Aside:

The default mesh size would yield adequate results for this model. However, because stress through the wall thickness is examined, the additional nodes will prove helpful.

Table 1 – Comparison of Finite Element Model Size

	Original Model (Default Mesh Size)	**Revised Model (½ Mesh Size)**	**Increase in Model Complexity**
No. of Nodes	16,052	88,037	Approx. 5.5 times larger
No. of Elements	9,337	55,857	Approx. 6 times larger

In this instance, following the general guideline, which suggests at least two solid elements across a part's minimum thickness, results in a significant increase in mesh density with a corresponding increase in solution time. This is a logical cause-and-effect consequence of a mesh size change.

Solution

Having defined restraints, loads, and a mesh, the thick-wall model is subjected to analysis as outlined below.

1. Right-click the study folder **Thick Wall Pressure Vessel (-Default-)** and from the pull-down menu, select **Run**. Solution time is significantly longer, approximately one minute on a Pentium 4® personal computer. To view actual "run time," right-click the **Results** folder and from the pop-up menu select **Solver Messages…** In the **Solver Message** window the **Total solution time** is listed. Click ☒ to close the **Solver Message** window.

2. Computed results, in the form of plots, are listed beneath the **Results** folder. Notice that plots contained in these folders revert to the system default plots.

Results Analysis

Displacement Analysis

To gain some insight into the deformation of the thick-wall pressure vessel subject to internal and external pressures, attention is first directed to the **Displacement1 (-Res disp-)** folder.

1. Right-click the **Displacement1 (-Res disp-)** folder and from the pull-down menu select **Show**. A displacement plot of the model appears as seen in Fig. 41.

2. In the Simulation manager tree, right-click **External Loads**, and from the pull-down menu select **Hide All**. This action hides all external loads acting on the model. Repeat for all **Fixtures**.

3. *If* the previous step removes the color-coded image of displacement in the pressure vessel, either double-click **Displacement1 (-Res disp-)** or right-click it and select **Show** from the pull-down menu. Fig. 41 is again displayed. *Orient the model in a front view.*

4. Move the cursor over the screen image to display an *un-deformed* outline of the model as super-imposed on Fig. 41. Placing the cursor near the mid-point of a cylindrical wall works well.

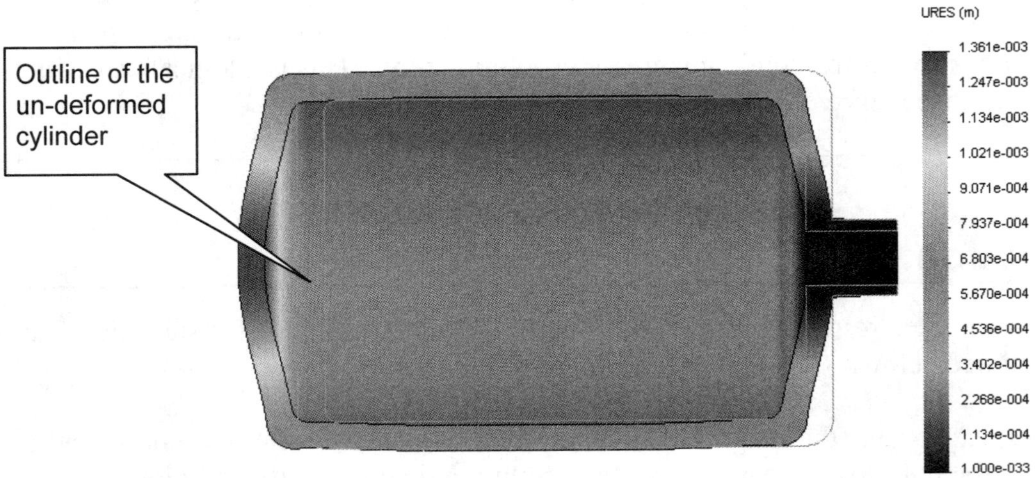

Figure 41 – Image of the model with symmetry and pressure boundary conditions "hidden." **Fixtures** are also hidden. The un-deformed shape of the model is superimposed on the image.

A comparison of the displacement plot with the un-deformed shape of the pressure vessel reveals the following, common sense, observations.

a. All axial displacements are away from the immovable pipe-end.

b. Bulging of both the left and right ends of the model contributes to longitudinal (axial) deformation *away* from the immovable end.

c. Longitudinal deformation (axial stretch) of the cylindrical section also contributes to overall axial deformation.

d. Slight radial deformation (bulging) of cylindrical walls is observed.

e. Virtually zero displacement occurs in the pipe connection.

Analysis Insight

Taking into account the fact that displacements depicted in Fig. 41 are greatly exaggerated (approximately 41.2 times larger than actual), briefly consider how the different boundary conditions (such as supports or a fixed wall at the left-end of the pressure vessel) described in an earlier **Analysis Insight** section, would impact results of the current example.

The effect of correct or incorrect boundary conditions (i.e., loads and fixtures) on finite element analysis results cannot be overemphasized!

von Mises Stress Analysis

The next topic for investigation is interpretation of stresses occurring within the model.

1. Double-click the **Stress1 (-vonMises-)** folder to display the plot shown in Fig. 42.

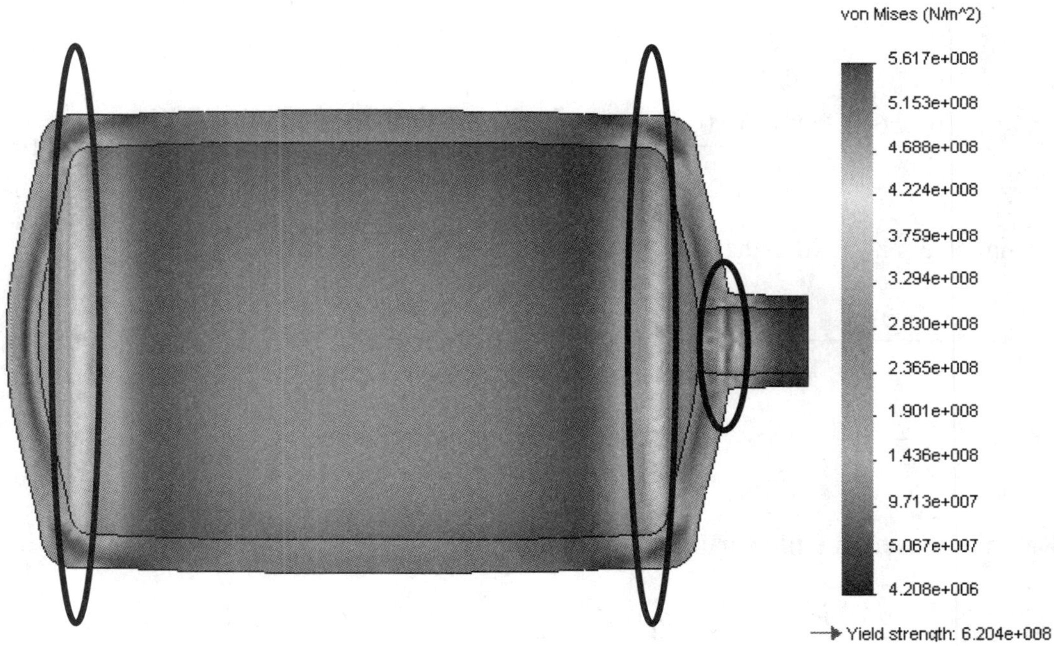

Figure 42 – Regions of high vonMises stress on the thick-wall pressure vessel model.

Regions of high vonMises stress at fillet radii on both ends of the cylinder and in the vicinity of the pipe-to-cylinder connection are circled on Fig. 42. All von Mises stresses are below the material yield strength listed beneath the color coded stress chart.

Tangential Stress Analysis

The next focus of this study is on tangential and radial stress distributions typically associated with analysis of pressurized thick-wall cylinders. However, before examining stress plots, it is helpful to have some expectation of magnitudes associated with these two stresses. Therefore, solutions based on Lame's equations for values of tangential and radial stresses at both the inside and outside surfaces of a thick-wall cylinder are included below.

Tangential stress at outside surface:

$$(\sigma_t)_o = \frac{p_i r_i^2 - p_o r_o^2 - r_i^2 \cancel{r_0^2}(p_o - p_i)/\cancel{r_o^2}}{r_o^2 - r_i^2}$$

$$= \frac{16.0e6(0.15)^2 - 0.101e6(0.175)^2 - (0.15)^2(0.101e6 - 16.0e6)}{(0.175)^2 - (0.15)^2} = 87.9 \text{ Mpa} \qquad [6]$$

Tangential stress at inside surface:

$$(\sigma_t)_i = \frac{p_i r_i^2 - p_o r_o^2 - \cancel{r_i^2} r_0^2(p_o - p_i)/\cancel{r_i^2}}{r_o^2 - r_i^2}$$

$$= \frac{16.0e6(0.15)^2 - 0.101e6(0.175)^2 - (0.175)^2(0.101e6 - 16.0e6)}{(0.175)^2 - (0.15)^2} = 103.8 \text{ Mpa} \qquad [7]$$

Radial stress at inside surface:

$$\sigma_{r_i} = \frac{p_i r_i^2 - p_o r_o^2 + \cancel{r_i^2} r_0^2(p_o - p_i)/\cancel{r_i^2}}{r_o^2 - r_i^2} = \frac{p_i r_i^2 - \cancel{p_o r_o^2} + \cancel{p_o r_o^2} - p_i r_o^2}{r_o^2 - r_i^2}$$

$$= \frac{-p_i(r_o^2 - r_i^2)}{(r_o^2 - r_i^2)} = -p_i = -16.0 \text{ Mpa} = \text{(internal pressure)} \qquad [8]$$

Radial stress at outside surface:

$$\sigma_{r_o} = \frac{p_i r_i^2 - p_o r_o^2 + r_i^2 \cancel{r_0^2}(p_o - p_i)/\cancel{r_o^2}}{r_o^2 - r_i^2} = \frac{\cancel{p_i r_i^2} - p_o r_o^2 + p_o r_i^2 - \cancel{p_i r_i^2}}{r_o^2 - r_i^2}$$

$$= \frac{-p_o(r_o^2 - r_i^2)}{(r_o^2 - r_i^2)} = -p_o = -0.101 \text{ MPa} = \text{(external pressure)} \qquad [9]$$

Two alternative ways of viewing these results in SolidWorks Simulation are investigated below. We begin with what might be considered the most intuitive method of viewing stress results and then proceed to a second method that makes use of the *Section Clipping* capability of the software. Begin by adding a plot of first principal stress to the **Results** folder. Try this on your own or follow the steps outlined below.

1. Right-click the **Results** folder and from the pull-down menu, select **Define Stress Plot…** The **Stress Plot** property manager opens.

Figure 43 – Plot of 1st principal stress distribution throughout the thick-wall pressure vessel.

2. In the **Display** dialogue box, click to open the **Component** pull-down menu and from the list of available stresses, select **P1: 1st Principal Stress.**

3. Verify that **Units** are set to **N/m^2**.

4. Click **[OK]** ✓ to close the **Stress Plot** property manager.

Figure 43 shows a front view of the distribution of 1st principal stress throughout the model. Once again notice regions of high stress at both end fillets where the cylinder and flat ends join. Unfortunately, Fig. 43 does not provide good delineation of stress variation through the central, thick-wall portion of the cylinder. That is to say, the mid-section of the cylinder appears a fairly uniform shade of light blue.

Analysis Insight

Regions of high principal stress and maximum vonMises stress are typically most important to the designer or stress analyst whose focus is on product safety. However, because a primary objective of this example is to investigate stresses associated with thick-wall pressure vessel theory and to learn different ways to display these results, the following section describes how to better examine these stresses while simultaneously discovering additional software plotting capabilities.

Adjusting Stress Magnitude Display Parameters

A quick review of previous calculations for tangential stress variation from the inside to the outside cylindrical surfaces of the model, equations [6] and [7] above, reveals:

Tangential stress at inside: $(\sigma_t)_i = 103.8$ Mpa

Tangential stress at outside: $(\sigma_t)_o = 87.9$ MPa

Comparing the above values with the range of 1st principal stress magnitudes displayed in the color-coded stress legend adjacent to the model (currently displayed on your screen) reveals that the above stresses occupy only a small portion of the full range of stress values displayed; see circled portion of the stress legend in Fig. 43. Thus, if it is desired to verify values of 1st principal stress between 87.9 MPa to 103.8 MPa, in the cylinder wall, then the stress display can be adjusted to bracket these stress values. The following steps outline a procedure to accomplish this.

1. Right-click **Stress2 (-1st principal-)** and from the pull-down menu select **Chart Options…** A portion of the **Chart Options** property manager opens as shown in Fig. 44.

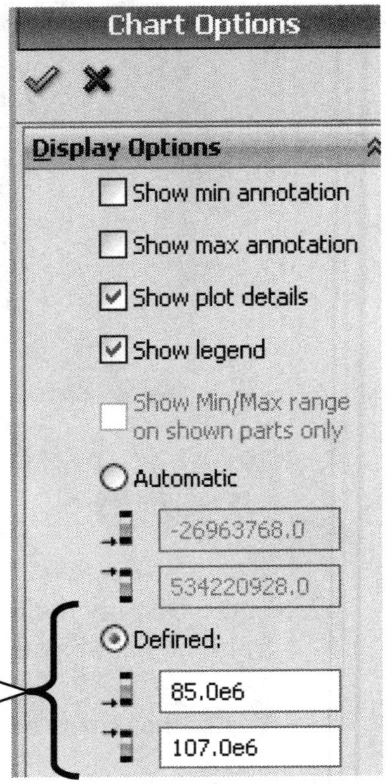

Figure 44 – Controlling the range of stresses displayed using the **Defined** option.

2. At the bottom of the **Display Options** dialogue box, select **⦿Defined:** This option provides a means of setting the desired upper and lower bounds for stress magnitudes to be displayed. In the upper box, type **85.0e6**, which is slightly lower than the *minimum* 1st principal stress value of $(\sigma_t)_o = 87.9$ MPa expected at the outside surface.

3. Similarly, in the bottom box, type **107.0e6**, which is slightly higher than the *maximum* 1st principal stress value of $(\sigma_t)_i = 103.8$ MPa expected at the inside surface of the cylinder.

4. Click **[OK]** ✓ to close the **Chart Options** property manager. Figure 45 (a) displays 1st principal stress magnitudes in the defined range.

5. Next, zoom-in on the boxed region, shown in Fig. 45 (a), to obtain a close-up view of stress variation through the cylinder wall as illustrated by the multiple color fringes in Fig. 45 (b). Notice that this region is well removed from effects of end-conditions caused by fillets at both ends of the cylinder.

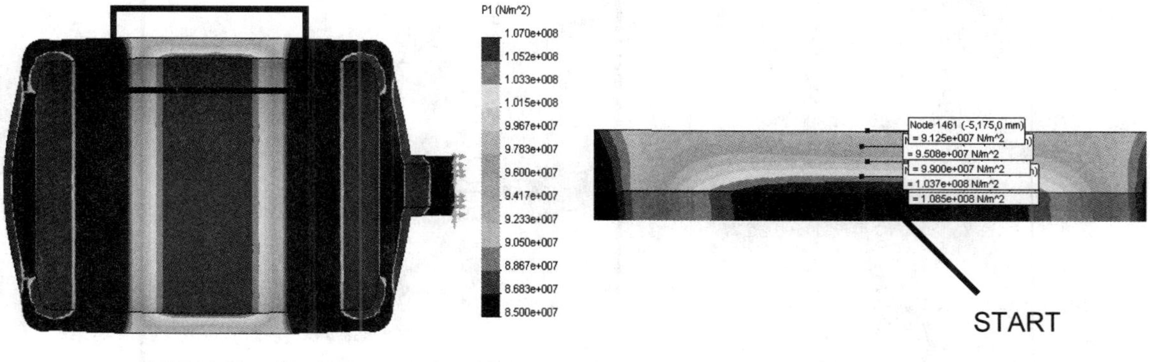

(a) (b)

Figure 45 – (a) 1st principal stress plot after magnitudes are restricted to the range: 85.0 MPa < σ_t < 107.0 MPa; (b) close-up of tangential stress distribution (σ_t) through the thick-wall.

The **Probe** feature is used next to determine actual values of 1st principal stress at various nodes across the wall thickness.

6. Right-click **Stress2 (-1st principal-)** and from the pull-down menu select **Probe**. The **Probe Result** property manager opens as shown in Fig. 46 (a). *Initially no values appear in the table.*

7. Begin at the inside of the cylinder wall, as near as possible to the middle of the cylinder; see "**START**" label on Fig. 45 (b). Then successively click and move the cursor slightly upward (moving in as straight a line as possible) and repeat until five node points are selected across the wall thickness. Stress values at each node point are simultaneously displayed on the model [also shown in Fig. 45 (b)] and in the **Results** dialogue box, Fig. 46 (a). *If difficulty selecting nodes is experienced, see the **ASIDE** section below.*

ASIDE:
If difficulty is experienced selecting the *unseen* nodes, temporarily close the **Probe Result** property manager, by clicking **X**, and turn "on" the mesh display as follows.

a. Right-click **Stress2 (-1st principal-)** and from the pull-down menu select **Settings…**

b. Within the **Settings** property manager, click to open the pull-down menu beneath **Boundary Options** and select **Mesh**. Click **[OK]** ✓.

A mesh displayed on the model should facilitate selecting corner *and* mid-side nodes on each element across the wall thickness. Repeat steps 6 and 7 with the mesh displayed.

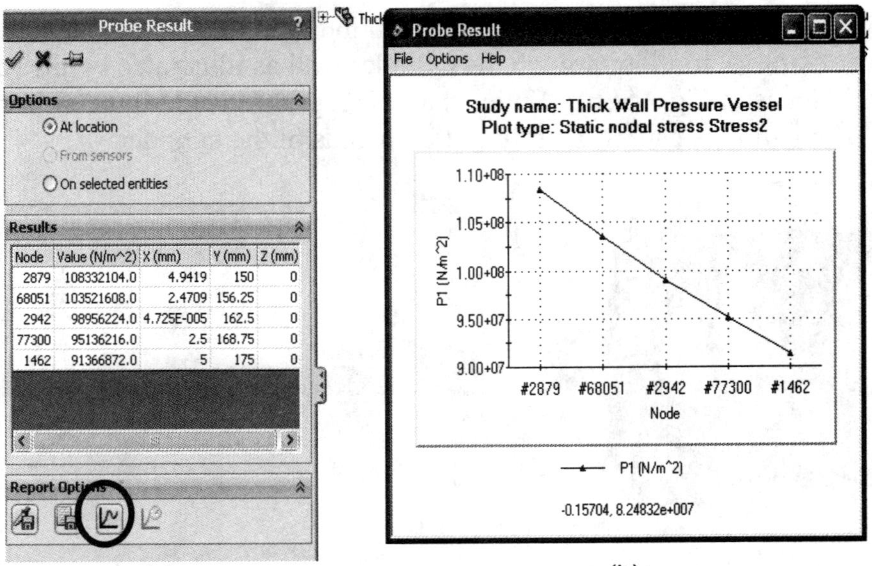

(a) (b)

Figure 46 – (a) **Probe** window displays values of $\sigma_1 = \sigma_t$ at node locations across the thick-wall; (b) the **Probe Result** window shows a graph of tangential stress variation from the inside surface (high stress) to the outside surface (lower stress) of the thick-wall pressure vessel.

8. After using the **Probe** feature to select nodes, click the **[Plot]** button at bottom of the **Probe Result** property manager to display a graph of tangential stress variation through the wall thickness as shown in Fig. 46 (b).
9. Click ☒ to close the **Probe Result** graph.
10. Click **[OK]** ✓ to close the **Probe Result** window.
11. If the mesh is still displayed on the model, right-click **Stress2 (-1st principal-)** and from the pull-down menu select **Settings…** In the **Boundary Options** dialogue box, open the pull-down menu and select **Model.**
12. Click **[OK]** ✓ to close the **Settings** property manager.

A quick comparison of classical results, found using Lame's equations, and finite element results for tangential stress magnitudes at the inside and outside wall surfaces yields the following.

For tangential stress at the inside surface:

$$\%\text{ difference} = \left[\frac{\text{FEA result} - \text{ classical result}}{\text{FEA result}}\right]100 = \left[\frac{108.3e6 - 103.8e6}{108.3e6}\right]100 = 4.15\% \quad [10]$$

Tangential stress at the outside wall surface:

$$\% \text{ difference} = \left[\frac{\text{FEA result} - \text{ classical result}}{\text{FEA result}}\right]100 = \left[\frac{91.36e6 - 87.9e6}{91.36e6}\right]100 = 3.78\% \quad [11]$$

Both these percent difference values are low enough that the analyst should have reasonable confidence in the finite element analysis results.

This concludes examination of tangential stress variation through the cylinder wall by conventional methods. The next section examines an alternate means of viewing these same results by using **Section Clipping** plots.

Using Section Clipping to Observe Stress Results

Use of *Section Clipping* is introduced in this section. Section plots are used where it is desirable to view stresses interior to a solid model, such as in an assembly of multiple parts, or if a solid model of the cylinder were used for this example rather than a cut-section of the model. Steps below outline use of the *Section Clipping* feature.

1. If the previous close-up view of the pressure vessel wall, appearing in Fig. 45 (b) remains on the screen, use the **Zoom to Fit** icon to restore the graphic display to a full image of the model. Then click the **Trimetric** icon to orient the model in an view similar to that shown in Fig. 47.

2. Right-click **Stress2 (-1st principal-)** and from the pull-down menu select **Section Clipping...** The **Section** property manager opens as shown in Fig. 48.

3. In the **Section1** dialogue box, notice that **Front Plane** is selected as the default viewing plane. Also, the **Distance** field, located immediately below **Front Plane** in Fig. 48, is set at **0.00 mm**, thereby indicating that the section view is currently displayed *on* the front surface.

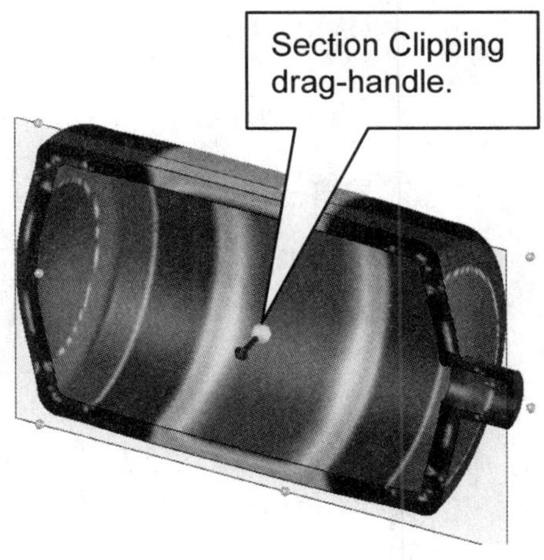

Figure 47 – Trimetric view of model showing 1st principal stress and the **Section Clipping** drag-handle.

4. In the **Options** dialogue box, clear the "✓" from ☐ **Show contour on the uncut portion of the model**. Immediately the interior and exterior surfaces of the model are shaded the default model color (typically grey). This makes for easier viewing of stress contours on cut sections.

5. Next, click-and-drag the *Section Clipping* drag-handle shown in Fig. 47. This action permits dynamic viewing of stresses within the model at any depth from the **Front Plane**.

6. Undo step 4 by checking ☑ **Show contour on the uncut portion of the model**, and again move the *Section Clipping* drag-handle.

A similar effect to that created in step 4 can be obtained as outlined next.

7. In the **Options** dialogue box, check to select ☑ **Plot on section only**. This action restricts plotted stresses to the **Front Plane** *at* the current depth. Once again, move the *Section Clipping* drag-handle and observe the resulting display.

8. To display stress distribution on a mid-plane through the model, type **0** in the **Distance** field of the **Section 1** dialogue box as shown in Fig. 48, and press **[Enter]**. This action creates the display shown in Fig. 49.

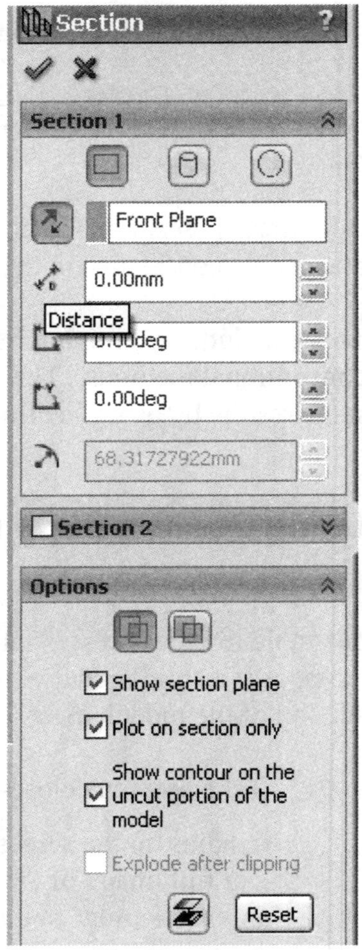

Figure 48 – The **Section** property manager is used to control display of stress contours *within* a model.

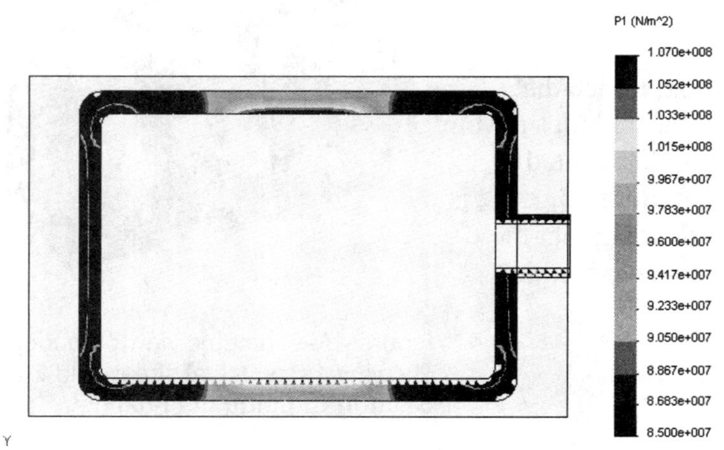

Figure 49 – Image of tangential stresses in the cylinder wall with the ☑ **Plot on section only** option active.

Section Clipping options demonstrated in steps 4 through 8 are convenient for masking stress contours which otherwise might make it difficult to differentiate between desired stress contours and other nearby colored fringes.

9. Within the **Section1** dialogue box, experiment by clicking the down arrow ▼adjacent to **0.00mm** in the **Distance** spin box. The down arrow moves the

section away from the front plane in the negative z-direction. Click-and-*hold* the down arrow ▼ to observe the section plane move progressively away from the cut section and *into* the model. Conversely, if the up arrow ▲ is clicked, the section viewing plane moves away from the model (+ z-direction). For values greater than **0.00mm**, the section plane is located *in front* of the model, thus the model is not sectioned. It is also possible to examine stress at a particular depth within the model by typing any desired location into the **Distance** spin-box.

10. Reset **Distance** to **0.00** mm and clear the check-mark "✓" from ☐ **Plot on section only**.

As a final demonstration of the *Section Clipping* feature, tangential stress variation through the cylinder wall is viewed by sectioning the cylinder as outlined below.

11. Either rotate the model to display its right-side view or, from the SolidWorks toolbar select the right-side view icon. A right-side view, looking down the axis of the cylinder from the pipe connection-end, appears in Fig. 50.

12. In the **Section 1** dialogue box, click to activate (light blue) the **Reference entity** field (top field that currently shows **Front Plane**).

13. Next, click the "+" sign adjacent to the **SolidWorks** flyout menu, at top-left of the graphics screen, and from the pull-down menu, select **Right Plane**.

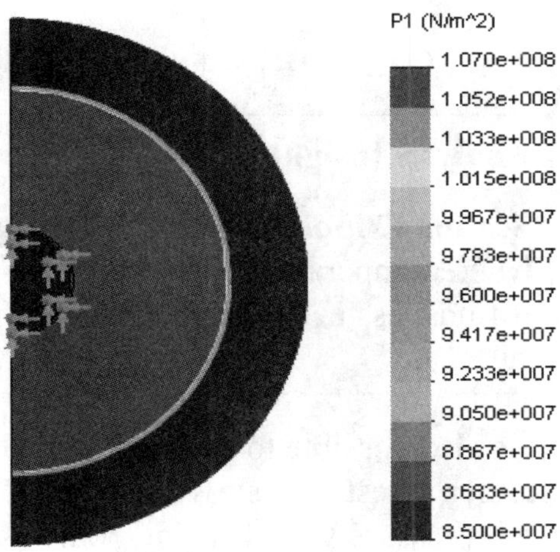

Figure 50 – Right-side view of model prior to taking a section view.

14. Notice that **Right Plane** now appears in the highlighted **Reference entity** field and, because the origin of the Cartesian coordinate system is located at the middle of the model, the right plane bisects the model at its mid-section. As a result, tangential stress variation through the wall thickness is shown as illustrated in Fig. 51. Rotate the model to verify this view.

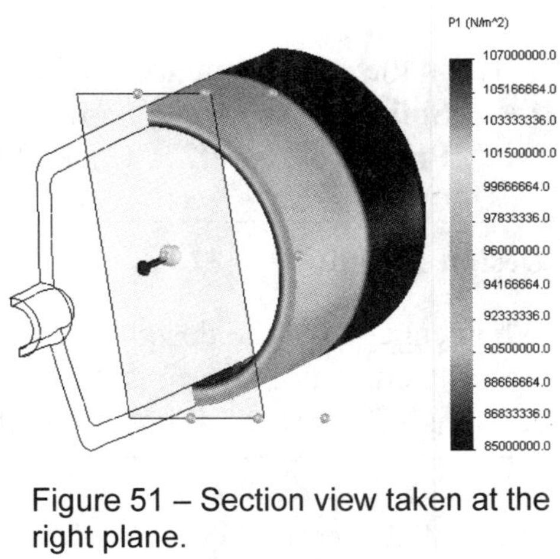

Figure 51 – Section view taken at the right plane.

15. Once again, to aid in examining stresses in the wall only, in the **Options** dialogue box, click to check ☑ **Plot on section only**. The resulting display shows stress contours on the cut section only. See Fig. 52.

Figure 52 shows stresses on the cut section only and the section clipping drag-handle. The model is rotated to reveal the location of the section on an outline of the model.

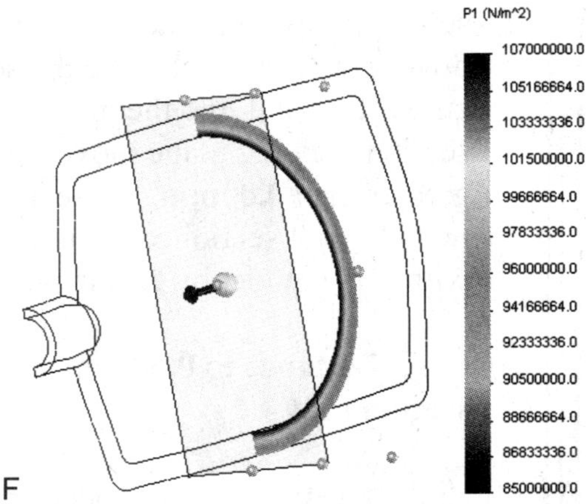

F

Figure 52 – Tangential stress display on mid-section of the model.

16. In the **Section 1** dialogue box, experiment by clicking the up ▲or down ▼ arrows on the **Distance** spin box to observe the effect on stresses displayed in the model.

17. Click **[OK]** ✓ to close the **Section** property manager.

Analysis Insight

Section Clipping is most advantageous for heat transfer and fluid flow problems where temperature or pressure variation throughout a model is of primary importance. It finds less use for stress analysis problems because maximum stresses occur on part surfaces.

It is also possible to use the **Probe** feature in combination with any of the *Section* plots to further investigate stresses within a model. This concludes the analysis of thin and thick-wall pressure vessels using both *shell* and *solid* elements, respectively. Alternate ways to examine results were also explored.

The current model need not be saved. Therefore, exit and discard the solution as follows.

1. In the main menu, select **File**. From the pull-down menu select **Close**. A **SolidWorks** window opens and prompts: **"Save changes to Thick Wall Pressure Vessel?"** Click **[NO]**.

Design Insight

When engaged in the design of any sort of pressure vessel, ASME Boiler and Pressure Vessel Codes[2] must be consulted. The Professional version of SolidWorks Simulation contains a Study type aligned with ASME codes.

---

[2] The ASME Boiler and Pressure Vessel Code, Sections I-XI, American Society of Mechanical Engineers, New York, NY, 1995.

EXERCISES

EXERCISE 1 – Thick Wall Pressure Vessel

The cylinder in Fig. E 4-1 allows three separate pipe connections. The connection on top of the cylinder is considered **Fixed** due to its rigid external attachment (not shown). However, both pipes on the flat end are connected to flexible pipe segments (also not shown) that permit movement in the X (axial) and Y (vertical) directions. Movement in these directions is permitted to accommodate axial and circumferential expansion when the tank is pressurized. In other words, movement is only restricted in the Z-direction at these pipe connections. Perform a finite element analysis of this cylinder subject to the following guidelines. Open the file: **Pressure Vessel 4-1**.

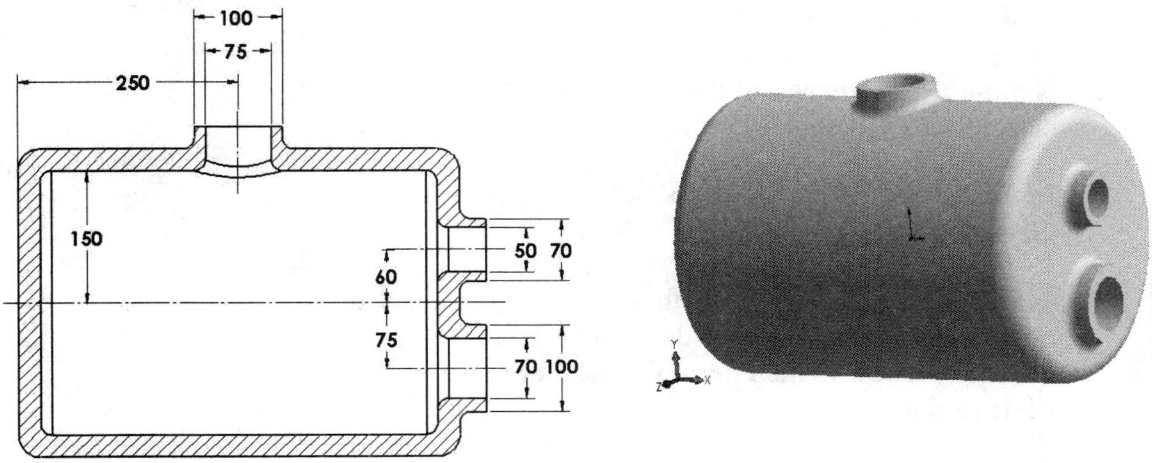

Figure E4-1 – Cylindrical pressure vessel with three pipe attachments. Wall thickness t = 25 mm.

- Material: **AISI Type 316L stainless steel** (Use S.I. units)
- Mesh: **High Quality** tetrahedral elements (NOTE: Determine whether $t \leq r_i/20$. Substituting yields, $25 \leq 150/20$. Since t is *not* $\leq r_i/20$, therefore thick-wall equations apply to classical calculations of stress in the cylinder walls.
- External Loads: **P = 14.5 MPa,** Internal pressure. External pressure: Negligible
- Fixtures: The pipe connection on top of the cylinder is **Fixed/Immovable.**

  Pipes on right end of the tank restrain movement in the **Z**-direction only. This restraint and its direction are somewhat arbitrary, but are included to demonstrate how alternative restraints might be applied.

  Assistance dealing with these pipe restraints is included in the ***Solution Guidance*** *box below.*

  Apply **Symmetry** restraints on cut surfaces of the cylinder.

Solution Guidance

Begin by reducing the model to half of the tank geometry as follows.

- In the SolidWorks Feature manager locate **Half-Model of Cylinder** and **Unsuppress** it.
- Also in the SolidWorks feature manager, defeature the model. **Supress** fillets at all pipe connections.

To apply restraints in the Z-direction on end surfaces of the horizontal pipe connections, proceed as follows.

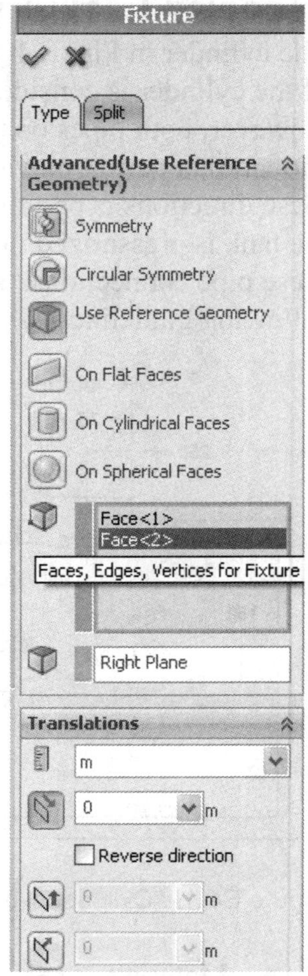

Fig. E4-2 – Restraints applied to prevent motion in the Z-direction.

i. Right-click **Fixtures** and from the pull-down menu, select **Fixed Geometry…**

ii. In the **Advanced** dialogue box, select **Use Reference Geometry**.

iii. Click the right *end face* of both pipe extensions located on the right-side of the cylinder. **Face<1>** and **Face<2>** appear in the **Faces, Edges, Vertices for Fixture** field.

iv. Activate the **Face, Edge, Plane Axis for Direction** field and in the SolidWorks flyout menu, select **Right Plane**.

v. In the **Translations** dialogue box, select the **Along plane Dir 1** icon. The field is highlighted (white) and "**0**" appears. This value indicates zero translation is allowed in the selected Z-direction. See Fig. E 4-3

v. Click **[OK]** ✓ to close the **Fixture** property manager.

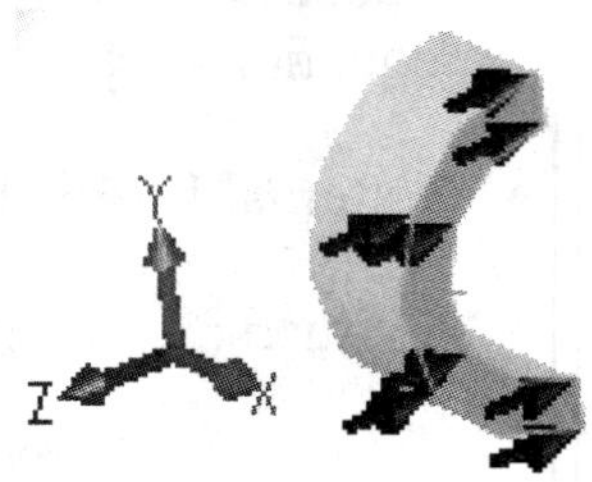

Fig. E4-3 – Restraint symbols in Z-direction.

Vectors displayed on the model should be oriented in the Z-direction, see Fig. E 4-3. Either the $\pm$ Z-direction is acceptable since displacement = 0.

Develop a finite element model that includes: material selection, fixtures, external loads, mesh the model (two elements are required across the cylinder wall thickness; one element thickness is permitted on pipe extensions), and a solution.

Determine the following:

a. Create a stress contour plot of von Mises stress in the cylinder and all its connecting entities. Include automatic labeling of maximum von Mises stress on the plot. Does the maximum von Mises stress exceed material yield strength?

b. Use classical equations to calculate magnitudes of tangential and radial stresses at both the inside and outside surfaces of the cylinder. Make these calculations in a region well removed from the cylinder ends and pipe connections.

c. Use finite element analysis to determine tangential stress in the cylinder wall opposite the top pipe connection. When determining this stress, reduce the range of stress values plotted to magnitudes slightly above and slightly below tangential stress magnitudes anticipated on the inside and outside surfaces. Plot the *appropriate stress* contours to show tangential stress in the cylinder wall.

d. Use the **Probe** feature to produce a graph of tangential stress variation through the cylinder wall from inside to outside. Choose node points at the middle of the cylinder (i.e. midway between its left and right ends.) Add a descriptive title and axis labels to this graph.

e. Repeat step (c), but replace "tangential" stress with "radial" stress.

f. Repeat step (d), but replace "tangential" stress with "radial" stress.

g. Compare the percent difference between FEA results and results obtained from classical pressure vessel calculations determined in part (b). Results to be compared include the tangential stress at inside and outside surfaces of the cylinder and also radial stress at inside and outside surfaces. Use the following equation to compute the percent difference between results.

$$\%\text{ difference} = \frac{(\text{FEA result - classical result})}{\text{FEA result}} * 100 = \qquad [1]$$

h. Comment upon the "goodness" of agreement between results of part (g). If classical and FEA results differ by more than 8%, explain why.

EXERCISE 2 – Analysis of a Sheet Metal Bracket Using Shell Elements

The bracket shown in Fig. E 4-4 is one of two brackets used to attach a "carry all" to a motorcycle frame. **Chrome Stainless Steel** is used for the bracket to enhance appearance and to provide corrosion resistance. Three bolts attach the bracket to the frame through holes on the vertical (left) leg at holes illustrated in Fig. E 4-4. A downward design load of 14 lb is applied at the hole on tab **A**. This load represents the portion of load carried by tab **A** in a fully loaded "carry all." Perform a finite element analysis of this part using *shell* elements applied at the mid-surface of the part.

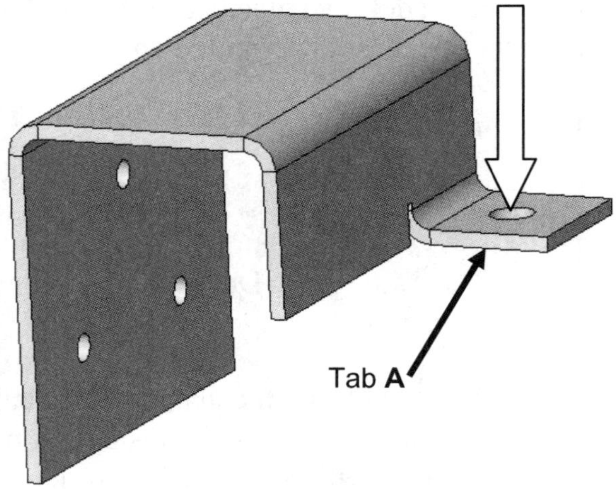

Figure E4-4 – Bracket used to attach a cargo case to a motorcycle frame.

Open the file: **Bracket 4-2**.

- Material: **Chrome Stainless Steel** (Use English units)
- Mesh: **High Quality** *shell* elements defined on the mid-surface. Use default mesh size. NOTE: For the **Shell mesh using mid-surface** option, thickness of the elements is automatically extracted from the SolidWorks model geometry.
- Fixtures: Apply a **Fixed** restraint to the three bolt holes. This fixture can be applied to either the hole edge or to its inner surface.
- External Load: **14 lb** applied vertically downward to the top surface of Tab A.

This exercise is used to demonstrate application of shell elements to a sheet metal part. Recall from the chapter introduction that sheet metal parts are automatically treated as shell elements by the software. As such, this exercise provides insight into a second way of creating a shell model. Guidance used to create a shell model of the bracket using this second method is provided below.

How is it known that the current model is a sheet metal part? To answer this question, open the part file and examine the SolidWorks Feature manager tree. In the tree, **Sheet-Metal1** is listed along with several SolidWorks features that pertain exclusively to sheet metal parts. Also, in the Simulation manager tree observe that **Bracket 4-2** is represented by a "thin sheet" icon Bracket 4-2 rather than by a solid body icon Bracket 4-2.

Solution Guidance

a. Apply **Fixtures** to the three holes. **Fixed** restraints can be applied to either the edges or surfaces within each hole. Restraints are automatically transferred to edges of the shell element model.

b. Applying a downward force on tab **A** is similar to that of applying a directed force on a split-line. The 14 lb downward force can be applied to either an *edge* or the *inner surface* of the hole in tab **A**.

Method #2 for Defining a Shell Model

a. Right-click **Bracket 4-2 (-Chrome Stainless Steel-)** (or) choose whatever filename was specified by you. From the pull-down menu, select **Edit Definition…** The **Shell Definition** property manager opens as seen in Fig. E 4-5.

b. In the **Type** dialogue box, choose ⊙ **Thin** and set **Unit** to **in**. The grayed-out number appearing in the **Shell Thickness** field **0.1046** corresponds to the sheet metal thickness specified in SolidWorks. This step permits the user to view the part thickness.

c. Click **[OK]** ✓ to close the **Shell Definition** property manager.

d. Right-click **Mesh** and select **Create Mesh…** The **Mesh** property manager opens.

e. In the **Advanced** dialogue box, verify that ☐ **Draft Quality Mesh** is *not* checked.

Figure E4-5 – Checking Shell thickness as specified in the original SolidWorks drawing file.

f. Accept remaining default settings and click **[OK]** ✓ to close the **Mesh** property manager.

Note the few number of steps required to create a shell mesh on this sheet metal bracket [three steps (a) to (c) above] as compared to approximately twenty five steps required to specify the mid-surface and then shell mesh the thin wall pressure vessel example. This streamlined procedure is realized because the original model was defined as a sheet metal part and the software automatically recognizes this fact. Models classified as "surface parts" are equally simple to convert to a shell mesh.

Develop a finite element model that includes: material specification, fixtures, external loads, mesh generation, and solution.

Determine the following:

a. Plot von Mises stress on the top surface of the shell face; include the applied load and fixtures on this plot. Consider the top surface to be that shown facing upward in Fig. E 4-4 (i.e., the top side of the model is the side to which the external 14 lb load is applied). Include automatic labeling of maximum and minimum von Mises stress on this plot.

   NOTE: If the "top" surface, as defined above in Fig. E 4-4, appears orange in color (recall orange denotes the "bottom" surface), then **Flip Shell Elements** as outlined in the example problem. However, remember to hold the **[Shift]** key while selecting *all* surfaces of the model.

b. Repeat part (a) for the "bottom" surface of the bracket. By what percent do the maximum von Mises stresses on the top and bottom surfaces differ.

c. Question: On what surface does the maximum von Mises stress occur? Does this stress exceed the material yield strength? Describe factors, such as part geometry, location of the applied load, etc. that cause the maximum stress to occur where it does on the model.

EXERCISE 3 – Joist Hanger Analysis Using Shell Elements

"Joist" is the name commonly applied to beams used to support floors in residential and commercial construction. So called "joist hangers" are often used to connect the ends of joists to a "header beam." For individuals unfamiliar with floor joists, header beams, and joist hangers, these items are labeled in Fig. E 4-6. Common nails are used to fasten joist hangers beams and joists. However, this exercise is simplified to examine only loads transferred to a joist hanger by a single joist (i.e., by a single floor beam). Also, nails used to fasten a joist to the joist hanger are ignored. The joist hanger to be analyzed is shown in Figs. E 4-7 (a) and (b).

Open the File: **Joist Hanger**

Figure E 4-6 – A joist hanger and related beams are identified in the image above.

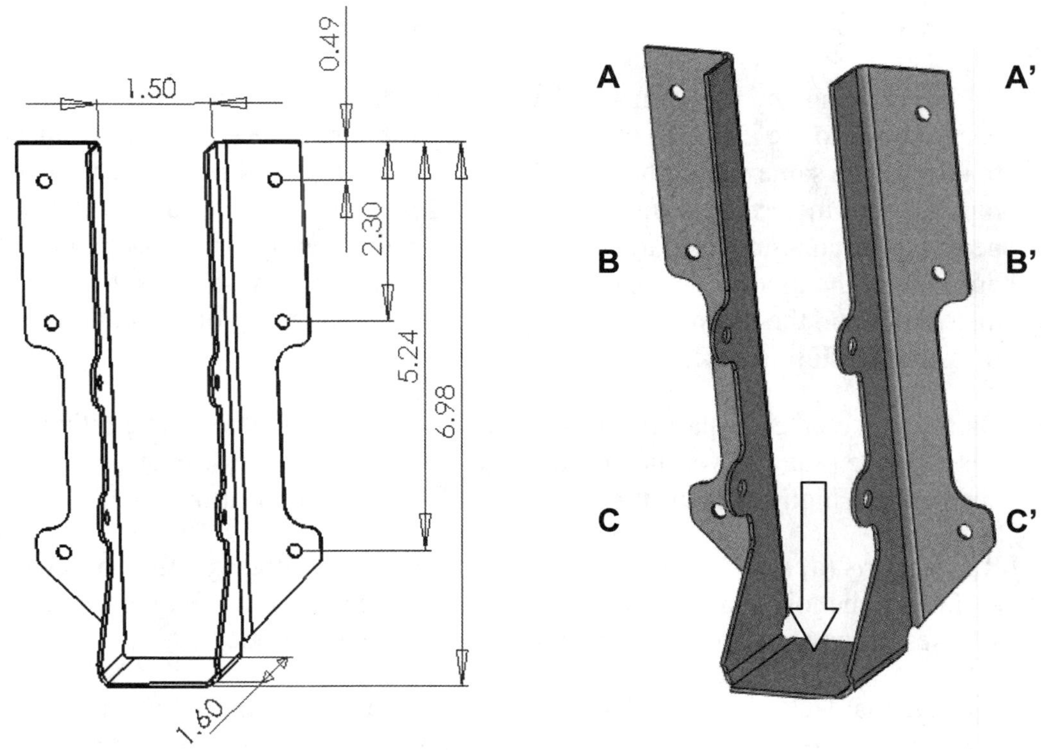

Figure E4-7 – Typical joist hanger used to support 2"x8" floor joists. A load of 320 lb is distributed over the bottom surface.

- Material: **Galvanized Steel** (Use English units) Galvanized material is used because joist hangers are also used under porches, decks, and in other exposed exterior environments.

- Mesh: **Shell Mesh**

- Fixture: **Fixed** restraints applied *only* to nail holes attached to the header beam at **A, A', B, B', C, C'** in Fig. E 4-7. A typical header beam is labeled in Fig. E4-6.

- External Load: **320** lb downward load applied normal to the bottom surface of the joist hanger. This load accounts for lumber weight plus the weight of furnishings, appliances, and people on the floor above. It is *uniformly distributed* over the bottom of the joist hanger.

Develop a finite element model that includes: material specification, fixtures, external load, mesh generation, and solution as specified below.

Determine the following:

a. Before creating any plots, ensure that the top side of the meshed model corresponds to the inside of the "U" shaped joist hanger. Recall that *all* surfaces that share the same *side* of the model must be specified as the same surface (i.e., top and bottom surfaces cannot be mixed together on the same surface). It may be necessary to imagine the part flattened-out to help identify surfaces common to one side of the model. Then, create a von Mises stress plot showing the stress distribution on the top surface of the joist hanger. For this plot, turn on the **Show max annotation** feature.

b. On the plot created in part (a), identify all regions of high stress by circling them. Also, on the plot, answer the question: "Is the material yield strength exceeded at any of these high stress locations?" If "yes" label these locations as "FS < 1."

c. Repeat parts (a) and (b), but create a plot of von Mises stress on the bottom surface of the joist hanger. On this plot, state whether the largest von Mises stresses occur on the top or bottom surface of the shell model.

d. Assume that lack of attention to detail, carelessness, rushing to finish the job, or just plain laziness, results in fewer than all nails being driven through holes **Fixed** to the header beam at holes **A, A', B, B', C, C'**. On your own create two additional scenarios. In scenario 1, omit one nail from *each side* of the joist hanger where it is attached to the header beam. In scenario 2, omit two nails from *each side* of the joist hanger. Do this by editing the **Fixtures** folder as follows.

  - In the Simulation manager tree, select **Fixture-1** and from the pull-down menu, select **Edit Definition…**

  - In the **Standard (Fixed Geometry)** dialogue box right-click the nails to be eliminated and then from the pull-down menu select **Delete**.

  - Click **[OK]** ✓ to close the **Fixture** property manager.

e. For both scenarios 1 and 2, repeat parts (a) and (b) of this problem. Does the joist hanger become unsafe for either of these two scenarios? If "yes" identify the unsafe scenario(s) and label areas where the safety factor is exceeded as "FS < 1."

Textbook Problems

In addition to the above exercises, it is highly recommended that additional problems involving pressure vessels and/or thin parts be worked from a design of machine elements textbook. Textbook problems provide a great way to discover errors made in formulating a finite element analysis because they typically are well defined problems for which the solution is known. Typical textbook problems, if well defined in advance, make an excellent source of solutions for comparison.

CHAPTER #5

INTERFERENCE FIT ANALYSIS

This example examines modeling of an interference fit between two mating parts. For purposes of discussion, the generic term "interference fit" is considered synonymous with the terminology "force fit" or "shrink fit." However, SolidWorks Simulation documentation refers to all these fits as "shrink fits." These fit classifications are often used to join two members together without the need for other fastening devices such as set-screws or keys and keyways. Interference fit analysis is often considered together with pressure vessel analysis since the internal member exerts the equivalent of an outward pressure on the part into which it is force fit. And, conversely, the external member exerts the equivalent of an external pressure onto the part it surrounds.

Although this example solves an interference fit problem for a single set of part dimensions, it is important to recognize that, in practice, maximum and minimum stress levels occur due to tolerance variations of mating part dimensions. For example, a minimum level of interference must be ensured in order to transfer a desired torque between mating components. This case results when the smallest shaft is inserted into the largest hole. Conversely, when tolerances are such that the largest shaft is inserted into the smallest hole, maximum interference results. Stress levels correspond directly to the amount of interference. Another factor to consider occurs when different materials are used for mating parts. In these instances the effects of differential dimension changes due to thermal expansion or contraction may also have to be considered. The above scenarios are cited to alert the user to other factors that affect interference fits. However, because the emphasis of this text is on mastering use of SolidWorks Simulation capabilities, these other factors are not considered in this example.

Learning Objectives

Upon completion of this example, users should be able to:

- Set-up and analyze an *interference fit* in an assembly.
- Define and use a *cylindrical* coordinate system.
- Examine results in a *local (cylindrical)* coordinate system.
- Generate a *report* summarizing results of a study.
- Apply alternative means of *controlling rigid body motion.*

Problem Statement

A partially dimensioned section view of a wheel and its axle are shown in Fig. 1. The wheel is part of an overhead traveling crane, which is used to transport heavy materials from point-to-point on a factory floor. The 2.5041 inch diameter shaft is shrink fit into a wheel-hub with inside diameter of 2.5000 inches resulting in a 0.0041 inch diametral interference. This example is the first to involve analysis of an *assembly* of more than one part. Analysis of this model begins below.

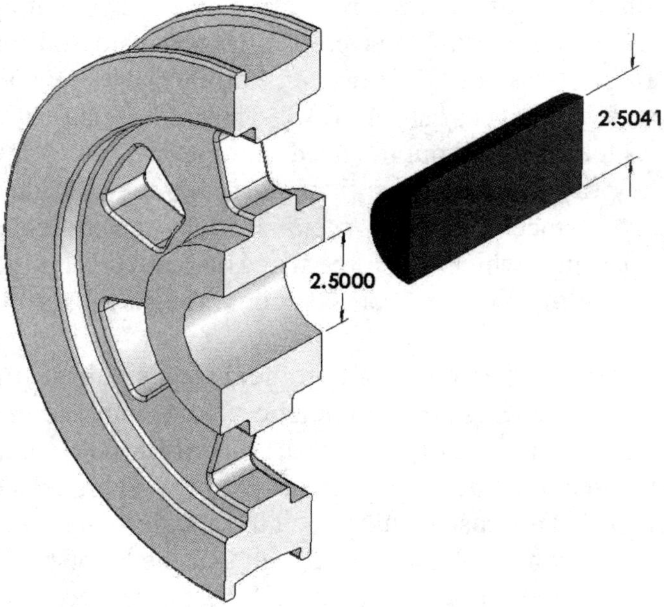

Figure 1 – Maximum shaft size and minimum hole size (minimum bore) for an interference fit between a shaft and crane wheel.

1. Open SolidWorks by making the following selections. (*Note:* "/" is used to separate successive menu selections.)

Start/All Programs/SolidWorks 2009 (or) Click the **SolidWorks** icon on your screen.

2. When SolidWorks is open, select **File / Open** and open the file named **Wheel Shaft Assembly**. If the **Assembly** menu opens, click-and-drag it to a convenient location, perhaps on the menu bar, at the top of your screen.

Interference Check

Before beginning an analysis of this assembly, confirm that part interference does indeed exist. Proceed as follows to check for interference.

1. In the Main menu, click **Tools** and from the pull-down menu select **Interference Detection…** The **Interference Detection** property manager opens as illustrated in Fig. 2.

2. In the **Selected Components** dialogue box observe that the **Wheel Shaft Assembly.SLDASM** is pre-selected as the assembly to be checked for interference. Also notice that the **Results** dialogue box currently indicates that interference is **Not calculated**.

3. In the **Selected Components** dialogue box, click the **[Calculate]** button. Immediately the *volume* of interference between the shaft and wheel is calculated and listed in the **Results** dialogue box as 0.06 in^3. Also, the interference region between the shaft and wheel is highlighted as illustrated in Fig. 2.

4. Click **[OK]** ✓ to close the **Interference Detection** property manager.

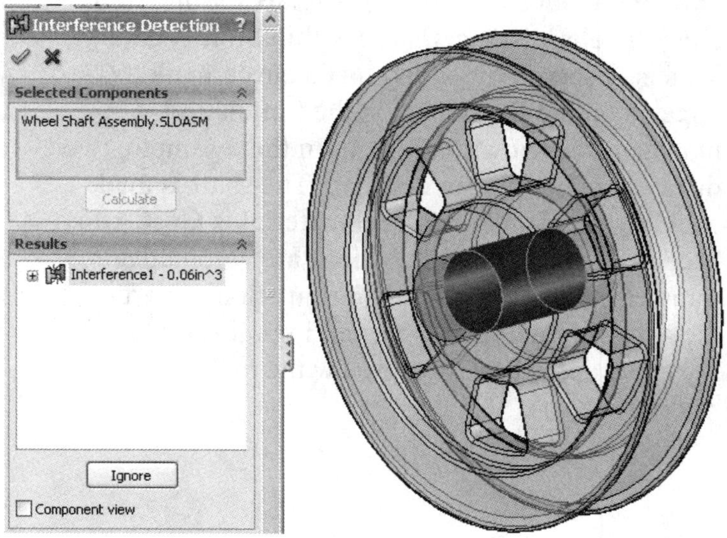

Figure 2 – The interference fit region is highlighted during an Interference Check of parts in the shaft and wheel assembly.

Creating a Static Analysis (Study)

1. In the main menu, select **Simulation** and from the pull-down menu choose **Study…** The **Study** property manager opens as shown in Fig. 3.

2. In the **Name** dialogue box type "**Force Fit Analysis**" as a descriptive name for this Study.

3. In the **Type** dialogue box select **Static** as the analysis **Type**.

4. Click **[OK]** ✓ to close the **Study** property manager.

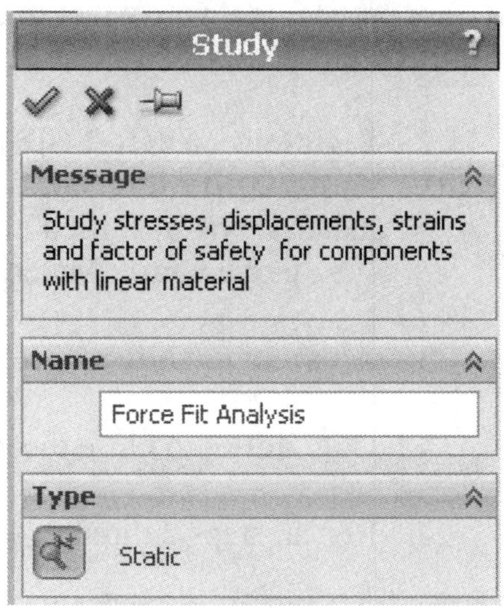

Figure 3 – Initial steps to create a Study in SolidWorks Simulation.

Assign Material Properties to the Model

Unlike previous examples, materials for the **Shaft** and **Wheel** are *pre-assigned* within SolidWorks. This is observed by noting that a check mark "✓" appears on the **Parts** icon in the Simulation manager tree shown in Fig. 4. In this example, two different materials are defined. The shaft is made of **Alloy Steel** and the wheel material is **Cast Alloy Steel**. These material selections are automatically transferred into SolidWorks Simulation as part of the assembly definition created in SolidWorks. The next step describes how to view the material settings.

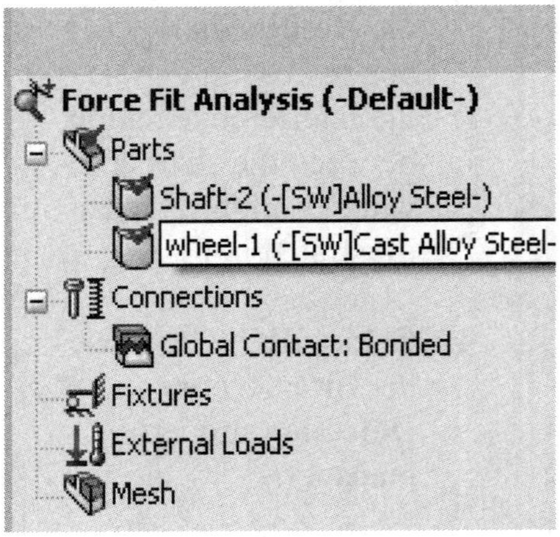

Figure 4 – Manager tree showing that materials for the Shaft and Wheel assembly are pre-selected in SolidWorks.

1. Click the "+" sign adjacent to the **Parts** icon. This action reveals that material for **Shaft-2** is designated as **(-[SW]Alloy Steel-)** and for **wheel-1** it is designated as **(-[SW]Cast Alloy Steel-)** as shown in Fig. 4.

Before proceeding, verify that material properties are specified in English units as outlined below.

2. Right-click **Shaft-2 (-[SW]Alloy Steel-)** and from the pull-down menu select **Apply/Edit Material...** The **Material** window opens. However, because material was specified in SolidWorks, the left side of the window is inactive (i.e., grayed out). Material properties appear in the right-half of the window.

3. Adjacent to **Units:** select **English (IPS)** units (if not already selected).

4. Click **[OK]** to close the **Material** window.

5. Repeat steps 2 through 4 for **wheel1 (-[SW]Cast Alloy Steel-)**.

Analysis Insight

The procedure outlined in steps 1 to 4 above can be used to alter the material selection for either component by selecting alternate materials **From library files** as done in previous examples.

Defeature the Model

An enlarged view of the shaft and wheel assembly is shown in Fig. 5. Careful observation reveals numerous small fillets and rounds on various edges of the model. Knowing in advance that the current assembly is to be analyzed using finite element methods, the developer of the original SolidWorks model expedited the defeaturing process by creating all the small fillets and rounds in a single step. Therefore, the defeaturing steps outlined below are very efficient.

Note: Larger fillets at the four "corners" of the spoke cut-outs are *not* removed from the model because, if removed, they might be a source of significant stress concentration. This judgment is based upon engineering insight. Proceed as follows to defeature the model.

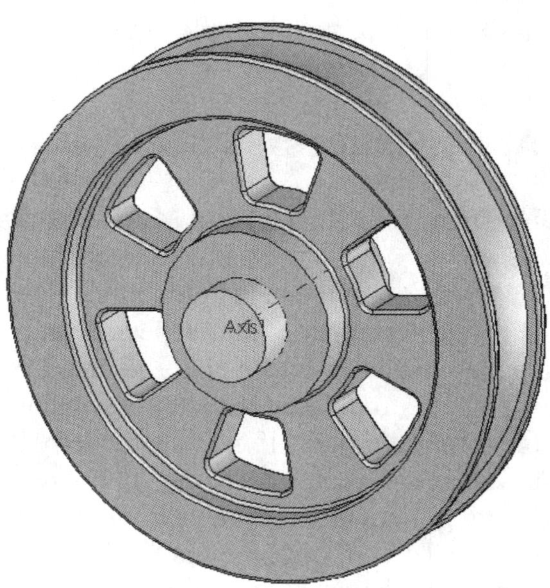

Figure 5 – Observe multiple fillets and rounds on various edges of the model.

1. If necessary, click-and-drag the lower boundary of the SolidWorks Feature manager tree downward to reveal its full contents. See striped arrow in Fig. 6.

2. Click the "+" sign adjacent to the **wheel<1>** folder, circled in Fig. 6, to display steps used to create the wheel model in SolidWorks.

3. Right-click the "**0.10 inch Fillets & Rounds**" highlighted near the bottom of the feature manger in Fig. 6. The pop-up menu, pictured to the right of the feature manager tree, also appears in Fig. 6.

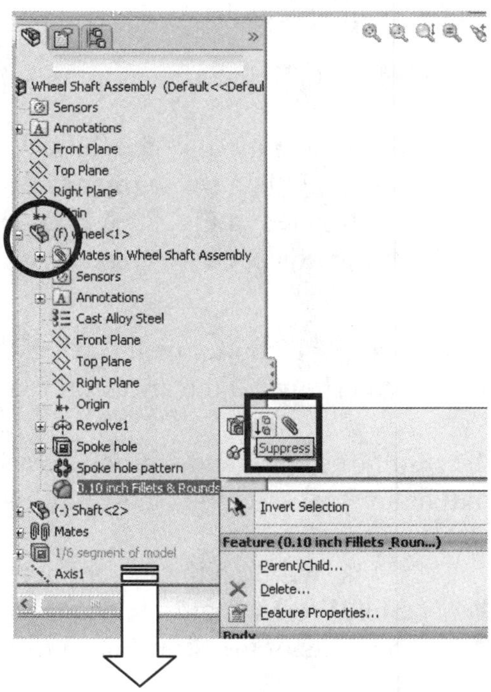

Figure 6 – Selections in the SolidWorks feature manager tree to simplify wheel geometry (i.e., defeature it).

4. Within the pop-up menu, select the **Suppress** icon, boxed in Fig. 6, to remove all small fillets and rounds from the wheel as seen in Fig. 7. This step simplifies wheel geometry prior to meshing the model.

Had other size fillets or rounds been specified on the model, the above process might have to be repeated multiple times.

Apply Fixtures

Unsuppress Part of the Model to Use Symmetry

Examination of the defeatured model, shown in Fig. 7, reveals symmetry in the repeated pattern of spokes and holes on the crane wheel. Once again, it is possible to reduce the solution size and speed up the solution process if model symmetry is used to advantage. Because there are six spokes and six openings, it is obvious that a 60° slice (360°/6 = 60°), or 1/6th of the model, is the smallest segment that should be used. It would be possible to select other fractions of the assembly for analysis as well. Other convenient segments would be 1/3, 1/2, or 2/3. Proceed as follows to apply the preceding symmetry observation.

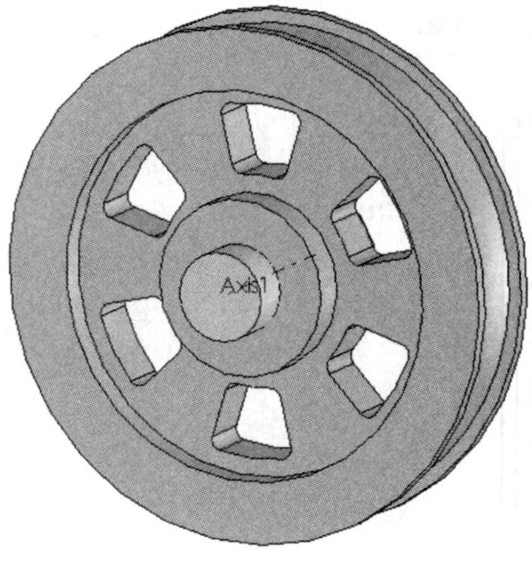

Figure 7 – Observing symmetry of the defeatured shaft and wheel assembly.

1. Near the bottom of the SolidWorks manager tree, *left*-click the "**1/6 segment of model**" icon highlighted in Fig. 8. A pop-up menu, also shown in Fig. 8, appears.

2. From the pop-up menu, select the **Unsuppress** icon shown at the arrow on Fig. 8.

The result of steps 1 and 2 produces a 1/6th segment of the shaft and wheel assembly shown in Fig. 9.

3. Click-and-drag the lower boundary of the SolidWorks Feature manager *upward* to reveal contents of the **Simulation** manager.

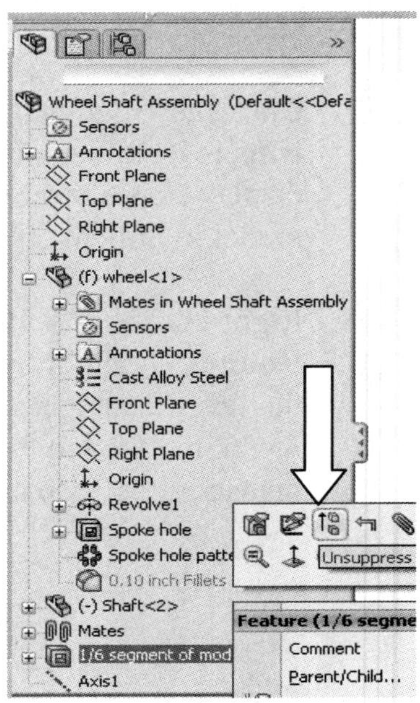

Figure 8 – Unsuppressing the 1/6th model of the shaft and wheel assembly.

Analysis Insight
Due to model symmetry, it is possible to select a "slice" of the model that either intersects openings between wheel spokes (as illustrated in Fig. 9) or one that intersects spokes on both sides of an opening.

The decision to model the segment shown in Fig. 9 is based on an understanding that a full picture of stresses in a spoke is more revealing than a split image of the stress distribution in half a spoke on either side of an opening.

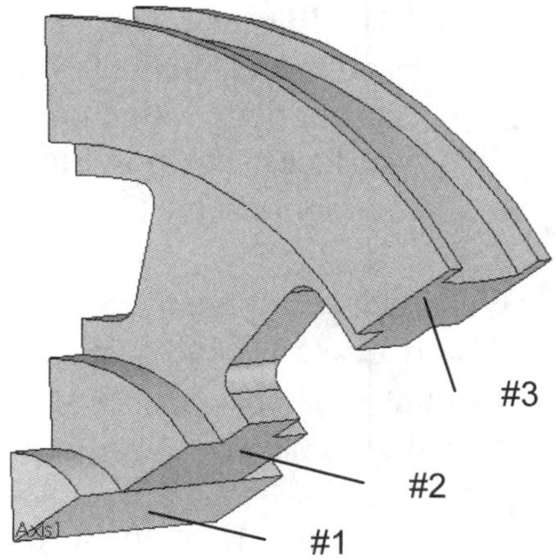

Figure 9 – Symmetry applied to yield a 1/6th segment of the shaft and wheel assembly.

Define Symmetry Restraints (Fixtures)

Symmetry restraints were first introduced in the previous chapter where segments of thin and thick-wall pressure vessels were considered. Symmetry restraints serve the purpose of making the cut portion of a symmetrical model behave *as if* the entire model were still present. Therefore, symmetry restraints must be applied to all surfaces created when the model was cut. Figure 9 shows one surface (#1) on the shaft and two surfaces (#2 and #3) on the hub and outer rim of the wheel, respectively. Of course, duplicate surfaces exist on the opposite side of the model. Therefore, symmetry restraints must be applied to a total of six surfaces. Proceed as follows to apply symmetry restraints.

1. In the Simulation manager tree, right-click the **Fixtures** icon and from the pull-down menu select **Fixed Geometry...** The **Fixture** property manager opens.

2. Open the **Advanced** dialogue box and select the **Symmetry** icon as shown in Fig. 10.

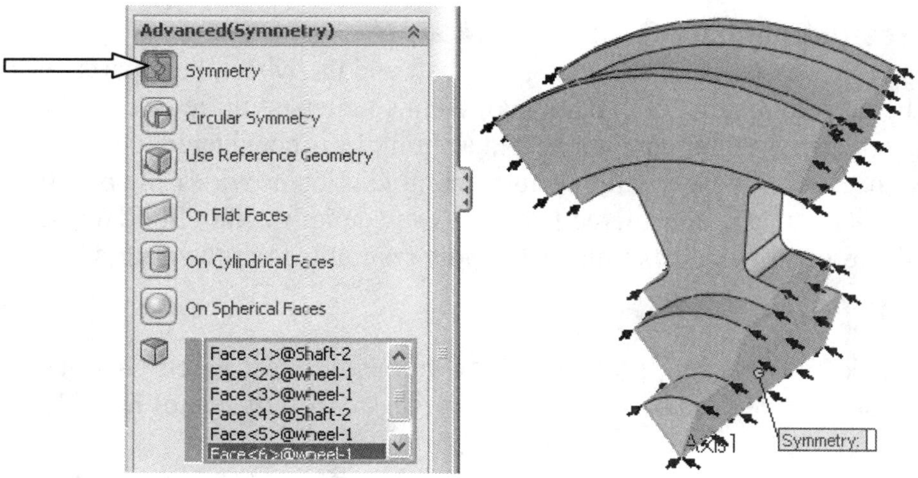

Figure 10 – **Symmetry** restraints applied to all cut surfaces of the shaft and wheel assembly.

3. The **Planar Faces for Fixture** field is highlighted (light blue) to indicate it is active and awaiting specification of surfaces to which symmetry restraints are to be applied. Move the cursor over the model and select the three numbered surfaces shown in Fig. 9. Also select their counterparts on the opposite side of the model. Rotate the assembly as necessary to select all faces.

With each selection, a new surface is highlighted and is listed as **Face<1>@wheel-1** (or **@Shaft-2** etc.), **Face<2>**, … **Face<6>** in the **Planar Faces for Fixture** field. Also, restraint symbols appear on the model as illustrated in Fig. 10. (Symbol size was increased to enhance visibility).

4. Click **[OK]** ✓ to close the **Fixture** property manager. **Fixture-1** appears beneath the **Fixtures** icon in the Simulation manager tree.

Analysis Insight
As noted in the thick-wall pressure vessel example, while assignment of symmetry boundary conditions applies proper restraints to model missing portions of the part, those same boundary conditions may not provide sufficient restraints to prevent "rigid body motion" of the model.

For this example, note the following two facts: (a) All restraints shown in Fig. 10 are applied normal to the cut surfaces; and (b) *If* each restraint vector were broken into components, then each vector could be replaced by its X and Y components. Rotate and view the model to convince yourself of these two facts. Therefore, an obvious conclusion is that *no restraint* exists in the axial Z-direction. Thus, rigid body motion of the model is not restrained in the axial direction.

Because rigid body motion is not allowed in finite element studies, additional restraints must be added to the model as outlined next.

Apply Fixtures to Eliminate Rigid Body Motion

Because the assembly consists of two parts, the shaft and the wheel, both parts must be restrained. The need to restrain both parts may seem counter-intuitive since a shrink fit is being defined between the shaft and wheel and a shrink fit is considered to be an immovable connection. However, this seeming contradiction provides an opportunity to note that shrink fit contact is considered frictionless by default within SolidWorks Simulation. Therefore, proceed as follows to apply restraints to prevent rigid body motion.

1. Right-click **Fixtures** and from the pull-down menu, select **Fixed Geometry…** The **Fixture** property manager opens as shown on the left side of Fig. 11.

2. Open the **Advanced** dialogue box and select **Use Reference Geometry**. Reference geometry will be selected in a future step.

3. In the **Advanced** dialogue box the **Faces, Edges, Vertices for Fixture** field is active (light blue). Proceed to select two vertices on the model (one on the shaft and the other on the wheel). Selected vertices are shown by two dots circled on Fig. 11. After selecting these vertices, **Vertex<1>@Shaft-2** and **Vertex<2>@wheel-1** appear in the active field. The actual number within < > depends on the order of selection.

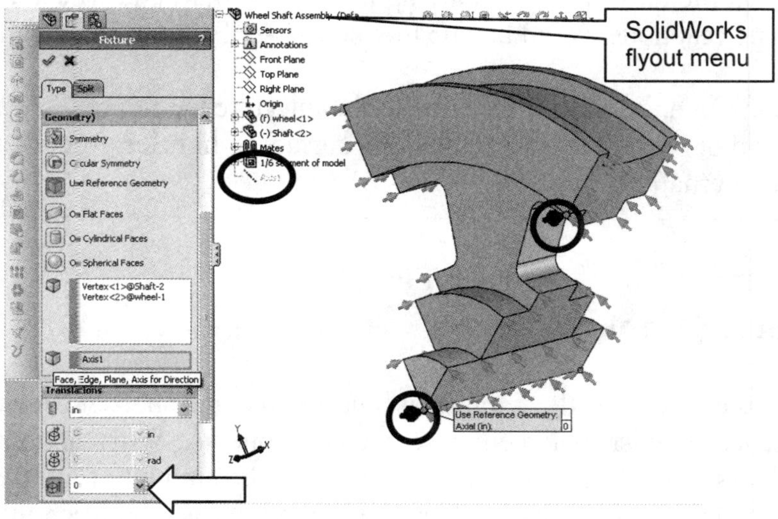

Figure 11 – **Restraint** property manager and selections of vertices and reference geometry needed to prevent rigid body motion of the shaft and wheel assembly.

4. Next, click to activate (light blue) the second field from top in the **Advanced** dialogue box. The identifier **Face, Edge, Plane, Axis for Direction** appears when the cursor is passed over this field as illustrated in Fig. 11.

5. Click to open the SolidWorks "flyout" menu, and select **Axis1** located at the bottom of this menu. **Axis1** is selected because it is oriented in the Z-direction, the direction in which rigid body translation is to be prevented. After making this selection, **Axis1** appears in the highlighted field. (Note: Your flyout menu may appear different than that shown in Fig. 11 depending upon what SolidWorks folders are open or closed). After selecting **Axis1**, close the SolidWorks flyout menu by selecting the "-" sign at top of the menu.

6. Open the **Translations** dialogue box (if not already open) and set **Unit** to **in**. Then, at the bottom of this dialogue box (see arrow in Fig. 11), select the **Axial** icon and accept the zero value shown. This value implies *no* translation is permitted in the **Axial** direction. Restraint symbols appear at the two locations in Fig. 11. Different colors and sizes are used to accentuate their presence.

7. Click **[OK]** ✓ to close the **Fixture** property manager. **Fixture-2** appears beneath the **Fixtures** folder in the Simulation manager tree.

8. Right-click **Fixtures** and from the pull-down menu select **Hide All**. This action temporarily hides restraint symbols to reduce clutter on the model.

The above steps ensure that the assembly is restrained against rigid body translation in the axial Z-direction.

> **Aside:**
> The focus of this example is on modeling and analyzing an interference fit. Therefore, no *external* loads or *reactions* are applied to the shaft and wheel assembly. External loads and reactions would be due to wheel-to-rail contact and shaft support reactions.
>
> As a consequence, only forces due to the interference fit are included. These forces are equal and opposite between contacting surfaces. In brief, forces caused by interference fits are internally balanced.

Define a Shrink Fit

Because the wheel inside diameter is smaller than the shaft outside diameter, an interference fit exists between these two components. When analyzing shrink fits in SolidWorks Simulation you are cautioned that the amount of interference should be greater than 0.1% of the larger diameter at the interface between mating parts. This restriction is imposed because the amount of overlap between mating parts should be sufficiently large to overcome approximations introduced during meshing. This is due to the fact that mesh size also includes a permissible tolerance range. If the amount of interference is too small, inaccurate solutions may result.

During the process of establishing a shrink fit between the shaft and wheel, it is necessary to specify the surfaces where interference occurs. To facilitate selecting these surfaces, components of the assembly are separated by creating an exploded view as follows.

1. From the Main menu select **Insert**. Then from the pull-down menu select **Exploded View…** The **Explode** property manager opens as illustrated in Fig. 12.

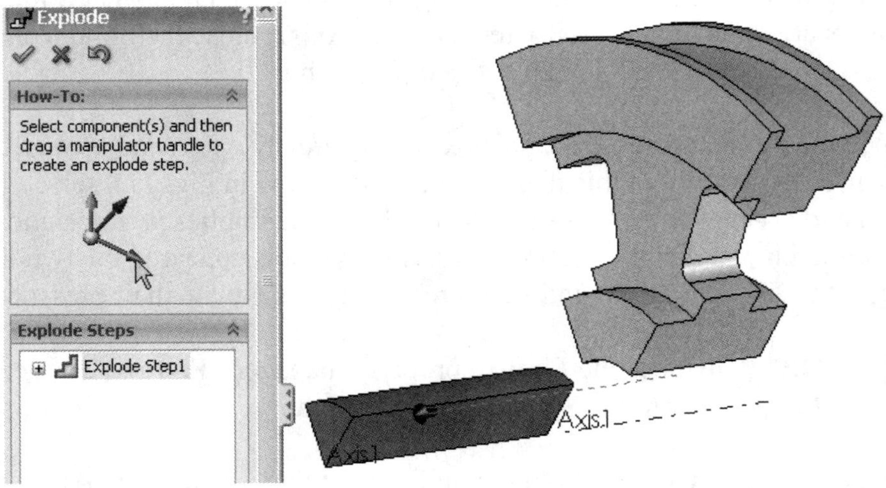

Figure 12 – Manually creating an exploded view of the shaft and wheel assembly.

Read the **How-To:** instructions at top of the **Explode** property manager and proceed as follows.

2. For this example, move the cursor onto the graphics screen and click to select the *shaft*. Immediately, an X, Y, Z coordinate triad appears to "float" near the shaft. Click-and-drag the vector aligned with the direction of the shaft axis and drag the shaft away from the wheel as illustrated in Fig. 12. This action is recorded in the **Explode Steps** table as **Explode Step1**.

3. Click **[OK]** ✓ to close the **Explode** property manager. Note: Either component could be moved in any direction to create an acceptable exploded view.

4. Within the Simulation manager, right-click the **Connections** icon. A pull-down menu appears. This is the first time this icon is used.

5. From the pull-down menu select **Contact Set…** The **Contact Set** property manager opens as illustrated in Fig. 13.

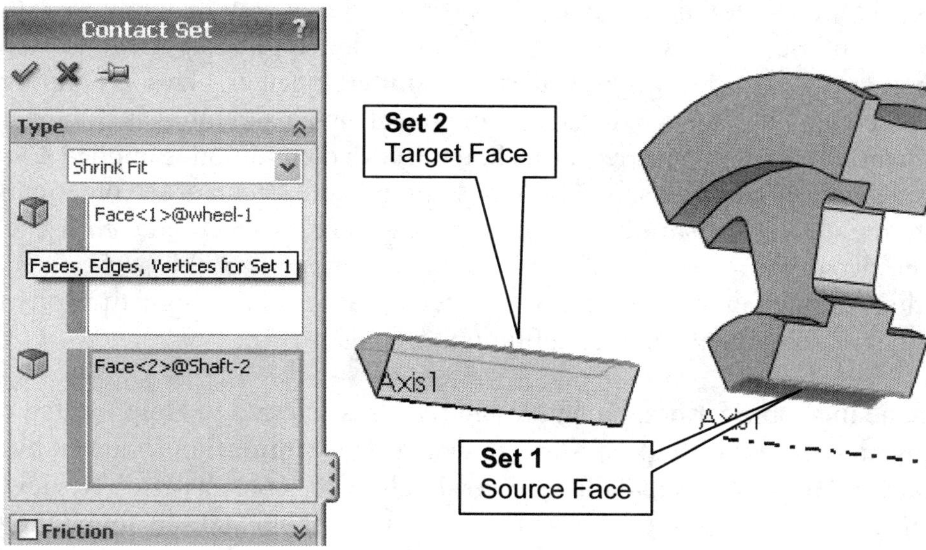

Figure 13 – Defining faces where a shrink fit occurs between the shaft and wheel. For this example the **Target** and **Source** faces can be interchanged without consequence.

6. At the top of the **Type** dialogue box, click to open the pull-down menu and select **Shrink Fit** as the type of contact to be modeled between the shaft and wheel.

7. The **Faces, Edges, Vertices for Set 1** field is activated (light blue) and awaits input. Rotate the model as necessary and select the *inside* surface of the hole as the **Set 1**. **Face<1>@wheel-1** appears in the active field of Fig. 13. **Set 1** entities are also referred to as the "source."

8. Next, click to activate the second field beneath the pull-down menu. This is the **Faces for Set 2** field. Move the cursor over the model and select the *cylindrical*

surface of the shaft as the **Set 2** surface, also shown in Fig. 13. **Face<2>@Shaft-2** appears in the active field. NOTE: In this example either surface can be designated as the **Set 1** or **Set 2**. However, this observation is not valid in all cases. See item (c) in the Analysis Insight section below for more details about "source" and "target" designation. **Set 2** is also referred to as the "target."

Analysis Insight:

a) Refer to the **Contact Set** property manager in Fig. 13 and note the **Friction** dialogue box at the bottom of this property manager. As noted earlier, interference fits are considered frictionless by default. However, if our goal were to investigate torque transmitted by the interference fit joint, then friction between mating surfaces would be defined here. This example does not examine **Friction** effects.

b) Also before closing the **Contact Set** property manager, briefly revisit the pull-down menu that lists the various types of connections available. Understanding these criteria and a built-in hierarchy that accompanies them is essential to proper modeling for a variety of design and analysis situations. For example, in *assemblies* of multiple parts, SolidWorks Simulation applies a system default assumption that all contacting surfaces are **Bonded** together. This assumption treats all contacting faces of different components in an assembly as if they are permanently "glued" together. As such, the **Bonded** condition is applied *Globally* to all contacting parts. This assumption is applied unless one of the other contact conditions, such as the shrink fit used in this example, is specified *locally* (i.e., between two or more contacting components in a larger assembly). Contact conditions defined in the **Contact Set** property manager have higher priority than do Global or component contact definitions.

   To pursue this topic further, the interested reader is referred to **Help** located on the main menu. From the **Help** pull-down menu, select **Simulation** followed by **Simulation Help Topics** and on the **Search** tab, type "contact sets." Review the multiple help topics listed there. Virtually all types of contact sets found there are excellently described and illustrated by animated examples.

c) The use of "source" and "target" is interchangeable in this example since both contacting surfaces are *faces*. However, the true definition of **Set 1** "source" entities refers to faces, edges, vertices, points, or beam joints. Whereas the definition of a **Set 2** "target" *only* refers to a face. Thus, in terms of the shrink fit modeled here, contacting faces satisfy the criteria for both a "source" and a "target." On the other hand, if a specific contact were to be defined between the surface of the shaft and the *edge* of the wheel hub, then the shaft *face* must be **Set 2**, the "target," while the hub *edge* must be **Set 1**, the "source."

9. Finally, click **[OK]** ✓ to close the **Contact Set** property manager.

Mesh the Model and Run the Solution

Although a correct solution is obtained with the model in either the exploded or unexploded state, return it to its *un*exploded state before meshing the model. This is done to permit observation of node alignment, or lack thereof, between nodes on the shaft and wheel after meshing. One way to un-explode the model is accomplished as follows.

1. Click the **Configuration Manager** icon, located at top of the SolidWorks Feature manager, shown circled in Fig. 14.

2. Within the Configuration manager, click the "+" signs adjacent to + **Wheel Shaft Assembly Configuration(s)** and adjacent to + **Default <Default>_PhotoWorks Display State [Wheel Shaft Assembly]**, (if not already selected).

3. Right-click **ExplView1**. Then, from the pull-down menu shown in Fig. 14, select **Collapse** to return the model to its assembled view.

4. Toggle back to the **SolidWorks Feature Manager** icon, shown boxed in Fig. 14.

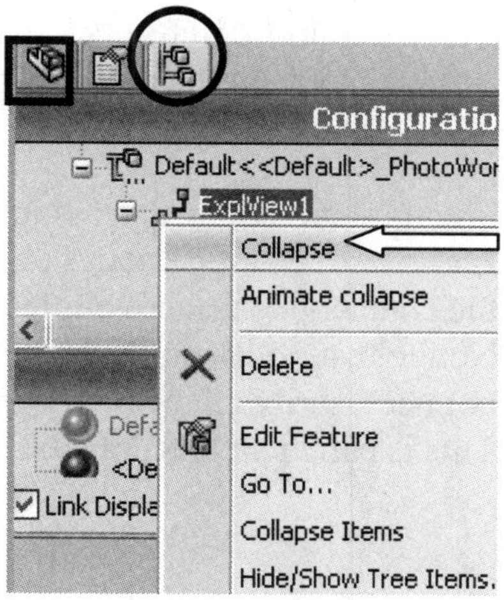

Figure 14 – Accessing the **Configuration Manager** tree to "collapse" (*un*explode) the shaft and wheel assembly.

5. In the Simulation manager tree, right-click the **Mesh** icon and from the pop-up menu select **Create Mesh…** The **Mesh** property manager opens.

6. Check ☑ **Mesh Parameters** to open the **Mesh Parameters** dialogue box and verify that inches (**in**) are shown in the **Units** field.

7. The default mesh size is considered acceptable for this analysis. However, before meshing, click to open the **Options** dialogue box. One of the options listed there is ☐ **Run (solve) the analysis**. *If* this option is selected, the software proceeds directly to the Solution after meshing the model. While this action eliminates one step in the solution process, it is typically *not* recommended because, if an error occurs, the user does not know if it is due to a failure to mesh the model or due to an error in the solution process. Therefore, click **[OK]** ✓ to close the **Mesh** property manager.

8. Finally, right-click **Force Fit Analysis (-Default-)** and from the pull-down menu select **Run**. The solution process takes slightly longer when solving for an interference fit (approximately 30 seconds).

9. If the mesh is not displayed after the solution, right-click the **Mesh** icon and from the pull-down menu, select **ShowMesh**.

The meshed model appears in Fig. 15. Zoom in to examine nodes on the edge of the contacting surfaces circled in this figure. Notice that nodes on the shaft and wheel are not necessarily aligned with one another. This is called an "incompatible mesh."

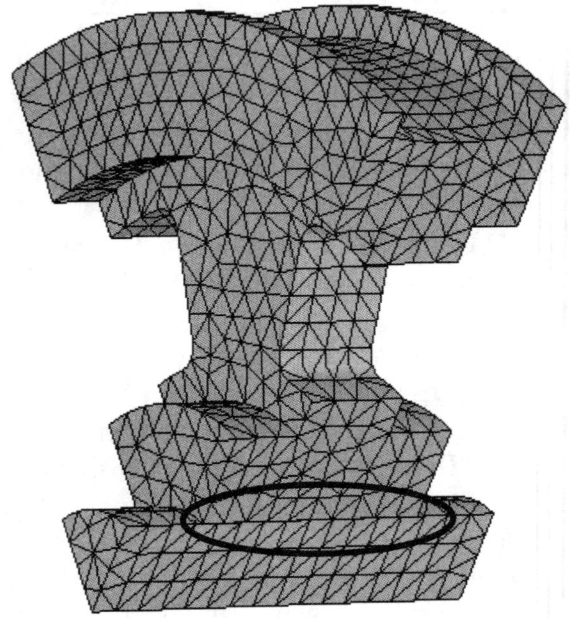

Figure 15 – Meshed model of the shaft and wheel assembly. Approximately eleven nodes exist along the contacting surfaces circled above.

Examination of Results

Default Stress Plot

Begin by examining the vonMises stress plot to gain an overview of results. Desired appearance attributes for this plot are defined below so that they can be copied when producing additional plots.

1. If necessary, click the "+" sign adjacent to the **Results** folder to display a list of the three default plots, **Stress1**, **Displacement1**, and **Strain1**.

2. Double-click **Stress1 (-vonMises-)** to display this plot. Zoom-in on the model to observe deformation between the shaft and wheel hub in the interference fit region. If the deformed model does *not* appear or if units on the stress legend are *not* psi, follow steps 3 to 5. Otherwise skip to step 6.

3. Right-click **Stress1 (-vonMises-)** and from the pop-up menu, select **Edit Definition…** The **Stress Plot** property manager opens.

4. In the **Display** dialogue box, change **Units** to **psi**.

5. In the **Deformed Shape** dialogue box, check ☑ **Deformed Shape** (if not already selected); also select ⊙ **Automatic**. Then click **[OK]** ✓ to close the **Stress Plot** property manager. The system default, exaggerated deformation scale, is applied to an exploded view of the image.

6. After examining the deformed model, right-click **Stress1 (-vonMises-)** and from the pop-up menu, select **Edit Definition…** The **Stress Plot** property manager opens.

7. In the **Deformed Shape** dialogue box, select ⊙ **True Scale**. This action displays distortions between the shaft and wheel parts at true scale (1:1).

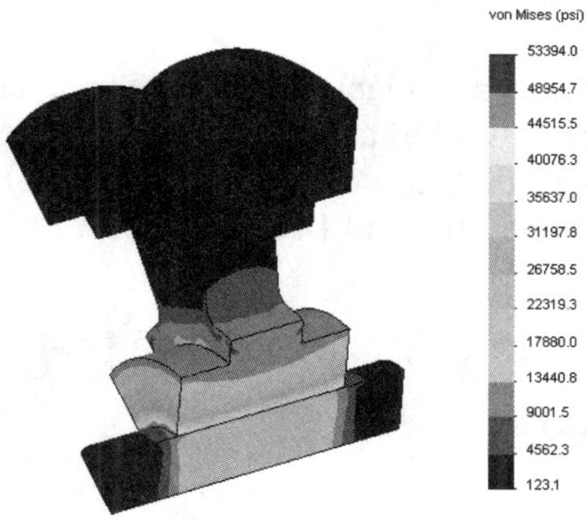

Figure 16 – vonMises stress plot incorporating modified display characteristics outlined in this section.

Next, adjust appearance of the von Mises plot so that, at the conclusion of this process, the plot appears as shown in Fig. 16. Proceed as follows.

8. Click to open the **Advanced Options** dialogue box. Then, click to *clear* the check from ☐ **Average results across boundary for parts**. This action is *very important* because parts of this assembly are made of two *different materials*. Also, the shaft is loaded in compression while the inside of the wheel is subject to tension. Therefore, it is not appropriate to average stress results across these two different parts. The resulting value would be meaningless.

9. Also within the **Stress Plot** property manager, click to open the **Property** dialogue box. In this dialogue box, click to "check" ☑ **Include title text** and in the empty field, type your name followed by a descriptive title for the plot.

10. Click **[OK]** ✓ to close the **Stress Plot** property manager.

11. Once again, right-click **Stress1 (-vonMises-)** and from the pop-up menu select **Settings…** The **Settings** property manager opens.

12. In the **Fringe Options** dialogue box, click the pull-down menu and select **Discrete** as the display mode for fringes.

13. Within the **Boundary Options** dialogue box, open the pull-down menu and select **Model** to display a black outline on the model. (This item is a user preference).

14. Click **[OK]** ✓ to close the **Settings** property manager.

Observation of Fig. 16 clearly reveals that stress levels in the vicinity of the shrink fit (53,394 psi) *exceed* Yield Strength of the wheel material, which is 35000 psi. Figure 17 shows a summary of properties for the wheel in the **Material Details** window. The material yield strength **SIGYLD** = 34994 psi ≈ 35000 psi is listed adjacent to the arrow. Another way to examine this fact is explored in the "Aside" section below.

Aside:
Recall that material information is available at any time by clicking the "+" sign adjacent to the **Parts** folder to reveal **Shaft-2** and **wheel-1**. Next, right-click **wheel-1 (-[SW]Cast Alloy Steel-)** and in the pull-down menu, shown in Fig. 17, and select **Details…** This action opens the **Material Details** window located at the right side of the Fig. 17.

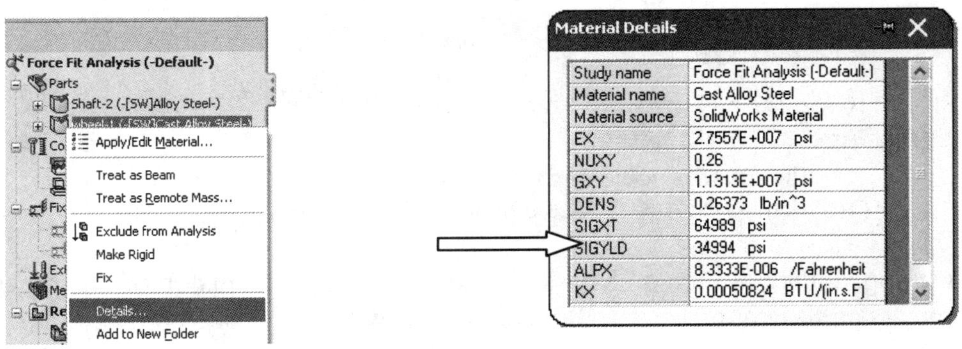

Figure 17 – Accessing material property details for the wheel to permit comparison of material Yield Strength with resulting stress in the component.

Notice that material yield strength does not appear on the vonMises stress plot as occurred in earlier examples. The reason for this is that assemblies involve multiple parts, which are often made of different materials. Therefore, the potential for different material properties prohibits the display of any single yield strength value. Because of this, an alternative procedure to that of using the *Safety Factor* check can be applied to display regions where yield strength is exceeded. To apply this method, begin by making a *temporary* change in the **Chart Options** property manager outlined below.

a) If **Stress1 (-vonMises-)** plot is not displayed, double-click its name to display it.

b) Right-click **Stress1 (-vonMises-)** and from the pull-down menu select **Chart Options…** The **Chart Options** property manager opens.

c) Near the bottom of the **Display Options** dialogue box click to select **⦿Defined:**. Then, in the bottom box (corresponding to maximum stress) type a value somewhat greater than the yield strength for the wheel as **38000** (or **3.8e4**).

d) Do *not* close the **Chart Options** property manager at this time.

A new plot of vonMises stress within the shaft and wheel assembly is shown in Fig. 18. However, this plot highlights (in red) the entire region where stress due to the interference fit exceeds the yield strength. Examination of the colored stress chart reveals that stresses above approximately 34840 psi are shown in red. Therefore, the stress region above the yield strength (35,000 psi) is easily identified. Next, reset to the original plot settings as follows.

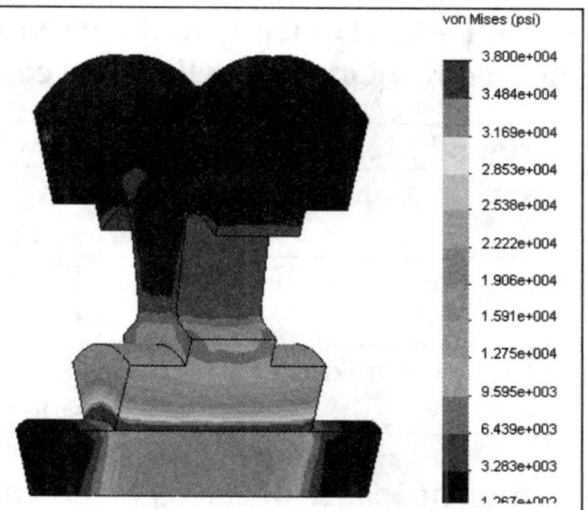

Figure 18 – Locating regions where yield strength is exceeded by re-defining chart **Display Options.**

e) Return to the middle of the **Display Options** dialogue box and select ⦿ **Automatic**.

f) Click **[OK]** ✓ to close the **Chart Options** property manager. The image is reset to display the full-range of von Mises stress throughout the assembly.

The fact that yield strength of the wheel is exceeded is a reasonable cause for redesign of the interference fit and/or selection of an alternative wheel material. However, since the goal of this example is to focus on defining interference fits and interpreting results of those fits, a re-design of the shaft and wheel assembly is not pursued here. We now return to investigate alternative means to display results.

Stress Plots in a Cylindrical Coordinate System

Circumferential (Tangential or Hoop) Stress

Circumferential (or) hoop stress is one of two stresses easily calculated using classical stress equations for a shrink fit. Because traditional stresses like σ_X, σ_Y, σ_Z, σ_1, σ_2, σ_3, τ_{xy}, τ_{yz}, τ_{zx}, etc., in a Cartesian (X, Y, Z) coordinate system are not conducive for representing circumferential stress in cylindrical parts, a cylindrical coordinate system is introduced below to facilitate the examination of results.

When establishing a cylindrical coordinate system, *any* axis can be used to define the axis of a local cylindrical coordinate system. However, once an axis is selected, the stresses usually associated with SX = σ_x, SY = σ_y, and SZ = σ_z take on new meanings as summarized in Table 1.

Table 1 – Correspondence between stresses in a Cartesian coordinate system and their equivalents in a cylindrical coordinate system.

Original Meaning of Stress	New Meaning in the Cylindrical Coordinate System
SX = stress in X-direction σ_X.	SX = stress in *radial* direction (σ_r) relative to the selected reference axis.
SY = stress in Y-direction σ_Y.	SY = stress in *circumferential* direction (σ_t) relative to the selected reference axis.
SZ = stress in Z-direction σ_Z.	SZ = stress in *axial* direction (σ_a) relative to the selected reference axis.

In brief, no matter what axis is chosen to be the reference axis[1] of a cylindrical coordinate system, the correspondence between radial, circumferential, and axial stresses listed in Table 1 remains valid.

Before selecting an axis to define a cylindrical coordinate system, a *copy* of the existing vonMises stress plot is made. The primary reason for making a copy of the stress plot is to save the time it would take to recreate all of the graphic settings defined above. Copy the plot as follows.

1. Right-click **Stress1 (-vonMises-)** and from the pop-up menu select **Copy**.

2. Right-click the **Results** folder and from the pop-up menu select **Paste**. A plot named **Copy[1] Stress1 (-vonMises-)** is added to the list of plots beneath the **Results** folder. Recall that an alternative means of making this copy is to click-and-drag **Stress1 (-vonMises-)** onto the **Results** folder.

3. Double-click **Copy[1] Stress1 (-vonMises-)** to display an *identical* plot of the vonMises stress including all previously defined plot display options.

Next, a cylindrical coordinate system is defined. **Axis1**, aligned with the shaft centerline, is the logical choice for the axis of a cylindrical coordinate system. However, since the goal is to display circumferential (hoop) stress in the cylindrical coordinate system, two changes must be made to the *copied* plot. First, **SY** must be specified as the stress to be viewed in this plot because, according to Table 1, **SY** = *circumferential* stress in a cylindrical coordinate system. And second, **Axis1** must be defined as the axis of a cylindrical coordinate system. Proceed as follows to alter the copied plot.

4. Right-click **Copy[1] Stress1 (-vonMises-)** and from the pop-up menu select **Edit Definition…** The **Stress Plot** property manager opens as shown in Fig. 19.

5. In the **Display** dialogue box, click to open the stress **Component** pull-down menu and change it to **SY: Y Normal Stress**. This action also opens the **Advanced Options** dialogue box also shown in Fig. 19. Recall that according to Table 1, stress **SY** represents *circumferential* stress in a cylindrical coordinate system.

[1] Reference axis refers to the axis aligned with the centerline of the cylindrical coordinate system.

6. Move the cursor over the top field in the **Advanced Options** dialogue box to identify it as the **Plane, Axis, or Coordinate System**. This field is highlighted (light blue) to indicate it is active and awaiting user input.

7. In the graphics screen, either click to select the center-line of the shaft axis (or) click to open the SolidWorks flyout menu and select **Axis1** shown circled on Fig. 19. This selection establishes **Axis1** as the reference axis of the cylindrical coordinate system. The name **Axis1** appears in the top field of the **Advanced Options** dialogue box.

8. Verify that ⊙ **Node Values** is selected and click **[OK]** ✓ to close the **Stress Plot** property manager.

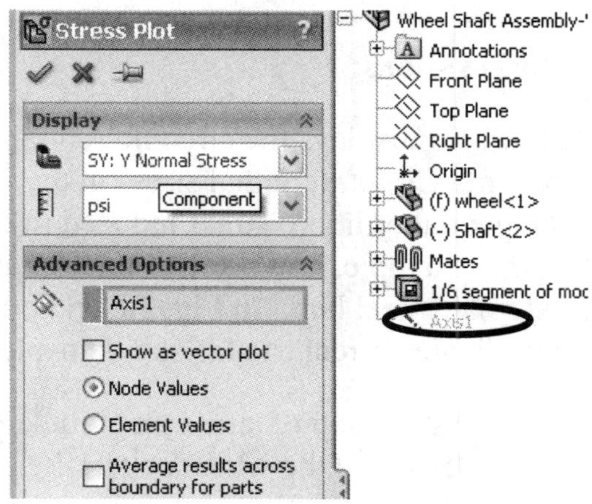

Figure 19 – Selections to define a cylindrical coordinate system and circumferential stress.

The circumferential stress distribution, as it appears in the cylindrical coordinate system, is shown in Fig. 20. Most of the model should appear green.

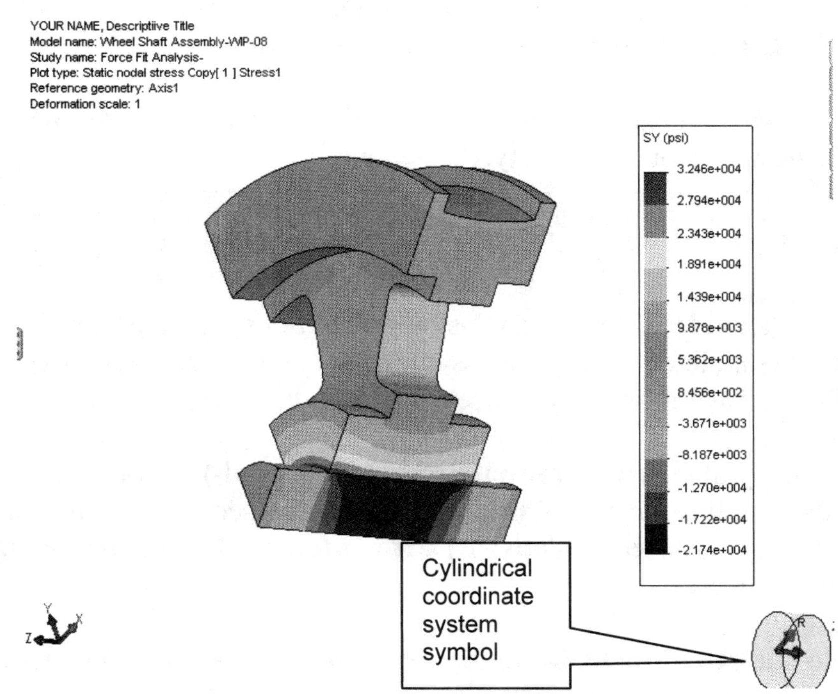

Figure 20 – Illustration showing circumferential stress distribution in the shaft and wheel in a cylindrical coordinate system.

9. Once again move the cursor onto **Copy[1] Stress1 (-Y normal-)** and click-*pause*-click to select this name. Then within the name field, type "**Circumferential Stress**" and press **[Enter]**. The plot name is changed to **Circumferential Stress (-Y normal-)**.

Observations:

Figure 20 displays the circumferential stress distribution in a cylindrical coordinate system. Circumferential stress in the wheel hub is analogous to circumferential (tangential or hoop) stress induced in a thick-wall cylinder subject to internal pressure. In this example, however, an interference fit is the cause of internal pressure on the external wheel hub. In Fig. 20, and on your screen, notice that the Global X, Y, Z coordinate system triad is supplemented by a cylindrical coordinate system symbol.

Also, observation of stress magnitude reveals that maximum circumferential stress does *not* exceed the wheel material yield strength. However, recall that vonMises stress of Fig. 16 and given by equation [1], is made up of *all* components of principal stress at a point. For simplicity, consider only a two-dimensional state of stress within the wheel hub, then both circumferential *and* radial stress components contribute to vonMises stress (σ') as follows.

$$\sigma' = \sqrt{\sigma_t^2 - \sigma_t \sigma_r + \sigma_r^2} \qquad [1]$$

where - σ_t = circumferential stress (tangential or hoop stress)
σ_r = radial stress

This brief digression emphasizes the need to consider the *appropriate* stress when reaching conclusions about part safety.

Radial Stress

The above observation leads to the conclusion that *radial* stress must also be examined in order to obtain a complete picture of stress due to the interference fit between the shaft and wheel. Proceed as follows to produce a plot of radial stress.

1. Make a copy of **Circumferential Stress (-Y normal-)** by following either procedure outlined in steps 1and 2 of the previous section. Try this on your own. The new copy is listed as **Copy[1] Circumferential Stress (-Y normal-)** beneath the **Results** folder.

2. Double-click **Copy[1] Circumferential Stress (-Y normal-)** to open a new copy of the previous (identical) plot.

3. Right-click **Copy[1] Circumferential Stress (-Y normal-)** and from the pull-down menu select **Edit Definition…** The **Stress Plot** property manager opens as shown in Fig. 21.

Because the preceding steps copied a plot that already includes a cylindrical coordinate system, there is no need to repeat steps required to define that coordinate system. Verify this by observing that **Axis1** appears in the top field of the **Advanced Options** dialogue box shown in Fig. 21.

4. In the **Display** dialogue box, click to open the **Component** pull-down menu and from the stresses listed, select **SX: X Normal Stress** which, according to Table 1, represents the *radial* stress in a cylindrical coordinate system.

5. Click **[OK]** ✓ to close the **Stress Plot** property manager.

Before proceeding, change the name of the plot currently named **Copy[1] Circumferential Stress (-X normal-)** to reflect that it now contains a plot of *radial* stress. Try this on your own or see the following step.

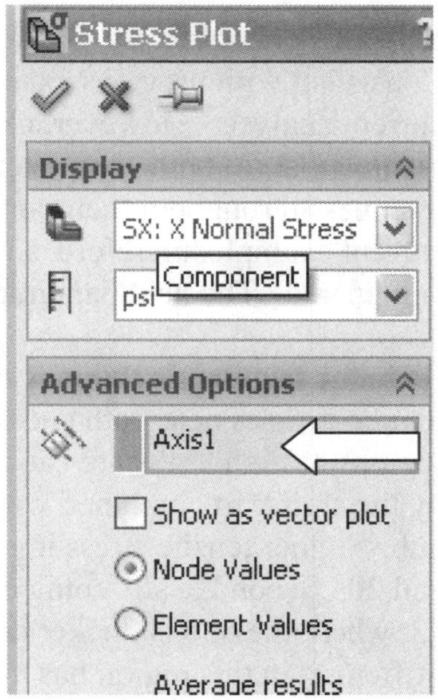

Figure 21 – Selecting SX: X Normal to display *radial* stress in the cylindrical coordinate system.

6. Click-*pause*-click the current folder and type **Radial Stress**. Then press **[Enter]**. The revised plot name should appear as **Radial Stress (-X normal-)**.

The resulting plot of radial stress is shown in Fig. 22. Radial stress represents stress normal to the two contacting surfaces. As such, radial stress represents the contact pressure between the shaft and wheel bore. Also observe the ± sign of radial stress magnitudes. Virtually all radial stress magnitudes are negative. Negative signs indicate compressive stresses acting on the outer surface of the shaft and on the inner surface of the wheel hub in the vicinity of the interference fit. This result is consistent with a general understanding of what happens in a shrink fit.

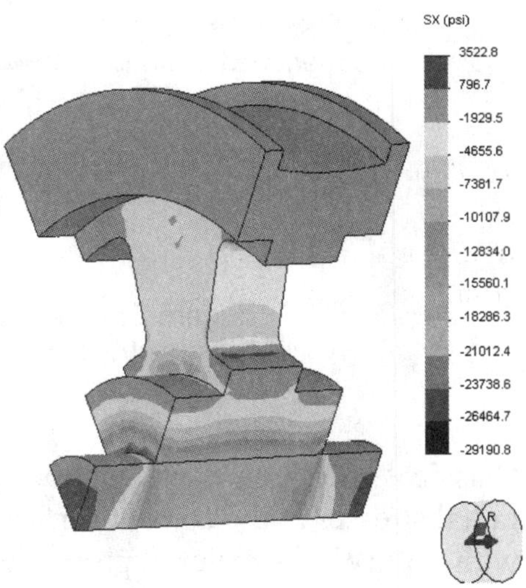

Figure 22 – Plot of *radial* stress distribution throughout the shaft and wheel assembly caused by the interference fit.

Verification of Results

Stress Predicted by Classical Interference Fit Equations

Consistent with previous examples, a check is made to determine validity of results of the current analysis. However, classical equations for interference fits between mating parts assume that (a) both components are of equal length, and (b) components are uniform thickness throughout their contact length. Both of these assumptions are violated in the current example, therefore, some differences between classical and FEA results are anticipated. The next paragraph describes two reasons for the expected differences.

First, the fact that both inner and outer members are not of equal length gives rise to higher stresses near both ends of the wheel hub at locations indicated in Fig. 23. These regions of high stress are caused by stress concentration effects due to pressure induced by the shrink fit combined with the geometric discontinuity where the shaft meets the hub. Higher tensile stress in this region of the hub was previously observed in Figs. 16 and 20. Second, a stiffening effect occurs in the central region of the hub, circled in Fig. 23, where the hub is thicker due to spokes and a built-up section located near its center. Stiffening in this region has the effect of altering magnitudes of all stresses examined thus far (hoop stress, vonMises stress, and radial stress).

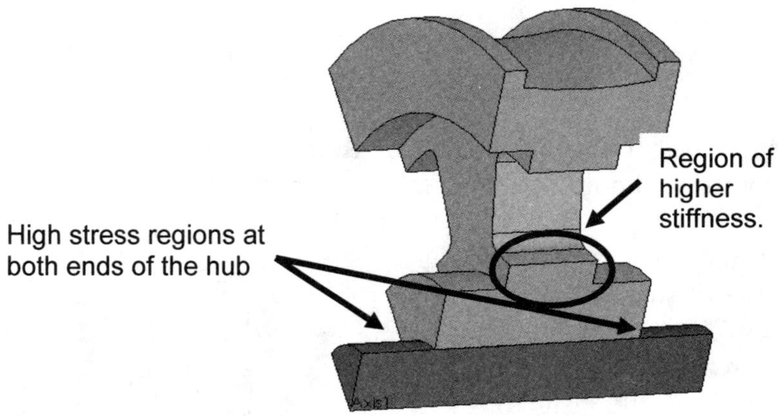

Figure 23 – Geometric differences between the actual model and assumptions of classical interference fit equations.

Classical interference fit equations are applied below to determine circumferential and radial stresses at the contact surface. Nominal part dimensions, given in Fig. 1, combined with SolidWorks material properties for the shaft and wheel are used in equation [2] to determine the common contact pressure "p" between mating parts.

Solution for common contact pressure between force fit parts.

$$\delta = \frac{pR}{E_o}\left(\frac{r_o^2 + R^2}{r_o^2 - R^2} + \nu_o\right) + \frac{pR}{E_i}\left(\frac{R^2 + r_i^2}{R^2 - r_i^2} - \nu_i\right) \qquad [2]$$

$$0.00205 = \frac{p(1.25)}{27.6e6}\left(\frac{(2.5)^2 + (1.25)^2}{(2.5)^2 - (1.25)^2} + 0.26\right) + \frac{p(1.25)}{30.5e6}\left(\frac{(1.25)^2 + 0^2}{(1.25)^2 - 0^2} - 0.28\right)$$

Solving equation [2] for contact pressure between the wheel and shaft yields p = 17,530 psi = radial stress at the contact surface = σ_r.

Where: δ = radial interference
p = the *unknown* contact pressure between mating parts
R = common radius at contacting surfaces
r_i = inside radius of inner member (r_i = 0 for a solid shaft)
r_o = outside radius of external member (wheel hub radius is used)
E_i = modulus of elasticity for inner member (shaft)
E_o = modulus of elasticity for outer member (wheel)
ν_i = Poisson's ratio for inner member (shaft)
ν_o = Poisson's ratio for external member (wheel)

Next, using the contact pressure "p" that exists between the shaft and wheel hub, circumferential stress at the outer surface of the inner member (i.e., on the shaft surface) is computed in equation [3].

$$(\sigma_t)_i = -p\frac{R^2 + r_i^2}{R^2 - r_i^2} = -17530\left(\frac{(1.25)^2 + 0^2}{(1.25)^2 - 0^2}\right) = -17{,}530\,psi \qquad [3]$$

Finally, the circumferential stress at the inner surface of the outer member (i.e., circumferential stress on inner surface of the wheel hub) is given by equation [4].

$$(\sigma_t)_o = p\frac{r_o^2 + R^2}{r_o^2 - R^2} = 17530\left(\frac{(2.5)^2 + (1.25)^2}{(2.5)^2 - (1.25)^2}\right) = 29{,}200\,psi \qquad [4]$$

Stress Predicted by Finite Element Analysis

Radial Stress Comparison

Given the prior observations about obvious differences between classical equation assumptions and the actual model, it is logical to expect differences between results predicted by classical equations and the finite element analysis (FEA). This section focuses on comparing results at contact locations predicted by classical equations [2] through [4]. Proceed as follows to determine radial stress (i.e., the contact pressure) between the shaft and wheel. Begin by reproducing the exploded view as follows.

*As of this writing, second time access to the **Explode** feature of SolidWorks (service pack 2.1) is not working properly. Thus, follow steps 1 to 5 below to turn exploded views "on" or "off".*

1. Click the **Configuration Manager** icon at top of the Feature manager tree. Click successive "+" signs until ExplView1 appears

2. Right-click **ExplView1** and from the pull-down menu, select **Explode.**

3. Return to the **Radial Stress (-X normal-)** and double click its name. The **Stress Plot** property manager opens.

4. Click **[OK]** ✓ to close the **Stress Plot** property manager and the model appears as an exploded view.

5. In the Simulation manager, right-click **Radial Stress (-X normal-)** and from the pull-down menu choose **List Selected**. The **Probe Result** window opens as shown in Fig. 24.

6. In the **Options** dialogue box, choose ⊙ **On selected entities.**

7. In the **Results** dialogue box the **Faces, Edges, or Vertices** field is highlighted and awaiting selection of the item for which results are to be displayed. On the graphics screen, rotate and zoom-in on the inner surface of the wheel hub shown "boxed" in Fig. 24, then click to select it. **Face<1>@wheel-1** appears in the field.

8. In the **Results** dialogue box, click the **[Update]** button.

Immediately the table is populated with data occurring on the selected surface. The **Value (psi)** column contains values of *radial* stress at all nodes on the inside surface of the wheel hub. Also included are node numbers, X, Y, Z locations of each data point, and a column identifying the **Components**, in this case **wheel-1**, to which the data applies. NOTE: to accurately view tabulated data it may be necessary to click-and-drag the right margin of the manager tree as well as column-edges within the table to increase their width.

Immediately the table is populated with data occurring on the selected surface. The **Value (psi)** column contains values of *radial* stress at all nodes on the inside surface of the wheel hub. Also included are node numbers, X, Y, Z locations of each data point, and a column identifying the **Components**, in this case **wheel-1**, to which the data applies. NOTE: to accurately view tabulated data it may be necessary to click-and-drag the right margin of the manager tree as well as column-edges within the table to increase their width.

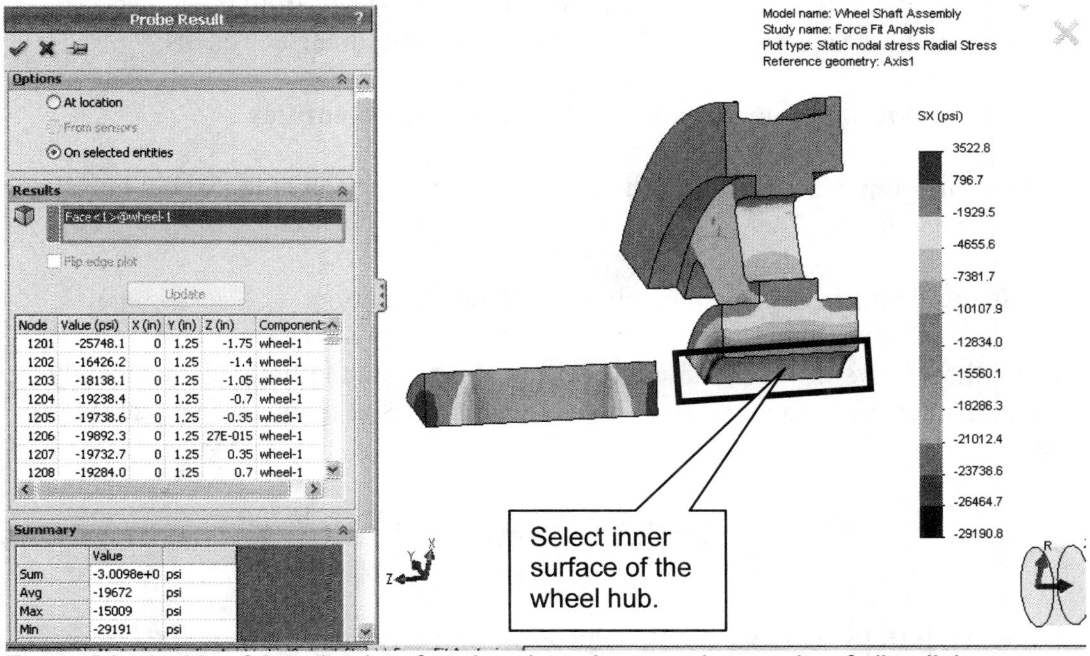

Figure 24 – Inside of the wheel surface is selected to examine results of all radial stresses acting on that surface. Results are summarized in the **Probe Result** table.

In the **Summary** dialogue box, located at the bottom of the **Probe Result** property manager, observe that radial stress values on the selected surface are summarized in several different forms (**Sum**, **Avg**, **Max**, **Min**, and **RMS**). For this example, consider only the **Avg** value listed as **-19672 psi** for the radial stress. Using this value, a comparison with the result of classical equation [2] above yields-

$$\% \text{ difference} = \frac{\text{FEA result - classical result}}{\text{FEA result}} * 100 = \frac{19672 - 17530}{19672} * 100 = 10.9\ \% \qquad [5]$$

While the percent difference found in equation [5] exceeds desired expectations, it is probably reasonable given the differences between assumptions associated with use of classical equations and the actual model geometry. This larger than desired difference is clearly a case where St. Venant's principle, once again, influences the final results.

9. Select the **[OK]** ✓ to close the **Probe Result** property manager.

Circumferential Stress Comparison

Next return to the **Circumferential Stress (-Y normal-)** plot and repeat the above procedure, except this time determine the circumferential stress on the inner surface of the wheel hub. Try this on your own. If needed, follow the steps outlined below.

1. Right-click **Circumferential Stress (-Y normal-)**, then from the pull-down menu select **Show**. Alternately, double-click **Circumferential Stress (-Y normal-)**.

2. Right-click **Circumferential Stress (-Y normal-)** and from the pull-down menu choose **List Selected**. The **Probe Result** property manager opens.

3. In the **Options** dialogue box, select ⊙ **On selected entities**.

4. On the graphics screen, click to select the inner surface of the wheel hub shown "boxed" in Fig. 24.

5. In the **Results** dialogue box, click the **[Update]** button.

Compare the **Avg** value for the circumferential stress from the finite element analysis with that predicted by equation [4] above. The comparison is shown in equation [6] below.

$$\%\ \text{difference} = \frac{\text{FEA result - classical result}}{\text{FEA result}} * 100 = \frac{28775 - 29200}{28775} * 100 = 1.48\ \% \quad [6]$$

6. Click **[OK]** ✓ to close the **Probe Result** property manager.

These results represent much better agreement between the Finite Element Analysis stress prediction and the classical equation solution. It might appear that the next logical step would be to compare finite element results for circumferential stress on the outer surface of the shaft with results predicted by equation [3]. However, because the process outlined above selects data at *all* nodes on the selected surface, poor agreement would result because a considerable area, on both ends of the shaft surface, lies outside the contact area defined by the interference fit. For this reason, these results are not compared here. However, if desired, *Split Lines* could be added to the shaft to limit comparison to the contact region only.

Quantifying Radial Displacements

Through additional application of the **List Selected** feature, SolidWorks Simulation provides a convenient means to verify the interference fit imposed on the mating parts of this example. Note: Because the shaft and wheel hub are of different lengths, results obtained from the following analysis are expected to differ from those predicted by classical equations. However, in instances where inner and outer members are of the same length, such as Exercise 1 at the end of this chapter, excellent agreement of results is obtained (< 2% difference). Proceed as follows to determine the deformation of each part.

1. In the Simulation manager, right-click the **Displacement1 (-Res disp-)** plot icon, and from the pull-down menu, select **Show**. The **Displacement** plot is displayed.

2. Again, right-click **Displacement1 (-Res disp-)** and from the pull-down menu, select **Edit Definition…** The **Displacement Plot** property manager opens as shown in Fig. 25.

3. In the **Component** field of the **Display** property manager, select **UX: X Displacement**. According to Table 1, **UX: X Displacement** corresponds to *radial* displacement in a cylindrical coordinate system.

4. Click to open the **Advanced Options** dialogue box. The **Plane, Axis or Coordinate System** field is highlighted (light blue) and awaits selection of an axis to define a cylindrical coordinate system.

5. Open the SolidWorks flyout menu (if not already open) and click to select **Axis1** to define it as the reference axis for a cylindrical coordinate system. **Axis1** should appear in the highlighted field.

6. In the **Display** dialogue box, verify that **Units** are set to **in** and that ⊙ **True scale** is selected in the **Deformed Shape** dialogue box.

7. Click **[OK]** ✓ to close the **Displacement Plot** property manager.

8. If the plot produced in the preceding step does not appear on the graphics screen, double-click **Displacement1 (-X disp-)** to display the plot.

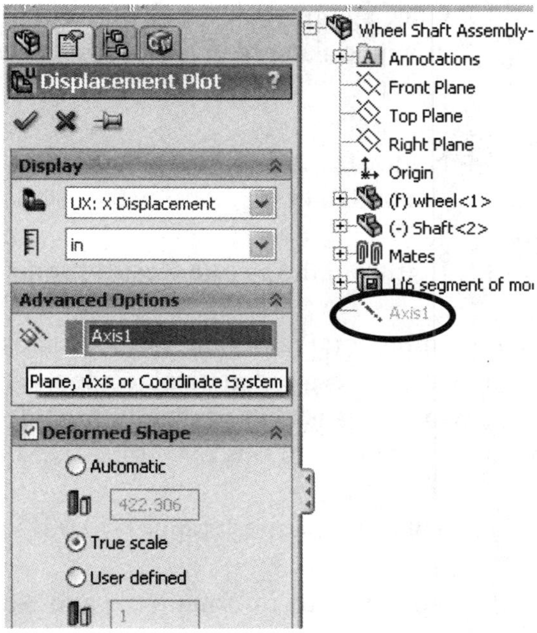

Figure 25 – Set-up of the **Displacement Plot** property manager to produce a plot of radial displacement.

9. Right-click **Displacement1 (-X disp-)** and from the pull-down menu choose **List Selected**. The **Probe Result** property manager opens.

10. In the graphics area, click the inner surface of the wheel hub shown "boxed" in Fig. 24. Then in the **Results** dialogue box, click the **[Update]** button.

The preceding step causes radial displacements at every node on the selected surface to be listed in the table of the **Results** dialogue box. Once again it may be necessary to click-and-drag to adjust column widths so that complete numerical values of displacement can be observed.

Of primary importance to this analysis is the **Avg** value of displacement listed in the **Summary** dialogue box. The value shown there corresponds to *radial* displacement of the inner surface of the wheel hub after the interference fit is accomplished. The **Avg** value of deformation on the inside surface of the wheel is listed as **0.0015174 in.** Without exiting the **Probe Result** property manager, proceed to examine deformation on the shaft surface as follows.

11. In the **Faces, Edges or Vertices** field, top field in the **Results** dialogue box, right-click **Face<1>@wheel-1** and from the pop-up menu select **Delete.**

12. Next, rotate the model so that the cylindrical surface on top of the shaft is visible and click to select it. **Face<2>@Shaft-2** appears in the active field.

13. Once again, click the **[Update]** button in the **Results** dialogue box. The table is now populated with values of the *radial* displacement on the outer surface of **Shaft-2**.

14. Notice the **Avg** value of radial displacement listed in the **Summary** table is **-0.00031449 in.**

15. Exit from the **Probe Result** property manager by clicking **[OK]**✓.

To determine total radial interference between the shaft and wheel, the absolute values of the above two **Avg** radial displacements are added together in equation [7]. The sum of these two values is approximately equal to the original radial interference specified in the opening statement of this example.

$$\text{Total radial interference} = |0.0015174\,| + |-0.00031449| = 0.0018319 \text{ in} \qquad [7]$$

And, from the given information, page 5-2, for this example,

$$\text{radial interference} = \tfrac{1}{2} * \text{diametral interference} = \tfrac{1}{2} * 0.0041 = 0.00205 \text{ in} \qquad [8]$$

The difference between total radial interference for equation [7], based on displacement plots, and the given interference from equation [8] is,

$$\text{Difference} = 0.00205 - 0.00183 = 0.00022 \text{ in (rounded values)} \qquad [9]$$

Knowing that the *entire* shaft surface is selected, but only that portion of the shaft surface within the contact region *should* be considered, the above difference is deemed acceptable.

This concludes the analysis portion of the current example. The following section describes a semi-automated method of generating a **Report** within SolidWorks Simulation.

Generating a Report

SolidWorks Simulation provides a pre-defined **Report** format for quickly generating and sharing information related to any Study. The **Report** folder contains a basic outline of items that the user can choose either to include or to exclude from a report. A report also provides a means for sharing information with others either via the internet (an HTML file) or in print form (a Word® file). The process for including or excluding items from a report is outlined below.

1. Before generating a report, adjust the model size and orientation on the screen to best display graphical characteristics of interest to the user. This is done because the orientation of all plots produced within the report is identical to their current screen image.

2. In the main menu, click **Simulation**. From the pull-down menu select **Report...** and the **Report Options** window opens as seen in Fig. 26.

At the top-center of this window, adjacent to **Report style:**, it is possible to select between **Contemporary** (default), **Professional**, and **Elegant** style reports. These options are accessible via a pull-down menu. Because only slight font and layout differences exist between these report formats, accept the default **Contemporary** report style and proceed as follows.

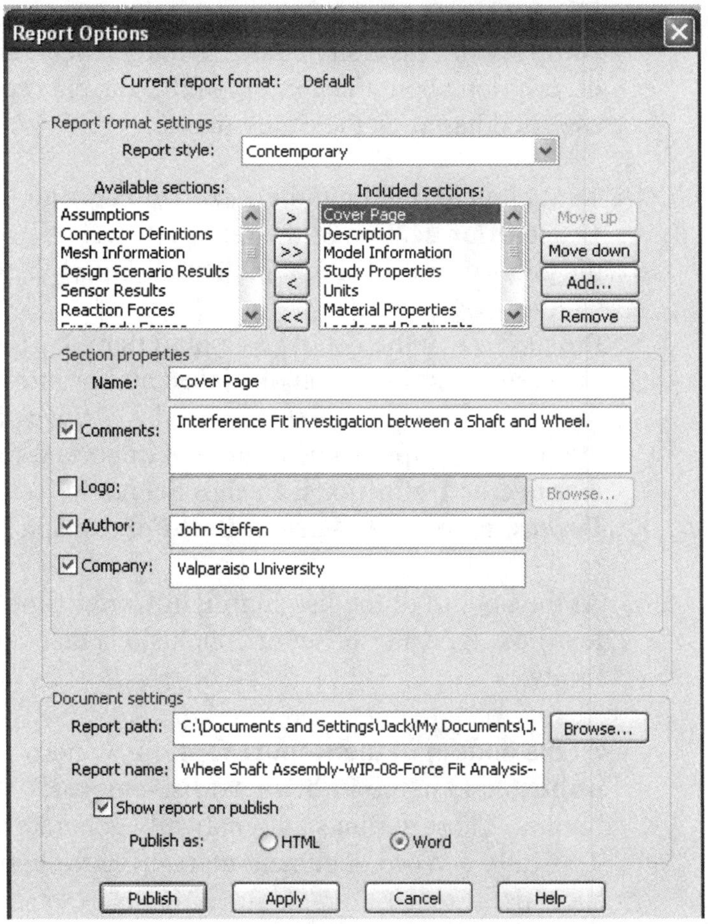

Figure 26 – Initial window of the **Report** folder showing a list of possible items that can be included or removed from a sample report.

Immediately below the **Report style:** pull-down menu are two scrollable columns. When first opening the **Report Options** window the left-hand column is typically empty and the right-hand column contains a list of all items that can be included in a report.

To remove an item from a report the item is highlighted (by clicking to select it) and then pressing the **[<]** button to move the selected item into the left-hand column. To move *all* items from the right column to the left column the **[<<]** button is pressed. Conversely, if one or all items are to be moved from the left-hand column into the right-hand column the **[>]** or **[>>]** buttons are used respectively. *Experiment with the above.*

The order of items within a report can also be changed by highlighting the item to be moved and clicking either the **[Move up]** or **[Move down]** buttons located to the right of the columns. Based on this brief introduction, we next proceed to generate a brief report. *Try the above, then restore the list to its original order.*

In the report generated below, several items are removed for the sake of brevity.

3. Begin by highlighting the **Cover Page** (if not already selected). Then, check the ☑ **Author:** field and type your name. Next, check ☑ **Company:** and enter your company or university name. Finally, check ☑ **Comments:** and provide a brief description about the content of the current report. A report title is automatically assigned based on the Study name.

4. Next click to highlight the *word* **Description**. This action activates the **Description** section of the report. Check ☑ **Comments:** and type a description of the goals of this example in the text-box.

5. Proceed down the list of remaining items by highlighting each item and briefly viewing the information displayed and/or information you can add. The following list suggests sections to be *removed* [<] from this report because they either are not applicable or are not important to this Study. **Assumptions**, **Connector Definitions**, **Design Scenario Results**, **Sensor Results**, **Reaction Forces**, **Free-Body Forces**, **Bolt Forces**, and **Pin Forces**.

6. At the bottom of the list, highlight **Conclusion**. Check ☑ **Comments:** and in the text-box, type a brief set of conclusions that can be drawn from the results of this Study.

7. At the bottom of the **Report Options** window check the ☑ **Show report on publish** and in the **Publish as:** list choose ⦿ **Word**, then press the **[Publish]** button. These settings automatically generate a Word® version of the report. Typically a Word document containing the completed report opens after a few seconds.

Take several minutes to scroll through the report and review the information you entered and the information automatically recorded in the report folder. Notice the variety of details relevant to the current example that are saved. Items such as the mesh type, mesh quality, and mesh size, are included along with data about the FEA solver used, material specifications, fixtures, and full color plots, etc. are *summarized* in the **Report**. While this file contains much useful data, it cannot replace the engineering insight that goes into evaluating results of a Study.

This concludes the present example. Unless instructed to save results of this example, proceed as follows to exit SolidWorks Simulation without saving the solution.

1. Select **File** from the main menu at top of screen and from the pull-down menu select **Close**.

2. A **SolidWorks** window opens and prompts: **Save changes to Wheel Shaft Assembly?** Click **NO**.

EXERCISES

╬ *Designates problems that introduce new concepts. Solution guidance is provided for these problems.*

EXERCISE 1 – Interference Fit Between a Bushing and Machine Frame

A bronze bushing is to be force fit into a hole in the cast iron wall of a machine frame. A bushing of this type serves as a bearing in a journal bearing set. The journal (i.e., the shaft) and bearing are separated by a thin film of lubricant, typically oil. Only the bushing and a portion of the machine frame are shown in Fig. E 5-1; the shaft is not shown. Important dimensions of the bushing and wall are included. The wall thickness and bushing length are equal. It is assumed that a sufficiently large segment of the machine frame is included in the model below so that boundary effects, due to influences of St. Venant's principle, are insignificant. Create a finite element analysis of the interference fit between these two mating parts.

Open the file: **Bushing and Frame 5-1**.

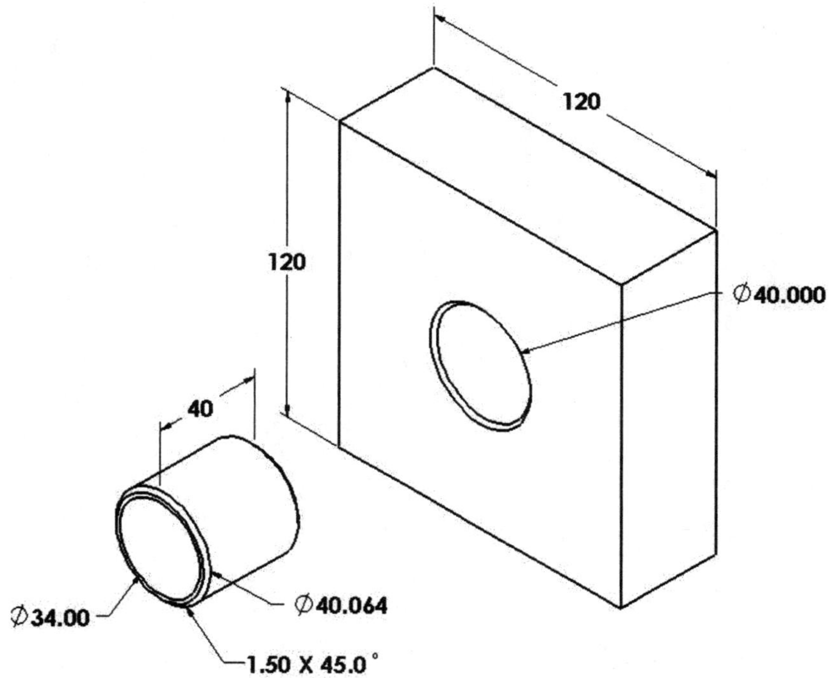

Figure E5-1 – Bushing and a portion of a machine frame wall. A comparison of the bushing outside diameter (o.d. = 40.064 mm) and the hole inside diameter (i.d. = 40.000 mm) in the machine frame reveals an interference fit between these mating parts.

- Material: Machine frame – **Gray Cast Iron** (Use S.I. units)
  Bushing – **Tin Bearing Bronze** (listed beneath "**Copper Alloys**")

- Mesh: **High Quality**, default size tetrahedral elements

- Fixture: Set **Connections / Contact Set** to **Shrink Fit** between the bushing and machine frame. If necessary, add restraints to prevent rigid body motion.

Solution Guidance
Discussion below provides general guidance (i.e., hints and reminders) for the solution to this problem. In particular instances where this solution differs from the example problem of this chapter, specific steps are provided.

Materials for this example are *not* pre-specified in SolidWorks. Therefore, after creating a **Study** in SolidWorks Simulation, assign *different* materials to each part as follows.

- In the Simulation manager, click the "+" sign adjacent to the + **Parts** folder. The **Bushing-2** and **Frame-1** folders appear.
- Right-click the **Bushing-2** folder to open the pull-down menu shown in Fig. E 5-2.
- From the pull-down menu, select **Apply/Edit Material…**
- In the **Material** window, specify the bushing material in the usual manner.
- Repeat the above steps to define **Gray Cast Iron** for the machine frame.

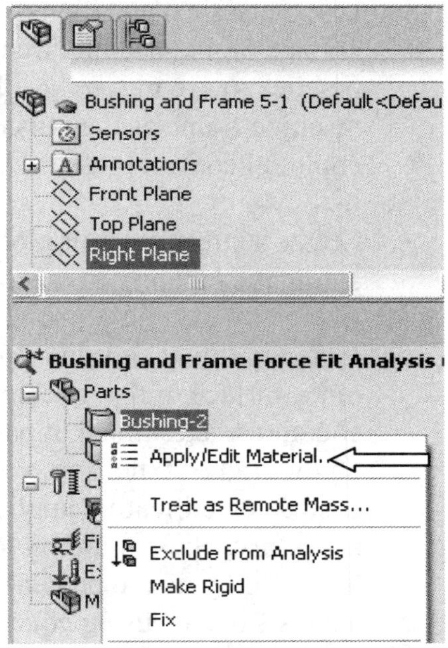

Figure E5-2 – Menu selections used to specify *different* materials for different parts of an assembly.

The above procedure applies individual material characteristics to parts contained in each sub-folder. In this instance there is only a single part in each sub-folder.

Next defeature the model. Also, use load and geometric symmetry to reduce the model to ¼ of the given assembly.

- Expand the SolidWorks Feature manager tree and beneath + **Frame<1>**, **Suppress** the **Frame Chamfer**. Similarly, beneath **Bushing<2>**, **Suppress** the **Bushing Chamfer**
- Also in the SolidWorks manager tree, right-click **Quarter Model – Assembly** and from the pop-up menu select the **Unsuppress**  icon.

When applying restraints to the model, consider carefully what restraint(s), if any, must be specified to prevent rigid-body-motion.

Develop a finite element model that includes: material specification, fixtures, a meshed model, and a solution. Defeature the model prior to analysis.

Determine the following:

a. Perform an interference check between the bushing and machine frame. Plot the resulting image.

b. Using classical equations, compute circumferential and radial stresses at the inner surface of the machine frame and the outer surface of the bushing. It is common practice to use the *radius* of a circle tangent to the inside of the block representing machine frame as the outside "radius" of the outer member. Also determine the common contact pressure between these surfaces.

c. Create a stress contour plot of von Mises stress in the assembly. Include automatic labeling of maximum and minimum von Mises stress on this plot.

d. In a cylindrical coordinate system, plot and compare circumferential stress at the inner surface of the machine frame with results calculated using classical equations determined in part (b). The value to be used for the finite element stress on the frame is the **Avg.** value of circumferential stress determined by using the **List Selected** feature applied to the inner surface of the hole in the frame. If necessary, click-and-drag to adjust column widths to show all digits of tabulated data. Compute the percent difference between classical and finite element analysis results using equation [1].

$$\% \text{ difference} = \frac{(\text{FEA result - classical result})}{\text{FEA result}} * 100 = \qquad [1]$$

e. Repeat part (d) for circumferential stress at the outer surface of the bushing.

f. In a cylindrical coordinate system, plot and determine the average value of radial stress (contact pressure) between mating surfaces; use the **List Selected** feature. Apply the **List Selected** feature to the inner surface of the hole and outer surface of the bushing. Although, theoretically, these values should be the same, some differences may occur. Therefore, determine the average of these two values and compare it with the classical result predicted for contact pressure determined in part (b). Then determine the percent difference by again using equation [1].

g. Because length of inner and outer members is equal, determine the radial displacement of the bushing (inner member) and machine frame (outer member) using the average **(Avg.)** value determined using the **List Selected** option. Determine the total radial interference and compare it with the given interference. Comment upon whether or not they check, and if not, explain why.

╬ EXERCISE 2 – Stress Variation in a Saw Blade due to Centrifugal Force (Special Topics: Centrifugal Force, Soft Spring Supports)

A saw blade of the type used on table saws, miter saws, or radial arm saws is shown in Fig. E 5-3. This part is considered to be a thin rotating disk provided (a) its thickness is constant, (b) its outside radius is large compared to its thickness, and (c) stresses are constant through its thickness. Blades of this type are labeled with a maximum rotational speed limit, which in this case is 5500 rpm. Additional external loads, due to cutting forces between the saw blade and work-piece, are not considered in this exercise. Despite the hole at the center of the saw blade, both stress concentration and interference fits are *ignored* in this exercise.

Develop a finite element model that includes material specification, applied centrifugal force, mesh generation, and solution. Because *centrifugal loading* and use of *soft springs* to support the part are not topics of the current chapter, guidance is provided to deal with these two aspects of the solution.

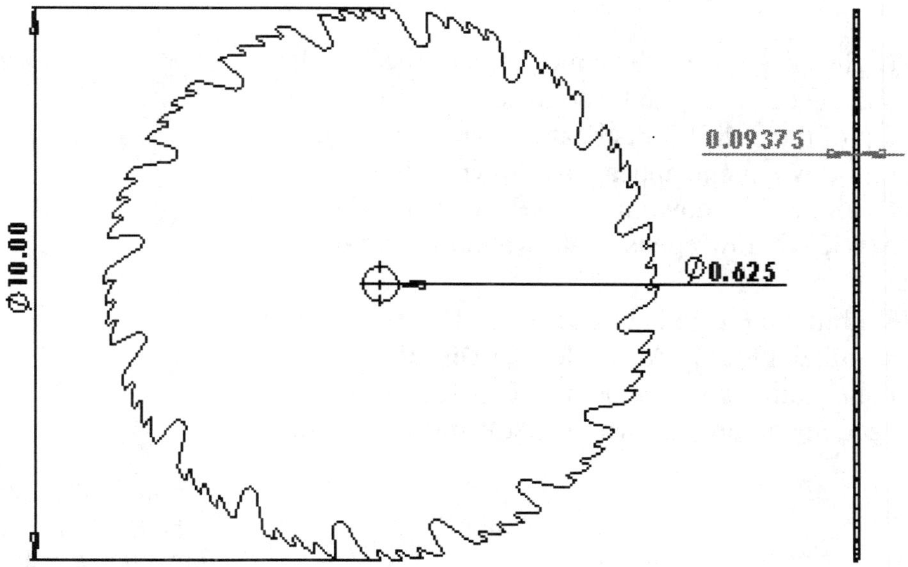

Figure E5-3 – Front and side views of a typical circular saw blade used in wood cutting applications.

Open the file: **Circular Saw Blade**

- Material: **Chrome Stainless Steel** (Use English units), steel density ρ = 0.282 lb/in^3
- Mesh: **High Quality** tetrahedral elements
- Fixture: **Soft Springs** See Solution Guidance section below.
- External Load: None. Load due to centrifugal force caused by 5500 rpm.

Solution Guidance

Guidance is provided below regarding (a) the use of soft springs to restrain the model, and (b) the application of a centrifugal force to load the model. Steps below presume that the **Circular Saw Blade** file is open and a Simulation Study has been initiated.

Rigid Body Motion Prevention

As noted above, **Soft Springs** must be applied to stabilize the model. Model stabilization is necessary because (a) **Fixed** or other common restraints are not appropriate for a part that is considered to be rotating, and (b) the centrifugal force applied to the blade does not provide restraints in the X, Y, or Z directions. Simply stated, static restraints are not consistent with assumed rotation of the saw blade.

For additional discussion about soft springs, see Chapter 1, pages 1-35 (top) to 1-36 (bottom). Soft springs can be assigned any time before the solution is run.

- Right-click the Study name at top of the Simulation manager tree (not to be confused with the name at top of the SolidWorks Feature manager tree). A pull-down menu appears as shown in Fig. E 5-4. From the pull-down menu, select **Properties…** The **Static** window opens as shown in Fig. E 5-5.

- Within the **Options** tab, select ☑ **Use soft spring to stabilize model**. Also select ⊙ **Direct Sparse** as the equation solver method. This solver must be used in conjunction with the soft spring option.

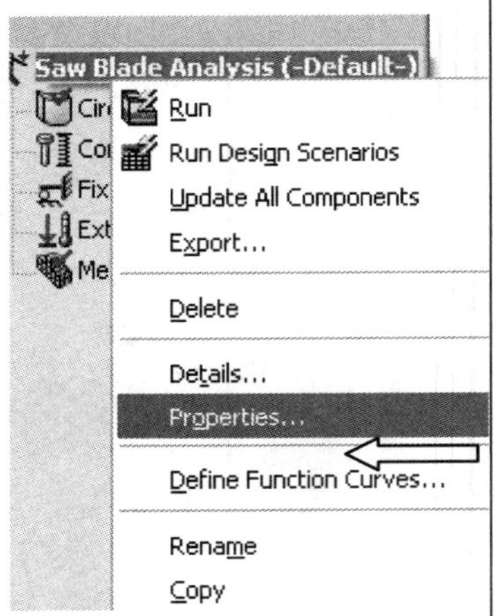

Figure E5-4 – Accessing the Study level pull-down menu to assign **Soft Spring** support to the model.

- Click **[OK]** to close the **Static** window

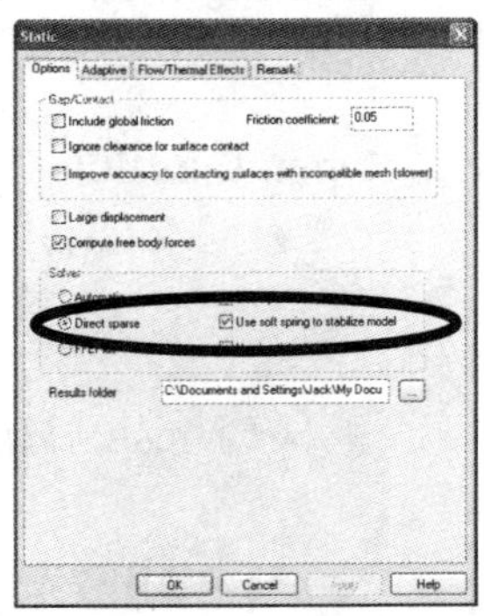

Figure E5-5 – Selecting **Soft Spring** support in the **Static** window.

Solution Guidance (continued)

<u>Centrifugal Force Specification</u>

- Right-click **External Loads** and from the pull-down menu select **Centrifugal...** The **Centrifugal** property manager opens. See Fig. E 5-6.
- In the **Selected Reference** dialogue box the **Axis, Edge, Cylindrical Face for Direction** field is highlighted (light blue). Select the *inside* cylindrical *surface* of the hole.

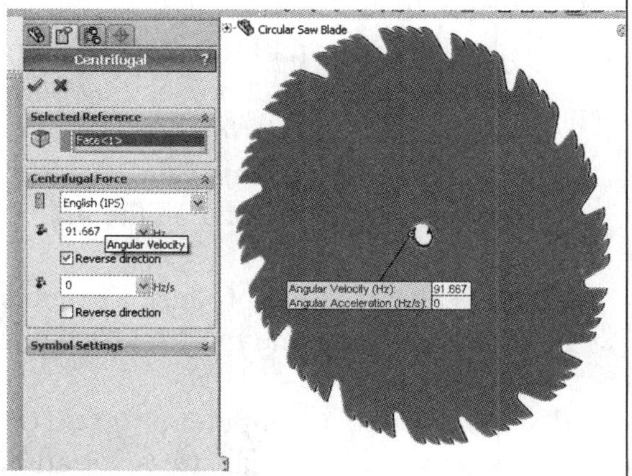

Figure E5-6 – Specifying a **Centrifugal** force on a saw blade rotating at 5500 RPM.

- In the **Centrifugal Force** dialogue box, type the rotational speed into the **Angular Velocity** field. Convert 5500 rpm to **Hz** (i.e., cycles/second = rev/sec). After typing this value, a red arrow appears inside the hole to indicate the direction of rotation. If the arrow is opposite the direction in which the saw teeth are "leaning," then select ☑ **Reverse Direction**. The notation **Centrifugal-1** appears beneath the **External Loads** folder.
- Click **[OK]** ✓ to close the **Centrifugal** property manager.

Determine the following:

Develop a finite element model that includes: material specification, soft springs, applied external load (centrifugal force), mesh generation, and solution.

a. After running the solution and obtaining the **Results** folder, edit the **Stress1 (-vonMises-)** plot by doing the following.
   - Turn off the ☐ **Deformed Shape**. You will know when the deformed shape is turned off because the centrifugal force arrow will again appear at the central hole.
   - Display **Discrete** fringes on the model
   - Display the **Mesh** on the model
   - Turn on ☑ **Show max annotation**
   - Next, *copy* the **Stress1 (-vonMises-)** plot. Then change the copied plot to display **P1: 1st Principal Stress**. Also, re-name this plot to reflect its true identity. HINT: Does the 1st principal stress represent *tangential* or *radial* stresses caused by rotation?

- Repeat the preceding step, except create a plot of **P2: 2nd Principal Stress.** HINT: Does the 2nd principal stress represent *tangential* or *radial* stresses caused by rotation?

b. Zoom in on the saw blade that displays a plot of **P1: 1st Principal Stress**. Then, use the **Probe** tool to select all corner and mid-side nodes beginning at the edge of the center hole and proceeding outward to as near as possible to the tip of any tooth. When selecting nodes, traverse the model in the straightest line possible. Create a graph of this data. Alter the graph title and axes labels to better describe information contained on the graph.

c. Repeat step (b) to produce a graph showing the variation of **P2: 2nd Principal Stress** at the same location on the model.

d. Either write a computer program or set up a spreadsheet to calculate both the tangential and radial stress variation from the central hole outward to the blade tip. Calculate the two stress magnitudes at 0.20 inch increments beginning at the hole inside radius and proceeding outward to the 5.00 inch outside radius. Also, within the spreadsheet, plot and label graphs of stress variation for both stress types. Use the following equations to compute tangential and radial stresses.

Tangential stress in a rotating disk.

$$\sigma_t = \rho\omega^2\left(\frac{3+\nu}{8}\right)\left(r_i^2 + r_o^2 + \frac{r_i^2 r_o^2}{r^2} - \frac{1+3\nu}{3+\nu}r^2\right) \qquad [2]$$

Radial stress in a rotating disk.

$$\sigma_r = \rho\omega^2\left(\frac{3+\nu}{8}\right)\left(r_i^2 + r_o^2 - \frac{r_i^2 r_o^2}{r^2} - r^2\right) \qquad [3]$$

Where,

ρ = mass density of the saw blade = density/(386 in/sec^2)
ν = Poisson's ratio
r_i = inside radius (inches)
r_o = outside radius (inches)
r = radius to the point of interest, variable (inches)
ω = angular velocity in cycles/sec = rev/sec

e. Use equation [1], repeated below, to compare percent differences between maximum stresses calculated using equations [2] and [3] with maximum stress values **P1: 1st Principal Stress** and **P2: 2nd Principal Stress** calculated using the finite element approach. Based on comparisons of calculated values and graphs, identify which finite element stress (**P1** or **P2**) corresponds to the tangential stress in the saw blade. Does the other finite element stress correspond to the radial stress in the saw blade? If "yes," state the basis for this conclusion. If "no," state why not.

$$\% \text{ difference} = \frac{(\text{FEA result - classical result})}{\text{FEA result}} * 100 = \qquad [1]$$

Textbook Problems

In addition to the above exercise, it is highly recommended that additional problems involving interference fits between mating parts be worked from a design of machine elements textbook. Textbook problems provide a great way to discover errors made in formulating a finite element analysis because they typically are well defined problems for which the solution is known. Typical textbook problems, if well defined in advance, make an excellent source of solutions for comparison.

NOTES:

CHAPTER #6

CONTACT ANALYSIS

Examples up to this point have included models for which various preliminary steps, such as suppressing or un-suppressing certain model features, were pre-planned so that examples could proceed quickly to introduce new principles and techniques. However, a real analysis is not often delivered in such a "ready to go" condition unless the user, or a CAD technician, plans ahead to prepare a model in the desired format. Either case requires the finite element analyst either to develop the model according to his or her own expectations or to inform a CAD expert about special modeling needs. To better prepare FEA users for these more realistic scenarios, this example include*s* many of the necessary preparatory steps thereby creating a more realistic example from beginning to end.

Learning Objectives

Upon completion of this example, users should be able to:

- Assign loads to a *non-flat surface* in *specified direction*(s)
- Define *Contact/Gap* conditions with *no penetration*
- Use *Animation* to understand deformation and stress development as load(s) are applied
- Apply *Iso Clipping* to view model stresses
- Display *Contact Pressure* plots

Problem Statement

A trunion mount, of the type used to attach hydraulic or pneumatic cylinders to a fixed surface, is shown in Fig. 1. Both the trunion and pin are made of **Alloy Steel**. The pin is subject to an 800 lb force acting upward to the right at 60° from the horizontal as shown in a right-side view, Fig. 2. The goal of this analysis is to determine maximum von Mises stress and its location on the trunion mount and to determine contact pressure distribution between the pin and holes in the trunion.

Figure 1 – Typical trunion mount.

Contacting surfaces occur where the pin passes through holes in the side-plates of the trunion and where the mid-portion of the pin is acted upon by a cylinder force (the cylinder attachment is not shown). For this reason, it is necessary to create separately identifiable contacting surfaces on the pin. *Split Lines* are used to divide the pin surface.

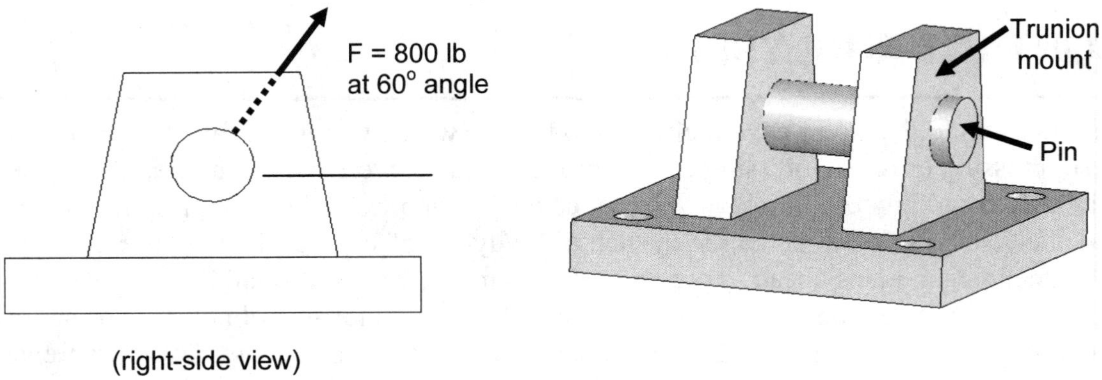

Figure 2 – Right-side view of trunion mount and pin showing direction of applied force.

The procedure outlined below is not the only way to apply *Split Lines* to the pin. It is, however, deemed simpler to demonstrate this aspect of model preparation on the pin alone, before joining it with the trunion base to form an assembly. Proceed as follows. *(Because a personal goal should be to develop independent competence using SolidWorks Simulation, many steps below are abbreviated where prior experience should be sufficient).*

Preparing the Model for Analysis

1. Open **SolidWorks 2009**.

2. Select **Files / Open…** and open the part file named "**Trunion Pin**."

All steps related to locating and creating *Split Lines* occur within SolidWorks, therefore a new Study is not started at this time. Three *Split Lines* are to be added to the trunion pin at locations illustrated on Fig. 3. It is important to know that the origin of the coordinate system is located at the center of the pin and that the pin is centered in the trunion mount. Given this information, those who are comfortable in their ability to locate the necessary reference planes and *Split Lines* are encouraged to proceed on their own. These individuals can skip the next two sections, titled "Add Reference Planes" and "Insert Split Lines." However, all necessary steps are provided below if guidance is desired.

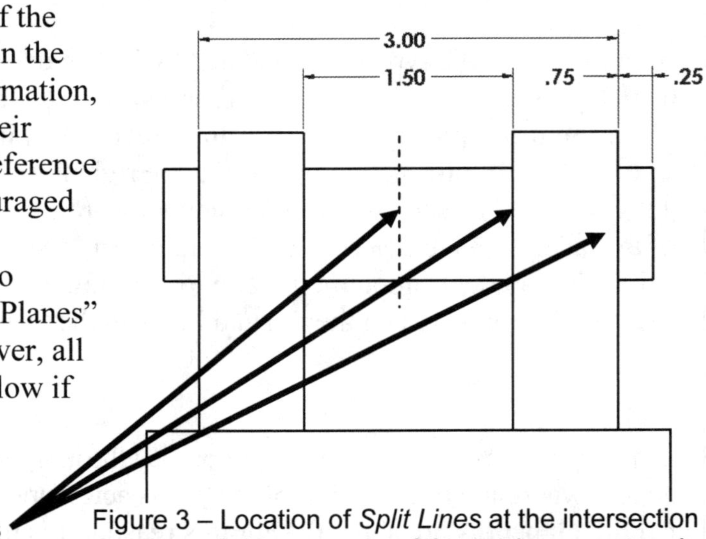

Figure 3 – Location of *Split Lines* at the intersection of the pin and side supports of the trunion mount and at the center of the pin.

Add Reference Planes

1. From the main menu select **Insert**.

2. In the pull-down menu, highlight **Reference Geometry ▶** and from the subsequent pop-up menu, select **Plane...** The **Plane** property manager opens and the SolidWorks flyout menu appears as seen in Fig. 4. If the flyout menu is not open, click the "+" adjacent to the **Trunion Pin** icon at top of the flyout menu to open it.

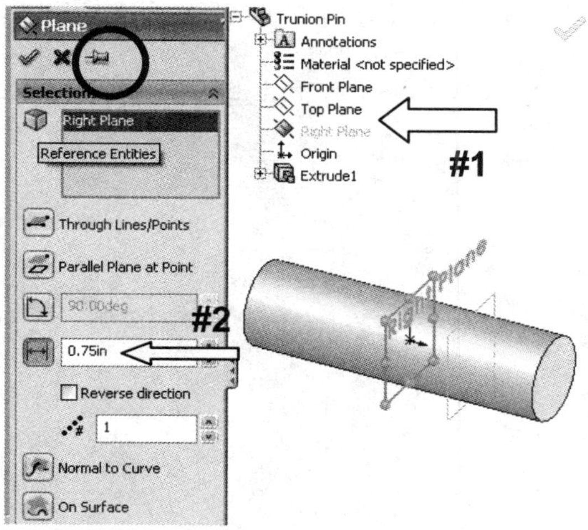

Figure 4 – Selecting the **Right Plane** as a starting point, the first **Reference Plane** is located 0.75 in to its right.

3. Click the **Keep Visible** "push-pin" at top of the **Plane** property manager (circled on Fig. 4). This action keeps the **Plane** property manager open so that multiple steps can be performed without the need to re-open it for each change.

4. In the **Selections** dialogue box the **Reference Entities** field is active (light blue). In the SolidWorks flyout menu, select **Right Plane**. See arrow **#1** in Fig. 4.

5. In the **Offset Distance** spin box, at arrow **#2**, type **0.75** as the distance from the **Right Plane** to the location of the first **Reference Plane**. Click mouse in the graphics screen and an outline of the **Reference Plane** appears on the pin.

6. Click **[OK]** ✓. **Plane1** is listed at the bottom of the SolidWorks flyout menu and is labeled on the pin.

7. Because the **Keep Visible** push-pin is active, **Plane1** is also listed in the **Selections** dialogue box.

8. By coincidence, the next reference plane is located at its desired position 0.75 in to the right of **Plane1** and is displayed on the model. Click **[OK]** ✓ to accept this new reference plane and **Plane2** is also added to the bottom of the SolidWorks flyout menu and is labeled on the pin.

9. Click to deselect the **Keep Visible** push-pin.

10. Repeat steps 4 to 6 again, but this time type **0.0** as the distance from the **Right Plane** in step 5. In other words, the third reference plane is added *at* the location of the **Right Plane**. This plane is located at the pin center because symmetry is used later in this example and both the trunion mount and the pin are cut at this location.

11. Click **[OK]** ✓ to close the **Plane** property manager.

A model of the pin and its three **Reference Planes** should appear as shown in Fig. 5.

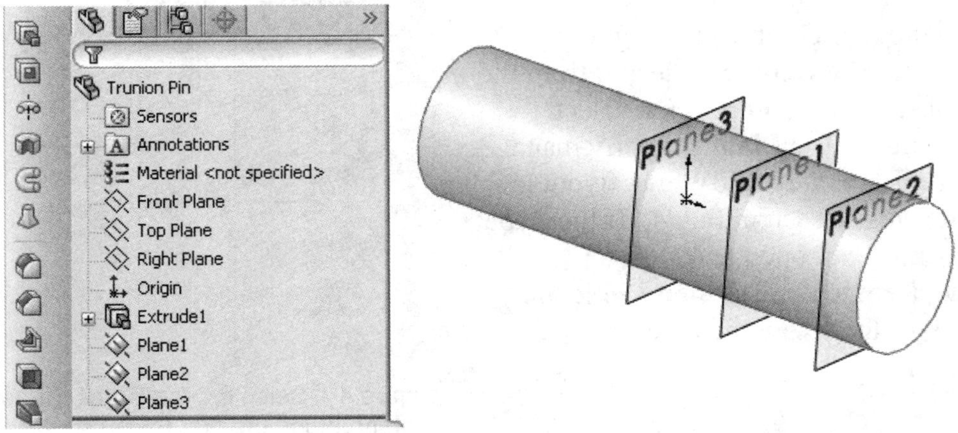

Figure 5 – Three **Reference Planes** are created to denote locations where *Split Lines* are to be added to the part.

Insert Split Lines

Intersections of **Plane1**, **Plane2**, and **Plane3** with the pin are used to locate *Split Lines* on the model as outlined below.

1. In the Main menu select **Insert**.

2. From the pull-down menu highlight **Curve ►** and from the pop-up menu, select **Split Line…** The **Split Line** property manager opens as shown in Fig. 6.

3. Because **Split Lines** are to be located where each plane intersects the pin, in the **Type of Split** dialogue box, choose ⦿ **Intersection**.

4. Click to select the upper field of the **Selections** dialogue box. The **Splitting Bodies/Faces/Planes** field is highlighted. Either select each of the planes appearing on the pin or click **Plane1**, **Plane2**, and **Plane3** in the SolidWorks flyout menu. Names of the three planes are listed in the upper field in the order selected.

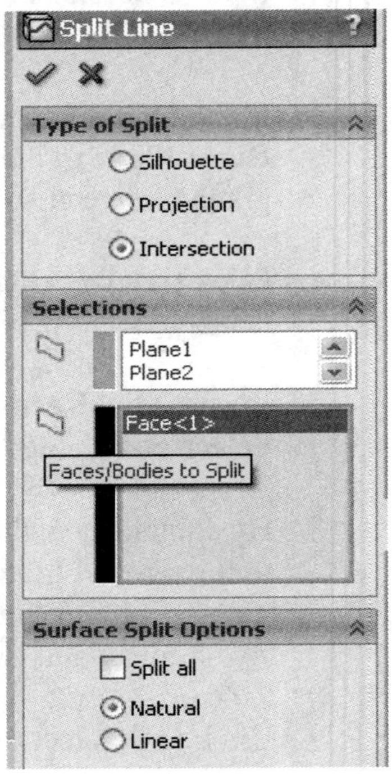

Figure 6 – The **Split Line** property manager is used to determine locations of *Split Lines* on the model.

5. Next, move the cursor onto the second field; its name appears as **Faces/Bodies to Split**. Click to activate this field. Then, move the cursor into the graphics area and select the *cylindrical* surface of the pin. **Face<1>** appears in this field.

6. In the **Surface Split Options** dialogue box, the setting should appear as ◉ **Natural**. If not, select it.

7. Click **[OK]** ✓ and three *Split Lines* appear on the pin as shown in Fig. 7. Also, **Split Line1** is listed at the bottom of the SolidWorks manager tree.

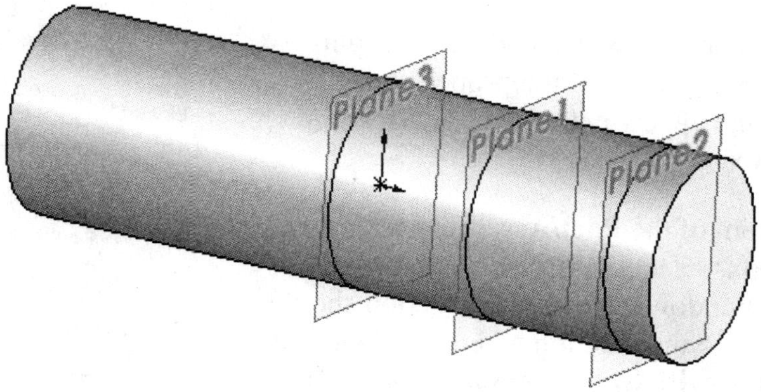

Figure 7 – *Split Lines* located on the trunion pin surface at intersections with the three **Reference Planes**.

Because symmetry exists, only the right-half of the pin is used for analysis. Therefore, no additional *Split Lines* need be added to the other half of the model. Save this file as outlined below.

8. From the main menu, select **File** followed by **Save As…**

9. In the **Save As** window, name the part "**Pin with Split Lines**" and **[Save]** the file to a PC, to network file space, or to temporary storage media such as a USB drive.

10. Close the file by selecting **File / Close**. (Do *not* close SolidWorks Simulation.)

Creating the Assembly Model

It is assumed that most SolidWorks Simulation users are already familiar with the SolidWorks work environment and the process of creating an *assembly* composed of two or more *parts*. Those individuals can proceed to join the **Trunion Base** and the **Pin with Split Lines** to form an assembly on your own and skip to the section titled **Create a Finite Element Analysis (Study)**. However, for users who are new to both SolidWorks and SolidWorks Simulation, a step-by-step procedure to create the assembly is outlined below.

In the assembly the pin is located concentric with holes in the trunion base and extends ¼ inch outside both of the two side supports shown in Fig. 3. This location will be replicated in the assembly created in the following steps.

1. In the main menu, click **File / New...** The **New SolidWorks Document** window opens.

2. Click the **Assembly** icon and then click **[OK]**. The **Begin Assembly** property manager opens as shown in Fig. 8.

3. Click to activate the **Keep Visible** push-pin circled at the top-right of the property manager. Also, read the upper sentence in the **Message** dialogue box.

4. At the bottom of the **Part/Assembly to Insert** dialogue box, select the **[Browse...]** button. The **Open** window appears. This action should take the user to the location where the **Trunion Base** and **Pin with Split Lines** are stored. If not, browse to other file storage locations as needed.

5. From the list of files, select **Trunion Base** and click **[Open]**.

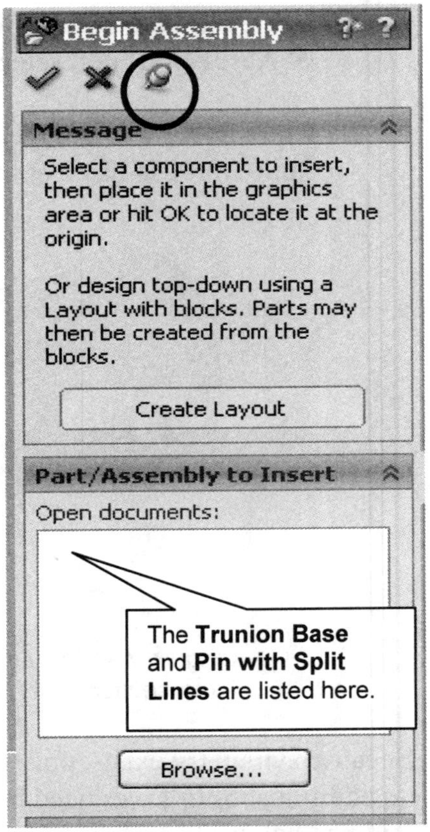

Figure 8 – The **Begin Assembly** property manager used to bring *parts* into an *assembly.*

6. The cursor and part appear and move together in the graphics area. Move the cursor to the top of the **Begin Assembly** property manager and click **[OK]** ✓. The trunion base automatically moves to the coordinate system origin. If the cursor is moved into the graphics area a second trunion base appears on the screen. ***Do not click again!***

Ignore the second trunion base that appears and proceed directly to the next step.

7. Move the cursor into the **Part / Assembly to Insert** dialogue box and again select the **[Browse...]** button. The **Open** window appears.

8. In the **Open** window, select the **Pin with Split Lines** and click **[Open]**. The cursor and pin appear and move together on the graphics screen.

9. Move the pin to a position above and to the left of the trunion base as illustrated in Fig. 9 and click to place it there. A small image of a mouse may appear with a green check-mark "✓" on the right mouse button, click the right mouse button to accept this position and simultaneously close the **Begin Assembly** property manager. *(The actual pin location is arbitrary, but first time users will gain greater insight into the assembly process if the pin and base do not initially intersect).*

The next task is to assemble the pin into holes on the trunion base. This requires use of a **Mate** definition between the parts to be joined. Because we are currently working in the *assembly* mode, the **Assembly** tab and its tool bar, shown in Fig. 10, should be displayed near the top of the screen. If not, two alternate methods of accessing the **Assembly** toolbar are outlined below.

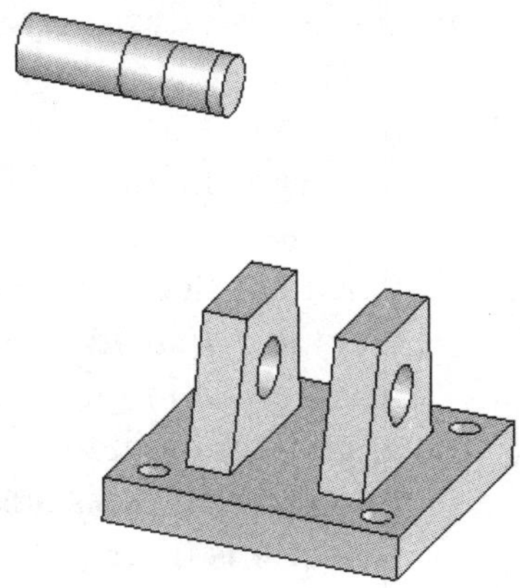

Figure 9 – Trunion base and pin (in an arbitrary position) prior to assembly.

Method 1

- Click the **Assembly** tab located near the upper left of the screen.
- An **Assembly** toolbar *similar* to that shown in Fig. 10 is opened.
- Skip to the "CAUTION" below Fig. 10.

Method 2

- Right-click anywhere in the toolbar at top of the screen. The **Command Manager** menu opens.
- From this menu select **Assembly** and the toolbar shown in Fig.10 should appear
- Skip to the "CAUTION" below Fig. 10.

Figure 10 – **Assembly** toolbar with the **Mates** icon circled. The **Mates** property manager is used to define geometric relationships (i.e., locations) of one part relative to another.

CAUTION: In the steps that follow the **Mate** icon is a single paper clip; it is *not* to be confused with the two paperclips labeled **Mates** located at the bottom of the SolidWorks feature manager tree.

10. Click the **Mate** icon .
11. The **Mate** property manager opens as seen in Fig. 11. The **Mate Selections** dialogue box is active (highlighted light blue). Passing the cursor over this field indicates it is to be filled with the **Entities to Mate**.

The first step is to position the pin so that it is concentric (aligned) with holes in the trunion base. To accomplish this, the two parts are selected as described next. NOTE: Because *Split Lines* are defined on the pin, its surface is effectively subdivided into segments at each *Split Line*. However, as described in the following step it is necessary to select *only one* cylindrical segment on the pin.

12. Click to select *any* cylindrical surface on the pin and the *cylindrical* surface *inside* either hole as highlighted in Fig. 12. The two parts move to align their cylindrical surfaces and names of the two selected faces appear in the **Mate Selections** dialogue box. The software is "smart" enough to guess that a concentric mate is probably desired, but this is not confirmed until the next step.

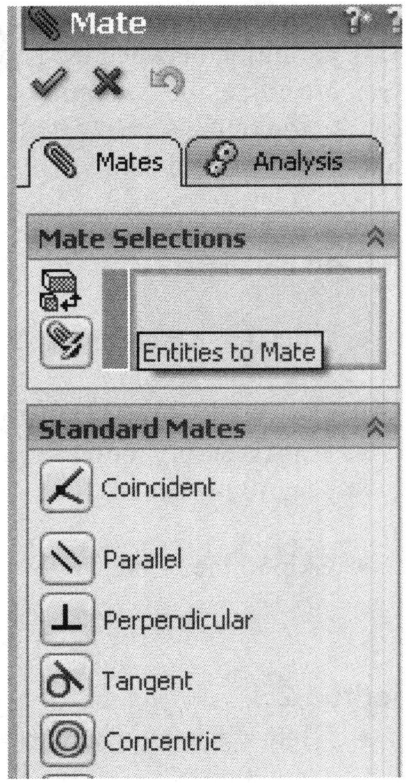

Figure 11 – Initial selection of surfaces to be specified as concentric is made in the **Mate** property manager.

A small pop-up icon bar appears as shown in Fig. 12. It shows icons of several possible mates that might be defined between the two cylindrical surfaces.

13. It is suggested that new users select the **Concentric** icon mate in the **Standard Mates** dialogue box because its name is listed adjacent to its icon. However, both icons are circled in Fig. 12 and either can be selected.

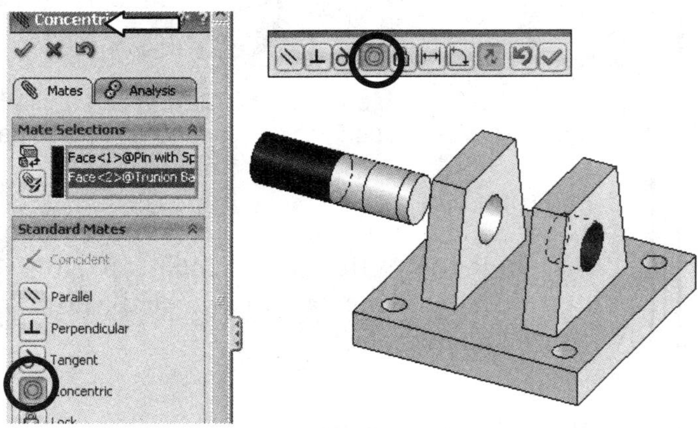

Figure 12 – Defining a **Concentric** mate between the pin and trunion base holes results in alignment between the two parts.

After selecting **Concentric**, the name **Concentric1** appears at the top of the property manager (see arrow in Fig. 12) and names of the two faces are listed in the **Entities to Mate** field.

14. Click **[OK]** ✓ to close the **Concentric1** property manager. *(Do NOT click **[OK]** twice; see next step).*

The property manager remains open, but its name changes back to the **Mate**. Proceed as follows to further define pin location within the holes

15. Click the right *end* of the pin *and* the right-face of the trunion support shown highlighted in Fig. 13. The pin-end is located flush with the trunion face.

However, because the 3.5 inch long pin is to be centered between the two supports (whose outside dimension is 3.00 in, see Fig. 3), pin location is altered as follows.

16. Type **0.25** in the **Distance** spin box indicated by an arrow on Fig. 13, and click anywhere in the graphics screen. This value ensures that the pin is offset 0.25 inch from the two selected surfaces. *See next step.*

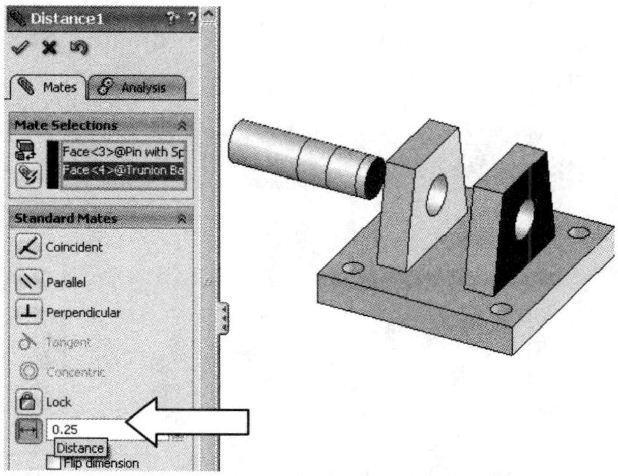

Figure 13 – Two faces are selected so that the appropriate **Distance** between them can be defined to center the pin between holes on the trunion base.

17. If the pin appears recessed within the right-side hole, or elsewhere on the assembly, it is necessary to check ☑ **Flip Dimension** located below the **Distance** spin box. The assembly should now appear as shown in Fig. 2, repeated below.

18. Click **[OK]** ✓ *twice* to close the **Distance1** and then the **Mate** property managers.

19. To protect the work invested in this example thus far, from the main menu select **File / Save As…** and in the **Save As** window, name the assembly "**Trunion and Pin Assembly**" then click **[Save]** to save the file.

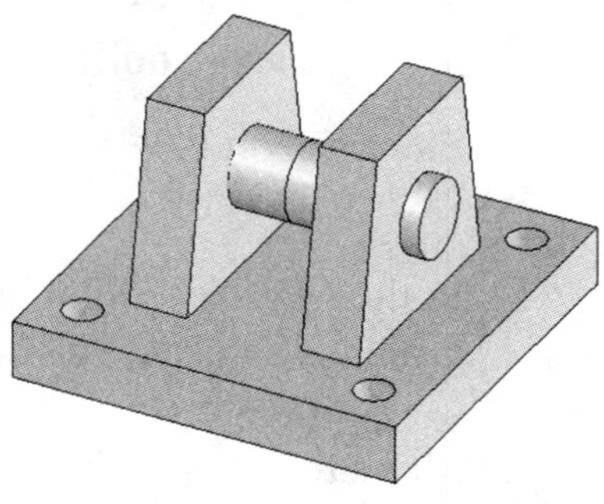

Figure 2 (Repeated) – Shows pin centered between two trunion sides.

Cut Model on Symmetry Plane

This example makes use of model symmetry to realize computational efficiencies associated with a smaller assembly and to provide additional practice using this powerful software feature. Steps below lead the user through one of several possible procedures used to create a symmetrical half-model.

1. In **View** the toolbar, click the **Front** view icon to rotate the front plane of the model into the plane of the screen.

2. Next, in the SolidWorks Feature manager tree, click to select **Front Plane**; see arrow in Fig. 14. The **Front Plane** is shown on an image of the model in Fig. 14.

NOTE: Additional top, front, and right planes exist for both the trunion base and for the pin. Although consistency of plane location was carefully coordinated for this example, it is important to realize that individual *parts* are created in their own local coordinate system. These individual local coordinate systems may be oriented differently once parts are brought together in the global coordinate system of an *assembly*.

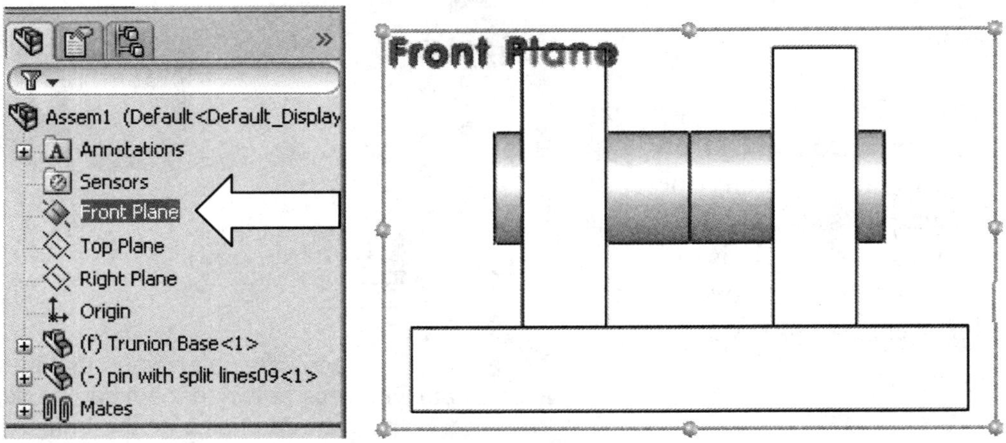

Figure 14 – The **Front Plane** is selected as the plane to sketch on as part of the process of cutting the model in half.

3. Click the **Sketch** icon to open a sketch on the front plane. If this toolbar does not appear on the screen, from the main menu, select **View**. From the pull-down menu, select **Toolbars►.** Then, scroll down in the toolbars menu and select the **Sketch** icon Sketch . This action opens the **Sketch** toolbar.

4. In the **Sketch** toolbar, select the **Line** icon and move the cursor onto the graphics screen. The cursor changes to a pencil symbol with a line adjacent to it.

5. Move the cursor above (or below) the *middle* of the assembly and a vertical dashed line appears to indicate alignment with the origin of the coordinate system. At this location, click and move the mouse to create a vertical line that extends completely through the model and extend it beyond its opposite border, then click again to end the line. Press **[Esc]** to terminate line drawing.

6. A screen image of the assembly should appear as shown in Fig. 15.

7. In the **Features** toolbar, select the **Extrude Cut** icon and the **Cut-Extrude** property manager opens. A portion of this property manager is illustrated in Fig. 16. *NOTE: If, instead, the* ***Extrude property manager opens****, click to select the vertical line again. Doing so opens the* ***Cut-Extrude*** *property manager.*

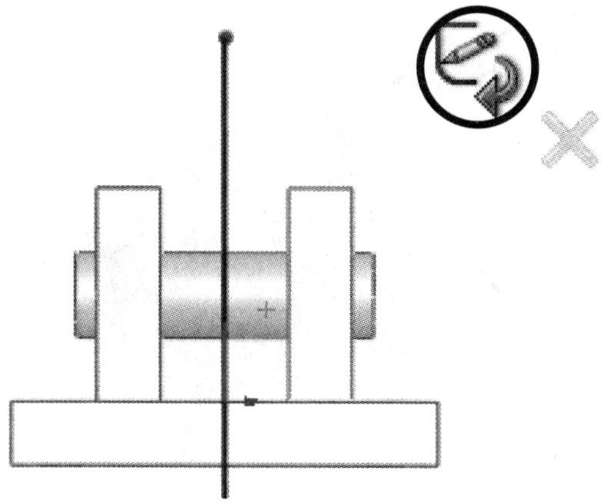

Figure 15 – Vertical line drawn on the **Front Plane** at center of the trunion and pin assembly. Also shown is the warning window that appears when closing a sketch.

8. The **From** dialogue box should indicate **Sketch Plane** and the **Direction1** dialogue box should indicate **Through All**.

9. If necessary, rotate the model so the surface created by extending the vertical line into a cutting plane is visible slicing through the model as shown in Fig. 17.

Three arrows appear on the plane. They point in directions in which the model is cut and material removed. Carefully observe the direction of the arrow *normal* to the plane. It should point *away* from the right-half of the model. Recall that the right-half of the pin was modified by the addition of *Split Lines*. Thus, the right-half of the model is to be saved.

10. If the normal arrow is directed toward the right-half of the model, click to change its direction by selecting ☑ **Flip side to cut**. See arrow in Fig. 16. When the normal arrow is directed toward the left-side of the assembly, proceed to the next step.

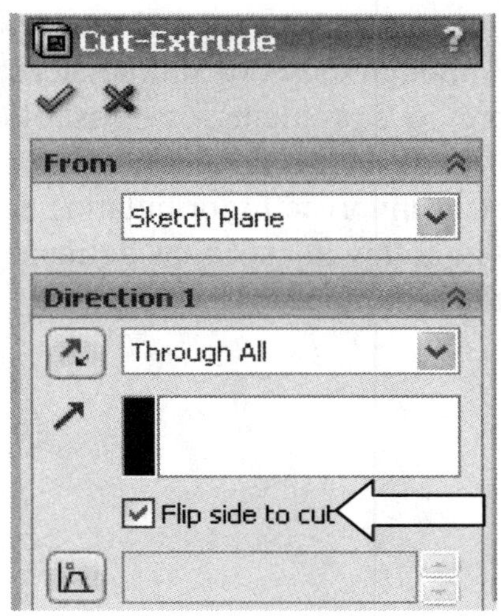

Figure 16 – **Cut-Extrude** property manager used to define direction for the portion of the assembly that is cut and removed by the sketch plane.

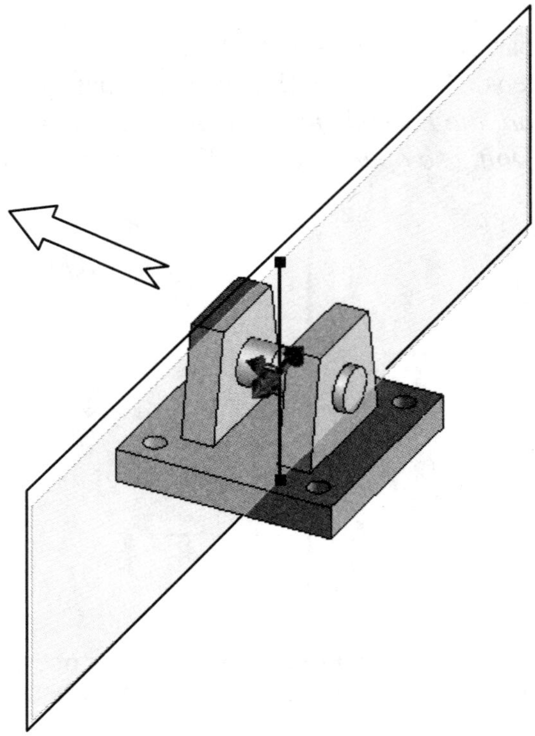

Figure 17 – The cutting plane created by extending the vertical line into a plane is shown along with arrows indicating the direction in which material is to be removed.

11. Click **[OK]** ✓ to close the **Cut-Extrude** property manager. The assembly should now appear as shown in Fig. 18.

This concludes the somewhat lengthy process of preparing a model for finite element analysis. Although these, or similar steps, were omitted from previous problems, one goal of the current example is to develop a comprehensive picture of typical tasks involved in formulating a complete analysis. The following sections define and solve the finite element model

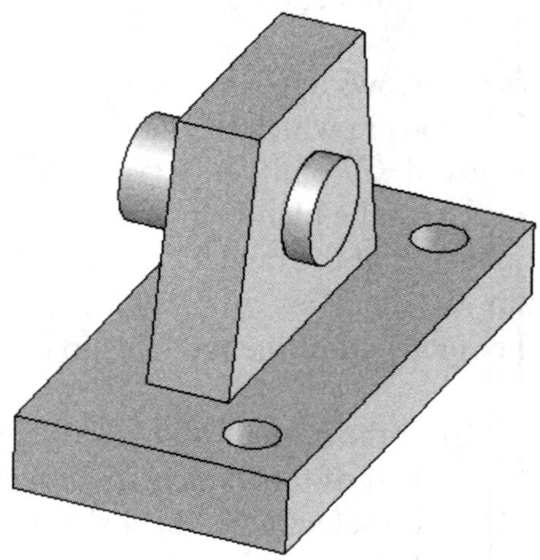

Figure 18 – Assembly after cutting it in half to make use of geometric symmetry.

Create a Finite Element Analysis (Study)

1. In the main menu, click **Simulation** and from the pull-down menu, select **Study...** The **Study** property manager opens.

2. In the **Name** field, type **Trunion and Pin Contact Analysis** to identify this study.

3. Verify that a **Static** analysis is selected then click **[OK]** ✓ to close the **Study** property manager. The Simulation manager appears on the left of the screen.

4. In the main menu, click **Simulation** and from the pull-down menu select **Options…** The **Systems Options - General** window opens.

5. Under the **Default Options** tab, select **Units** and set the following options:
   - In the right-half of the window under **Unit system**, select ⦿ **English (IPS)**
   - Under **Units** set **Length/Displacement:** to **in** and **Pressure/Stress:** to **psi**.

   Ignore remaining options.

6. Click **[OK]** to close the **Default Options - Units** window.

Assign Material Properties

1. In the Simulation manager tree right-click the **Parts** folder and select **Apply Material to All…**

2. In the **Material** window, select ⦿ **From library files:** and from the pull-down menu select **solidworks materials**.

3. From the list of available steels, select **Cast Alloy Steel**. In the right-half of the **Material** window, notice that **Units:** appear as **English (IPS)** as defined above.

4. Click **[OK]** to close the **Material** window.

Assign Fixtures and External Loads

The following section includes subtitles to identify specific restraint types applied to the model. Individuals who choose to use subtitles to guide their application of restraints are encouraged to do so on their own. Complete instructions are provided if needed.

Symmetry and Immovable Restraints

In the following steps, **Fixed** (immovable) and **Symmetry** restraints are applied at bolt holes on the trunion base and at cut (symmetrical) surfaces respectively. An outline of necessary steps is provided below.

1. Right-click the **Fixtures** folder and from the pull-down menu, select **Fixed Geometry…**

2. In the **Standard (Fixed Geometry)** dialogue box, ensure the **Fixed Geometry** icon is selected (gray highlight) and the **Faces, Edges, Vertices for Fixture** field is highlighted (light blue).

3. Move the cursor over the model and zoom in, as necessary, to select the *inside surface* of each bolt hole on the trunion base. Restraint symbols appear inside each hole as illustrated in Fig. 19.

4. Click **[OK]**✓ to close the **Fixture** property manager.

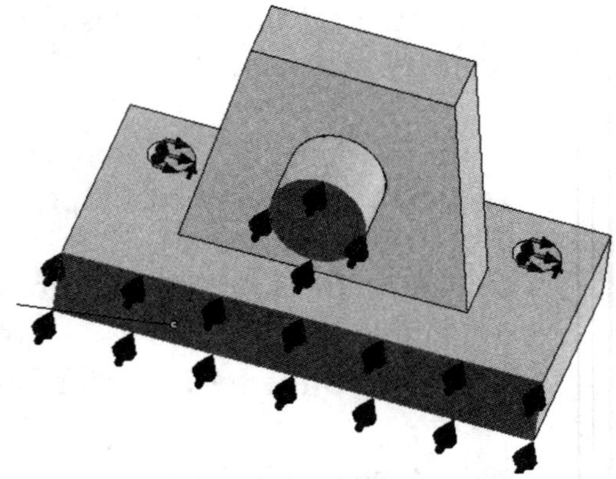

Figure 19 – **Fixed** restraints are applied to bolt holes and **Symmetry** restraints are applied to cut surfaces of the pin and trunion base.

5. Again, right-click the **Fixture** folder and from the pull-down menu select **Fixed Geometry…** The **Fixture** property manager opens.

6. Click to open the **Advanced** dialogue box and select the **Symmetry** icon from the list of available fixture types.

7. Apply this restraint by selecting both cut surfaces (highlighted on the model in Fig. 19). **Symmetry** restraints are applied normal to the cut surface, thereby preventing displacement in the X-direction. Compare directions with the coordinate system triad to verify this statement. NOTE: Restraint symbols are typically directed toward the cut surfaces.

8. Click **[OK]** ✓ to close the **Fixture** property manager.

Connections Define Contact Conditions

In the Simulation manager tree, Fig. 20, observe that a new folder, named **Connections**, appears. This folder is included any time an *assembly* is analyzed so that interactions (i.e., contact conditions) between mating parts can be defined. The **Connections** folder was also encountered in Chapter 5, where a Shrink Fit was analyzed. The following steps outline how **Connections** are used to define local contact between the pin and inner surface of the hole in the trunion base.

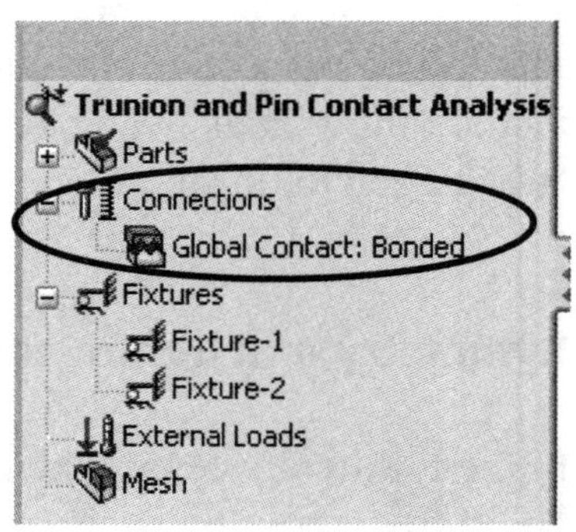

Figure 20 – **Connectors** folder in the Simulation manager tree.

To facilitate selection of the contacting surfaces, begin by creating an exploded view of the assembly. Proceed as follows.

1. In the main menu click **Insert** and from the pull-down menu select **Exploded View…** The **Explode** property manager opens with the message, "**Select component(s) and then drag the manipulator handle to create an explode step.**"

2. Click to select the pin. Then *drag* the manipulator arrow in the direction of the +X-axis (this direction corresponds to the pin axis) to move the pin away from the model as shown in Fig. 21.

3. Click **[OK]** ✓ to close the **Explode** property manager.

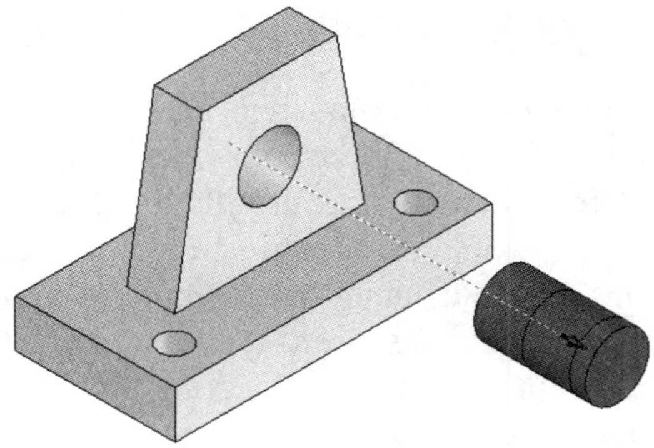

Figure 21 – Explode the assembly to facilitate selection of contacting surfaces.

4. In the Simulation manager tree, right-click the **Connections** folder and from the pull-down menu, select **Contact Set…** The **Contact Set** property manager opens as shown in Fig. 22.

5. In the **Type** dialogue box, select **No Penetration** from the pull-down menu to define the type of contact between the pin and hole surfaces.

6. Select the *inner surface* of the hole, highlighted in Fig. 22, and **Face<1>@ Trunion Base-1** is listed in the **Faces, Edges, Vertices for Set 1** in the upper field of the **Type:** dialogue box.

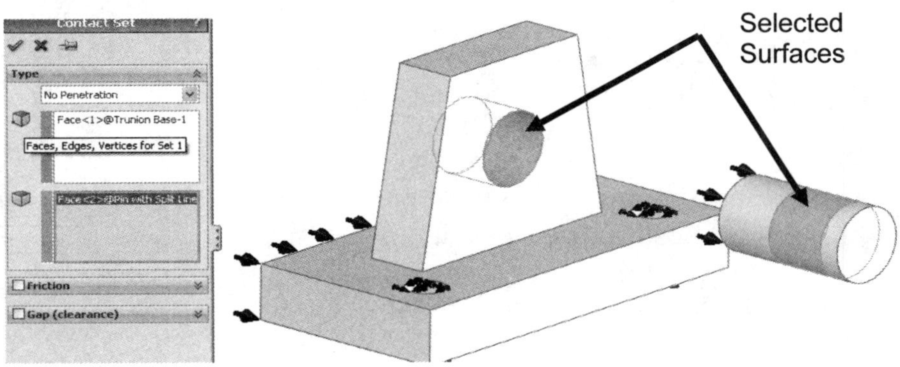

Figure 22 – Selecting surfaces between which the **Contact/Gaps** restraint is applied.

7. Next, click the **Faces for Set 2** field (second field from top) to activate it. Then, on the pin, select the corresponding surface, also highlighted in Fig. 22. **Face<2> @Pin with Split Line** appears in the **Faces for Set 2** field.

8. Click **[OK]** ✓ to close the **Contact Set** property manager. Highlighting disappears from the model and beneath the **Connections** folder appears an icon labeled, "**Contact Set-1 (-No Penetration<Trunion Base-1, Pin with Split Lines-1>-).**" Place cursor over this text to reveal the entire phrase.

Applying a Directional Load

This section outlines steps necessary to apply a directional load to the pin. In previous examples, only force components in the X, Y, and Z directions were applied to parts. Using that approach, the 800 lb force applied to the pin at a 60° angle from the horizontal, Fig. 1, would be represented by the Y and Z force components on the model. However, this example demonstrates application of these force components in a way not used in earlier problems. Further, because only half of the model is being analyzed, only half of the entire load is applied to the pin. However, before applying the load, the model is re-assembled as follows.

1. Select the **Configuration** manager icon  located at top of the SolidWorks feature manager tree.

2. At top of the **Configuration manager**, click the "+" sign adjacent to **Default <Display State-1> [Trunion Pin and Assembly]** to display additional folders.

3. Next, right-click **ExplView1** and from the pull-down menu, select **Collapse**.

After the model is re-assembled, proceed as follows to apply the load.

4. In the Simulation manager, right-click the **External Loads** folder, and from the pull-down menu select **Force…** The **Force/ Torque** property manager opens; see Fig. 23.

5. In the **Force/Torque** dialogue box, select the **Force** icon. It appears shaded dark gray.

6. Also in the **Force/Torque** dialogue box, choose ⊙ **Selected direction**. The property manager changes to look like that shown in Fig. 23.

7. The **Faces, Edges, Vertices, Reference Points for Force** field is highlighted and awaits selection of the entity to which the force is applied. Rotate the model as necessary and click the pin surface shown highlighted in Fig. 24. **<Face1>@Pin with Split Lines-1** is listed in the active field.

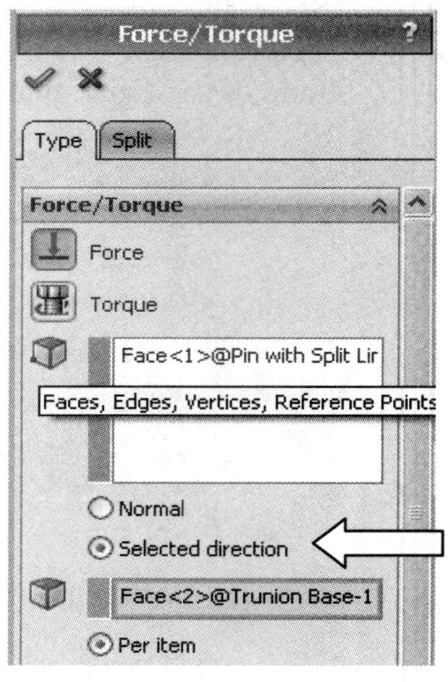

Figure 23 – Selecting faces to define force component direction in the **Force/Torque** property manager.

8. Also in the **Force/Torque** dialogue box, click to activate the **Face, Edge, Plane, Axis for Direction** field (second field from top) and proceed to select the trunion support face highlighted in Fig. 24. **Face<2>@Trunion Base-1** appears in the active field.

> **Aside:** It is also possible to select any other face, edge, plane or axis that is aligned with the direction of the applied force components. Other surfaces that could be selected include: the cut-end of the pin; the cut-face of the trunion base; or the **Right Plane** from the SolidWorks flyout menu (the plane selected *must* be at the assembly level, *not* at the component level).

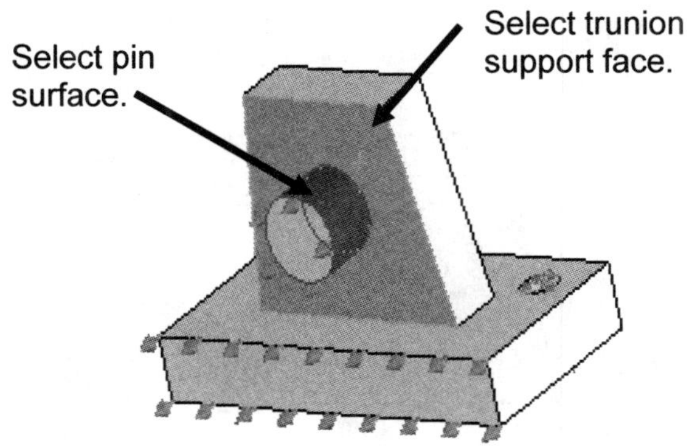

Figure 24 – Selecting the surface for force application and a face to define its direction.

The bottom portion of the **Force/Torque** property manager is shown in Fig. 25. In the **Force** dialogue box, three choices are available for defining magnitude and direction of a force. Icons adjacent to the top two fields show two different directions for applying forces parallel to the selected face while the bottom field indicates a force applied perpendicular to the selected face.

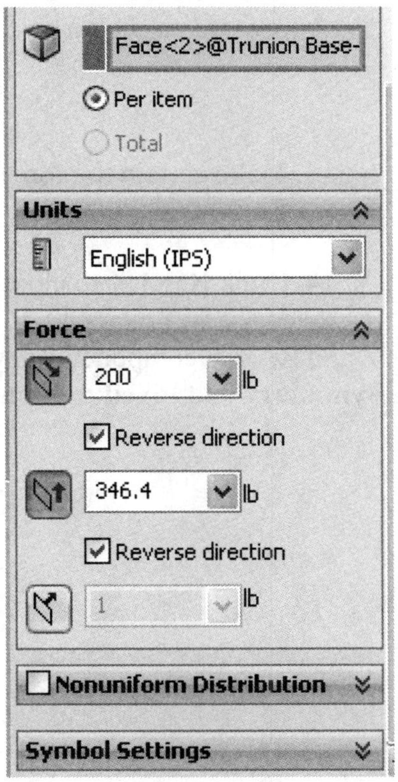

Figure 25 – Specifying magnitude and direction of force components.

9. In the **Force** dialogue box, move the cursor over the top field. It is label **Along Plane Dir 1**. Click the icon adjacent to this field to activate it. Immediately, force vectors are displayed on the center segment of the pin. *(Ignore their direction for now.)*

10. These vectors are parallel to the trunion face selected above. Use the coordinate system triad to verify that these vectors lie in the Z-direction. This direction corresponds to the horizontal component of the 400 lb force[1]. Therefore, in the top field, type **200**, which is determined from:

$$F_Z = 400*\cos 60^o = 200 \text{ lb}$$

[1] Recall, only half the total force of 800 pounds, or 400 pounds, is applied to the half-model.

Figure 1 (repeated below) shows geometry related to the above calculation. Also observe on-screen "flags" that display direction, units, and magnitude of force components.

11. If force vectors are oriented in the incorrect direction, check ☑ **Reverse direction**. Refer to Fig. 26 for proper directions of force components.

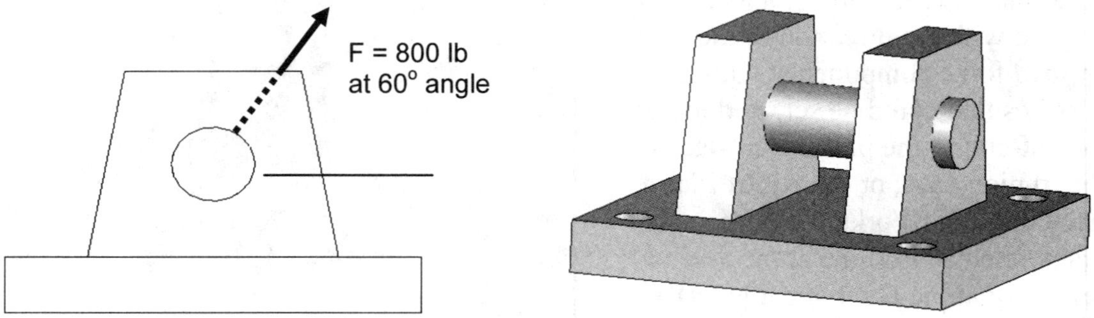

(right side view)

Figure 1 (repeated) – Right-side view of trunion mount and pin showing direction of applied force.

12. Enter the Y-component of force on your own and verify that its direction is upward as shown on Fig. 26. Use a force magnitude of:

$$F_Y = 400 * \sin 60^\circ = 346.4 \text{ lb}$$

13. Make certain the force **Normal to plane** is deselected (i.e., the bottom field in the **Force** dialogue box is "grayed" out).

14. Click **[OK]** ✓ to close the **Force/Torque** property manager.

Y and Z force components applied to the pin should now appear as shown in Fig. 26. **Symmetry** and **Fixed** restraints are temporarily hidden to reduce clutter.

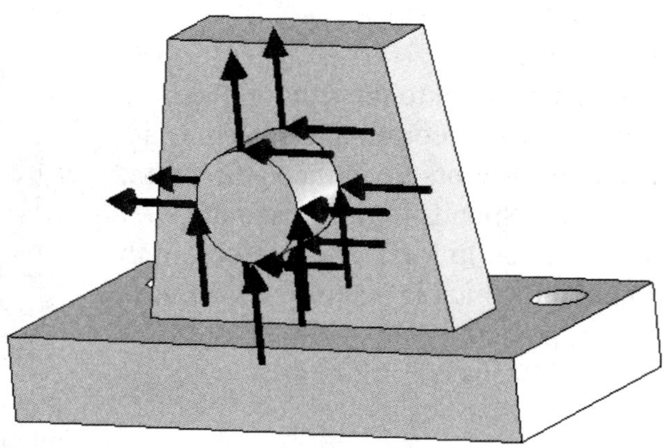

Figure 26 – To improve visibility, the Y and Z components of force applied to the pin are illustrated to a somewhat enlarged scale.

At this point the model is ready for meshing as outlined next.

Meshing the Model and Running the Solution

1. Right-click the **Mesh** folder and from the pull-down menu select **Create Mesh…**

2. Accept the default mesh size settings and in the **Options** dialogue box, check ☑ **Run (solve) the analysis** then click **[OK]** ✓. This option causes the software to automatically run the solution after meshing..

Notice that the solution takes longer to run (approximately 25 seconds) especially during the **Solving contact constraints:** portion of the analysis.

Results Analysis

A primary goal of this example is to introduce tools used to observe contact pressure (stress) between mating components. As such, and because the state of stress is too complex to model with simple classical stress equations, little attention is focused on other stress results in the current model. However, because von Mises stress is widely used to compare stress magnitude against material Yield Strength, its results are examined briefly below.

Von Mises Stress

1. If von Mises stress is not displayed on the model, double-click **Stress1 (-vonMises-)** located beneath the **Results** folder. An image of von Mises stress distribution in the model is displayed in Fig. 27 and on your screen.

2. If the model does not appear as a deformed view, right-click **Stress1 (-vonMises-)** and select **Edit Definition…** Within the **Stress Plot** property manager, verify that a check appears adjacent to ☑ **Deformed Shape** and select ⊙ **Automatic** as the scaling method.

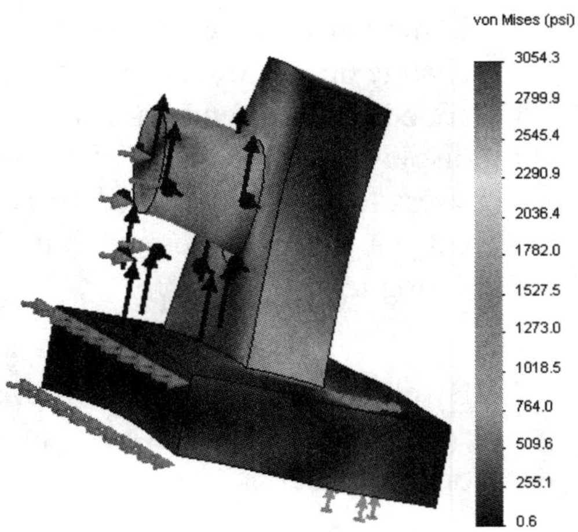

Figure 27 – von Mises stress contours displayed on the deformed shape of the trunion and pin assembly.

3. Click **[OK]** ✓ to close the **Stress Plot** property manager. The displayed image should appear similar to that shown in Fig. 27.

Observe that the maximum von Mises stress (3,054 psi) is well below the material Yield Strength (34,994 psi). Recall that Yield Strength is *not* displayed on assembly plots because dissimilar materials might be used for different components in an assembly.

Iso Clipping

Unlike **Section Clipping** that permits stepping through a model at user specified increments of *distance* to view stresses on different "slices" of the model, **Iso Clipping** permits a variety of display options based on the *stress level* to aid interpretation of study results. These options are investigated below.

1. Right-click **Stress1 (-vonMises-)** and from the pull-down menu select **Iso Clipping…** A partial view of the **Iso Clipping** property manager is illustrated in Fig. 28.

The **Iso 1** dialogue box contains a sliding scale whose two extreme values correspond to the minimum and maximum values of the quantity displayed at top and bottom of the color-coded stress legend appearing on the graphics screen. In the present case, von Mises stress magnitudes are displayed.

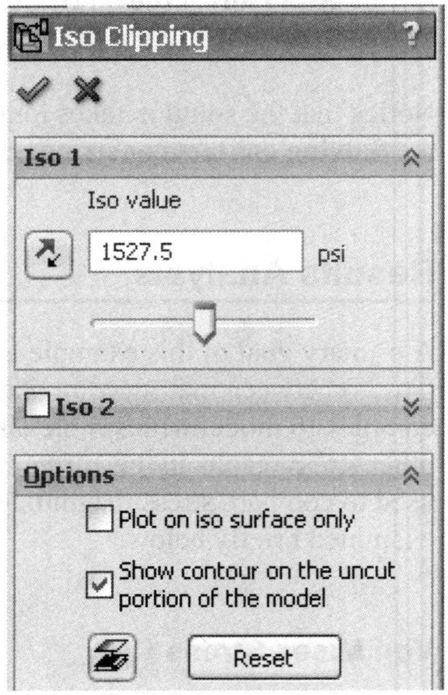

Figure 28 – Sliding stress scale in the **Iso Clipping** property manager.

2. In the **Iso 1** box, click-and-*drag* the sliding scale pointer and observe stress levels change on the model. Simultaneously, a moving arrow, adjacent to the color-coded stress legend, indicates the *lowest* magnitude of stresses currently being displayed on the image. Sliding the pointer from left-to-right results in lower stress levels being peeled away such that only areas of high stress remain. The current value of stress magnitude also appears in the **Iso value** box in the **Iso 1** dialogue box.

3. By clicking the **Reverse clipping direction** icon and then moving the sliding scale pointer from left-to-right, gradually increasing levels of stress are displayed on the model.

4. Next, in the **Options** dialogue box, located at bottom of the **Iso Clipping** property manager in Fig. 28, check ☑ **Plot on iso surface only** and once again move the sliding scale pointer. This time observe that *only* stress of a certain magnitude is plotted. This result is *not* pictured on the model in Fig. 29. Return **Iso Clipping** to its original setting by again clicking the **Reverse clipping direction** icon

The above option permits easy identification of regions where stress is *at* a certain level.

5. Clear the check mark from ☐ **Plot on Iso surface only**, before proceeding.

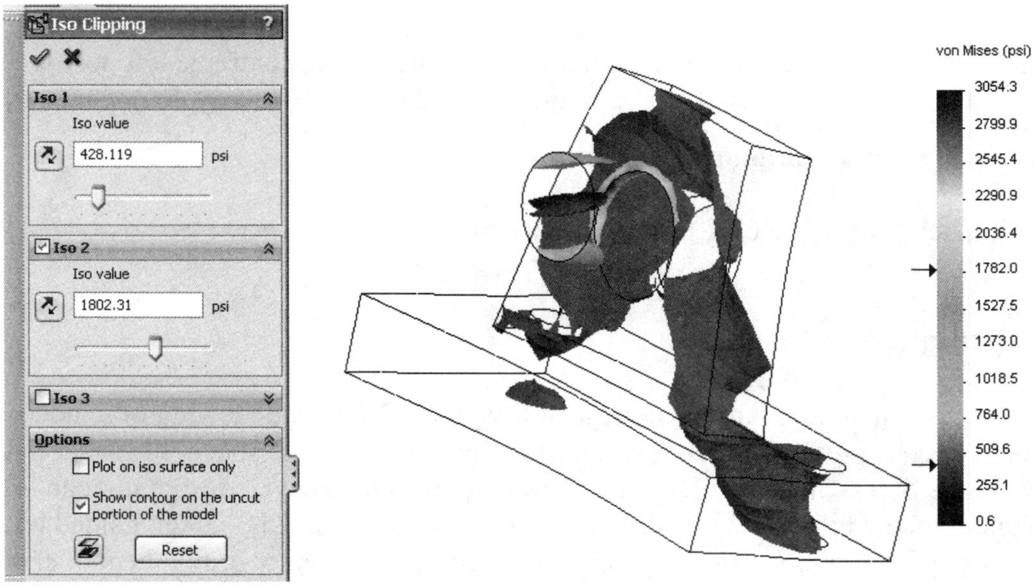

Figure 29 – **Iso Clipping** is set to display stresses *between* values set in the **Iso 1** and **Iso 2** dialogue boxes. Max. and Min. stress magnitude labeling is also turned on.

6. Next, check ☑ **Iso 2** to open a second dialogue box in the **Iso Clipping** property manager and click the **Reverse clipping direction** icon for **Iso 2**. See Fig. 29.

7. Use the sliding scale in each dialogue box to set a lower bound and an upper bound for stress magnitudes to be displayed. In Fig. 29 **Iso 1** is set at **428** psi and **Iso 2** is set at **1802** psi. *Any approximations of these values are acceptable.*

The corresponding plot, shown at the right side of Fig. 29, displays stress values *between* approximately 428 psi to 1,802 psi. Also observe two arrows adjacent to the color-coded stress legend. These arrows mark the lower and upper bounds of stress magnitudes currently displayed. NOTE: It may be necessary to click the **Reverse clipping direction** icons to properly set upper and lower bounds.

Analysis Insight

Iso Clipping permits easy identification of regions where stress levels are *above or below* a given value.

Iso Clipping also permits isolating and displaying stresses *between* certain lower and upper limits.

Before proceeding, return the full display of von Mises stress contours to the model as follows.

8. Clear the check-mark "✓" from the ☐ **Iso 2** dialogue box.

9. In the **Iso 1** dialogue box, slide the scale pointer to the extreme left position to display the full range of stress contours on the model. If they do not appear, click the **Reverse clipping direction** icon.

10. Click **[OK]** ✓ to close the **Iso Clipping** property manager.

Animating Stress Results

SolidWorks Simulation **Animation** capability permits dynamic viewing of a model due to applied loads provided ☑ **Deformed Shape** was checked, as specified earlier in the "**von Mises Stress**" section. During animation the model is cycled from no load to maximum load while stress, displacement, or strain is displayed. Insight gained by viewing these variations can be valuable in determining whether or not the model is behaving as expected based on applied loads and restraints. Proceed as follows to animate the von Mises stress results.

1. Right-click **Stress1 (-vonMises-)** and from the pull-down menu select ►**Animate…** The **Animation** property manager opens as shown in Fig. 30.

2. If the model is animated, click the **Stop** button at top of the **Basics** dialogue box.

3. Within the **Basics** dialogue box, the top field controls the number of **Frames** (i.e., the number of still images that are played back in sequence to simulate continuous motion). Set the **Frames** spin-box value to **10**. This value is a user preference. Higher values create smoother, but slower, animations.

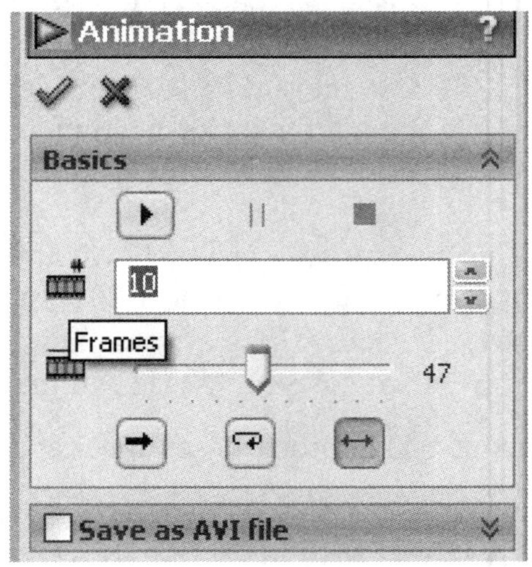

Figure 30 – A portion of the **Animation** property manager showing the **Frames** and **Speed** controls.

4. The slide-scale, located at the bottom of the **Basics** dialogue box, controls the **Speed** of animation. Moving the slide to the left slows the animation and, conversely, movement to the right increases animation speed.

Experiment with these capabilities on your own. The model can be rotated to view it from different angles while animation is proceeding. Use the **Start**, **Pause**, and **Stop** buttons, located from left to right across the top of the **Animation** dialogue box, to control animation. If desired, an animated sequence can be saved as an AVI File.

5. After experimenting with this capability, click **[OK]** ✓ to close the **Animation** property manager.

Animation of stress variation in the trunion mount corresponds to each power stroke of a cylinder. The cycling of stress from minimum to maximum should emphasize the need for fatigue analysis of many machine components.

Displacement Results

Displacement results can be displayed and examined in like manner to that described above for the von Mises stress plot. Users are encouraged to examine the displacement display and animate it on their own.

Analysis Insight

For those familiar with the actual hardware used in a trunion mounted hydraulic or pneumatic cylinder, the displacement animation should raise questions about the validity of loads applied to the pin. A photograph of a complete trunion mount, shown in Fig. 31, reveals that the central portion of the pin passes through a close fitting hole on the cylinder base similar to holes at both ends of the trunion base. A far superior model of the trunion mount and pin assembly should include additional geometry and a **Contact Set** definition applied along the center portion of the pin.

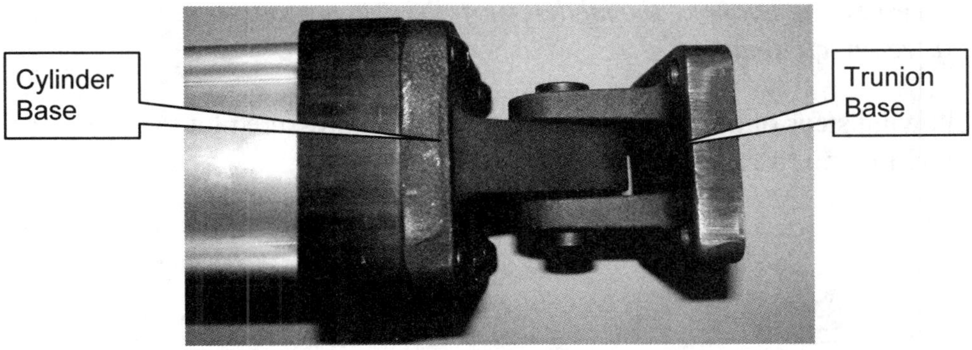

Figure 31 – Close-up view of a trunion mount attached to the base of a pneumatic cylinder.

This insight is introduced to emphasize, once again, the significant influence of *proper boundary conditions* upon accurate finite element results. On your own, consider whether or not the accuracy of boundary conditions (i.e., **Loads** and **Fixtures**) applied to this model could be further improved. For example, knowing that the trunion mount is to be bolted down, should another restraint be applied to the bottom surface of the trunion mount to prevent deflection *into* a rigid surface beneath it? Also consider how additional restraints applied to the bottom surface of the trunion depend on the stiffness of the surface to which it is fastened.

Proper finite element analysis requires its users to carefully consider numerous factors that directly influence the validity of results. The ability to easily create and model these alternate design scenarios is clearly one of the strengths of the finite element approach.

Contact Pressure / Stress

The final section of this example explores use of the **Contact Pressure** plot. This plot displays, in a unique graphical format, the contact pressure developed between mating parts for which **Contact Set** conditions are specified. Proceed as follows to display this plot.

1. Begin by turning off the display of loads and restraints on the model. Right-click the **Fixtures** folder and from the pull-down menu, select **Hide All**. Do the same for the **External Loads** folder.

2. Next, right-click the **Results** folder and from the pull-down menu, select **Define Stress Plot…** The **Stress Plot** property manager opens.

3. Within the **Display** dialogue box, click to open the stress **Component** pull-down menu and from the list of options, select **CP: Contact Pressure**.

4. Click **[OK]** ✓ to close the **Stress Plot** property manager. A new plot named **Stress2 (-Contact pressure-)** is listed beneath the **Results** folder.

5. If the contact pressure plot is not displayed, double-click **Stress2 (-Contact pressure-)**. *Examine the model carefully. The default display of contact pressure is relatively small.*

The following steps outline how to adjust the contact pressure plot to appear as illustrated in Figs. 32 (a) and (b).

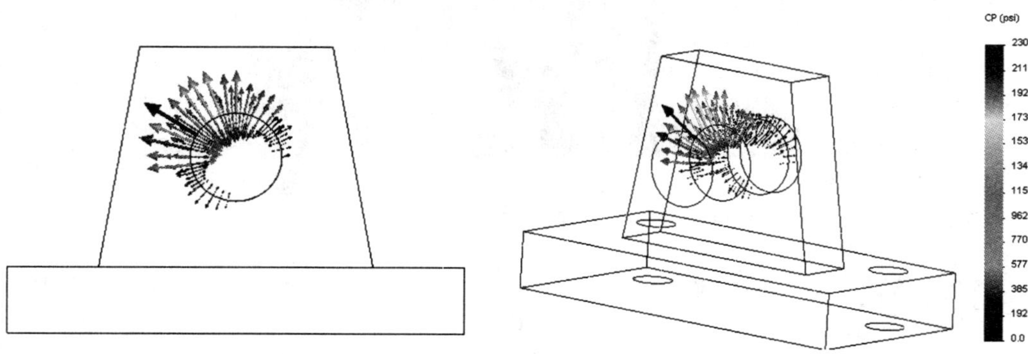

(a) (b)

Figure 32 – (a) Left-side view of **Contact pressure** between the pin and hole in the trunion mount; (b) view showing three-dimensional nature of **Contact pressure** between mating surfaces.

6. Right-click **Stress2 (-Contact pressure-)** and from the pull-down menu select **Vector Plot Options…** The **Vector plot options** property manager opens as shown in Fig. 33.

7. Within the **Size** field (upper spin-box in the **Options** dialogue box), type **600** to enlarge the contact pressure vectors displayed on the current plot. The value chosen for the **Size** field is a user preference and should be selected to create a meaningful display.

8. Make certain that ⦿ **Match color chart** is selected. This option adds color to the vector plot such that, in addition to vector size indicating magnitude of the contact pressure, the vector color also corresponds to that displayed in the accompanying color-coded legend.

9. Click **[OK]** ✓ to close the **Vector plot options** property manager. Your display should now appear similar to that shown in Figs. 32 (a) and (b).

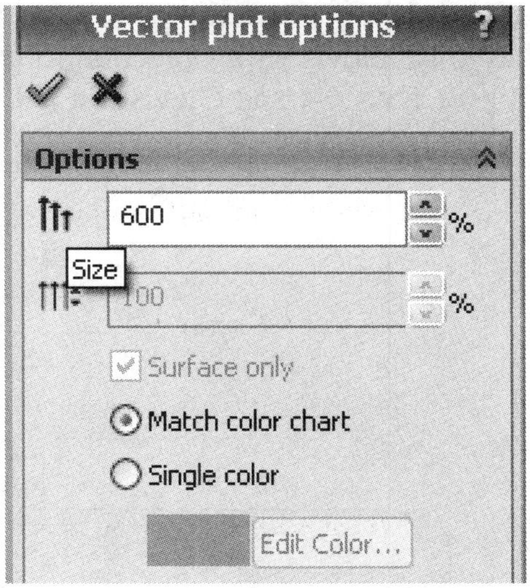

Figure 33 – Magnitude of the vector display is controlled within the **Vector plot options** property manager.

10. Rotate and zoom-in on the model to gain a better appreciation of the three-dimensional nature of contact pressure variation between the pin and hole in the trunion mount. Observe that higher contact pressure exists toward the loaded side (i.e., the middle) of the pin.

A **Contact Pressure** plot is somewhat unique because it displays both magnitude and direction of pressure between the contacting surfaces. Existence of this plot is dependent on the **Contact Set** condition defined earlier in this example.

This concludes the analysis of contact pressure developed between the trunion base and a pin subject to an external load. This example file can either be saved or closed without saving at the discretion of the user. If file space is of a premium, delete the file.

11. In the main menu, select **File/Close** (or) **File/Save As** and proceed accordingly.

Analysis Insight

In closing, consider how methods of this chapter could have been applied to the pin used to attach the roller to the cam follower in the example of Chapter #1 or to determine contact stress in the vicinity of the pin hole in the curved beam model of Chapter #2.

EXERCISES

EXERCISE 1 – Contact Pressure Between a Clevis and Pin

At the push-rod end of a hydraulic or pneumatic cylinder (opposite end from the trunion mount) is a part that connects the push-rod to a driven component. This connector, commonly called a "clevis," takes many different forms, one of which is pictured in Fig. E 6-1. A clevis is typically threaded onto the end of a cylinder push-rod. It then is connected to a driven device by means of a pin. The figure below shows the geometry of a typical clevis with a reaction force, F = 12400 N, applied to its clevis pin. Open the files **Clevis 6-1** and **Clevis Pin 6-1** and perform a finite element analysis to determine the items requested below.

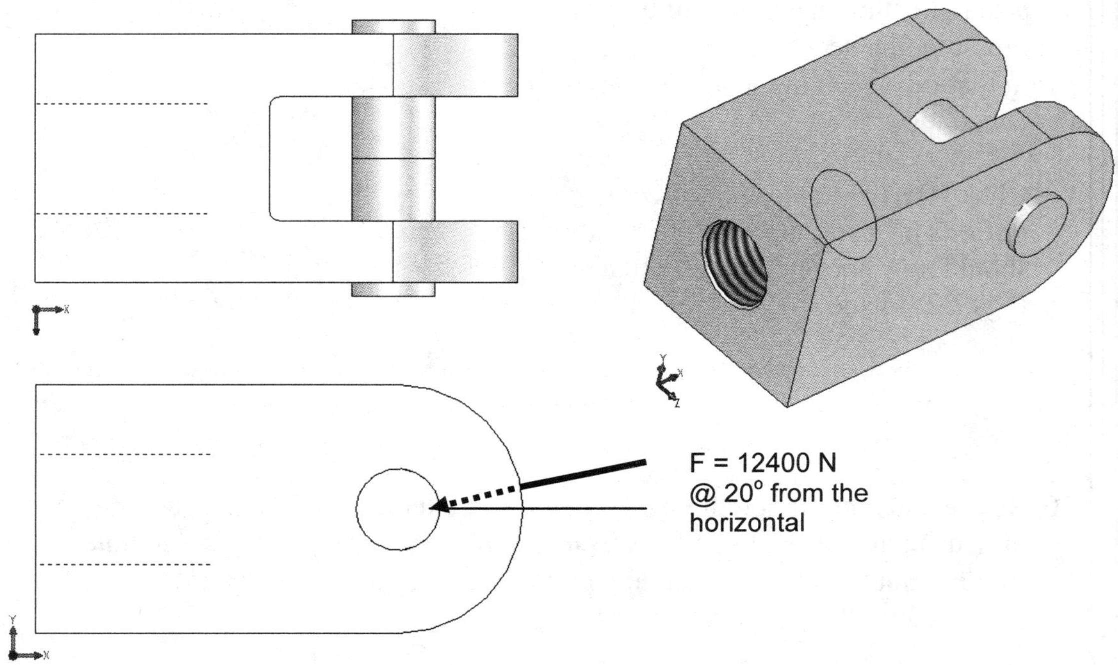

Figure E6-1 – Top, front, and isometric views of a clevis and pin assembly. A force of 8600 N is applied to the pin as shown in the front view.

- Material: **1045 Steel, cold drawn** (Use S.I. units), consider steel to be ductile.
- Mesh: **High Quality** tetrahedral elements
- Fixtures: **Fixed (immovable)** (appropriate for a push-rod threaded into the hole)
  Symmetry as instructed below
  Contact Set define between the pin surface and the clevis hole, specify **No penetration**.
- External Load: Apply "appropriate" force components to model the applied load.

- Assumptions:
  - ➢ The pin (40 mm long) is centered between sides of the clevis (clevis height and depth = 36 mm, square).
  - ➢ Use symmetry to model half of the clevis and pin assembly.

Determine the following:

Develop a finite element model that includes: material specification, fixtures, external load(s), mesh, and a solution. Defeature the model as needed and delete the "cosmetic threads" as outlined below. *Reminder: Assuming the example of the current chapter was worked, recall that system default units were changed to English at the outset of the example. Refer to section* "**Create a Finite Element Analysis (Study)**", *page 6-13 steps 4 to 6 to define SI units for the current exercise.*

Cosmetic Threads

So called "cosmetic threads" are included on the Clevis model to provide insight into its means of attachment to a cylinder push-rod end. Cosmetic threads are a symbolic representation of screw threads rather than actual geometric shapes cut into the model. As such, they serve their intended purpose of conveying information, but do not affect results. For example, they do not cause stress concentration due to thread profiles cut into the model. It is often desirable to **Delete** cosmetic threads because, if not deleted, they cause a circle and/or dashed lines to appear on various views of the model as shown in top, front, and isometric views in Fig. E 6-1. Although this remnant of the thread profile does not affect results, it is found bothersome by some individuals. *At the start of this exercise*, delete cosmetic threads as follows.

1. Open the file **Clevis 6-1**.
2. Contents of the SolidWorks feature manager are shown in Fig. E 6-2.
3. Near the bottom of the SolidWorks feature manger, click the "+" sign adjacent to **Threaded Hole Cut-Extrude2**.
4. Beneath this icon, right-click **Cosmetic Thread 4** and from the pull-down menu select **Delete**.
5. Return to the problem solution.

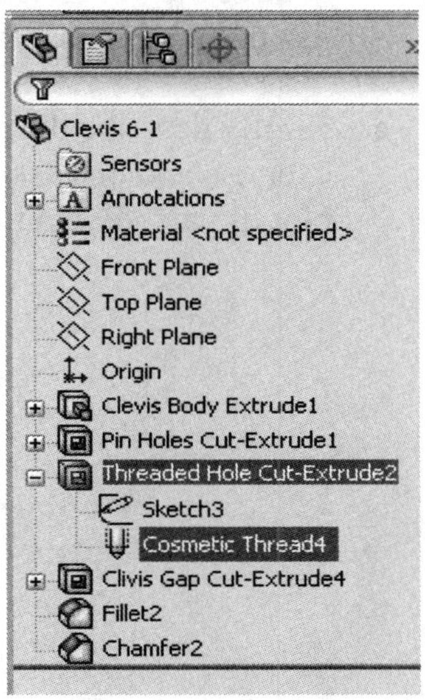

Figure E 6-2 – **SolidWorks** feature manager used to **Delete** the **Cosmetic Threads**.

a. Create a plot showing all restraints and loads applied to half of the assembly model. This image might be thought of as the finite element equivalent of a free-body diagram. Do not show stresses or a mesh on this plot. Adjacent to the image, hand write calculations used to determine the X and Y force components acting on the pin. Also, on a small sketch oriented the same as the model, draw and label magnitudes of the X and Y force components applied to the model.

b. Create a plot showing **Contact Pressure** between the pin and clevis. Enlarge vector size to make vectors easily visible, but in reasonable proportion to the overall image. Select a view that clearly shows the three dimensional nature of contact pressure variation.

c. Create a plot of von Mises stress contours displayed on a deformed image of the pin and clevis assembly. Show the deformed model by checking ☑ **Deformed Shape** and select ⊙ **Automatic** as the scaling method. Also, incorporate automatic labeling of the maximum von Mises stress.

d. Create a safety factor plot based on von Mises stress. Identify region(s) of the assembly that have a safety factor less than 2.0 based on the material yield strength.

e. Use **Iso Clipping** to create a plot that shows regions of the model where von Mises stress exceeds the material yield strength (if any such regions exist). Include automatic labeling of the maximum von Mises stress on this plot.

f. Discuss **Fixtures** applied to the clevis and pin model. Provide sound reasoning and justification for restraints applied at the threaded clevis attachment location. If you believe the suggested restraints are incorrect or can be improved, provide a detailed discussion that justifies the opinion expressed.

g. Briefly describe the procedure used to plot the stress magnitudes for part (e) of this exercise and discuss the correspondence, or lack thereof, between the safety factor plot of part (d) and the Iso Clipping plot of part (e).

EXERCISE 2 – Contact Pressure in a Hip Prosthesis

Hip replacement joints are frequently used for individuals who suffer from severe arthritis or hip bone fractures. Fig. E 6-3 illustrates the stem and cup for a typical hip prosthesis. The femur (upper leg bone) is prepared by reaming an appropriate size cavity into which the stem is cemented. To further distribute load to the femur and relieve shear forces in the cement between the stem and femur, a lip, labeled in Fig. E 6-3 (b), transfers a compressive load due to body weight to the upper end of the femur. Similarly, the cup is fixed to the hip bone by bone adhesive and projections that protrude into receiving holes drilled into the hip bone. These protrusions stabilize the cup and prevent cup rotation relative to bone tissue. A screw connector is also provided. Specific surface areas of the stem and cup are porous (not illustrated below). Re-growth of natural bone tissue into these porous areas promotes development of a stronger bond between the prosthesis and bone. The cup liner provides a low friction surface between stem and cup.

Open File: **Stem and Cup Assembly**

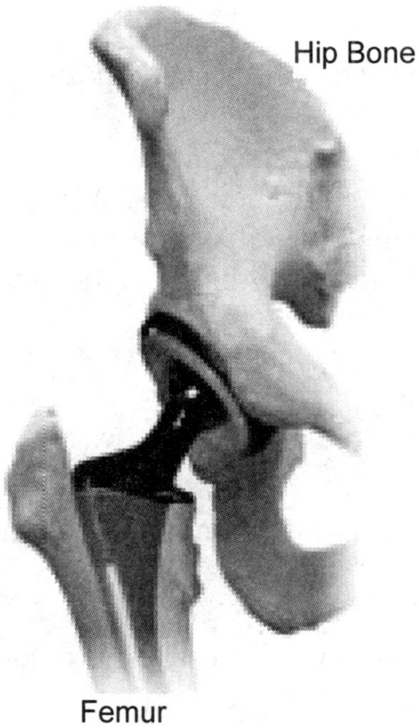

(a)

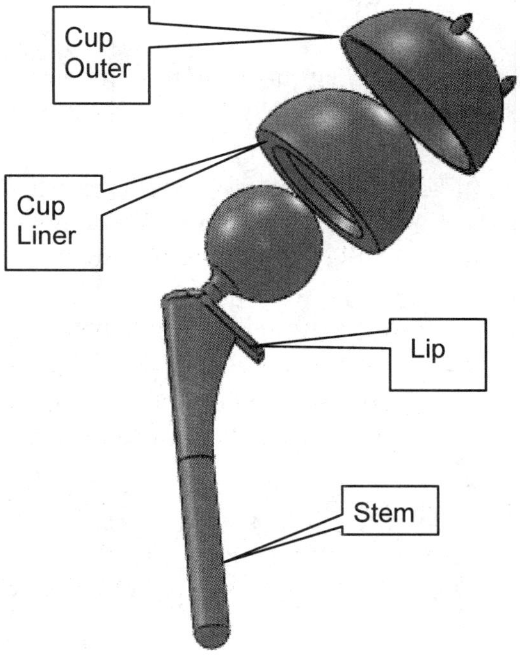

(b)

Figure E 6-3 – Figure (a) shows a hip prosthesis as it would appear in implanted in the human body.[2] Figure (b) is an exploded view showing the three main components of the **Stem and Cup Assembly**.

> **Disclaimer**
> Actual part dimensions and materials are considered proprietary information. Therefore, none of the dimensions or part materials used in this exercise are representative of actual provider data.

[2] Photo [Fig. E 6-3 (a)] courtesy of Zimmer Inc., Warsaw, Indiana

- Material[3]: **Cup Liner** – Locate under **Plastics** then choose **PTFE (general)**
  Stem and **Cup Outer** – Locate under **Titanium Alloys** then choose **Commercially Pure Grade 2 Textured (SS)**

- Mesh: High quality tetrahedral elements

- Fixture: To be specified by the user based on experience gained in previous exercises and an understanding of the hip replacement process described above. Carefully consider how and where restraints are applied to the model relative to how and where external loads are applied.

- External Load: Person's weight = **145** lb. You may decide to use a different external load. If so, include the reason for that decision in part (a) of the exercise listed below.

Determine the following:

Develop a finite element model that includes: material specification, realistic fixtures, external load(s), mesh generation, and solution.

a. On the upper half of one page, create a plot showing all fixtures and loads applied to stem and cup assembly. This image represents the finite element equivalent of a free-body diagram. Do not show stresses or a mesh on this plot. On the lower half of the page, provide:

   - sound reason(s) and justification used to specify the fixture(s) or external load(s) applied to the cup outer.

   - sound reason(s) and justification used to specify the fixture(s) or external load(s) applied to the stem.

   - If an external load other than the person's given weight is used, provide insight into the reasoning used to determine an alternate weight.

b. Create a plot of von Mises stress contours displayed on a deformed image of the stem and cup assembly. Show the deformed model by checking ☑ **Deformed Shape** and select ⦿ **Automatic** as the scaling method. Also, incorporate automatic labeling of the maximum von Mises stress.

c. Create a plot showing **Contact Pressure** between the "ball," at the upper end of the stem and the cup liner. Enlarge vector size to make vectors easily visible, but in reasonable proportion to the overall image. Select a view that clearly shows the three dimensional nature of contact pressure variation.

---

[3] Materials and their associated properties shown here in *no way* reflect actual manufacturer's specifications.

EXERCISE 3 – **Stress Concentration Analysis using Part Symmetry**

Exercise No. 1 of Chapter 3 is repeated here. However, make use of techniques mastered in the current chapter to reduce the size of the **Plate With Hole 3-1** model by making use of model symmetry. For your convenience, all necessary parts of the previous exercise are repeated here. NOTE: The previous exercise need *not* have been worked.

Open the file: **Plate with Hole 3-1**.

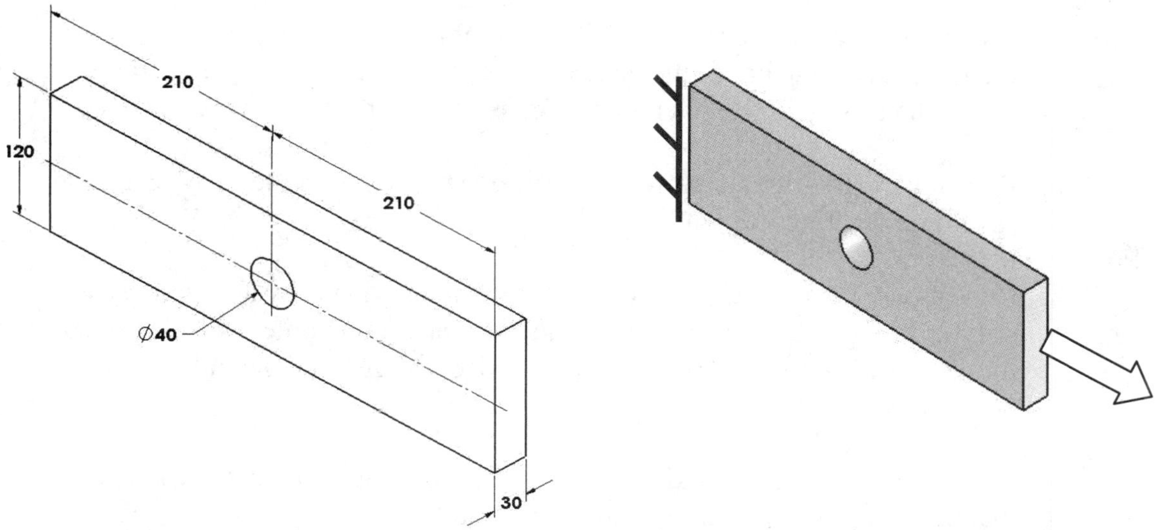

Figure E6-3 (Figure E3-1 repeated) – Aluminum bar with central hole subject to an axial force. A geometric discontinuity is present in the form of the 40 mm diameter hole.

- Material: **2018 Alloy** aluminum (Use S.I. units)
- Mesh: **High Quality** tetrahedral elements. Use three different meshes as specified in parts (a, c, and d) below.
- Fixtures: **Fixed** applied to left end.
- External Load: **370 kN** applied normal to the right-end causing tension in the bar.

Develop a finite element model that includes: material specification, symmetry restraints, external load, mesh generation, and solution as specified below. For this analysis use high quality meshes of the sizes specified below and perform the following.

Solution Guidance

- To simplify application of model symmetry, refer to the SolidWorks Feature manager tree.

When applying **Fixtures** to the model, open the **Advanced** dialogue box and select the **Symmetry** 

icon. Apply **Symmetry** restraints to all cut surfaces of the model.

Determine the following:

a. Using a *default* size mesh, create a contour plot of the *most appropriate stress* to permit comparison of its magnitude adjacent to the hole with that predicted by classical equations for stress computed at the same location; see part (e) for calculation of classical results. Include fixtures (symmetry restraints), external load, and mesh on this plot.

b. Use the **Probe** feature to produce a graph of the *most appropriate stress* from the top edge of the bar to the edge of the central hole. Note that a straight path should be available for this model because nodes must lie on the cut edge.

c. Repeat part (b) after resetting the mesh size to *fine*. Use the copy feature to save time creating this study.

d. Repeat part (b) a third time after resetting the mesh size by applying *mesh control* around both edges and the inner surface of the hole. Use the default mesh control setting: **Ratio a/b = 1.5**. Also use the copy feature to save time creating this study.

e. Use classical equations and available stress concentration factor charts to manually compute maximum stress at the hole.

f. Compare results predicted using the three different meshes with that predicted by classical stress equations. Compute the percent difference for each comparison using equation [1].

$$\% \text{ difference} = \frac{(\text{FEA result - classical result})}{\text{FEA result}} * 100 = \qquad [1]$$

g. Comment upon which FEA results are in best agreement with predictions of the classical equations? Which method of mesh refinement is usually preferred and why?

h. If Exercise 1 of Chapter 3 was worked, compare magnitudes of the maximum *appropriate stress* at the hole location. Compare magnitudes *only* for the case when *Mesh Control* is used. Then answer the question, "Which FEA model (i.e., the *complete* model or the *symmetrical* model) is in best agreement with calculation of stress at the hole location using classical equations and stress concentration factor charts? If differences exceeding 5% are obtained, explain the reason for this difference.

i. Symmetry is used to reduce model size and computation time, especially for large, complex models. For the current exercise, is it possible to further reduce model size through the application of symmetry principles? If "yes," sketch the reduced model and show symmetry restraints acting on the model.

Textbook Problems

In addition to the above exercises, it is highly recommended that additional problems involving contact between mating parts be worked from a design of machine elements textbook. The parts need ***not*** be cylindrical. Textbook problems provide a great way to discover errors made in formulating a finite element analysis because they typically are well defined problems for which the solution is known. Textbook problems, if well defined in advance, make an excellent source of solutions for comparison.

NOTES:

BOLTED JOINT ANALYSIS

Machine screws, bolts, and/or nuts and bolts in combination, are some of the most frequently used means of joining mechanical components. Bolted joints are commonly used in non-permanent connections where access to and removal of components for repair or replacement is essential to the maintenance of mechanical devices. This example examines steps involved to successfully model bolted connections. Bolted connections are but one of many connection types available in SolidWorks Simulation. Other connector types not examined here include: springs, rigid, pins, links, spot welds, and bearing connections between components.

Learning Objectives

Upon completion of this example, users should be able to:

- Define *bolt connectors*
- Define *custom material properties* for bolt connectors
- Identify when mesh refinement is necessary based on *high stress gradient*
- Define *contact sets* between mating parts without the use of Split Lines.

Problem Statement

An angle bracket is attached to a long, rigid support plate as illustrated in Fig. 1. Both the support plate and angle bracket are made of **ANSI 1020 Steel**. For purposes of this example, the support plate is shortened by arbitrarily cutting it in the vicinity of the two dashed lines on either side of the angle bracket. Four **M 12 x 1.75** bolts with nuts (i.e., 12 mm diameter metric bolts with a thread pitch = 1.75 mm) fasten the two parts together through the four holes shown. Bolts and nuts are not shown in the accompanying figure. All bolts are tightened to a preload of **24000** N. The goal is to determine bolt loads when the joint is loaded by a force of **5000** N acting normal to the top surface of the tab at the right end of the angle bracket. The force acts both toward and away from the tab surface shown on Fig. 1, but is not a cyclic load.

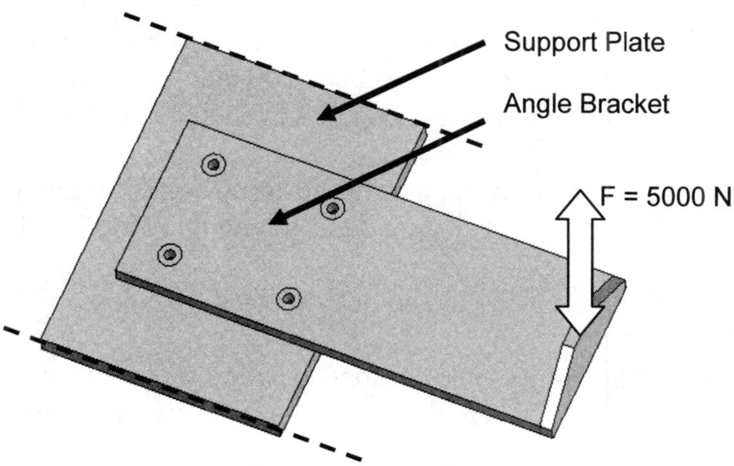

Figure 1 – Basic geometry of the angle bracket and support plate, showing bolt hole locations.

1. Open SolidWorks by making the following selections. (*Note:* "/" is used to separate successive menu selections.)

Start/All Programs/SolidWorks 2009 (or) Click the **SolidWorks** icon on your screen.

2. When SolidWorks is open, select **File / Open**. Then use procedures common to your computer environment to open the file named "**Support Plate and Angle Bracket.**" The screen image should look similar to Fig. 1.

Create a Static Analysis (Study)

1. In the main menu, select **Simulation** and from the pull-down menu select **Study...** Alternatively, select the **New Study** icon from the SolidWorks Simulation toolbar. Either action opens the **Study** property manager.

2. In the **Name** dialogue box, type "**Bolted Joint-DOWNWARD Load.**"

3. Verify that a **Static** analysis is selected and click **[OK]** ✓ to close the **Study** property manager. An outline of the study is created in the Simulation manager.

Assign Material Properties to the Model

Material properties of the support plate and angle bracket are assigned in this section. Because both components are the same material, this procedure is quite straightforward. Try it on your own. Steps are provided below if guidance is desired.

1. Right-click the **Parts** folder and from the pull-down menu, select **Apply Material to All...** The **Material** window opens.

2. In the **Material** window, select ⦿ **From library files:** and select **solidworks materials** in the pull-down menu. From the list of materials, click the "+" adjacent to **Steel (32)** and from the pull-down menu, choose **AISI 1020**.

3. In the right-half of the **Material** window, verify that **Units:** are set to **SI** and verify the material Yield Strength is **351571000** N/m^2.

4. Click **[OK]** to close the **Material** window.

Notice that bolt material is not specified at this time. Bolt material is specified independently when other bolt characteristics are defined.

Apply External Load and Fixtures

Traditional Loads and Fixtures

This section outlines the application of restraints and an external load using procedures similar to those encountered throughout this user manual. Those wishing to apply fixed/immovable restraints to cut edges of the support plate and a 5000 N load normal to the tab on the right end of the angle bracket are encouraged to proceed on their own. However, steps are provided below if guidance is desired.

1. In the Simulation manager, right-click the **Fixtures** folder and from the pull-down menu, select **Fixed Geometry...** The **Fixture** property manager opens.

2. In the **Standard (Fixed Geometry)** dialogue box, select the **Fixed Geometry** icon (if not already selected).

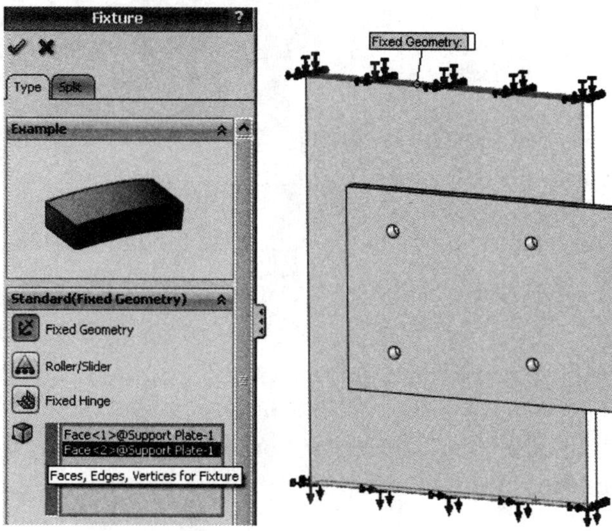

Figure 2 – Application of restraints to cut-surfaces at top and bottom of the support plate.

3. The **Faces, Edges, Vertices for Fixture** field is highlighted (light blue). Move the cursor into the graphics screen and rotate and zoom-in on the model as necessary to select the two cut surfaces of the support plate shown in Fig. 2. **Face<1>** and **Face<2>@Support Plate-1** appear in the highlighted field.

4. Click **[OK]** ✓ to close the **Fixture** property manager.

Next apply a downward force on top of the tab at the right-end of the angle bracket.

5. Right-click the **External loads** folder and from the pull-down menu, select **Force...** The **Force/Torque** property manager opens as illustrated in Fig. 3.

6. In the **Force/Torque** dialogue box, verify that the **Force** icon is selected (gray highlight) and that force direction is selected as ⦿ **Normal.**

7. The **Faces and Shell Edges for Normal Force** field is highlighted (light blue) and awaits input. Proceed to select the top surface of the angle bracket shown in Fig. 3.

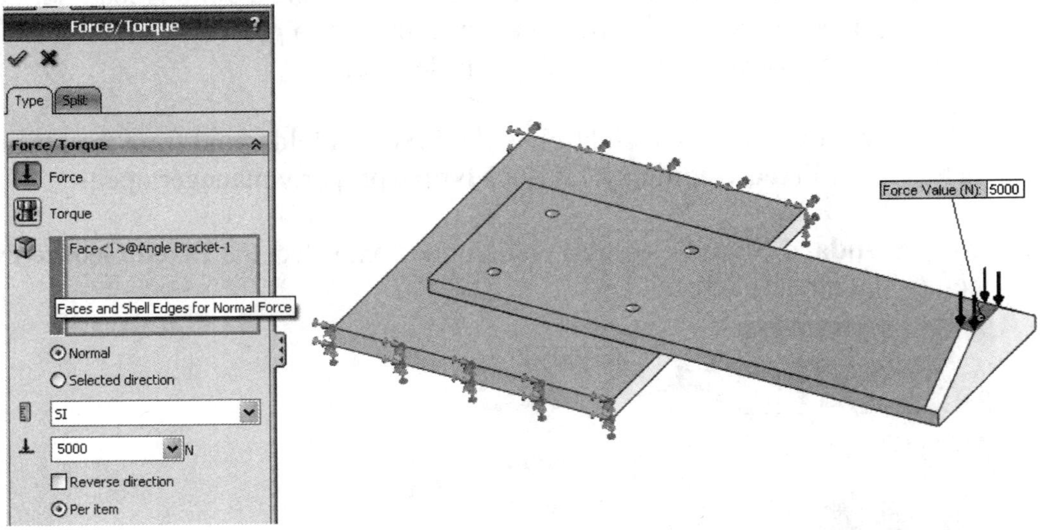

Figure 3 – Application of a downward force normal to top surface of the tab located at the right-end of the angle bracket.

8. In the **Unit** dialogue box, verify that units are set to **SI**.

9. In the **Force Value** field, type **5000** N and select ⦿ **Per item**. The force should act downward, if not check ☑ **Reverse Direction**.

10. Click **[OK]** ✓ to close the **Force/Torque** property manager.

Define Bolted Joint Restraints

Individual bolted fasteners used to join the angle bracket and support plate are defined next. Discussion below assumes the bolt-head is located on top of the angle bracket while the nut is located against the bottom surface of the support plate as identified in Fig. 4. Definition of bolted joints also takes place within the **Connections** folder located in the Simulation manager tree.

Carefully and sequentially work through the following steps to define *one bolt at a time.* NOTE: If all bolt clamping surfaces are selected in a single step, software ability to isolate *individual* bolt reactions is lost. Also, while proceeding through the following steps, place the cursor onto each field or icon to reveal its name. This approach enhances insight into understanding the function of each option.

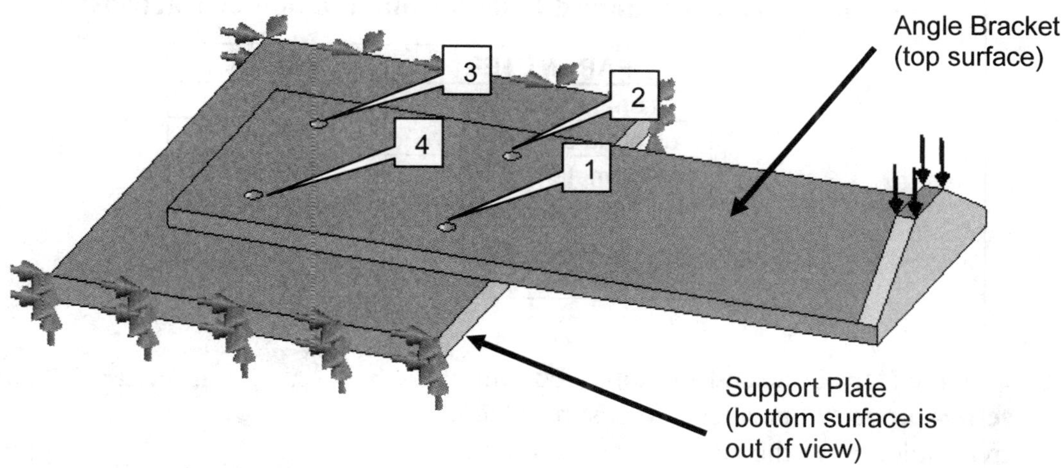

Figure 4 – Angle bracket and support plate showing bolt holes numbered from 1 to 4 in counterclockwise order.

1. Right-click **Connections** and from the pull-down menu select **Bolt…** The **Connectors** property manager opens; a partial view is shown in Fig. 5.

2. Begin by clicking the **Keep Visible** "push-pin" located at the top-right of the **Connectors** property manager and circled in Fig. 5.

3. At top of the **Type** dialogue box, open the pull-down menu to examine the various connector types listed. Then, from the list of possible connectors, select **Bolt**.

4. Select the **Standard or Counterbore with Nut** fastener shown boxed in Fig. 5. Move the cursor over the remaining icons to get a quick overview of other connector types available within the **Bolt** connector sub-group.

Within SolidWorks Simulation there exist multiple ways to define bolted connectors. The most direct method is outlined below. In order to define a nut and bolt, the parameters listed in Table 1, on the next page, are needed. Table 1 shows values applicable to grade 5.8 metric **M 12 x 1.75** bolts and nuts used in this example. Information shown in Table 1 is readily available in most design of machine elements texts.

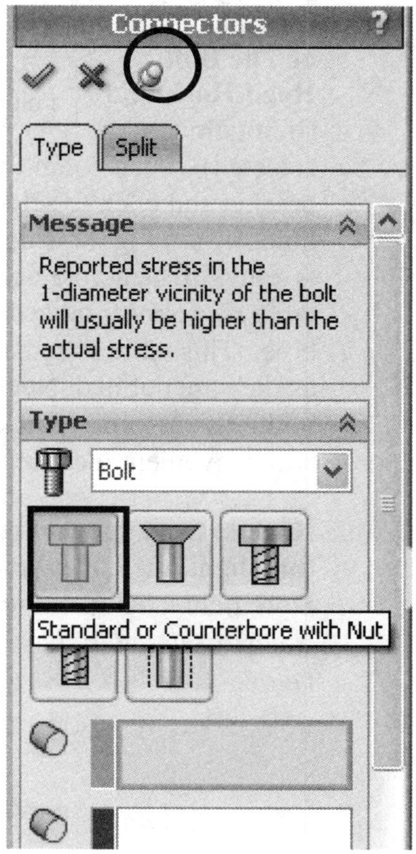

Figure 5 – Partial view of the **Connectors** property manager with the **Keep Visible** push-pin and connector type selected.

Table 1 – Values required to define nut and bolt characteristics.

PARAMETER	VALUE
Bolt shank diameter	12 mm
Bolt head diameter	18 mm
Nut diameter	18 mm
Bolt Elastic Modulus	207e9 N/m^2
Bolt Poisson's Ratio	0.292
Bolt Pre-load	24000 N

The following steps proceed from top to bottom of the **Connectors** property manager. To ensure selection of the correct field, move the cursor over each field to reveal its name. Also recall that the bolt head is located on the angle bracket, considered to be the top of the model, and the nut is located on the support plate (bottom side of the model) in Fig. 8.

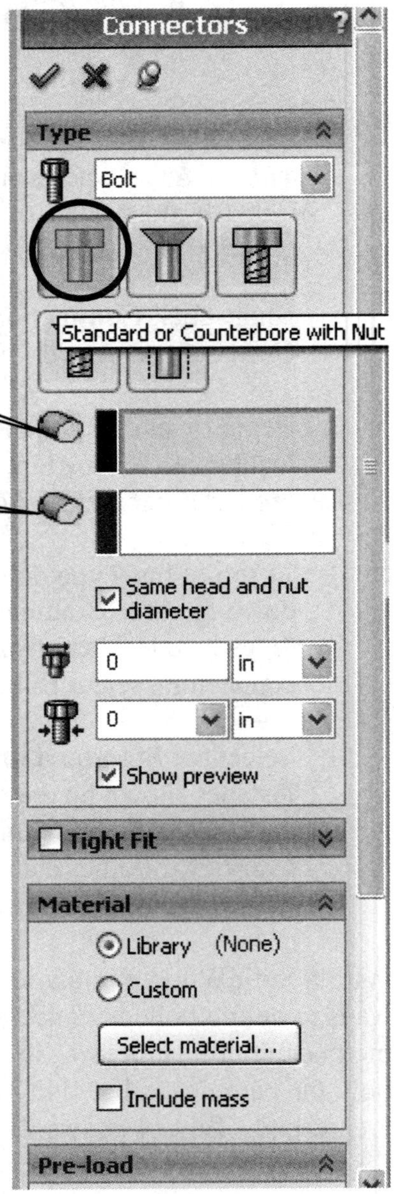

Figure 6 – The **Connectors** property manager after selecting **Bolt** as the connector type.

5. Click to activate (light blue) the **Circular Edge of The Bolt Head Hole** field (if not already selected). Then zoom-in on the *top* of the angle bracket and click to select the *top edge* of bolt hole #1; see Fig. 8. **Edge<1>@Angle Bracket-1** is listed in the active field, see Fig. 7. A flyout table *may* appear adjacent to the selected bolt hole. This table summarizes all bolt parameters as they are defined. Neglect initial values shown in the flyout table. Click and drag the flyout table to a convenient location on the screen.

6. Next, in the **Type** dialogue box, click to activate (highlight) the **Circular Edge of The Bolt Nut Hole** field labeled in Fig. 6. *CAUTION: This step is easily missed in the repetitive process outlined below*

7. Rotate and zoom-in on the *bottom* of the support plate to select the corresponding bottom *edge* of bolt hole #1. **Edge<2>@ Support Plate-1** is listed in the active field.

8. Immediately beneath this field, check ☑ **Same head and nut diameter**. This step matches the nut and bolt head diameters as is common for standard bolt connections.

9. In the next field from the top, click to open the **Unit** pull-down menu and select **mm**. ***Units*** *must be specified prior to entering the bolt head diameter.*

10. To the left of the **Unit** field, type **18** mm in the **Head Diameter** field.

11. Next, adjacent to the **Bolt Shank Diameter** field, click to change **Unit** to **mm**.

12. In the **Bolt Shank Diameter** field, type **12** mm.

13. Clear the check mark "✓" from ☐ **Tight Fit** (only if checked). This option does not pertain to bolts inserted through clearance holes such as are used in this example.

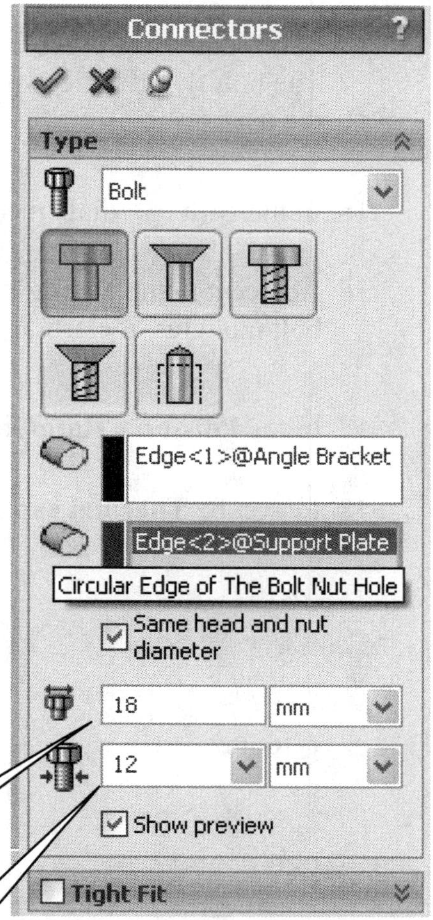

Figure 7 – Top portion of the **Connectors** property manager showing selections used to define bolts and nut contact faces.

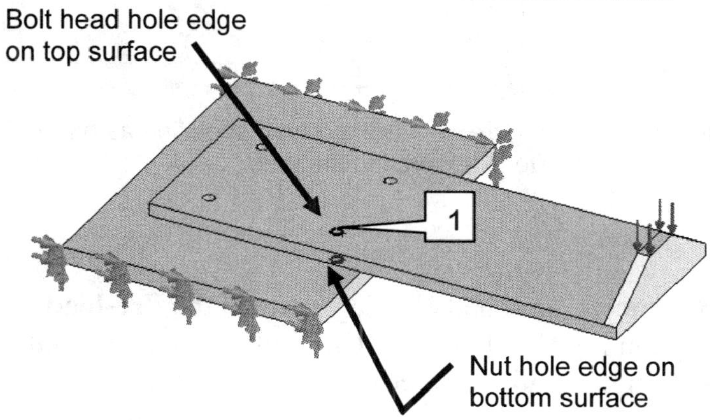

Figure 8 – Model showing selection of hole edges for the bolt head and nut contact faces for bolt #1.

Next, direct your attention to the **Material** dialogue box. In this dialogue box it is possible to select bolt material from the **Material** window, as has been done in all previous examples, or to specify custom material properties as outlined below.

14. Scroll down to the **Material** dialogue box shown in Fig. 9, select ⦿ **Custom**. The bolt flyout table expands to display additional information to be specified by the user.

15. In the **Unit** dialogue box, select **SI** (if not already selected).

16. Adjacent to the **Young's Modulus** E_x field, type **207e9** N/m^2 to identify the bolt modulus of elasticity.

17. In the **Poisson's Ratio** field, type **0.292**.

18. Leave the **Thermal expansion coefficient** α blank. Temperature is not a factor.

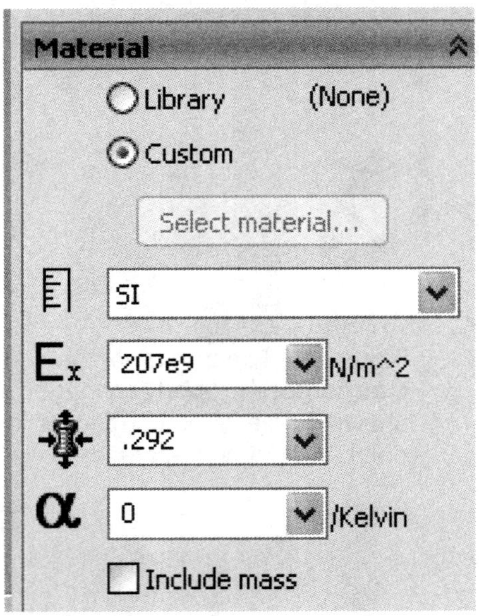

Figure 9 – Specifying custom material properties for bolts in the **Material** dialogue box.

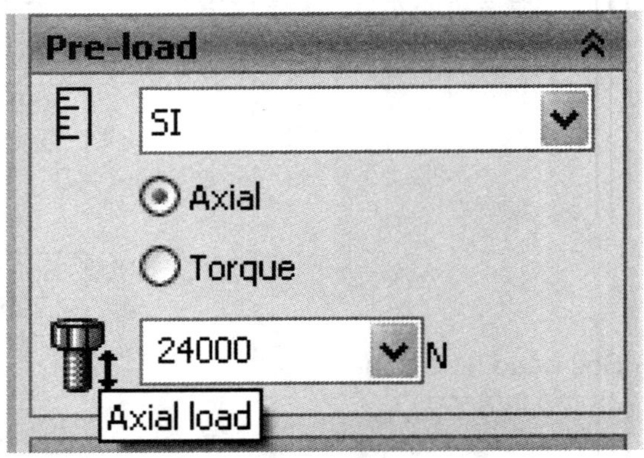

Figure 10 – Bolt preload specified as an axial (tensile) force in the bolt.

19. Scroll to the bottom of the **Connectors** property manager where the **Pre-load** dialogue box appears as shown in Fig. 10. Open the **Unit** pull-down menu and from the list, again select **SI** (if not already selected).

20. Next, select ⦿ **Axial**. This selection indicates that the bolt preload is expressed by an axial (tensile) load in the bolt.

21. In the **Axial load** field, type **24000** N.

22. Return to the top of the **Connectors** property manager and click **[OK]** ✓. This action applies all of the above settings to bolt #1.

As specifications are entered for each remaining bolt and nut, symbols representing bolt connectors appear at each hole location as illustrated in Fig. 11.

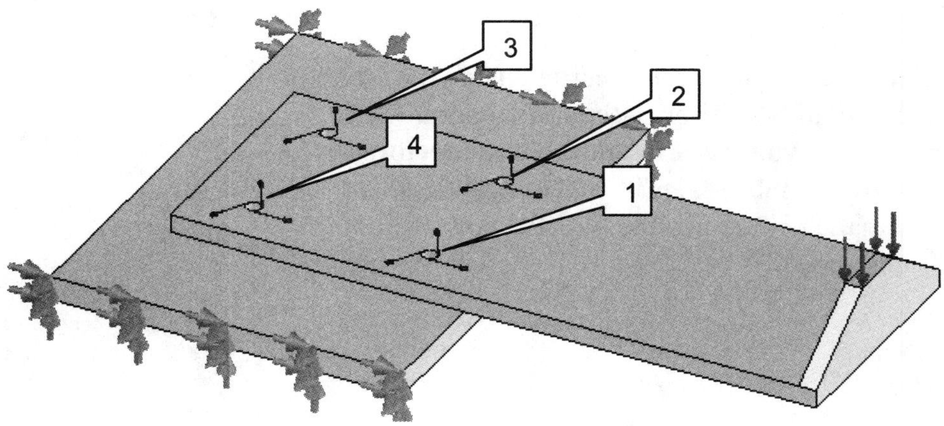

Figure 11 – Bolt connector symbols appear at locations of the Head and Nut Contact Faces. Rotate the model to view symbols on bottom of the support plate.

Because the **Keep visible** push-pin was selected, the **Connectors** property manager remains open and all values entered to describe the first bolt are retained. Unless changed by the user, the software assumes that additional identical bolts are used. Thus, it only remains to select the top and bottom hole-edges for the remaining bolts and nuts in the *counterclockwise order* shown numbered in Fig. 11. Proceed as follows.

23. Within the **Type** dialogue box the **Circular Edge of The Bolt Head Hole** field should again be highlighted. On the *top* surface of the angle bracket, select the *edge* of hole #2. The hole edge is highlighted.

24. Beneath the above field, click to activate the **Circular Edge of The Bolt Nut Hole** filed. Rotate the model and zoom-in on the *corresponding* hole on the *bottom* of the support plate. Click to select the edge of this hole and bolt connector symbols appear on the model. In the property manager, scroll down and notice that all other data entries remain as previously defined.

25. Return to the top of the **Connectors** property manager, and click **[OK]** ✓. This action applies the previous settings to the currently selected bolt location.

Repeat steps 23 through 25 for *each* remaining bolt. Follow the counterclockwise order shown in Fig. 11.

26. After defining bolt #4 (and clicking **[OK]** ✓ in step 25), select **Cancel** ✖ to close the **Connectors** property manager.

At this point, **Bolt Connector-1** through **Bolt Connector-4** should be listed beneath the **Connections** folder in the Simulation manager tree as illustrated in Fig. 12.

NOTE: If all bolts had been specified using the **Hole Series** feature of SolidWorks, then Simulation would have asked "**Do you want to add bolt connectors to all holes in the Hole Series?**" Selecting **Yes** would have automatically applied the selected bolt to all holes in the same series.

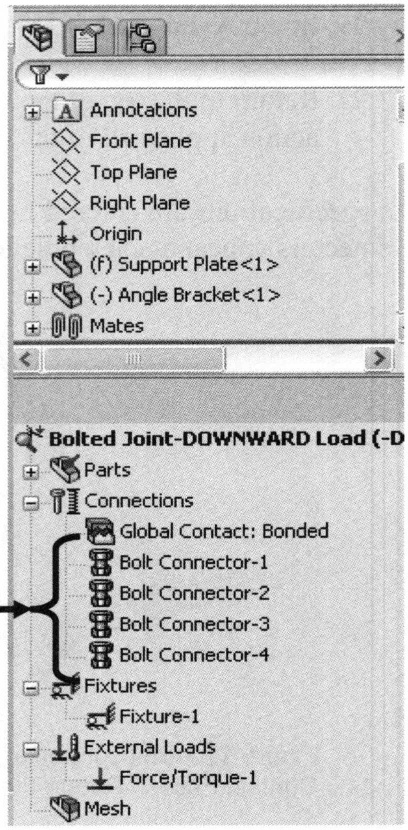

Figure 12 – Individually defined bolt connectors listed beneath the **Load/ Restraint** folder.

Analysis Insight

Instead of specifying bolt preload as an **Axial** force, in the **Pre-load** dialogue box, it is also possible to specify bolt preload in terms of torque applied to tighten the nut as shown in the **Pre-load** dialogue box of Fig. 13.

When bolt torque is specified, the software uses a rearranged form of equation [1] to compute axial preload. Notice that the torque coefficient **K**, listed as "**Friction Factor (K)**" at the bottom of the **Pre-load** dialogue box, can be changed to account for specific joint conditions.

A variety of joint and bolt characteristics, such as: surface finish (painted, plated, clean, etc.); alignment (parallelism of surfaces and/or flatness under the bolt head and nut); and thread condition (dry, lubricated, coated, etc.) all affect the torque coefficient **K**.

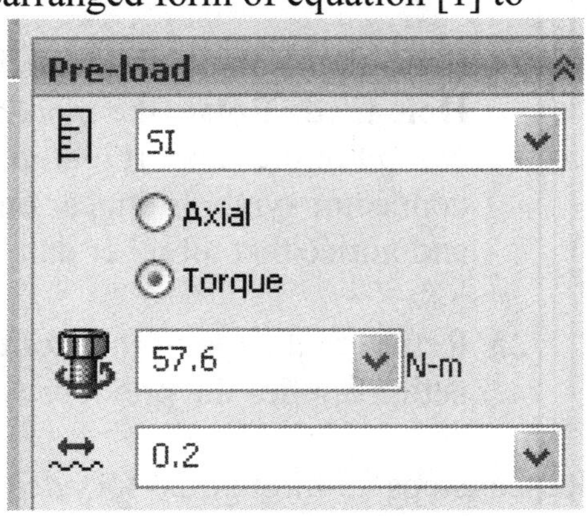

Figure 13 – **Preload** dialogue box showing specification of bolt **Torque** rather than an axial preload value.

The relationship between bolt preload and bolt torque is typically defined in a design of machine elements text by the following equation.

$$\mathbf{T = KF_i d} \quad [1]$$

Where: $\mathbf{F_i}$ = desired bolt preload (the initial axial tensile force in the bolt)
$\mathbf{T}$ = applied torque required to develop a desired preload $\mathbf{F_i}$
$\mathbf{K}$ = torque coefficient (K = 0.20 is a generally accepted value)
$\mathbf{d}$ = nominal bolt diameter

For this example, if ⦿ **Torque** were selected rather than O **Axial** preload, then the torque used to tighten the bolt is given by:

$$\mathbf{T = KF_i d} = (0.20)(24\ \text{kN})(0.012\ \text{m}) = 57.6\ \text{N-m}$$

See the entry typed into the **Torque** field in Fig. 13.

This completes the definition of individual bolt connectors. However, because we are dealing with an assembly, it is also necessary to define contact conditions between the two members that are bolted together. This task is addressed in the following section.

Define Local Contact Conditions

Contact between the angle bracket and support plate must also be defined. Because there are only two components in this assembly, it would be possible to define contact between mating surfaces on these two parts using a *Global* contact specification (i.e., a specification that applies to all contacting surfaces). However, it is more instructive to define contact in a *Local* sense (i.e., specific to the two contacting surfaces). This approach provides the user with greater control when defining contact situations and prepares the user to deal with more unique situations should they be encountered in other modeling applications. Begin by switching to an exploded view.

1. In the main menu, select **Insert** and from the pull-down menu choose **Exploded View…** The Explode property manager opens.

2. Click to select the angle bracket (top part) in Fig. 14. A coordinate system triad appears on the part. Drag the Y-axis of the triad upward. Release the mouse button when the figure looks similar to Fig. 14. (Alternatively, drag the support plate downward).

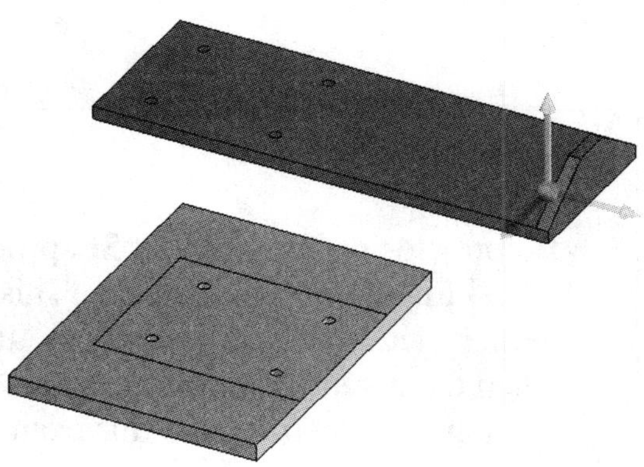

Figure 14 – Exploded view prior to defining contact conditions.

3. Click **[OK]** ✓ to close the **Explode** property manager.

4. In the Simulation manager tree, right-click the **Connections** folder and from the pull-down menu select **Contact Set...** The **Contact Set** property manager opens as shown in the middle of Fig. 15.

5. In the pull-down menu at top of the **Type** dialogue box, select **No Penetration.**

6. The **Faces, Edges, Vertices for Set 1** field is highlighted (light blue) and awaits input. Move the cursor into the graphics screen and rotate the model to select the bottom, left-end of the angle bracket shown highlighted in Fig. 15 (a). **Face<1>@Angle Bracket-1** is listed in the active field. A *Split Line* is provided to facilitate selecting only the contact surface.

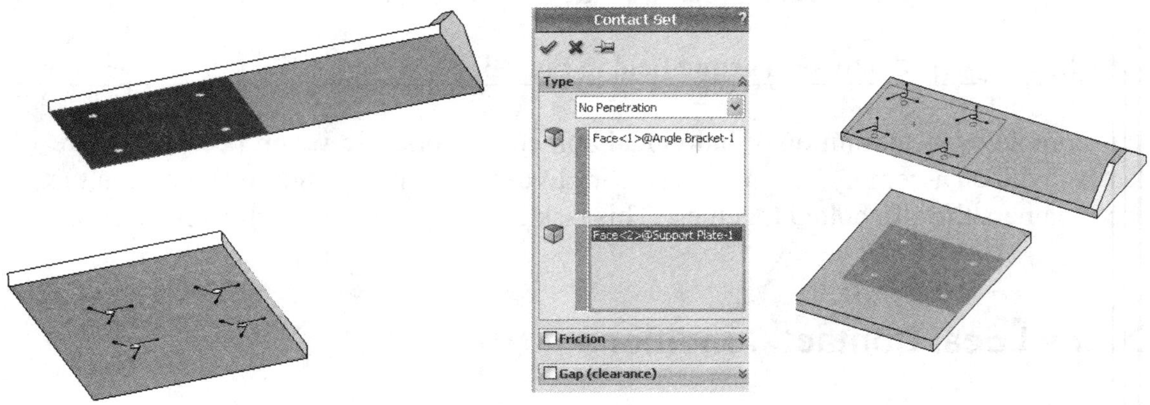

(a) Select bottom of Angle Bracket.

(b) Select top of Support Plate.

Figure 15 – Selection of equal and opposite faces defined to be in contact with **No Penetration**.

7. Click to highlight (light blue) the **Faces for Set 2** field, located at the bottom of the **Type** dialogue box. Then, proceed to select the contact face in the vicinity of bolt holes on top of the support plate. See highlighted face in Fig. 15 (b). **Face<2>@Support Plate-1** is listed in the active field. Once again *Split Lines* are provided to permit selection of only the contact surface.

Analysis Insight:

Before closing the **Contact Set** property manager, click to place a check mark in the ☑ **Friction:** dialogue box. This dialogue box reveals that it is possible to define friction between the contacting surfaces. This option is typically applied when the potential for movement is investigated between mating parts. Since friction is not pertinent to this example, clear the ☐ **Friction** check-box before proceeding.

8. Click **[OK]** ✓ to close the **Contact Set** property manager. Highlighting disappears from the model and beneath the **Connections** folder appears an icon labeled, "**Contact Set-1 (-No Penetration<Angle Bracket-1, Support Plate-1>-).**" Place cursor over this text to reveal the entire phrase.

Before proceeding, the model is returned to its original, un-exploded, state as follows.

9. Toggle to the **Configuration Manager** by clicking its icon at top of the SolidWorks manager tree.

10. Click the "+" sign adjacent to **Default<Default Display State-1> [Support Plate and Angle Bracket]**.

11. Right-click ExplView1 and from the pull-down menu, select **Collapse**.

12. Toggle back to the SolidWorks by clicking the **SolidWorks** icon.

Mesh the Model and Run Solution

1. In the Simulation manager right-click the **Mesh** folder and from the pull-down menu select **Create Mesh…** The **Mesh** property manager opens.

2. Within the **Mesh Parameters** dialogue box, set **Unit** to **mm**, and accept the default mesh size.

3. Click to open the **Advanced** dialogue box and verify that **Jacobian points** is stet to **[4 Points]**, the default setting.

4. Click **[OK]** ✓ to close the **Mesh** property manager.

5. Right-click the Study name, **Bolted Joint-DOWNWARD Load**, and select **Run**.

Notice the significant increase in time required to solve this problem (approximately five to seven minutes). The primary time increase occurs during multiple iterations required to solve the contact restraints portion of the solution where contact conditions between mating parts are determined. The following paragraph provides a non technical description of the equation solution process.

To help understand the reason for this time increase, consider that deformation of one part causes (or transfers) that deformation to the mating part at the contact surface. Also, think of the parts starting from an un-deformed state and gradually transitioning to the fully deformed state. Throughout this incremental deformation process, the governing equations between mating parts must be satisfied at all times (i.e., consistent deformations must exist throughout the model and across the contact area). Thus each small change of deformation is accompanied by a new iteration of calculations that begins where the previous calculations ended. Therefore, the governing equations are solved and satisfied multiple times as the deformation "grows" to its final condition.

Results Analysis for the Downward External Load

Von Mises Stress

Briefly examine a plot of von Mises stress to gain an understanding of the magnitude and distribution of this stress throughout the assembly.

1. Click the "+" sign adjacent to the **Results** folder (if not already selected).
2. Right-click **Stress1 (-vonMises-)** and from the pull-down menu, select **Show**. A plot of von Mises stress is displayed on the model (if not already displayed by default).
3. Right-click **Stress1 (-vonMises-)** and from the pull-down menu select **Edit Definition…** The **Stress Plot** property manager opens.
4. In the **Display** dialogue box change **Units** to **N/m^2**.
5. In the **Advance Options** dialogue box, clear the check mark from ☐ **Average results across boundary for parts** and verify that ⊙ **Node Values** is selected.
6. At top of the **Deformed Shape** dialogue box, verify that ☑ **Deformed Shape** is checked. Also within this dialogue box, select ⊙ **Automatic** to apply the system default exaggerated deformation to the model display.
7. Click **[OK]** ✓ to close the **Stress Plot** property manager.
8. Right-click **Stress1 (-vonMises-)** and from the pull-down menu select **Chart Options…** The **Chart Options** property manager opens.
9. In the **Display Options** dialogue box, check both ☑ **Show min annotation** and ☑ **Show max annotation**.
10. In the **Position/Format** dialogue box, select **scientific (e)** as the **Number Format** and **3** as the **No of Decimals** to be displayed.
11. Click **[OK]** ✓ to close the **Chart Options** property manager. A plot of von Mises stress on the deformed model should appear as illustrated in Fig. 16.

Observe that the maximum von Mises stress, indicated on the model and in the color-coded legend as 2.094e+008 N/m^2, is considerably less than the material Yield Strength of 3.5157e+008 N/m^2.

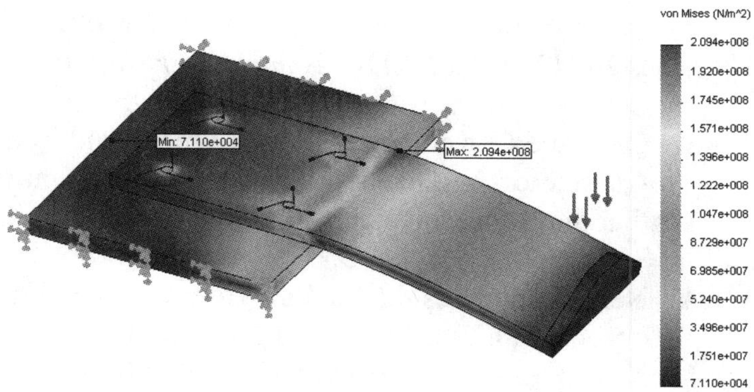

Figure 16 – von Mises stress distribution as seen in a top view of the assembly corresponding to a downward acting load on the model.

Bolt Forces (for Downward Load)

A primary feature of a bolt analysis is the ability to determine forces acting at each bolt. In the assembly analyzed in this example, it is reasonable to expect similar bolt forces in bolts #1 and #2, which are equidistant from the applied load. Similarly for bolts #3 and #4, which are located a further, but equal, distance from the applied load. Axial bolt force is the algebraic sum of its preload plus effects due to external load(s) acting on the joint. Bolt forces are examined as follows.

1. Right-click the **Results** folder, and from the pull-down menu, select **List Pin/Bolt /Bearing Force…** The **Pin/Bolt/Bearing Force** window opens as shown in Fig. 17.

Examination of this window reveals the **Study name:** in the upper left corner. Beneath the study name is a pull-down menu where it is possible to select results for **All pins**, **All bolts**, **All bearings** or results for each individual bolt. From this pull-down menu, select **Bolt Connector-1**. Adjacent to the bolt number is the current set of units. Set **Units:** to **SI**. Finally, at the bottom of the window, the **X**, **Y**, **Z**-components and the **Resultant** are listed for the **Shear Force (N)**, **Axial Force (N)**, and **Bending moment (N-m)** that act on the bolt number 1.

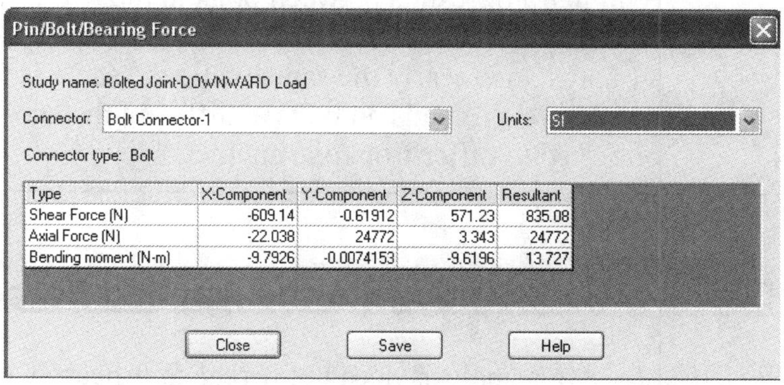
Pin/Bolt/Bearing Force

Study name: Bolted Joint-DOWNWARD Load

Connector: Bolt Connector-1 Units: SI

Connector type: Bolt

Type	X-Component	Y-Component	Z-Component	Resultant
Shear Force (N)	-609.14	-0.61912	571.23	835.08
Axial Force (N)	-22.038	24772	3.343	24772
Bending moment (N-m)	-9.7926	-0.0074153	-9.6196	13.727

Close Save Help

Figure 17 – The **Pin/Bolt/Bearing Force** window summarizes all Shear Force, Axial Force, and Bending moments that act on each bolt in the joint.

2. In the **Axial Force** row, observe the **Resultant** in the far right column. Its value is **24743** N. *Note: Values may differ slightly due to computational round-off.*

3. Click the **Connector:** pull-down menu and from the list of connectors, select **Bolt Connector-2**. This bolt is positioned adjacent to bolt #1 on the model. Observe that the **Resultant** bolt force is **24780** N.

4. Next, display results for **Bolt Connector-3** and **Bolt Connector-4**. Again observe values of the **Resultant** axial bolt forces. For bolt #3, Resultant = 23949 N, and for bolt #4, Resultant = 23948 N.

5. Close the **Pin/Bolt/Bearing Force** window by clicking the **[Close]** button.

Observations

a. Forces at both bolts in the same row are nearly identical in magnitude (allowing for some computational variation).

b. Forces at bolts #1 and #2 differ at most by 3.25 % from the specified bolt preload (24000 N) and both loads are slightly *higher* than the given preload.

c. Note the small difference (only 1 N) between resultant forces in bolts #3 and #4 that are located in the row furthest from the applied load. These values differ by 0.20 % from the specified bolt preload of 24000 N. But, due to joint loading, these values are both slightly *less* than the original bolt preload.

d. The bolted joint is well designed because most of the load is carried by the material clamped between the bolt head and nut. This observation is based on the fact that bolt load differs only slightly from the bolt preload value of 24000 N.

e. Symmetry of results between bolts in the two different rows lends credence to the fact that the problem is formulated correctly. That is to say, loads on bolts #1 and #2 are nearly the same while the same is true for loads on bolts #3 and #4. However, loads on bolts at different distances from the applied load are observed to differ from one another.

Define a New Study with the Applied Force Reversed

Because the above analysis does not reveal significantly different results at the two rows of bolts, the example is next re-worked with an upward force applied to the angle bracket as shown in Fig. 18. Rather than *copying* various items from the existing study into a new study, as demonstrated in Chapter 3, the procedure below will produce a *duplicate* of the current study and then alter the new study to reflect changes indicated above.

1. Beneath the graphics area of the screen, right-click to select the Simulation Study *tab* labeled **Bolted Joint-DOWNWARD Load** and from the pop-up menu, select **Duplicate**. The **Define Study Name** window opens as shown in Fig. 18.

2. In the **Study Name:** field, type **Bolted Joint-UPWARD Load** and click **[OK]**. This action creates an exact duplicate of the former study.

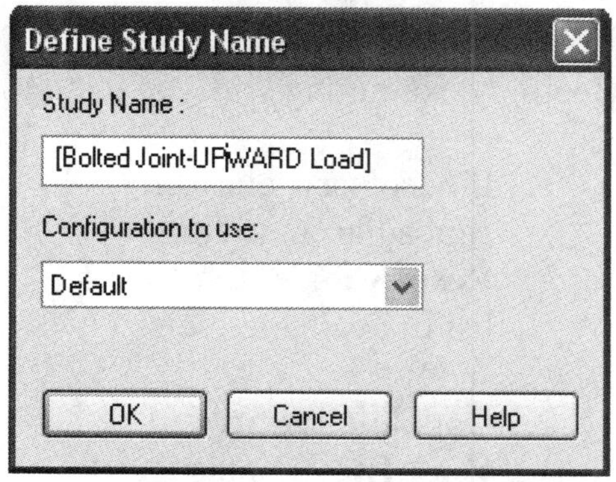

Figure 18 – A *duplicate* of the existing study is assigned a new **Study Name**.

To differentiate this study from its predecessor, it is only necessary to reverse the load applied to the angle bracket. To accomplish this, proceed as follows.

3. If necessary, click the "+" sign adjacent to **External Loads** to reveal **Force/Torque-1** defined during the previous study.

4. Next, right-click **Force/ Torque-1** and from the pull-down menu select **Edit Definition…** The **Force/ Torque** property manager opens.

5. Just below the **Force Value** of **5000** N, click to check ☑ **Reverse direction**. Force vectors applied at the end of the angle bracket should now be directed upward as shown in Fig. 19.

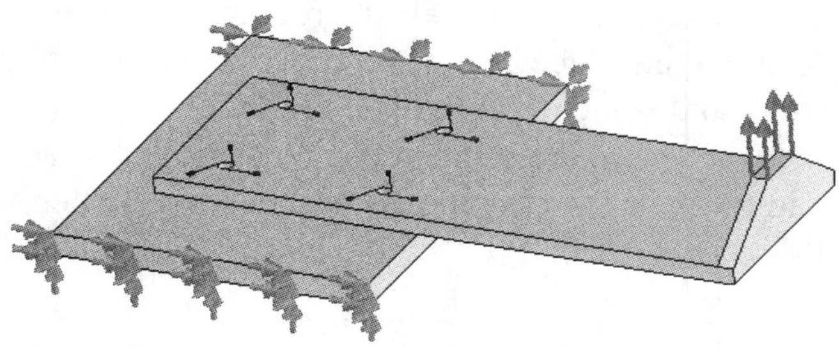

Figure 19 – Bolted joint model with the applied force reversed so that it acts upward.

6. Click **[OK]** ✓ to close the **Force/Torque** property manager.

Because all aspects of the previous study were copied, nothing else need be done except to re-run the solution due to the altered loading condition. Re-running the solution eliminates the warning ⚠ symbol adjacent to the **Results** folder and the error ⚠ symbol adjacent to the **Copy of [Bolted Joint-UPWARD Load]** study name. Re-run the solution on your own, or execute the following step.

7. Right-click the study name, **Copy of [Bolted Joint-UPWARD Load] (-Default-)**, folder and from the pull-down menu, select **Run**.

Results for the bolted assembly subject to an upward acting load are examined below.

Results Analysis for the Upward External Load

Von Mises Stress

Begin by examining von Mises stress.

1. If necessary, click the "+" sign adjacent to the **Results** folder to reveal a list of available plots.

2. Double-click **Stress1 (-von Mises-)** to display this plot (if necessary). The plot illustrated in Fig. 20 appears. Note the small circled areas of high stress.

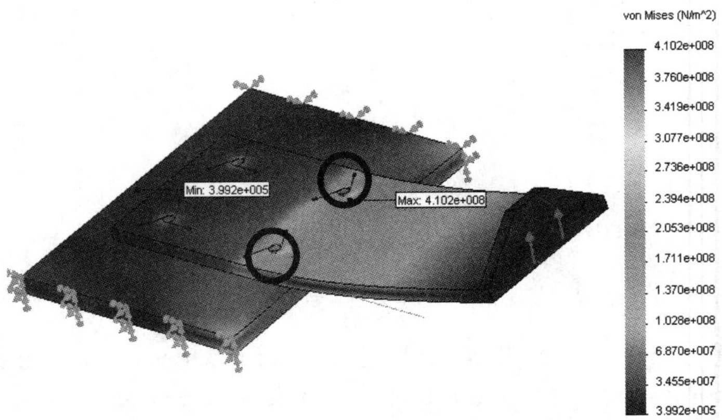

Figure 20 – von Mises stress distribution throughout the model corresponding to an *upward* acting load of 5000 N.

To obtain a good overview of stress distribution throughout the model, rotate the model to view all surfaces. Notice that, corresponding to an upward load, maximum stress within the model 4.102e008 N/m^2 (*values were observed to vary in subsequent analysis runs*) exceeds the material Yield Strength of 3.5157e+008 N/m^2 by approximately 17%. Close examination reveals the region of maximum stress is located adjacent to bolt hole #2 at the interface between the two parts. The region of maximum stress is exceedingly small and some ramifications of this finding are discussed in the **Analysis Insight** section below. The interested reader is encouraged to zoom in on the area of maximum stress and to apply iso-clipping, as outlined in Chapter #6, to view the high stress gradient in this region.

> **Analysis Insight**
>
> If the load is statically applied and the material is ductile, it can be argued that localized yielding occurs in the maximum stress region. A further argument is that localized yielding in the highly stressed area results in increased strength. This increase is due to the phenomenon commonly referred to as "cold-working" of the material. On the other hand, if the material is brittle or if loads are repeatedly applied and released (or reversed) failure by fracture or fatigue will likely occur.
>
> The most instructive way to investigate any high stress region is with the mesh displayed on the model. The reason for this is that the rate of change of stress magnitude, also known as "stress gradient," can be observed in relation to element size. However, the three dimensional nature of the mesh makes it difficult to obtain easily

interpreted textbook images in the region of maximum stress. Therefore, we next examine a region of high stress gradient on the surface of the angle bracket to demonstrate its significance relative to mesh size.

Begin by observing the two small *areas* of high stress that occur adjacent to bolt #1 and bolt #2 circled in Fig. 20.

To further emphasize the stress gradient in this region, Fig. 21 shows an enlarged view of the area adjacent to either bolt #1 or #2 with a mesh superimposed on the model. On your own, create a view like that shown in Fig. 21. The following steps are provided in the event that guidance is desired.

3. Right-click **Stress1 (-von Mises-)**. From the pull-down menu, select **Settings…** The **Settings** property manager opens.

4. Verify that the **Fringe Options** dialogue box is set to **Discrete**; if not change it. This action further emphasizes the small boundaries of the high stress (yellow) area relative to mesh size.

5. From the pull-down menu in the **Boundary Options** dialogue box, select **Mesh**. A mesh is superimposed on the model.

6. Click **[OK]** ✓ to close the **Settings** property manager.

7. Zoom-in on either of the high stress areas circled on Fig. 20 to obtain an image similar to Fig. 21. The high stress area is outlined for emphasis.

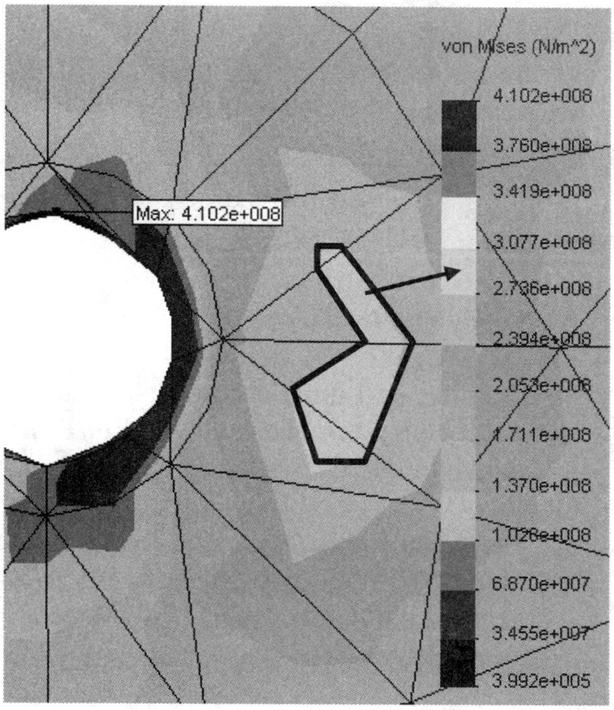

Figure 21 – Enlarged view showing the maximum stress region lies within a *portion* of the elements outlined in the figure. Stress magnitude is correlated to the color-coded stress scale.

Conclusion: Because the high stress region is *smaller* than any individual element (i.e., it occupies only a portion of three different elements), it is desirable to use a smaller mesh in this region. Recall that a finer mesh reveals stress levels more accurately. Because this small area occurs adjacent to a geometric discontinuity (the bolt hole), use of *Mesh Control* outlined in Chapter 3, should be considered.

The above observation is of paramount importance in any analysis where a high stress gradient occurs. However, because determination of bolt forces is the primary goal of this example, we return to analyze the bolted joint results without applying mesh refinement at this time.

Bolt Forces (for Upward Load)

The effect of altering direction of the applied load upon bolt forces is examined next.

1. Right-click the **Results** from the folder, and pull-down menu, select **List Pin/Bolt /Bearing Force...** The **Pin/Bolt/Bearing Force** window opens.

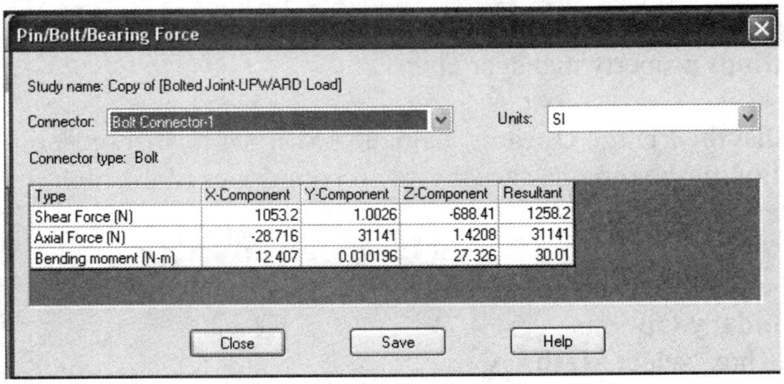

Figure 22 – Forces at **Bolt Connector-1** corresponding to an upward load applied to the angle bracket.

2. Verify that **Units:** are set to **SI**. If not, change to **SI** units.

3. Open the pull-down menu adjacent to **Connector:** and from the list of connectors, select **Bolt Connector-1**. The **Pin/Bolt/Bearing Force** window should appear as shown in Fig. 22. (Alternatively, select **All Bolts**, and scroll through the results.)

4. The **Axial Force (N)**, in the **Resultant** column at the far right of the table, is **31141** N (values may differ slightly). This value represents an increased axial (tensile) bolt load of 6361 N above that found for the downward load applied to the angle bracket

5. Open the pull-down menu adjacent to **Connector:** and from the list of connectors, select **Bolt Connector-2**. In the **Axial Force** row, the **Resultant** force in this bolt is now **31110** N, which is reasonably close (within 31 N) to the value obtained at bolt #1 in the previous step.

Recall that bolts #1 and #2 are located adjacent to one another at the same distance from the applied load. Theoretically, identical bolt loads are expected at these two locations. However, due to inaccuracies and round-off error, the small differences noted above are considered acceptable.

6. Repeat steps 3 and 4 for **Bolt Connector-3** and **Bolt Connector-4**. Axial bolt forces at these two locations are **24050** N and **24043** N respectively.

A side view of the model in Fig. 23 supports the finding of larger bolt tensile forces at bolts nearest to the applied load due to the additional upward "pull" resisted by bolts #1 and #2. Likewise, only a slight increase is expected at bolts #3 and #4, which are farthest from the applied load.

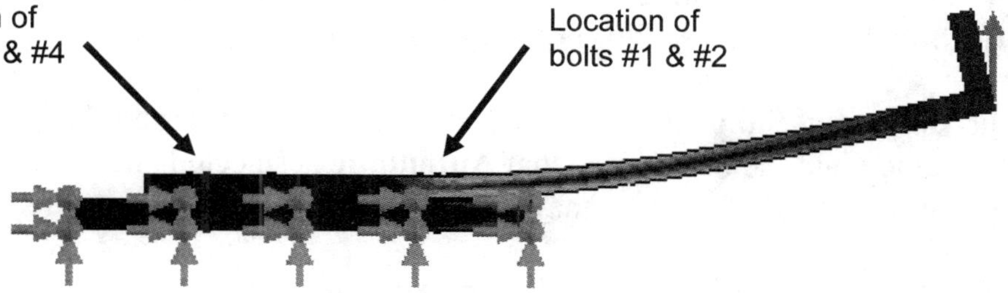

Figure 23 – Side view of the bolted joint with the angle bracket subject to an upward load at its right end.

Analysis Insight

Before closing the **Pin/Bolt Force** window, observe magnitudes of the **Shear Force** and the **Bending moment**. Whereas, **Bending moment** in the bolt is so small as to be almost negligible, the **Shear force** magnitude varies from a high of 1258.2 N at bolts #1 and #2 to a low of 892.63 N at bolts #3 and #4 respectively. Shear forces, while not negligible, are small compared to axial forces in the bolts. More importantly, however, shear stress in the bolt subject to the maximum shear force is small relative to bolt shear strength. The following calculation examines shear stress in the most heavily loaded bolt.

$$\tau = F_s/A_s = (1258.2\text{ N}) / (0.0763\text{ m}^2) = 16.5\text{ k N/m}^2 = 0.0165\text{ MPa} \qquad [2]$$

where:

F_s = maximum shear force at a bolt
A_s = minor area of screw thread (at root of thread profile) NOTE: For structural bolts, the nominal bolt diameter should be used.
τ = shear stress in bolt caused by maximum shear force

When compared to a conservative value of shear strength (S_{sy} = 234 MPa) for a Grade 5.8 metric bolt, a safety factor of approximately 15 is found. For this reason, shear stress is not considered significant in this example.

However, for many structural applications, shear in bolts is the *primary* mode of loading. In those instances, shear load on bolts is of prime importance. An end-of-chapter exercise examines a bolted joint where shear in the joint is the governing factor.

It may be possible to gain some insight into the origins of the X and Z components of shear force, by animating the model. To do this, proceed as follows.

7. Select **[Close]** to exit the **Pin/Bolt/Bearing Force** window.

8. If the von Mises stress plot is not displayed, double-click **Stress1 (-vonMises-)**.

9. Right-click **Stress1 (-vonMises-)** and from the pull-down menu, select **Edit Definition…** The **Stress Plot** property manager opens.

10. In the **Deformed Shape** dialogue box, make sure ☑ **Deformed Shape** is checked. In the same dialogue box, notice that **Automatic** is selected and the distortion scale factor is **7.95719** (values may differ slightly). This value is altered below.

11. Click **[OK]** ✓ to close the **Stress Plot** property manager.

12. Right-click **Stress1 (-vonMises-)** and from the pull-down menu, select ▶ **Animate…** If the model is animated, select the **Stop**  icon.

13. In the **Basics** dialogue box, increase the **Frames** to **10** and move the **Speed** control slide to the left. These actions smooth-out and slow the animation.

14. Click the **Start**.  icon.

15. Slowly rotate the model to examine its deformation due to the applied load. Pay particular attention to deformations in the region near bolts #1 and #2 where the angle bracket and support plate intersect.

16. Click **[OK]** ✓ to close the **Animation** property manager.

Because it may be difficult to observe deformations that cause shear forces in bolt #1 and bolt #2, steps 9 through 15 above are repeated, except replace step 10 with the following.

17. In the ☑ **Deformed Shape** dialogue box, select ⦿ **User Defined**. In the adjacent field, type **30**. Then continue at step 11. This action increases the magnitude of the deformation displayed.

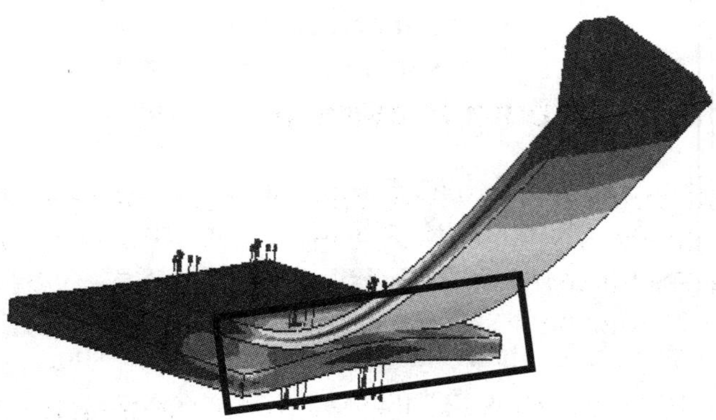

Figure 24 – Using animation to visualize origins of shear forces in the X and Z-directions at bolts #1 and #2.

The deformed model should appear similar to that illustrated in Fig. 24. In the following discussion, particular attention is focused on deformations between mating parts in the boxed region on this figure.

18. **Stop** the animation and click **[OK]** ✓ to close the **Animation** property manager.

Figure 25, below, represents a top view of the bolted joint where bolt connectors are represented by circles. Shear force components, directed according to their ± signs listed in the **Pin/Bolt/Bearing Force** connectors window, are shown at each bolt location. Using a combination of Fig. 25 and deformations viewed when animating the model, directions of the shear force components should begin to "make sense."

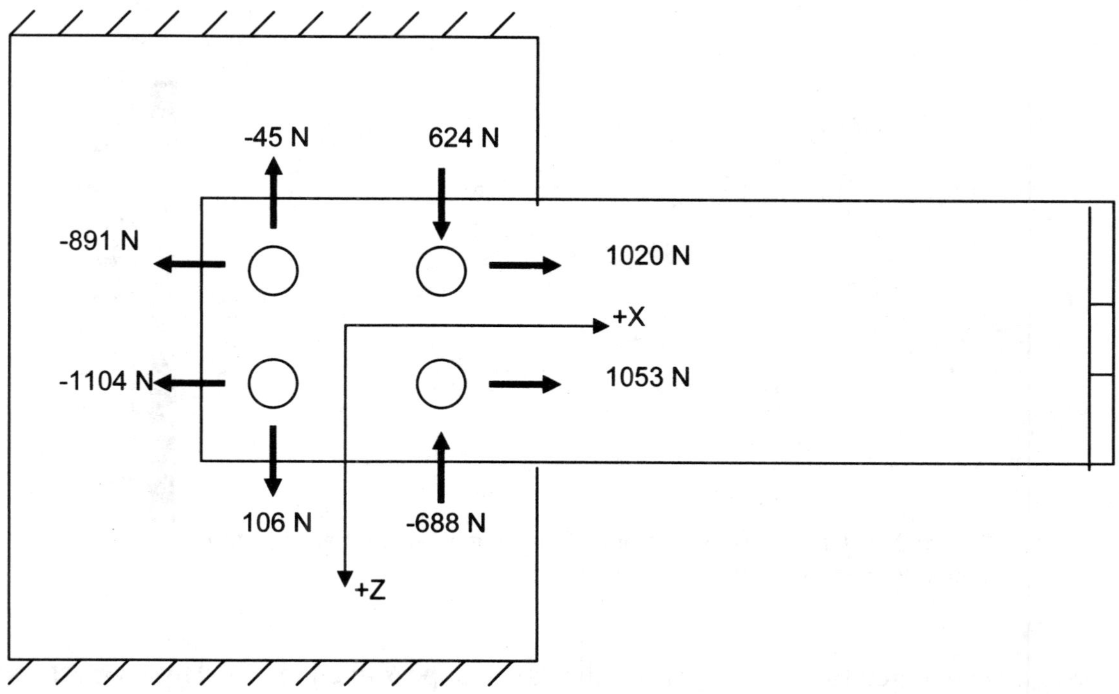

Figure 25 – Shear force components in the X and Z-directions developed in each bolt.

Bolt Clamping Pressure

Bolt preload is known to apply an equal and opposite clamping force on the joined members. Using software capabilities investigated in the previous chapter, contact pressure is investigated next. This analysis provides further insight into the intent of the bolted joint analysis capability within SolidWorks Simulation.

1. Right-click the **Results** folder and from the pull-down menu, select **Define Stress Plot...** The **Stress Plot** property manager opens.

2. In the **Display** dialogue box, click to open the pull-down menu adjacent to **VON: von Mises Stress** and from the pull-down menu select **CP: Contact Pressure.**

3. Verify that **Units** are set to **N/m^2**.

4. Next, in the **Advanced Options** dialogue box, clear the check-mark from ☐ **Average results across boundary for parts.**

5. Click **[OK]** ✓ to close the **Stress Plot** property manager. A new plot, labeled **Stress2 (-Contact pressure-)** is listed beneath the **Results** folder.

6. If not already displayed on the graphics screen, double-click **Stress2 (-Contact pressure-)** to display a contact pressure plot similar to that shown in Fig. 26.

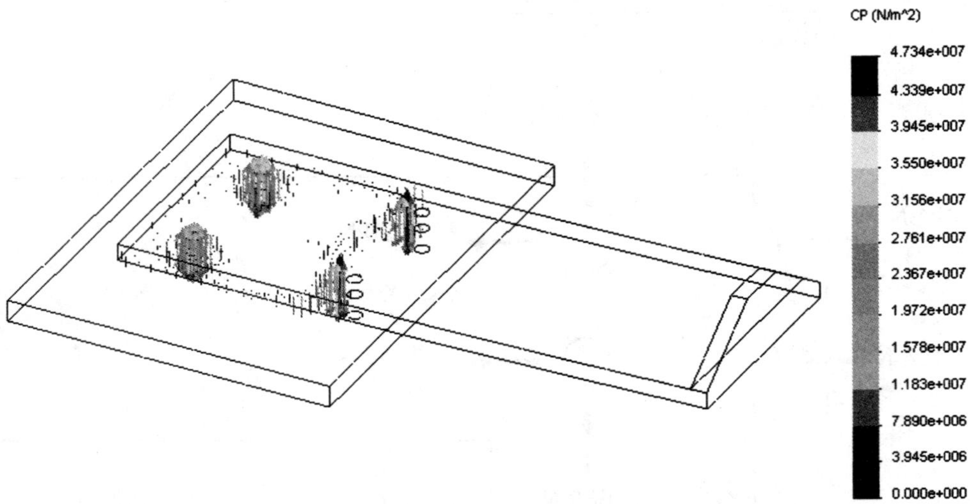

Figure 26 – Contact pressure plot showing interaction between the angle bracket and the support plate.

Users are encouraged to alter the graphic display to appear like Fig. 26. However, steps are provided below if guidance is desired.

7. Right-click **Stress2 (-Contact pressure-)** and from the pull-down menu, select **Settings...** The **Settings** property manager opens.

8. Within the **Boundary options** dialogue box, click to display the pull-down menu and from it select **Model**. An outline of the model appears. The **Fringe options** dialogue box can be set to either **Discrete** (preferred) or **Continuous.**

9. Click **[OK]** ✓ to close the **Settings** property manager.

Because bolt restraint symbols might obscure other pertinent graphical information, temporarily remove them from the display as follows.

10. In the Simulation manger tree, right-click **Connections** and from the pull-down menu select **Hide All**.

11. Repeat step 10 to temporarily hide **Fixtures** and **External Loads** (optional).

If the contact pressure vectors initially appear too small, which is often the case, increase their size as follows. Try this on your own or follow the steps listed below.

12. If necessary, double-click **Stress2(-Contact pressure-)** to again display the contact pressure.

13. Right-click **Stress2 (-Contact pressure-)** and from the pull-down menu select **Vector Plot Options…** The **Vector plot options** property manager opens.

12. In the **Options** dialogue box, type **800** in the **Size** field (upper spin-box) to enlarge the size of contact pressure vectors displayed. Vector **Size** is a user preference.

13. Accept other default settings in this property manager and click **[OK]** ✓ to close it. Your display should now appear similar to Figs. 26 and 27.

14. Rotate and zoom-in on the model to gain better insight into what is actually plotted.

Figure 27 shows three different views of contact pressure vectors in the vicinity of the bolt holes and throughout the assembly.

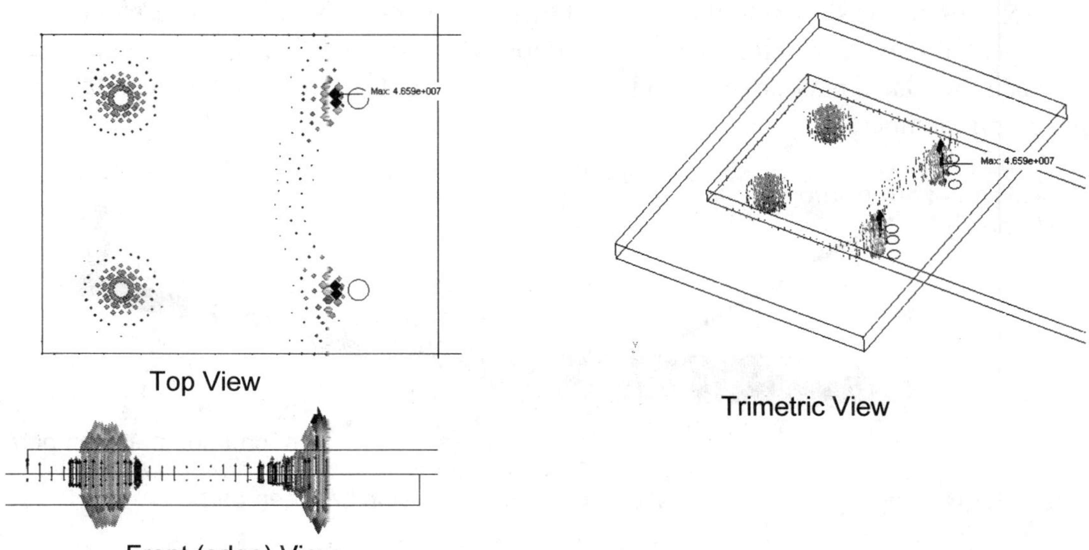

Figure 27 – Various views showing distribution of contact pressure between mating parts in the bolted joint subject to an upward load.

Analysis Insight

Do graphical results in Fig. 27 (currently displayed on your screen) correspond with what you expected to see? The answer might surprise many users. However, it is valuable to understand what these plots reveal in order to ensure that results are interpreted correctly. Some additional questions that might be asked are:

a. Is the contact pressure shown in Fig. 27 applied by the bolts onto the plates?

or

b. Is the contact pressure shown in Fig. 27 the pressure that exists between the plates themselves?

or

c. Do the plots represent the superposition of contact pressure due to bolt clamping forces (i.e., forces beneath the head of the bolt and nut) and due to plate contact?

The answer to question (a) is that, although bolt preload "grips" the parts together, a **Connections** condition was not specified between contacting faces of the bolt or nut and corresponding surfaces on the parts. For this reason, contact pressure between the bolt or nut and the plate surface is *not* illustrated.

Based on the above observation, it should be clear that the answer to question (b) is that contact pressure between the mating parts (i.e., between the plates) is shown in Fig. 27. Verify this by observing the direction of pressure vectors shown in the front view of the contacting surfaces. All vectors originate at the surface of each part and point away from the surface on which pressure acts. Also, in all views, notice that no contact pressure is shown to the right of bolts #1 and #2. This is consistent with Fig. 23, repeated below, which indicates a location where potential separation (i.e., a gap) between the plates may develop. This gap reduces contact pressure between the structural members.

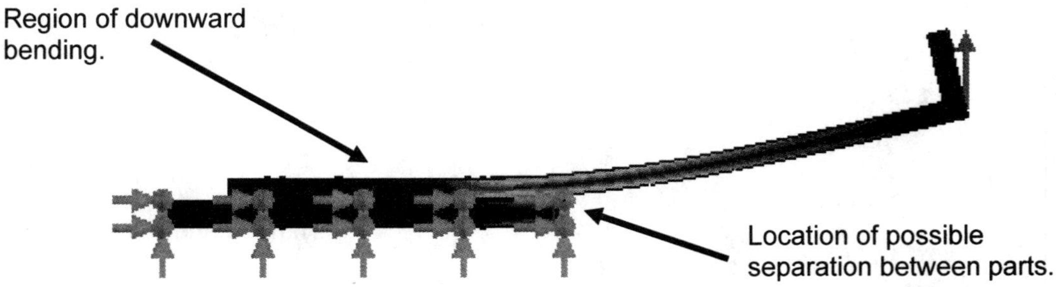

Figure 23 (repeated) – Probable location for a **Gap** to develop between parts.

Fig. 27 also reveals a "footprint" of pressure, in the form of an arc, created by downward bending of the bracket to the left of and between bolts #1 and #2 caused by the upward deformation of the part to the right of these bolts.

Analysis Insight (continued)

Question (c) is already answered in response (a) above. However, it is worthy to note that even if no external load were applied to the angle bracket, contact pressure would still result in both plates around all four bolt connectors. In other words, the images show that bolt preload causes contact pressure between the parts that are gripped rather than between the bolt connectors themselves and the gripped members.

Bolts #3 and #4 are relatively unaffected by the upward load applied at the right end of the bracket. Therefore, notice the fairly uniform shape of contact pressure distribution both in terms of magnitude (front view) and geometry ("ring" shapes in the top view) around these bolt holes.

Summary

Based on this example, it is evident that bolt force determination is one of the primary outcomes of a bolted joint analysis. This capability is useful for predicting and verifying design or analysis of bolt connections under load. Further, application of the **Contact Pressure** capability permits an analyst to determine contact pressure distribution in mating parts in the vicinity of connectors, such as bolts, thereby enhancing understanding of factors such as bolt spacing.

Exercises 1 and 2 on the following pages outline a different method for defining contact between mating parts that does not require the use of Split Lines.

This concludes the study of bolted joints, their definition, resulting contact pressure(s), and bolt reaction forces.

This example file can either be saved or closed, without saving, at the discretion of the user.

1. From the main menu, select **File / Close** (or) **File / Save As** and proceed accordingly.

EXERCISES

EXERCISE 1 – Eccentrically Loaded Bolt Joint

A steel plate is connected to a vertical column by means of four **M 16 x 2, Grade 8.8** steel bolts. Bolt material properties are: **E = 207 GPa** and **Poisson's Ratio = 0.292**. The column is a 254 mm x 76 mm structural steel channel. Both the column and plate are made of **ASTM A36 Steel**. The channel can be considered rigidly fixed (**immovable**) on cut surfaces above and below the connection location. Only a segment of the column is shown in the figures below. The plate is subject to a vertical load of **16** kN applied to its top-right *edge* as shown in Fig. E 7-1. Figure E 7-1 shows the basic geometry of parts in this assembly. For simplicity, detailed images of the bolts are not shown. Open files **Column 7-1** and **Plate 7-1** and perform a finite element analysis to determine items requested below.

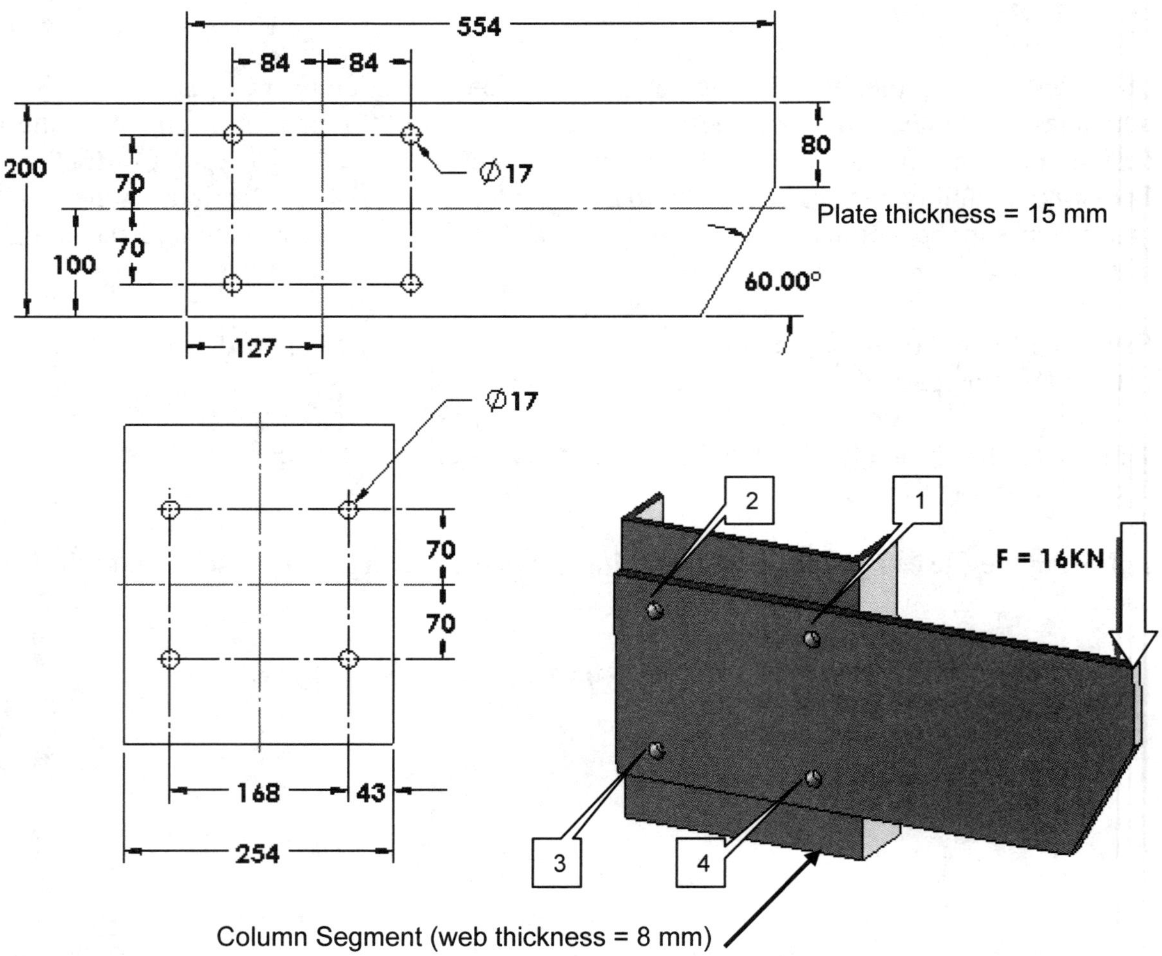

Figure E7-1 – Basic geometry of the column and plate. A 16 kN load is applied on the upper-right *edge* of the plate. Bolt numbers are shown in "call out" boxes.

- Material: **ASTM A36 Steel** (column and plate material properties)
  E = 207e9 Pa, and Poisson's ratio **ν = 0.292** (bolt properties)
- Mesh: **High Quality** tetrahedral elements
- Fixtures: **Fixed** as necessary on top and bottom cut surfaces of the column.

  Connections with **No Penetration** between the column and plate. A simplified method of defining contact between these two parts is outlined below.

  Bolt connector with **Nut**, use a washer diameter = 30 mm under the bolt-head and nut.
- External Load: **16 kN** downward at top-right *edge* of the plate.
- Assumptions: Bolts fit in clearance holes where D_{Hole} = 17 mm
  Bolts are field tightened to a torque T = 226 N-m
  Bolt torque coefficient K = 0.20

Determine the Following:

Begin by creating an assembly of the **Column 7-1** and **Plate 7-1** parts; see **Solution Guidance** below. Then develop a finite element model that includes: material specification, fixtures, external load(s), bolt connectors, mesh, and solution.

Solution Guidance

This section outlines a simplified means for defining contact between mating parts *without* the need for *Split Lines*. Perform steps below after creating an assembly of the **Column** and **Plate** and after defining **Mates** between these two parts. The model should appear as shown in Fig. E 7-2.

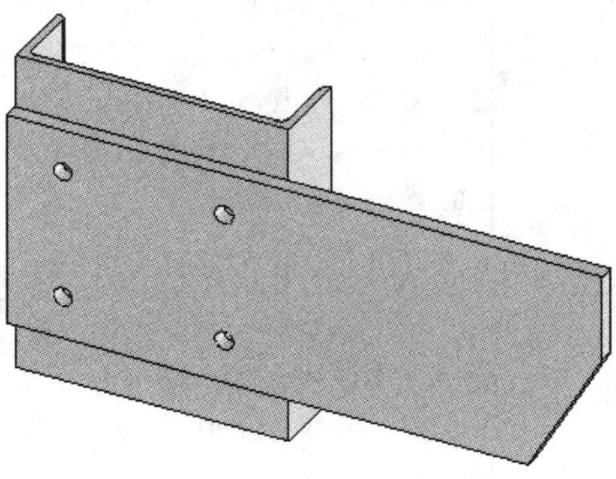

Figure E 7-2 – **Column** and **Plate** assembly prior to definition of contact conditions.

The following steps outline use of the **Find Contact Sets** capability to assist in the definition of contact characteristics between mating parts. Despite the power of this option, it should be used with care because, in complex assemblies, it may find extra contact sets that are not intended or it may not find a contact set that the user wants. As a case in point, the **Find Contact Sets** option is applied *prior* to defining bolted connectors. This is done because bolted connectors add the potential for contact under the bolt head and nut and between the bolt shank and the inside of the bolt holes. This procedure eliminates the possibility of unwanted contact sets being defined.

Solution Guidance (continued)
Proceed as follows to apply the simplified contact set capability. Steps below assume a Simulation Study has been started.

- In the Simulation manager, right-click the **Connections** and from the pull-down menu, select **Find Contact Sets…** The **Find Contact Sets** property manager opens as shown in Fig. E 7-3.
- In the **Options** dialogue box, select ⦿ **Touching faces** (if not already selected).
- In the **Components** dialogue box, the **Select Components or Bodies** field is highlighted (light blue). Move the cursor into the graphics screen and click to select *both* the **Column** and the **Plate**. Select parts in any order. Names of the selected parts, **Plate 7-1-1@Assem2** and **Column 7-1-1@Assem2** are listed in the active field; see Fig. E 7-3.
- Next click the **[Find Faces]** button and the software automatically identifies *any* contacting faces on these two parts. Within the **Results** dialogue box, names of the contacting faces are listed as **Contact Set-1 (-Plate 7-1-1, Column 7-1-1-)**. Word order maybe reversed.
- Also within the **Results** dialogue box, open the pull-down menu adjacent to **Type:** and select **No Penetration** to define the type of contact between the column and plate.
- Finally, at the bottom of the **Results** dialogue box, click the **[Create contact sets]** button.
- Click **[OK]** ✓ to close the **Find Contact Sets** property manager.

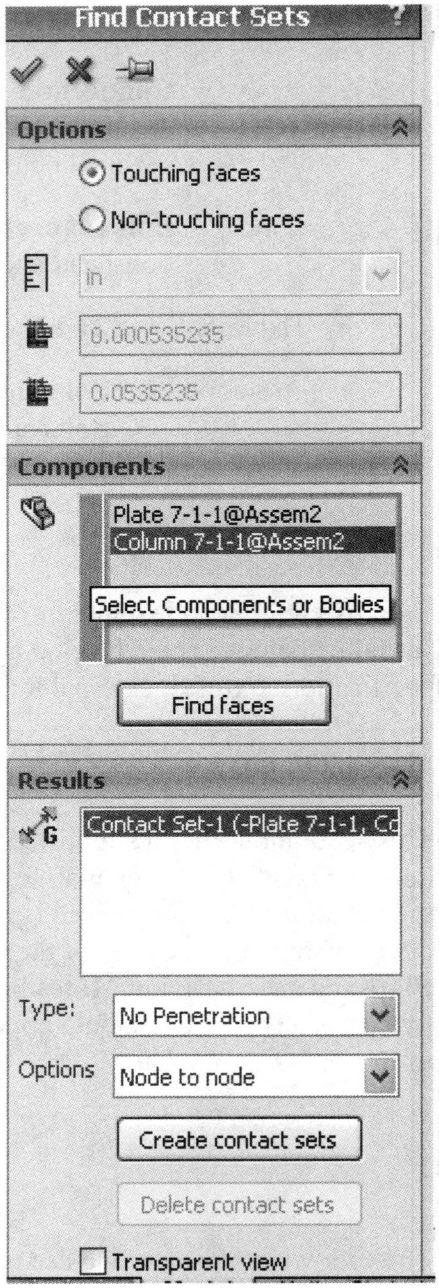

Figure E 7-3 – The **Find Contact Sets** property manager facilitates definition of contact between mating parts.

Although a number of selections were involved in defining contact between the column and plate, use of the single **Find Contact Sets** property manager is much simpler than creating an exploded view; outlining contact areas using *Split Lines;* and then defining contact using the **Contact Set** icon as yet another step. At this point, complete the definition of the finite element model and the analysis outlined below.

a. Create an isometric or trimetric plot showing all fixtures and external loads, including bolt connectors, applied to the model. This image is the finite element equivalent of a free-body-diagram. Do not show stresses on this plot. This plot should fill at least half of an 8 ½ x 11 inch page. [See also item (c) below.] Manually label bolt numbers 1 through 4 on this figure. Bolt numbers should be consistent with those shown on Fig. E 7-1

b. Due to loading on this model, shear forces create the primary loads on each bolt. Using SolidWorks Simulation, determine the shear loads at each bolt location. Then, plot a front view of the model and on it manually sketch each shear force component and the resultant shear force at each bolt. Label the magnitude and direction of each shear force component and the resultant shear force at each bolt.

c. Create a plot of contact pressure between the column and plate. Exaggerate the scale of contact pressure to best depict pressure distribution on the mating parts.

d. Check the solution by manually calculating the shear force(s) at each bolt. Compare manually calculated results with finite element results and compute the percent difference between resultant shear forces at each bolt using equation [1]. Cut-and-paste two **Pin/Bolt/Bearing Force** tables from the finite element solution onto a page accompanying the manual solution. Be sure to correlate these results with the corresponding manual calculations of bolt shear force.

$$\% \text{ difference} = \frac{(\text{FEA result - classical result})}{\text{FEA result}} * 100 = \qquad [1]$$

e. Question: Do directions of shear force components appearing in the **Pin/Bolt /Bearing Force** table correspond to shear forces acting *on* the bolt, or do they represent directions of shear forces exerted by the bolt on the members? Justify your answer in terms of sketches made in part (c).

EXERCISE 2 – Bolted Cylinder Head

The **Ductile Iron** "pipe-end" on a pressurized tank is sealed by an **Alloy Steel** cylinder head as shown in Fig. E 7-4. The cylinder head is held in place by eight **5/8 inch-11 UNC, SAE Grade 8.2** steel bolts for which the modulus of elasticity, **E = 30e6 psi**, and Poisson's ratio, **μ = 0.30**. The pipe-end is subject to an internal static pressure of 900 psi. A confined gasket seal (not shown) is located in the flange groove. Because the gasket is located in a confined groove rather than "sandwiched" between the cylinder head and flange, its low stiffness relative to other components can be ignored. Figure E 7-5 shows the basic geometry of parts in this assembly. Open files **Cylinder Head 7-2** and **Pipe End & Flange 7-2** and perform a finite element analysis to determine items requested below.

Figure E 7-4 – Bolted joint closing a "stub-end" on a pressurized tank.

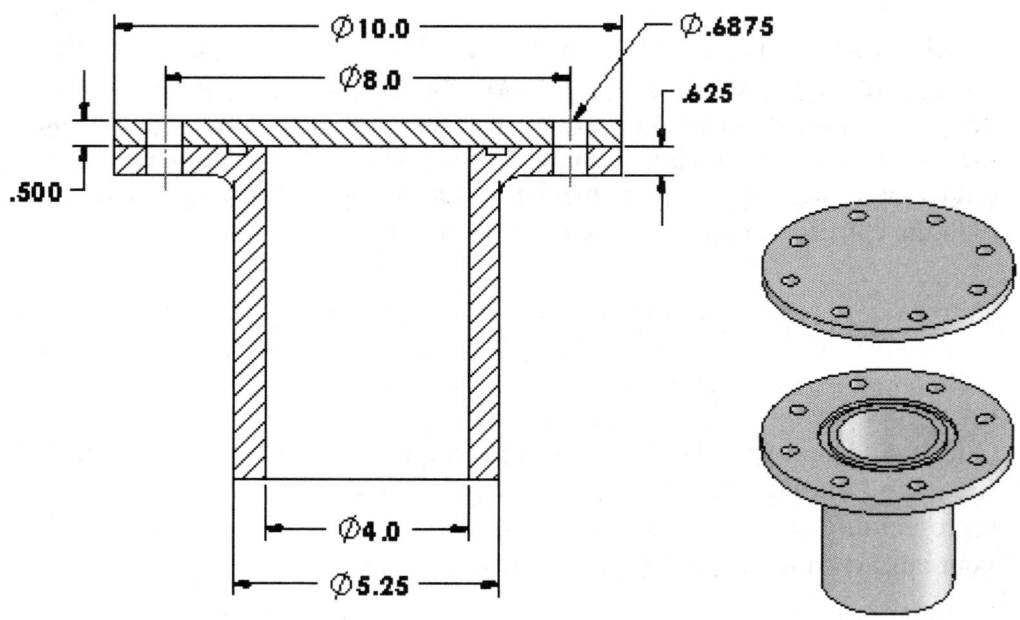

Figure E 7-5 – Basic geometry of the cylinder head and flanged pipe end. Assume the pipe segment is twice as long as shown above.

- Material: **Alloy Steel** (cylinder head)
  Ductile Iron (pipe-end and flange)
  E = 30e6 psi, and Poisson's ratio **ν = 0.30** (bolt material)

- Mesh: **High Quality** tetrahedral elements

- Fixtures: as necessary on the cut (bottom) pipe-end

  Contact Set between cylinder head and pipe flange. See **Solution Guidance** in Exercise 1, above, for a simplified method of defining contact between the cylinder head and pipe flange.

  Bolt connector with **Nut**: Assume the outside diameter under the bolt head and nut is 15/16 inch (0.9375 in).

- External Load: Pressure = **900 psi** on all internal surfaces

- Assumptions: Bolts fit in clearance holes where $D_{Hole} = 0.6875$ in
  Bolts are field tightened to a torque T = 2540 lb*in
  Bolt torque coefficient K = 0.20

Determine the Following:

Begin by creating an assembly of the **Cylinder Head** and **Pipe End & Flange**. Use the simplified **Find Contact Sets** procedure outlined in the **Solution Guidance** section of the previous exercise as you develop a finite element model. The complete model should include: material specification, fixtures, external load(s), bolt connectors, mesh, and solution.

a. Create a plot showing all restraints and loads applied to the model. This image is the finite element equivalent of a free-body-diagram. Do not show stresses on this plot. This plot should fill at least half of an 8 ½ x 11 inch page. On this plot, write a brief statement that clearly identifies the type of fixture(s) applied to the cut-end of the pipe segment shown in Fig. E7-5.

b. Create a plot of contact pressure between the cylinder head and the pipe flange. Exaggerate the scale of contact pressure to best depict pressure distribution on the mating parts. What can be stated about the uniformity of contact pressure between the mating surfaces (i.e., between the cylinder head and pipe flange)? In your answer pay particular attention to pressure distribution in spaces *between* bolts on the bolt circle that join these two parts together.

c. Due to loading on this model, each bolt is subject to its initial pre-load plus a portion of the load due to internal pressure. Use SolidWorks Simulation to determine the load in a representative number of bolts (at least four) by accessing results in the **Pin/Bolt /Bearing Force** window. Cut-and-paste screen images of four **Pin/Bolt/Bearing Force** windows onto an 8 ½ x 11 inch page. See also item (d) below.

d. Develop a set of manual calculations to determine the resultant tensile load in a typical bolt. Place these calculations on a page following the page created in item (c). Compare manually calculated results for axial bolt load with finite element results and compute the percent difference between resultant bolt tensile loads using equation [1].

$$\% \text{ difference} = \frac{(\text{FEA result - classical result})}{\text{FEA result}} * 100 = \qquad [1]$$

Textbook Problems

In addition to the above exercise, it is highly recommended that additional problems involving bolted connections be worked from a design of machine elements or a structural analysis textbook. Bolted assemblies can be loaded by axial loads, bending loads, shear loads, or a combination of all three. Textbook problems provide a great way to discover errors made in formulating a finite element analysis because they typically are well defined problems for which the solution is known. Typical textbook problems, if well defined in advance, make an excellent source of solutions for comparison.

APPENDIX A

ORGANIZING ASSIGNMENTS USING MS WORD®

This appendix is included to offer guidance in the use of Microsoft Word® for the preparation of deliverables associated with end of chapter exercises. It is assumed that users are familiar with Word® or some other word processor. However, a few procedures outlined below might be new even to seasoned Word® users. Although Chapter 5 demonstrates a semi-automated means to generate a **Report** using features embedded within the Simulation software, this section provides guidance for users needing to output, into a neat report, *only* those items requested in end of chapter exercises. A fringe benefit of this approach is that, in addition to a well organized assignment, the report (a) can be prepared simultaneously while working an exercise, and (b) can be printed on fewer pages, a real plus for students on a tight print quota.

The goal of this section is show, through example, how to combine features of Word® with capabilities of SolidWorks Simulation to produce a concise and well organized report. Techniques described herein are the same procedures used to create this text. An example of the "final report" demonstrated here can be found beginning on page A-8. Be advised that *only the basics* of document editing are described here.

Learning Objectives

Upon completion of this unit, users should be able to:

- *Copy and paste* images from SolidWorks Simulation into a word processor document. (It is presumed users already possess cut and paste capability).

- *Crop* and *Re-size* images extracted from SolidWorks Simulation.

- Apply *Text Wrapping* around images copied from SolidWorks Simulation.

- *Extract data* from **Probe Results** tables and include it in a document as an Excel® *spreadsheet* table.

- Append *Callouts* to images to label significant aspects of a model or stress results.

Problem Statement

The problem used in this example is based on the cam follower analysis performed in Chapter 1. As such, users should be familiar with technical aspects of the analysis thereby allowing us to focus on how results of that problem might be presented in a summary report. Assume the following items are requested as part of the finite element analysis.

Deliverables:

a. An image to document **Fixtures** and **External Loads** applied to the model. Label applied force magnitudes on this image.

b. On the same page as part (a) create a plot of the most appropriate stress in the cam follower.

c. A graph of the most appropriate stress at one inch below the top end of the cam follower. On this graph include descriptive titles and axis labels.

d. Beneath the graph of part (c) include a table (in Excel) of stress values determined using the **Probe** tool for the graph of the previous step.

Software Version

Because of the moderate adoption of Windows Vista® and upgraded versions of Word® and Excel® that accompany it, instructions below are based on Microsoft Word® 2003 in a Windows XP® operating system. Newer versions of Word® should function sufficiently similar to permit adapting instructions below to the newer environment.

Setting Up the Necessary Editing Tools

Before demonstrating how to create an organized report, the necessary editing tools are organized on the screen. Most of these tools are found in the **Drawing** toolbar. Assuming that this toolbar is *not* displayed in the Word© window proceed as follows to add it and modify its contents. NOTE: For many items demonstrated below there exist alternative ways to accomplish the same tasks. However, for the sake of brevity, only one method is demonstrated.

1. Right-click anywhere on the main menu and from the pull-down menu select ☑ **Drawing**. This action adds the **Drawing** menu to the bottom (typically) of the screen. The default **Drawing** menu is shown in Fig. 1.

Figure 1 – The default **Drawing** menu in MS Word®.

2. To relocate this menu, click-and-drag its "drag handle," circled in Fig. 1, to the desired location on the screen.

Next, several frequently used icons are added to the **Drawing** menu as follows.

3. Left click the **Toolbar Options** button, shown boxed in Fig. 1, and from the pop-up menu, first select **Add or Remove Buttons▼** followed by **Customize...** See Fig. 2.

Figure 2 – Menu selections to add buttons to the **Drawing** toolbar.

4. The **Customize** window opens in Fig. 3. Within this window, select the **Commands** tab circled in Fig. 3.

5. In the left column, beneath **Categories**, select **Drawing**, shown at arrow in Fig. 3.

6. On the right side of this window, scroll through tools listed beneath **Commands** and click-and-drag the commands listed in Fig. 4 onto the **Drawing** toolbar and drop them there.

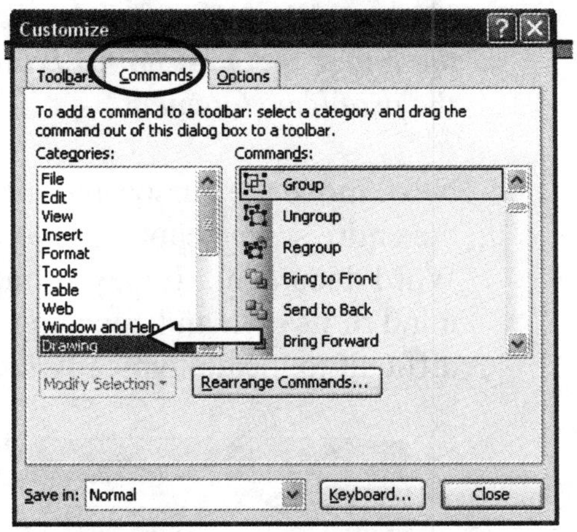

Figre 3 – Within the **Customize** window, buttons are selected to add to the **Drawing** toolbar.

Figure 4 – **Commands** copied onto the **Drawing** toolbar.

The **Drawing** toolbar now has sufficient tools to accomplish the tasks outlined in steps (a) though (d) of the **Problem Statement**. Thus, the process of creating a custom report begins below.

Creating a Custom Report (a demonstration)

Cutting and Pasting Images into a Word Document

Begin by assuming that both SolidWorks Simulation *and* a Word document are open, side-by-side, on the screen. Both these windows must be resized to fit on the monitor.

Also assume that the cam follower is displayed with **Fixtures** and **External Loads** applied to the model as shown in Fig. 5. *NOTE: It is also possible to switch from window to window by using the **Minimize** and **Restore** buttons at the top right of each window.*

1. Because it can be tricky to place text onto a page *after* an image is placed on the page, it is a good practice to type your name, date, and exercise number at the top of a blank sheet in Word®.

2. Next, capture the current SolidWorks Simulation screen image by simultaneously pressing the **[Ctrl] + [Print Screen]** buttons on the keyboard. For simplicity, refer to this image as a "screen capture." This step places a copy of the entire screen image onto the clip board as shown in Fig. 5. *Before performing this step, choose a view of the model that best displays its desired attributes. In this case, the image includes both **Fixtures** and **External Loads** as requested in part (a) of the problem statement.*

3. Next, move the cursor into the Word document and select **Paste**. Since a copy of the entire screen capture is on the clip board, that entire image now appears in the Word document. It may *not* appear at its desired location. The image often has a mind of its own and appears wherever it chooses on the page. If the image is difficult to locate, typically look *above* the location where you clicked to paste it.

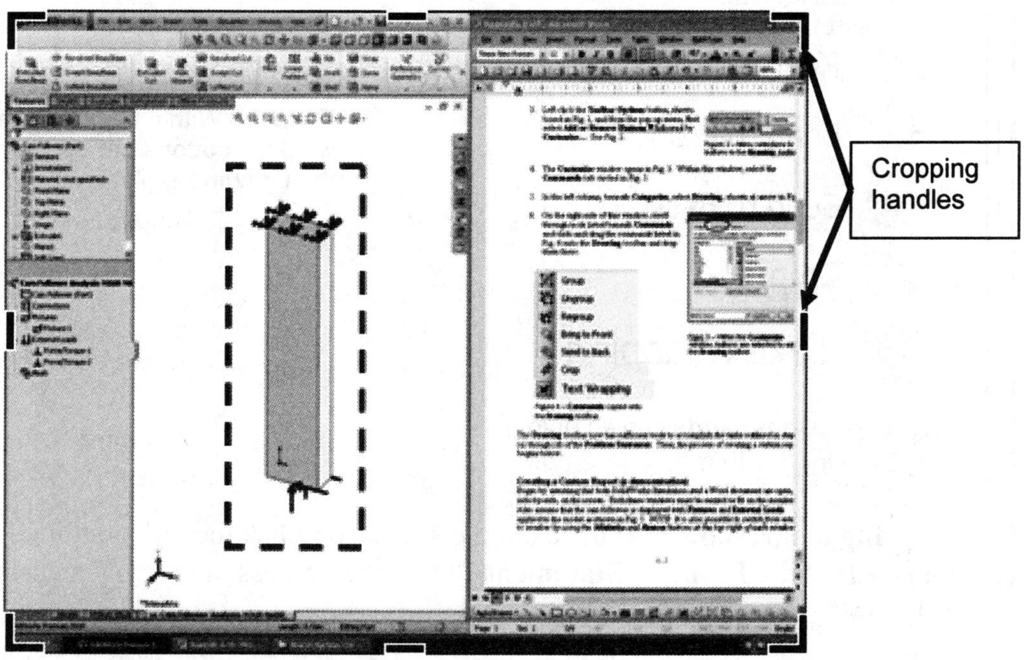

Figure 5 – The screen capture after it is pasted into a Word document. If both SolidWorks Simulation and Word are open simultaneously, images of both are pasted into the current document.

4. Click to select the image. When selected, "handles" (tiny circles) appear at each corner and at the middle of each side of the image. If desired, resize the image by clicking and dragging these handles.

5. Because it is desired to include only an image of the model along with its **Fixtures** and **External Loads**, the image is next cropped by selecting the **Crop** tool shown in Fig. 4. Once selected, the **Crop** tool replaces the cursor and bold corners and a short dash appears on each edge of the selected image as shown in Fig. 5.

6. Using the **Crop** tool, click and drag any of the dark bars appearing on the image boundaries to crop the model to the approximate size shown by dashed lines in Fig. 5. Click anywhere outside the image to end cropping.

7. After cropping, the image may be too small. Therefore, click the image again to select it. The handles (tiny circles) reappear. Click and drag any of these handles to re-size the image as desired. Because cropping occurs in finite steps, it is often helpful to enlarge the image, crop it again, and then return the image to its desired size.

Part (a) of the problem statement also requests that magnitudes of the force components be labeled. Labeling can be done manually or as outlined below.

8. In the **Drawing** toolbar, select the **AutoShapes** pop-up menu and from the list, select **Callouts**. Then select the **Callout** of your choice. For this example, the **Rectangular Callout** is used. See Fig. 6.

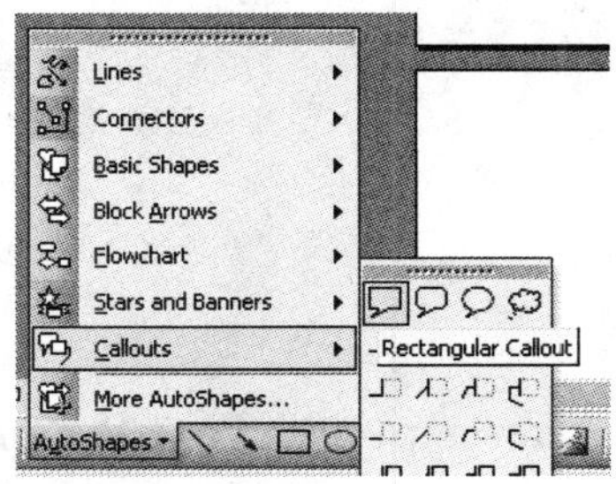

Figure 6 – Selecting a **Callout** to label the model.

9. Move the cursor near the model where the force component is to be labeled. The cursor symbol changes to a "+" sign. Click an drag the cursor to create a small text box. This box can be resized as needed by dragging its handles.

10. Click inside the **Callout** box and type a label for the X-component of force. Font style and font size can be changed by selecting these items on the Word® menu. Drag the pointer on the **Callout** box to identify the appropriate force component as shown in Fig. 7.

11. An identical procedure is used to label the Y-force component. It is not repeated here. To finalize this image, two additional steps are necessary. First, it is necessary to **Group** the image and its label. Grouping is necessary because the image and label are two different entities. As such, they *might* move independently and become separated during subsequent editing of the document. Any relative movement might separate the label from the force vector thereby rendering it useless. Proceed as follows to **Group** these items. Items can be un-

grouped and positions changed at a later time. However, un-grouping can get messy.

12. Simultaneously hold down the **[Shift]** key while clicking to select the **Callout** and the image. Selection handles appear around each object as shown in Fig. 7. Then in the **Drawing** toolbar, select the **Group** icon.

The second step required to finalize the image is only necessary if typed text accompanies the image. This text can be placed in several different locations relative to the image. In this text, the most typical arrangement is either for text to appear adjacent to the image, as shown in Fig. 7, or text can appear above and below an image as illustrated in Fig. 5. Either selection is made my choosing the **Text Wrapping** icon and selecting either **Tight** or **Top and Bottom** from the pop-up menu. Click the **Text Wrapping** icon now.

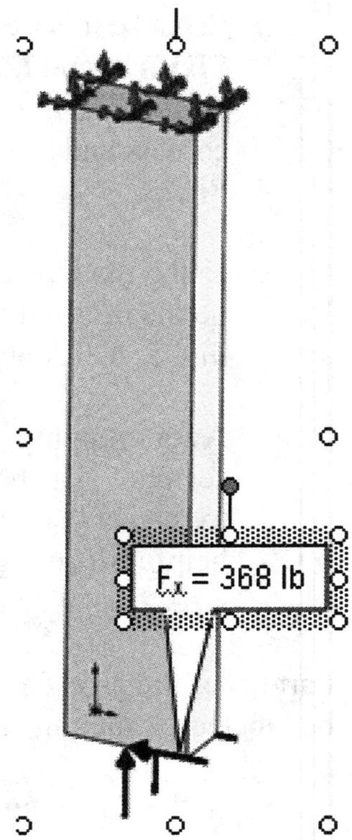

Figure 7 – Placing a label on an image and grouping the entities to effectively "lock" them together.

After applying **Text Wrapping** it is typically necessary to click the image and drag it to its desired location on the page. Reminder, *if* various parts of an image are not **Grouped** together, then they will need to be moved one at a time and re-organized in the final position. Grouping eliminates this extra task.

A Word of Caution and Encouragement

Using the cut, paste, crop, callout, and group commands takes some getting used to. It easily frustrates individuals with a low tolerance for ambiguity. In other words, all kinds of unexpected things can happen. For example, after grouping items together, it is not unusual for typed text to overlap the image. Don't panic, simply make a selection using the **Text Wrapping** tool and many things will get un-scrambled. Using **Ungoup** causes similar problems.

The procedures to cut and paste images from SolidWorks Simulation into a Word® document, to re-size those images, and to document them by the addition of labels is demonstrated above. The same procedure can be used to copy an image of the *most appropriate stress* [requested in part (b) of the problem statement] onto the same page as the image of Fig. 7. These two images are shown in Fig. 9 at the end of this example.

Incorporating an Excel Spreadsheet into a Word Document

Parts (c) and (d) of the problem statement request that graph of the most appropriate stress (σ_y) be placed onto the same page with an Excel® spreadsheet that contains data used to produce the graph. Therefore, the last item to be demonstrated here is to capture data from the **Probe Results** table, to export it into an Excel® spreadsheet, and finally to insert the spreadsheet into a Word document. The procedure to accomplish this is outlined in the following section.

Capturing Probe Results Data and Exporting it to an Excel Spreadsheet

The following steps assume that the **Probe** tool was used to select nodes from left to right across the model at a location 1 inch below the top (fixed end). It is also assumed that the **Probe Result** property manager is open and that stress values at each node location are stored in the **Results** table as shown in Fig. 8. One problem with the **Results** table is that, without resorting to scrolling through the data, its small size often prevents display of *all* values determined when using the **Probe** tool. This shortcoming is overcome by saving and displaying *all* the data in an Excel® spreadsheet. To capture this data into a spreadsheet, proceed as follows.

1. In the **Report Options** dialogue box, at the bottom of the **Probe Results** property manager, click the **Save** icon circled in Fig. 8. Immediately the **Save As** window opens and the **File name:** field contains the name assigned to the current Study. It is best to assign a descriptive name associated with this file such as: **"C: \My Excel\Cam Follower Data.csv"** Also, at the bottom of this window note that the **Save as type:** field shows **Excel File (*.csv)**. Finally, click the **[Save]** button.

2. Also, click **[OK]** ✓ to close the **Probe Result** property manager.

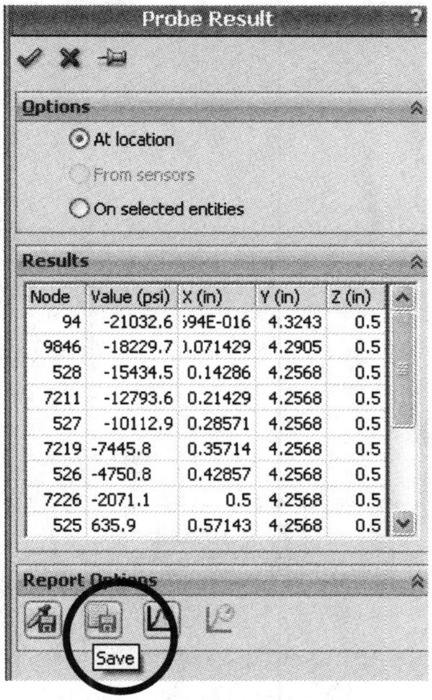

Figure 8 – The **Probe Result** table populated with stress values sampled across the cam follower face.

3. Next, open the file in Excel and copy the data by clicking and dragging over it and selecting, **Copy**. Carefully note the number of rows and columns of data.

4. Return to the Word document and download the Excel file by clicking the **Insert Microsoft Excel Worksheet** icon and sizing the spreadsheet with the proper number of rows and columns. Finally, **Paste** the data into the Word document.

5. Arrange the graph and Excel data table by clicking on the graph and dragging it to a desired location on the same page. See Fig. 10.

Exhibits of both pages, at reduced size, are shown below and on the following page.

EXAMPLE REPORT

NAME: ____________________

DATE: ____

Exercise 1, Chapter #1

Below are examples of figures requested in parts (a) and (b) of the example exercise used to demonstrate report preparation by copying and pasting multiple images from SolidWorks Simulation into onto a single page in a Word document. This space would ordinarily be used to include technical data bout the finite element models below.

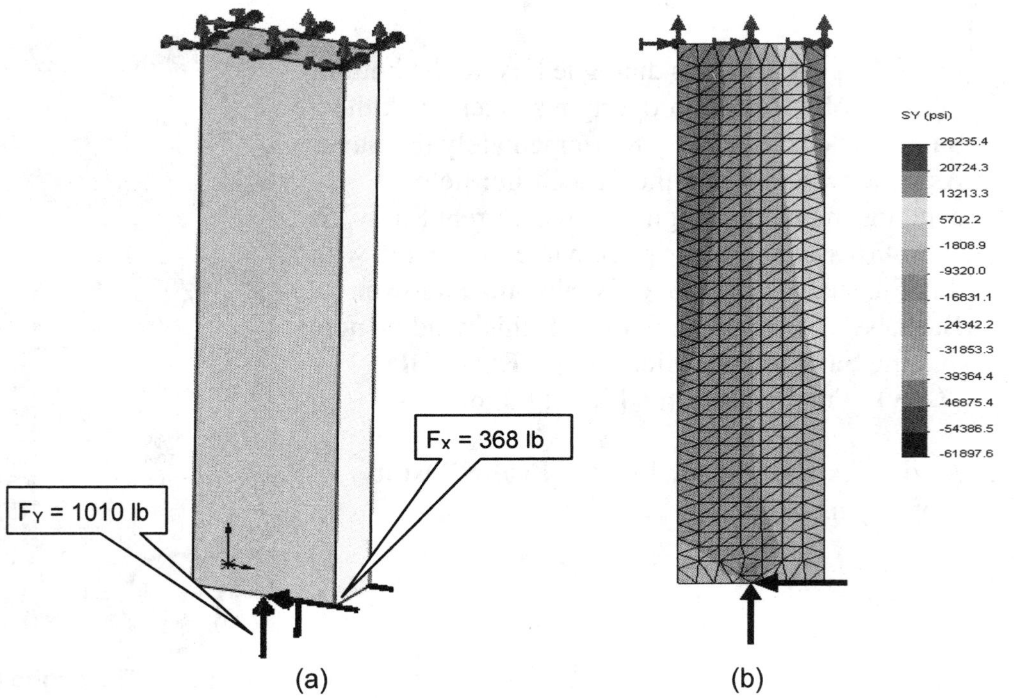

Figure 9 – Figure (a) shows the cam follower and its associated **Fixtures** and **applied External Loads**. Figure (b) shows a plot of σ_y due to combined axial and bending stress in the cam follower.

A descriptive figure caption can be placed beneath the figures and answers to questions relevant to the model can be typed in available space on the page along with the images. The above figures were cut and pasted from SolidWorks Simulation. Then, labels were added and all items were grouped together using techniques demonstrated here.

EXAMPLE REPORT (continued)

The spreadsheet below contains all the **Results** data found using the **Probe** tool. In spreadsheet format, it is possible to compare stress magnitudes on both sides of the cam follower with values calculated using classical stress equations. See notes appended at the left side of the Excel spreadsheet. .

Model name: Cam Follower (Part)				
Study name: Cam Follower YOUR NAME				
Plot type: Static nodal stress Stress1				
Result Type: SY				
Node	Value (psi)	X (in)	Y (in)	Z (in)
94[illegible]	-21032.6	-[illegible].27E-16	4.3243	0.5
9846	-18229.7	0.071429	4.2905	0.5
528	-15434.5	0.14286	4.2568	0.5
7211	-12793.6	0.21429	4.2568	0.5
527	-10112.9	0.28571	4.2568	0.5
7219	-7445.8	0.35714	4.2568	0.5
526	-4750.8	0.42857	4.2568	0.5
7226	-2071.1	0.5	4.2568	0.5
525	635.9	0.57143	4.2568	0.5
7232	3327.1	0.64286	4.2568	0.5
524	6034.1	0.71429	4.2568	0.5
7238	8720.3	0.78571	4.2568	0.5
523	11418.3	0.85714	4.2568	0.5
8794	14255	0.92857	4.2905	0.5
27[illegible]	17094.7	1	4.3243	0.5

Maximum compressive stress on top left side of the cam follower.

Maximum tensile stress on top right side of the cam follower

This space can be used to discuss trends observed on the graph or values determined using the **Probe** tool.

Additionally, calculations of stress determined using classical stress equations can be included here and compared with finite element analysis results.

All this can be accomplished in the neat and concise report format illustrated here.

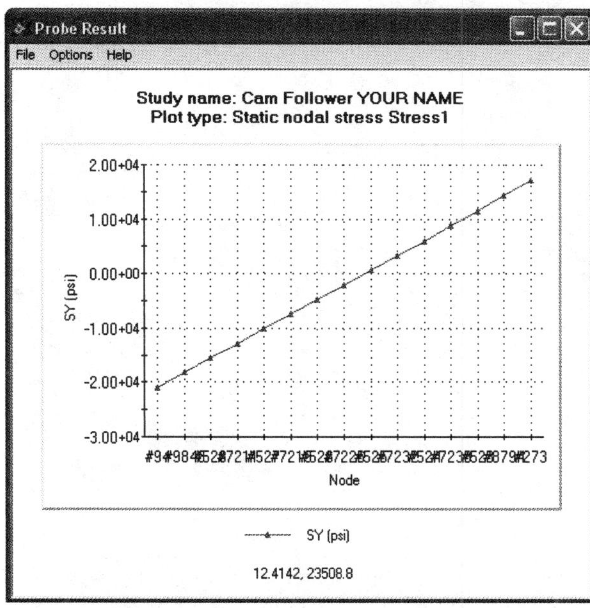

Figure 10 – Graph of combined axial compressive stress and bending stress across the face of the cam follower at 1" below the top (fixed) end.

NOTES:

INDEX

NOTES:

NOTES:

NOTES: